PASSIONATE INTELLECT
The Poetry of Charles Tomlinson

LIVERPOOL ENGLISH TEXTS AND STUDIES
General Editors: JONATHAN BATE and BERNARD BEATTY

This long-established series has a primary emphasis on close reading, critical exegesis and textual scholarship. Studies of a wide range of works are included, although the list has particular strengths in the Renaissance, and in Romanticism and its continuations.

Byron and the Limits of Fiction edited by Bernard Beatty and Vincent Newey. Volume 22. 1988. 304pp. ISBN 0–85323–026–9 *cased*

Literature and Nationalism edited by Vincent Newey and Ann Thompson. Volume 23. 1991. 296pp. ISBN 0–85323–057–9 *cased*

Reading Rochester edited by Edward Burns. Volume 24. 1995. 240pp. ISBN 0–85323–038–2 *cased*, 0–85323–309–8 *paper*

Thomas Gray: Contemporary Essays edited by W. B. Hutchings and William Ruddick. Volume 25. 1993. 287pp. ISBN 0–85323–268–7 *cased*

Nearly Too Much: The Poetry of J. H. Prynne by N. H. Reeve and Richard Kerridge. Volume 26. 1995. 224pp. ISBN 0–85323–840–5 *cased*, 0–85323–850–2 *paper*

A Quest for Home: Reading Robert Southey by Christopher J. P. Smith. Volume 27. 1997. 256pp. ISBN 0–85323–511–2 *cased*, 0–85323–521–X *paper*

Outcasts from Eden: Ideas of Landscape in British Poetry since 1945 by Edward Picot. Volume 28. 1997. 344pp. ISBN 0–85323–531–7 *cased*, 0–85323–541–4 *paper*

The Plays of Lord Byron: Critical Essays edited by Robert Gleckner and Bernard Beatty. Volume 29. 1997. 416pp. ISBN 0–85323–881–2 *cased*, 0–85323–891–X *paper*

Sea-Mark: The Metaphorical Voyage, Spenser to Milton by Philip Edwards. Volume 30. 1997. 236pp. ISBN 0–85323–512–0 *cased*, 0–85323–522–8 *paper*

A full list of available titles can be obtained from Liverpool University Press.

PASSIONATE INTELLECT

*The Poetry of
Charles Tomlinson*

MICHAEL KIRKHAM
University of Toronto

LIVERPOOL UNIVERSITY PRESS

Liverpool English Texts and Studies, Volume 31

First published 1999 by
LIVERPOOL UNIVERSITY PRESS
Senate House, Abercromby Square,
Liverpool, L69 3BX

Copyright © 1999 by Michael Kirkham

The right of Michael Kirkham to be identified as the
author of this work has been asserted by him in accordance
with the Copyright, Design and Patents Act 1988.

*All rights reserved. No part of this volume may be reproduced,
stored in a retrieval system, or transmitted, in any form or by
any means, electronic, mechanical, photocopying, recording or
otherwise without the prior written permission of the publishers.*

British Library Cataloguing-in-Publication Data
A British Library CIP record is available

ISBN 0–85323–543–0 *cased*
      0–85323–553–8 *paper*

Set in Monotype Garamond by
Wilmaset Limited, Birkenhead, Wirral
Printed and bound in the European Union by
Bell & Bain Limited, Glasgow

For Ruth

and in memory of
Alan Hancox and Denys Harding,
generous friends

We are endeavouring to knock out of ourselves all the preconceived ideas, emptying ourselves of everything except that nature is here to gather it and understand it if only we will be clean enough, healthy enough, and humble enough to go to it willing to be taught and to receive it not as we think it should be, but as it is, and then to put down vigorously and truthfully that which we culled.

    F. H. Varley (Canadian Painter), 1914

Each thing, living or unliving, streams in its own odd, intertwining flux, and nothing, not even man nor the God of man, nor anything that man has thought or felt or known, is fixed or abiding. All moves. And nothing is true, or good, or right, except in its own living relatedness to its own circumambient universe; to the things that are in the stream with it.

    D. H. Lawrence, 'Art and Morality' (*Phoenix*), 1925

I realized, when I wrote it, that I was approaching the sort of thing I wanted to do, where space represented possibility and where self would have to embrace that possibility somewhat self-forgetfully, putting aside the more possessive and violent claims of personality. The embrace was, all the same, a passionate one, or so it seemed to me.

    Charles Tomlinson, Preface to *Collected Poems*, 1985

Contents

Acknowledgements	viii
Introduction	1
1 An Ethic of Perception	25
2 One World	73
Meetings and Encounters	77
Prospects	91
Perfections	106
3 Manscapes 1958–1966	127
4 Manscapes 1969–1978	169
5 A Saving Grace	213
6 Art and Mortality	243
Bibliography	307
Index	329

Acknowledgements

Quotations from *Collected Poems*, *The Return*, and *Annunciations* (© Charles Tomlinson, 1987, 1987, 1989) are reprinted by permission of Oxford University Press. Parts of Chapters 5 and 6 have been adapted from 'An Agnostic's Grace', written for *Charles Tomlinson: Man and Artist*, edited by Kathleen O'Gorman (1988). Other passages have appeared previously in *British Poetry since 1970: A Critical Survey*, edited by Peter Jones and Michael Schmidt (1980), and *The New Pelican Guide to English Literature*, Volume 8, edited by Boris Ford (1983, 1995).

I am grateful to Ted Chamberlin for taking the time to read and to advise on the revision of an earlier version of this book. I would like to thank Cyrilene Beckles and Jean Smith for help in word-processing my text.

NOTE

Quotations from Tomlinson's poetry are either from the latest edition of *Collected Poems* (Oxford and New York: Oxford University Press, 1987) or from one of the collections published subsequently. Each reference to a poem is accompanied by the title and date of the collection in which it first appeared, followed by its page number in *Collected Poems*, identified by the abbreviation CP, or, for later work, in the collection identified in the text.

Introduction

Three books of criticism devoted to Tomlinson's poetry, two published in the United States and one in Canada, have preceded this one.[1] I have been reading Tomlinson for over forty years, and this study was written, in the long-standing conviction that he is a major poet, to support that conviction by a detailed examination of his work. Its aim is to show how these poems demand to be read and what they yield to close scrutiny. A critical 'reading' conveys, and invites other readers to share and ponder, the critic's experience of a poem, an *oeuvre*. Criticism can seem glib if, naming themes, labelling techniques, tracing influences and sources, identifying literary and historical contexts, it is only *about* the poetry; if it does not also try with its own language to enter *into* that experience. This study is addressed to two audiences: readers already interested in its subject and anyone who wishes to enquire into a reputation not yet tested.[2]

Charles Tomlinson was born in 1927 at Stoke-on-Trent, where with other working-class children he received an excellent grammar school education. He studied English at Cambridge (1945–48), where he met the poet and critic Donald Davie. He taught school for three years in London, and then spent a year in Italy (1951–52). He completed an MA thesis in the University of London in 1955, and in 1956 joined the Department of English at the University of Bristol as Lecturer (later Reader and finally Professor, holding a personal Chair). He retired in 1992. He brought out a pamphlet of verse, *Relations and Contraries*, in 1951, which he regards as prentice work and, except for one poem, has not been reprinted. In 1955 he published his first original poems, *The Necklace*, and received the first of many prizes and awards for his poetry. On the strength of this and its successor, *Seeing is Believing*, published first in the United States in 1958 and then, with additional poems, in England two years later, he was acclaimed by Hugh Kenner as 'the most original poet to come along in a generation'.[3] Since then he has averaged one collection every three years. His first *Selected Poems* appeared in 1978 and his first *Collected Poems* in 1985. He has translated from several languages, publishing volumes of translation from Fyodor Tyutchev, Antonio Machado, César Vallejo and Attilio Bertolucci, and in another volume a substantial selection of all his translations. He edited *The Oxford Book of Verse in English Translation* in 1980 and *Eros English'd: Classical Poetry in Translation* in 1992. He has written in quadrilingual collaboration with Octavio Paz, Jacques Roubaud and Edoardo Sanguineti (*Renga*, 1971) and, with Paz again, produced a bilingual sequence, *Airborn/Hijos del Aire* (1981). Translations of his poetry have appeared during the 1990s in Portugal, Spain, Germany, Italy and Mexico. He has edited collections of critical essays on Marianne Moore and William Carlos Williams, a selection of Williams's poems, a selection of poems by George Oppen, and a bilingual selection from the poetry of Octavio Paz. In 1981 he published *Some Americans*, a memoir of his personal meetings with some of the makers of American modernism. He delivered the Clark Lectures at Cambridge in 1982, which were published the following year as *Poetry and Metamorphosis*. Simultaneously or alternately he has been a painter. There have been exhibitions of his graphics, selections of which have been reproduced in *Words and Images* (1972), *In Black and White* (1976) and *Eden* (1986). He is an Honorary Fellow of Queens' College, Cambridge, and in 1974 was made a Fellow of the Royal Society of Literature.

In the study of a poet's *oeuvre* the relevant context for any given poem is that created by the existence of other poems, written before or after. A chronological survey of poetic development is not the only way of comprehending the meaning, quality and value of the work. There are other classes of relationship between the poems, which can be more clearly elucidated by various kinds of nonchronological arrangement. Of the six chapters in this book, only the third and fourth trace a historical progression; the others seek to illuminate different kinds of inter-relationship. I am convinced that, with some exceptions, critics in England have underestimated Tomlinson's achievement; frequently, it seems to me, this results from a failure to see—or hear—what is there in the poems. The plan of the book reflects, therefore, an expository intention: to open up understanding by presenting his work in an unfolding sequence—a particular grouping of poems and topics for discussion and ordering of chapters.

Tomlinson is both a poet and a painter, and the poet shares the painter's close and passionate interest in the 'appearances' of the material world. A large proportion of his work focuses its attention on objects, places, landscapes: poems based, as he writes in a key essay, 'The Poet as Painter', 'on exposure to and observation of the fleeting moments of visual sensation'. An understanding of Tomlinson's work must begin with these poems; they are therefore the subject of my first chapter 'An Ethic of Perception'. The developed habits of receptivity and minute attention, undistracted by 'the merely personal', referred to in that essay constitute a discipline of objectivity, 'an ethic of perception', which he says he recognized in Cézanne's painting and 'wanted to earn the right to use . . . as a basis for poetry'. Critics have found it convenient to divide his poetry into two groups: poems of the natural world, or the world of objects, and poems that deal directly with the human world. Though it may be critically convenient, it is also potentially misleading, for these records of sense experience invariably have an analogous human content; Tomlinson suggests that the artistic ethic he took from Cézanne made possible to him 'a range from natural landscape to civic landscape'.[4] The distinction, then, simplifies. More seriously, it ignores Tomlinson's *unified* vision of a natural-human world, a moral vision informing 'human' and 'natural' poems alike, centred in a common core of values, and in doing so it obscures the very basis of the poetry's originality. If one nevertheless accepts this classification, the reason for giving separate attention to the nature poems, or poems of observation, is to examine in all its parts and aspects the ethic of perception in its primary application.

The theme of Chapter 2, 'One World', is the unified vision of a natural-human world. It explores the common ground of sensory and mental experience, aesthetic and moral values. I have tried to show that certain forms of thought, organizing images and ideas pervasive in the poetry enable him to make of natural phenomena and human acts and works 'a single sphere'[5] of meaning.

While Chapter 2 investigates the relationship between 'nature poems' and 'human poems', Chapters 3 and 4 confine their attention to the latter. The linking title, 'Manscapes', a coinage adapted from Tomlinson, is meant to suggest, again, that in this poetry human scene and natural landscape belong to one vision. These chapters are, as I said, the exception in my exposition of Tomlinson's work. During the late 1950s, the 1960s and the 1970s, with each collection he added new areas of human experience, progressively enlarging his poetic range. This development, therefore, invites a historical approach. This is not to forget but to find a different way of drawing attention to the relationship between these and the neighbouring poems of perception.

The exploration of new areas and views of human experience did not, of course, halt in 1978. The reason for suspending my survey at that point is that I want to take a different approach to the later poetry, by which I mean everything written after *The Way of a World* (1969). Although the third and fourth chapters, like the second, are concerned to show the *relationship* between Tomlinson's interpretations of sense experience and human experience, they also concede the distinction. In Chapters 5 and 6 that distinction is ignored. Chapter 5, 'A Saving Grace', beginning with a brief chronological account of the poetry published in the 1950s and 1960s, discusses the poetry of the 1970s and 1980s as an entity. There are no breaks or sudden redefinitions of his material in Tomlinson's poetry, and a systematic dissection of his poetic career into periods would be artificial. Nevertheless it is both convenient and appropriate that an examination of his more recent work should harvest whatever lucidities have accrued from a partitioning of his previous work into categories and a discussion of how they are connected; the distinctions and divisions are for better understanding and appreciation, and the means can be dispensed with when the end is gained. There is, besides, a more objective reason for taking 1969–70 as the beginning of a new phase in his poetic development. After fifteen years of relative inactivity as a painter, at the end of the 1960s he started experimenting with surrealist techniques of improvisation and collage and produced during the next ten years a quantity of graphic work;[6] for a decade he worked alternately as painter and poet. He remembers those years as possessing 'a strange radiating sufficiency', and for the effect they had on his writing—'namely, of admitting into it a greater regard for chance and for the mysterious fullness of the given'. 'Though I have ceased to make pictures', he concludes, 'I feel that my poems still lie open to forces emanating from that now completed phase. It seems, in retrospect, to have been like a season in Eden.' His memoir of this fertile season, written in 1985,[7] by no means accounts for everything in the resulting poems, but in the recollection of its grace it catches the quality of mind and temper, a pervasive mood, that one had noticed and wondered at, first, in *The Way of a World* and then in the successive collections of the 1970s and the 1980s.[8]

The concluding chapter, 'Art and Mortality', discusses some new concerns and emphases emerging in the 1980s. Its purpose is also to sample and look closely at Tomlinson's poetic performance during that decade and to attempt some general conclusions about the character of his art.

Tomlinson has retired from university teaching but not from poetry. Two further collections have appeared in the 1990s. A new *Selected Poems* was published in 1997.

* * * * *

Since the publication of *Seeing is Believing* in 1958, it has been clear to me that Tomlinson is a major poet. Recognition of his importance came quickly in the United States, near the beginning of his career, and the appearance in recent years of translations of his work bears witness to a widening reputation outside Britain. In his own country, however, acceptance has been slow in coming; underrated and misunderstood in some quarters, as Donald Davie, Michael Edwards, Richard Swigg and others have claimed, he remains a controversial poet. I have stated my purpose in writing this critical study; to defend his poetry along lines dictated by misconceptions of it would be a digression from that purpose. Yet there is no denying that the history of Tomlinson's critical reception in Britain is peculiar—puzzling and depressing—and the fact cannot simply be passed over. Apologetics are inappropriate, but a consideration of some of the unsympathetic descriptions and adverse judgements of his work should be attempted. Since my own 'answers' to such criticism are also implicit in the discussion of particular poems in the following chapters, I think the reader will find it useful if here I present the views of his critics and my responses in conjunction with the poet's own conception of what he is doing in his poems, summarized from interviews and other public statements.

Before turning to those statements let me draw attention to a description of his work by a Hungarian friend, quoted in 'Over Elizabeth Bridge' (CP p. 226), a poem first published in *Written on Water* (1972).[9] In 1969 Tomlinson visited Budapest, and during the next three years, he writes, one image of the city continued to tease his memory with hints of uncertain meaning: 'Three years, now, the curve of Elizabeth Bridge / Has caught at some half-answering turn of mind'. He had always known that the image corresponded in some elusive way to the turbulence of the city's history, but it is characteristic, he tells his friend, that he should 'hesitate to fix a meaning':

> that uncertainty
> And restless counterpointing of a verse
> 'So wary of its I', Iván, is me.

'Uncertainty', like 'wary' in Ivan's phrase once it is echoed back to him, makes a gesture of modest self-deprecation, as if confessing or conceding something; it is a courtesy, but also a feint, as such courtesy sometimes is, concealing a challenge to habitual thinking. The challenge is to discover in circumspection a principle and an enabling discipline. As the poem goes on to demonstrate, 'uncertainty' and 'counterpointing' define the mode of relationship between subject and object in Tomlinson's verse: an *uncertainty* that is a form of vigilance against solipsism, the subjective absorption of the object; a *counterpointing* of object and subject (in that order of precedence—the image calls to the answering mind) which maintains their separateness in relationship. Both words indicate a habit of attention and respect for the other—attendance upon the experience—which allows an image gradually to release its meaning over a three-year interval without interference from an officious 'I'. The antithesis of 'I' and 'me', in Tomlinson's remarks to his friend, makes a riddling distinction between ego and self. Restraint of subjectivism is the means of enlarging the circumference of the perceiving self, an expansion of self which is not at the same time an inflation of ego.

That strong sense of the difference between the isolated ego and the larger self developed out of his experience of prolonged illness during youth. He has spoken about this in some of his interviews. He grew up in a working-class neighbourhood of Stoke, a street of 'blackened houses',[10] breathing 'sedimented air / From a landscape of disembowellings, underworlds / Unearthed among the clay'.[11] For two years pleurisy and then rheumatic fever kept him out of school and for nine months bedridden. The experience turned his attention not inward but, he says, 'away from myself and my illness'.[12] 'It made a contemplative of me, but it wasn't myself I was contemplating.'[13] Those months upstairs alone 'made me very aware of myself as a separate physical entity, but also ... of the world surrounding me of which I could see little but could hear through the window'.[14] His imagination fed 'on what Coleridge calls ... "all the numberless goings-on of life"' —the sounds of the house as well as sounds from the street and even 'the clink of shunting wagons from the sidings beyond'.[15] Tomlinson is an admirer of Coleridge, in particular the conversation poems and the notebooks, but it is significant that he could quote from one of those poems, 'Frost at Midnight', which starts from the poet's hinted sense of present estrangement and recalls his loneliness as a schoolboy boarder in Christ's Hospital, the blue-coat school at that time located in the City of London, and feel no need to comment on the resemblances between the situation of the young Coleridge and his own at about the same age: Coleridge 'reared', as he says, 'In the great city, pent 'mid cloisters dim', who 'saw nought lovely but the city and the stars'; Tomlinson, at Stoke, confined to that upstairs room, where 'for long periods you didn't see people'[16] and whence he could barely see 'the chimneys of the houses opposite'.[17] Whether or not during that period of extreme isolation Tomlinson at times felt a comparable sense of estrangement from the 'goings-on of life', his emphasis is not on that separation but on the effort to make connection. What Coleridge has missed and, in the form of a prayer, solicits for his baby son, to learn by sight and sound the 'eternal language' of Nature, is for Tomlinson the foundation of his art: behind the windows 'you were very conscious of the world pulsing as a fact quite distinct from yourself and yet in which you had a share . . . almost as if you were out there, but unseen yourself'.[18]

Seeing, the act of seeing and how things look, is a preoccupation of Tomlinson's poetry. But in his recollection of the circumstances of his illness, which he says permanently affected the set of his mind, the word that recurs is 'unseen'. The motivating 'effort away'[19] from self was, in the first place, the urge to join a world he could not see. Later, released from his confinement, the fascination of the *unseen* developed in the adolescent a determination to see, and record, what is not easily seen and takes *effort* to recover. Drawing trees made him aware of 'all that escaped one in rendering the tangled boughs, for instance', and that awareness, he adds, 'entered into my feeling for words as well, and the way aspects of reality escaped them also'.[20] But seeing is always potentially a metaphor for the mind's apprehension of reality; and in that sense too, as the unknown and perhaps unknowable, the unseen has continued to be a concern of his poetry. Recalling the experience of the boy 'alone upstairs' listening to the activities of the house or in the distance the noise of shunting wagons, he speaks of 'a peculiar transparency of consciousness' through which an exterior world is given an interior presence. He has a double sense of this experience. Either it is a 'sense of something over there—drawing me out of myself into a sort of balance',[21] or it is as if, by imagining, he could become an 'unseen' witness of 'what was happening down there and out there'.[22] Either the object or the subject is invisible. They are not, however, mutually exclusive alternatives: together they convey the paradox of a world that at once resists penetration and invites participation. Tomlinson sometimes uses the word 'mystery' to identify a certain quality in his experience of place, and I think this paradox is at the heart of its meaning for him. In drawing or writing it is what escapes one, the world beyond self that cannot be fully translated into visual or verbal language. He uses the word in describing his early passion for fishing: 'I fished all over the county, quietly, meditatively intent on the mysteries of weather and water'[23]—the variety and intricacy of phenomena but also, surely, the problem of penetrating the impenetrable, translating the untranslatable. When he uses the word again, in a discussion of the sense in which his poetry might be termed 'religious', it has the same reference to those aspects of reality that escape one: 'I am awed by things that escape my grasp and I am awed by the mystery of a universe that refuses to be tidied away.'[24] He thinks of his landscape poems as 'contemplations', a species of 'religious poetry', which record the discovery of what his friend, the French poet Philippe Jaccottet, calls *ouvertures*—openings through place into mystery'. 'Place', he continues, 'speaks to me ... of very fundamental things: time, death, what we have in common with the animals, what things are like when you stop talking and look, what Eden is like, what a centre is.'[25]

The enforced confinement and isolation of those two years, from which he sought imaginative release, had their parallel outside his room in the limiting conditions of life at Stoke. Meditating on that period over thirty years later, he recalled, in 'The Marl Pits', the felt need to free himself from 'a world / Whose stoic lethargy seemed the one reply / To horizons and to streets' closed in by 'a monotone fume, a bloom of grey'.[26] His liberation began at school with the study of languages. 'Languages meant another world out there', the world, for example, introduced to him by the refugee Jewish teacher of German, who had studied at Berlin and Heidelberg, 'where people talked about Rilke and Kafka and Mann as everyday facts'. He remembers, too, when his French teacher was explaining Aristotle's *Poetics*, his excitement 'at the thought that here I was in the fifth century B.C. Athens bandying about words like catharsis and anagnorisis' even as the view through the window showed him 'the same old pot bank smoking away down the street'. The acrid staleness of the air in the Potteries is associated in Tomlinson's mind with the 'stale stoicism'[27] of the region's inhabitants. The boy's strenuous effort to make connection with an outer world from which illness had banished him became, when he recovered and returned to it, also a cultural aspiration. It was to 'another world', wider 'horizons', that he imagined 'the unseen railway was leading' him—drawing him out of himself 'into a sort of balance'[28] between self and other places, other times. When a decade later the cultural insularity promoted by Larkin and Amis was influential in literary circles (under the slogan 'no more myth kitties and no more poems about foreign cities'), 'I felt', he told Alan Ross, 'that my world—the world I had been reaching out to since I was twelve—was under attack and I smelt in the air once more all the stalenesses I'd detested.'[29]

Tomlinson says that, as a result of his schooling in languages, he knew French poetry before he knew English poetry. It was not surprising, then, that in the process of mastering his own poetic craft he should turn his attention to translation.[30] His first book of translations, *Versions from Fyodor Tyutchev*, made in collaboration with his colleague at the University of Bristol, Henry Gifford, appeared in 1960, the same year as the supplemented edition of *Seeing is Believing*. Translation has remained a major concern, playing a significant role in Tomlinson's growth as a poet. Its value, he says, is that comparison of 'individual words in your own and another language' reveals 'just how radically language stylizes experience';[31] which is a lesson in objectivity, how not to mistake a way of saying for the object of sense or thought. 'It's also a marvellous way of getting beyond linguistic barriers', the enclosure of a single language, 'and discovering new forms'.[32] New forms, new modes of expression, are new views; as such the pursuit of them is another manifestation of Tomlinson's lifelong campaign to secure possession of a ground beyond self, to escape 'the fixities of self' (a purpose informing his reluctance, in 'Over Elizabeth Bridge', 'to fix a meaning' to experience). Conditioning by the structures and habits of one language need not be, but may well encourage, something like a linguistic solipsism. When he speaks of translation as one of the greatest challenges a poet can face, the challenge is what it was for the young man drawing trees, where, he says, 'the resistant detail challenged me ... to concentrate on the world beyond myself'.[33] If a sense of affinity drew him to the

Russian Tyutchev and the Spanish poet Machado, he was drawn to the Peruvian César Vallejo and the Mexican poet Octavio Paz by an attraction of opposites: 'here were two poets utterly different in temperament from myself and so challenged what I thought and felt'.[34]

In his interview with Alan Ross, in 1981, trying to re-enter the mind of his young self as he listened to the sounds of house and street, removed from yet sharing in 'the goings-on of life', he uses the phrase 'a peculiar *transparency* of consciousness', as if consciousness were a sheet of glass through which the objective world transmits an image of itself. He uses the same word to describe Gifford's contribution to their renderings of Tyutchev. This was the provision of a 'transparency',[35] (the word they had adopted at the time of their collaboration), that is, a literal translation of each poem alongside the original but also a transliteration which, with notes about sound effects and nuances of meaning, aimed to bring out as much as possible of the poem's 'physical feel'. 'Transparency', in this usage, denotes the mind's simultaneous separation from and identity with the source of its perceptions. It is the paradox which, I suggested earlier, is for Tomlinson the 'mystery' of the self's encounter with the other, whether it be the world of sense experience or another language, another mind.

Tomlinson's repeated use of the expression 'getting beyond' in explaining his poetic aims should be noted: getting beyond the egocentric self, beyond a cramping fatalism, beyond linguistic and cultural insularity. The limiting agents are all seen as forms of subjectivism; the goal is a larger, a less 'personal' self. One model he cites is William Carlos Williams, whose best poems demonstrate that 'intense personal excitement can be conveyed without heavyweight expressionist insistence, the poet's personality lost (as it were) in its object'.[36] Liberation from the personal, or self-regarding, self is the self's means of entry into a world ('out there') of negotiable relations. To gain admittance to it the self must embrace 'a certain anonymity';[37] it needs to feel the *resistance* of the other, whether natural or human, to the merely subjective. Tomlinson looks for resistance to the self-regarding self not only in subject matter but also in language.

'Poetry', he insists, 'stands by a certain ungainsayableness that religion knew before it went soft in the nineteenth century and then stayed soft.'[38] Since it cannot ignore the inexorable facts of existence, its words must be of a corresponding hardness, 'a medium in which you [can] (as it were) sculpt your meaning'.

'Playing with words as if they were plasticine', a toy for private use, his description of Dylan Thomas's practice, is by these standards, therefore, 'regressive'[39] and for the same reason, he says, referring to the social nature of words, 'a threat to what I should call a *civil* language'.[40] He points out that his own landscape poems, though usually unpeopled, 'are written in a language so dense in the usages of community that [he] can never think of them as being merely private or passive'.[41] They challenge the illusion of self-containment with their recognition of necessity and the necessary implication of humanity in its defining conditions, but do not surrender to 'a sapping fatalism'.[42] It is necessary to feel the resistance of fact, conditionality, but it is equally necessary for us to oppose the compulsions of time and place, seeking, as it were, an equilibrium of resistant forces. Tomlinson speaks of that search as a process of negotiation: his landscape poems are, he tells us, 'full of the weave of time'—a metaphor implying human accommodation not submission—and 'they map the continuous negotiation we all make in being involved in a world of things whose full nature keeps eluding us'.[43]

The conviction that feeds Tomlinson's determination to liberate himself from the narrowly personal and feel himself part of a world that 'exceeds [his] grasp', 'whose *full* nature keeps eluding us', is also D. H. Lawrence's. In a review of J. Hillis Miller's *Poets of Reality*, a study of modern writers from whose company Lawrence is conspicuously excluded, he quotes this sentence from 'Art and Morality': 'And nothing is true, or good, or right, except in its own living relatedness to its own circumambient universe; to the things that are in the stream with it.'[44] Nothing is good or true or right in isolation; specifically, self has its meaning in the context of what is not self, the human in the context of what is not human. It is ironic, therefore, that one of the misconceptions that has bedevilled criticism of Tomlinson is that a poetry of the physical universe must be a poetry divorced from the human world: he has been accused, as Ian Hamilton reminded him in 1964, of 'writing about things rather than human beings'. The antithesis is fallacious on two counts. In the first place, as Tomlinson pointed out, many of the 'things' he writes about—'houses, cities, walls, landscapes'—are 'saturated in human presence and tradition', and that is part of his reason for writing about them. Of course, there are poems in Tomlinson's *oeuvre* of which this is not true, where the non-human confronts the human with its difference. Yet where this is so the antithesis between things and human beings is equally inappropriate; confrontation is encounter and these poems too are about relationship, where, moreover, the relationship between self and the non-human other parallels the relationship between self and the human other. 'The terms on which I write about things are the same terms on which true relationship with people becomes possible; that's to say, in my "thing" poems, there is a sense of letting the other be, a containment of self, if you like.'

In this statement Tomlinson is rebutting not only the charge of scanting treatment of the human subject but an earlier suggestion that influence from *other* artists can erode originality. 'You can't have too much of it if you know what to do with it ... The trouble with most critics is that they have such shallow [and, one might add, romantic] notions of originality.'[45] In advocating openness to the in-flowings from other minds he is once again affirming the other's contribution to the enlargement, not the curtailment, of self. For 'containment' here means both restraint and inclusion in a larger ('circumambient') whole, perhaps the largest imaginable— elsewhere he speaks of 'a containing universe'.[46] Tomlinson's metaphor, like Lawrence's, is spatial; it is, however, characteristic of his art to create both spatial and temporal perspectives. Talking to Michael Schmidt in 1977, he instances 'Antecedents', an early sequence presenting 'a capsulated history of late romanticism' which, as the title makes plain, is implicitly an exploration of his own relationship with that movement. 'I was trying to bring to bear my sense of late romanticism on the situation as it existed in the London Bohemia of the 1950s. All this was an attempt to understand myself through history.'[47] Self-understanding has always been for Tomlinson an act of situating oneself in 'living relatedness' to the other. Here the other is a literary and cultural milieu, which is in turn 'placed' by its relation to an earlier one, the Paris of Jules Laforgue and Stéphane Mallarmé.

By the late 1980s, looking back over more than three decades of writing, he was able to discern in his poetic record of place a connecting purpose: to maintain both a freshness of relationship and a sureness of perspective. In an interview with Richard Swigg in 1987 he notes the motif of return. 'It's as if I have to keep faithfully going back and feeling once more all the links'—returning to La Serra in northern Italy, the scene of the earliest pieces in his *Collected Poems*, but also revisiting Oaxaca in Mexico, Alburquerque and Chimayó in New Mexico, and the desert landscape of the American Southwest. He has to renew his experience of these places, which is to 'feel out' the self's share in the reality of each place as an inseparable part of the self's own reality; but no less urgently he needs to weigh these experiences against each other. In the collection called *The Return*, just published at the time of this interview, 'the American experience', he says, 'is still being balanced up against those youthful days in Italy'.[48] He speaks of these returns, we notice, as acts of fidelity; 'faithfully going back', acknowledging unbreakable attachments, recognizing certain permanencies. In 1972 he had told his readers (in a *Poetry Book Society Bulletin*) that 'the search for forms, for patterns of order, for meaningful relationship with people and place, is the human act of faith'.[49]

Some critics have reservations about the 'patterns of order' that Tomlinson is intent on finding. An anonymous reviewer in *The Times Literary Supplement* points to the 'agreeable marriages' everywhere in his work between 'natural flux and aesthetic structure' and mildly 'wonders if Mr. Tomlinson's world is *too* harmonic'.[50] In illustration of the 'harmonic' he quotes from 'Written on Water',[51] but makes no mention of the tensions in that poem between wish and fact, the search for pattern and its elusiveness. Water is flux, but 'One returns to it *as though* it were a thread / Through the labyrinth of appearances'; note the tentativeness, the hesitation 'to fix a meaning'. Is even the assertion of the concluding lines quoted by the

Introduction 15

reviewer entirely unqualified? The title-phrase, repeated, gives us the paradox of water:

> 'Written on water', one might say
> Of each day's flux and lapse
> But to speak of water is to entertain the *image*
> Of its seamless momentum once again. (my emphasis)

Thus the poem begins the movement towards its final affirmation not of a certainty but a faith, a hoped-for disclosure: but 'its liquid friction of small sounds', giving the illusion of speech, is that paradox, a 'continuing revelation / Of itself, never to be revealed'. A. Kingsley Weatherhead, in a generally sympathetic account of Tomlinson's work, expresses a similar reservation with the comment, concerning the 'geometry' in his scenes, that 'if the discovery of the pattern reduces tangled reality [in the representation of a cityscape in 'The Tree'[52]] to a schema or a pictograph, it did at least have the effect of creating the reader's awareness'.[53] But that 'tangled reality', unmodified, regularly gets full recognition in the poems. Geometry does not reduce, it sets the form the eye discovers—an ascending, branching tree in a 'treeless street'—against what is, immitigably, also there, heightening our awareness of the tangle of 'gutter, gable, slates, and chimney-crowns'; to say 'at least' of the creation of such an awareness is to minimize a considerable achievement. This interdependence of form and the formless is the theme of a later poem, 'Snow Signs'.[54] The snow-lines left after a partial thaw, a 'white geometry' edging the contours of a hillside, reveal—by (so to speak) measuring—'the fortuitous / Full variety a hillside spreads for us'; it would have gone unnoticed without that accentuation. The variety of nature spreads itself *for us* only in the sense that, if the eye lives in relationship with what it sees, the seen (scene) enters our 'human universe', as it does in Wordsworth's poetry. (Tomlinson told Ian Hamilton that if we had retained relations with it, 'the world of Wordsworth, ... allied with the insights of the phenomenologists, might have given us back a human universe'.[55])

The counterpointing of geometry and flux is also, famously, a tactic of 'Swimming Chenango Lake'.[56] It leads in that poem to other counterpointings: the shaping spirit 'making a where in water' and 'The going elsewhere of ripples incessantly shaping'; the freedom of the eye and the dependence of the body; possession and relinquishment. All are versions of the balancings energetically practised in Tomlinson's poetry: supple evasions of bias, of 'the fixities of self'. Notoriously he has denounced extremity in poetry as in life. In 'Some Presences on the Scene: A Vista of Postwar Poetry', an essay contributed to a festschrift for Donald Davie in 1988, he echoes Yvor Winters in arguing that 'the surrender to impulse and the divine right of self-expression', which has led poets to suicide or a 'readiness to court self-destruction'[57] for self-expression's sake, is to misconceive the poetic vocation, drastically limiting its range by distorting the significance of self. Balance is not, as some reviewers of Tomlinson's work have supposed, the substitution of 'detachment' for involvement. Commitment to extremity is, simply, an incompleteness, entailing a massive exclusion of unexamined experience; the struggle to achieve balance is, for him, a struggle for wholeness, truth to all facets of an experience. He has a predilection for such figures of complementary opposition as 'sensuous abstraction' and 'passionate intellect'[58] to define the balances he looks for in poetry, his own or others'. When he was writing his first poems, poets were supposed to be 'creatures of feeling', but as a young man looking for an alternative to the excesses of Dylan Thomas and his followers, he welcomed Davie's insistence that the poet's 'trade ... is both to feel and to discriminate feeling. It was the discrimination part', he remembers, 'that seemed particularly tonic in the poetic climate of the fifties.'[59] Those critics who have accused Tomlinson of 'detachment' have apparently retained Matthew Arnold's prejudice against cerebration ('The poetry of Dryden, Pope, and all their school is conceived and composed in their wits, genuine poetry is conceived and composed in the soul'[60]); but the discriminating mind *focuses* feeling, it does not suppress it. Though he rejected the emotional incontinence of the neo-romantics, he did not therefore embrace its inversion by the Movement poets of the 1950s or their successors in the following decade—the ' "man-of-the-world" off-handedness' and 'rootless wit' of a poetry that did not 'commit itself to very deep emotion'.[61]

Those who favour the word 'detachment' in describing Tomlinson's poetry will also, more justifiably, refer to the influence of the Augustan school of poets held in such low esteem by Arnold. Davie, in his introduction to *The Necklace*, in 1955, was the first to draw attention to the 'sternly traditional, classical, almost Augustan morality'[62] revealed in it; since then 'Augustanism' has been a commonplace in summary descriptions of his work. The label identifies something that is there, related to what he himself calls 'civility' in the language and moral ethos of his poetry, but it gives a false impression if it is used without qualification and is not balanced by an equally clear perception of how much he owes to English romanticism. Tomlinson regards the subjectivist strain in romantic poetry not as its defining characteristic but as its Achilles' heel; for him, as for Jacques Barzun (*Romanticism and the Modern Ego*), its essential strength, as also its central endeavour, is its realism, its cultivation of perception, 'respecting what the eye saw, enumerating the streaks of that tulip which Johnson had found of so little interest to poetry, and greeting these perceptions with a renovated wonder and tact'.[63] The school of poetry founded by Wordsworth and Coleridge was certainly 'concerned with its feelings' but concerned also, self-critically, self-diagnostically 'to weigh those feelings over against the bodied presence of rocks and stones and trees, over against the outward-going eye'.[64] In stressing the part played by romanticism in the formation of his poetic outlook Tomlinson is anxious to correct a view of his art that, if it were true, would indicate a culpable absence of that balance and perspective which he has worked to achieve—a balance of classicism and romanticism, a perspective that combines a romantic judgement of classicism with a classical judgement of romanticism. 'So what critics call "Augustanism" in my case', he tells his interviewer, 'is probably the attempt to situate all I've learned from romanticism within reach of a distrust of the ego, within reach of a flexible awareness that ... you must respect what is other than you as you respect people in a conversation'; and what he learned from Wordsworth and Coleridge is itself, we recall, a confrontation of feeling with fact serving 'an awareness of things that is both passionate and balanced'.[65] The romanticism that Tomlinson values culminates in

Ruskin. He relates his poetic principles to 'a development out of romanticism in the prose of Ruskin's *Modern Painters* and of Hopkins's notebooks', a continuation but one that works 'against the grain of that subjectivism which too often aborted the romantic quest'.[66]

Tomlinson is, as one critic writes, 'a late exemplar of literary modernism' who, unlike Eliot, Joyce and Pound, however, 'has shown little interest in existential angst or spiritual deracination'.[67] In an art that seeks balance and wholeness and enacts a participatory relationship of subject with object, Tomlinson casts himself as a 'tutelary spirit / Of his own inheritance' and 'speaks to celebrate'[68] this relationship and this inheritance. As a poetry of persistent (selective) celebration it has incurred the criticism, as we have noted, of being 'too harmonic', too frequently a composition of 'agreeable marriages'. This is a superficial reading of the poems. It separates the 'harmonic'—treaties, compacts, accords—from other pressing awarenesses that complicate and temper his affirmations, and it forgets that in any collection there are poems of other moods, founded on a seasoned knowledge of hard truths, the devastations of time and human folly. Tomlinson has drawn attention to these polarities in his work. In a *Poetry Book Society Bulletin* he writes, of *American Scenes* (1966), that it moves 'between the solitudes, the misgivings of some of the opening pieces with the awareness of death, and the realisation of a range of possibilities of sensuous awareness, relationship and society, coming full circle ... with a quotation from Dante's *Paradiso*. The two poles of the book are "Snow Fences" and "Idyll", the one all death, coldness and desolation, and the other all continuity and humanity, permeated by a kind of secular grace.' He has pointed out similar confrontations in later collections. Over against what he is prepared to call 'a religious awareness' there is, in fact, in Tomlinson's work a pervasive, if unhistrionically displayed, consciousness of mortality and the pains of an intrinsically unfriendly universe. He informs us that while he was writing much of the opening section of *American Scenes*, which includes 'Snow Fences', he was 'haunted by "The entire creation sighs and throbs with pain"' (Romans viii, 22).[69]

We have learned from his account of his youth that there is for

Tomlinson a direct link between these antithetical mind-sets. The origins of his search for 'marriages' with a world 'going elsewhere' than where you want it to go were in his early experience of physical and cultural exclusion. He recognizes the presence of the same contraries, the same consequential relation between lack and 'the will to wish back Eden',[70] in the work of the French poet Jaccottet, 'its insights being the fruit both of deprivation and an awareness of plenitude'; in his friend's poetry, as in his own, 'humanity and landscape are held in imaginative rapport', therefore, 'with difficulty and hope'.[71] It was with this conjunction of toughness and vision that Tomlinson entered the post-war world: a Europe that felt, in his words, 'pretty smashed up and worn down', an England afflicted with what Ernest Bevin called at the time 'a poverty of desire'. Cinema then seemed to him 'vastly more important than the novel—the novel after Joyce and Lawrence, that is', but, an admirer though he was of the French directors whose films were making their way into England during the late 1940s, he 'came to feel and resent the terrible, sapping fatalism' of much of their work. His verdict on the surrealist cinema of the 1920s and 1930s, which visually interested him more, was finally the same: 'a mere surrender to the fortuitous and to a fluidity [of imagery] in which there was not enough resistance'.[72] His own resistance to the art of fatalism was part of his general dissatisfaction with and dissent from a common mood of the period. Against inertia and apathy he sets the example of Isaac Rosenberg, whose 'growing realisation of the need for tragic acceptance' led to the achievement of his finest poems. Tragic acceptance is not fatalism but a 'revolt against circumstances' which does not prevent a baring of consciousness to the full experience of war, an acceptance that incorporates resistance. In *Trench Poems*, 'however close or terrible the experience, it is recorded without accusation ... and with all the strength of inner calm'.[73] The meaning of such calm is made clear in Tomlinson's line, in 'Over Elizabeth Bridge', memorializing the Hungarian poet Attila József, who killed himself in the 1930s: 'His verse grown calm with all it had *withstood*'.[74] War is not Tomlinson's subject, though the violence of revolution sometimes is. He does share, however, Yeats's sense of the twentieth century as 'an age of demolition'—tragic in its violation of 'fine relationship and the literal and daily demolition of its inherited architecture'[75]—and he speaks of 'the tragic fall from plenitude in our own urban universe'.[76] Yeats is exemplary for Tomlinson 'both as a custodian of value and a poet who can experience and record the tragedy without flinching',[77] the acknowledgement and realization of loss equalling in intensity the passion of conviction he opposes to it.

In an earlier discussion of 'Over Elizabeth Bridge', I referred to Tomlinson's description of his poetic stance as one of restless uncertainty and wariness. I suggested that this apparently modest confession conceals an affront to conventional thinking, challenging the reader to discover in circumspection an enabling discipline for poetry. Throughout this Introduction I have been arguing that Tomlinson's effort to achieve balance and perspective is not aimed, ascetically, at self-limitation and detachment but is a struggle for wholeness, an enlargement of self by liberation from partial views. An energetic, passionate engagement with his material, not austerity, is the hallmark of his work. This is not obvious to all his critics, though it should be. Calvin Bedient, for example, in an appreciative essay,[78] nevertheless declares that Tomlinson's imagination is 'far from being ample, headlong, or richly empowering'. In considering this judgement one must decide what conception of imagination is implied by 'headlong' (is there a poetic virtue in undeliberated self-precipitation?). If we knew, it might tell us why he thinks Tomlinson's is 'unobtrusive and stopped-down'. A brief look at some lines in a poem of the late 1970s might help us in weighing the issues raised by this critic. 'For Danton' (*The Shaft*, 1978; CP p. 278) meditates upon the tragic irony of Danton's career: he who had instituted the Revolutionary Tribunal, but had striven to abate its pitiless severities, was tried and condemned by it. The poem pictures him back in Arcis-sur-Aube, his birthplace, two months before his arrest:

> He fronts the parapet
> Drinking the present with unguarded sense:
> The stream comes on. Its music deafens him
> To other sounds, to past and future wrong.

By implication, a guarded sense of the present is the standard by which Danton's attitude is being judged here. A guarded sense of things is surely what Bedient deprecates in a 'stopped-down' imagination. But 'guarded' in this context would mean not inhibited or defensive but circumspect—that is, attentive to all circumstances that may affect decision. Should circumspection seem a modest literary virtue, note its relevance to Eliot's definition of wit in his essay on Andrew Marvell: 'a constant inspection and criticism of experience. It involves, probably, a recognition, implicit in the expression of every experience, of other kinds of experience which are possible.' The 'unguarded' vision is one blind to the whole truth: conversely, a guarded vision would be one that opens the mind to all circumstances, to the present and its contraries. The critical, vigilant, self-doubting—in a word, circumspect—approach to experience recommended in these lines, far from bottling up imagination, is precisely what empowers and gives it ample range.

NOTES

'Schmidt' identifies a conversation with Michael Schmidt in *PN Review*, 5:1 (1977); 'Ross' identifies a conversation with Alan Ross first published in 1981 and reprinted in Kathleen O'Gorman (ed.), *Charles Tomlinson: Man and Artist* (Columbia: University of Missouri Press, 1988); 'Swigg' identifies a conversation with Richard Swigg published for the first time in the same collection of essays; 'Doce' identifies a conversation with Jordi Doce in *Agenda*, 33:2 (Summer 1995), an issue devoted to Tomlinson's work.

1. Kathleen O'Gorman (ed.), *Charles Tomlinson: Man and Artist* (Columbia: University of Missouri Press, 1988); Brian John, *The World as Event: The Poetry of Charles Tomlinson* (Montreal and Kingston, London and Buffalo: McGill-Queen's University Press, 1989); Richard Swigg, *Charles Tomlinson and the Objective Tradition* (Lewisburg: Bucknell University Press; London and Toronto: Associated University Presses, 1994).

2. Richard Swigg in *Charles Tomlinson and the Objectivist Tradition*, the most recent and the most comprehensive study of his work, traces the principal influences on Tomlinson's poetry and defines its position in a literary and intellectual Anglo-American tradition of factuality. It takes a very different approach from mine but

one that stands in an exactly complementary relation to the 'reading' I offer in these pages.

3. *Poetry*, xciii:5 (February 1959), pp. 335–40.

4. *Eden*, p. 14.

5. 'A Sense of Distance' (CP p. 175).

6. Reproduced in *Words and Images* (1972), in *In Black and White* (1976) and, with finer clarity of tone, in *Eden* (1985).

7. Appended to *Eden*, a volume of graphics and of poems selected from his published work.

8. See the last paragraph of my chapter on Tomlinson in *British Poetry since 1970: A Critical Survey*, ed. Peter Jones and Michael Schmidt (Manchester: Carcanet New Press, 1980).

9. CP p. 226.

10. 'Hokusai on the Trent' (CP p. 248).

11. 'The Marl Pits' (CP p. 243).

12. Doce, p. 22.

13. Ross, p. 24.

14. Doce, p. 22.

15. Ross, p. 24.

16. *Ibid*.

17. Doce, p. 23

18. Ross, p. 24

19. Doce, p. 22.

20. *Ibid.*, p. 23.

21. *Ibid.*, p. 22.

22. Ross, p. 24.

23. Doce, p. 23.

24. Swigg, p. 232.

25. Ross, p. 35.

26. 'The Marl Pits' (CP p. 248).

27. Ross, p. 23.

28. Doce, p. 22.

29. Ross, p. 23.

30. See Tomlinson's 'Metamorphosis and Translation' in *Poetry and Metamorphosis* (1983) and 'The Poet as Translator', the Introduction to his *The Oxford Book of Verse in English Translation* (Oxford and New York: Oxford University Press, 1980). See also Henry Gifford, 'The Poet as Translator', *Agenda* ('Charles Tomlinson: International Issue'), 33: 2 (Summer 1995).

31. Schmidt, p. 37.

32. Doce, p. 29.

33. *Ibid.*, p. 23.

34. *Ibid.*, p. 29.

35. Ross, p. 29.
36. 'Some Presences on the Scene: A Vista of Postwar Poetry', *On Modern Poetry: Essays Presented to Donald Davie*, ed. Vereen Bell and Laurence Lerner (Nashville: University of Vanderbilt Press, 1988), p. 222.
37. Ross, p. 35.
38. Swigg, p. 232.
39. 'Some Presences on the Scene', p. 214.
40. Schmidt, p. 35.
41. Ross, p. 35.
42. Swigg, p. 228.
43. Ross, p. 35.
44. Review of J. Hillis Miller's *Poets of Reality* in *Encounter*, XXX:5 (May 1968). Lawrence had an early and lasting influence on Tomlinson's values. Donald Davie comments on this influence in his personal Foreword to *Charles Tomlinson: Man and Artist*. See Tomlinson's 'The Middlebrow Muse', his review of *New Lines*, an anthology of contemporary English verse edited by Robert Conquest, for his employment of these values in his judgement of its contents.
45. 'Four Conversations', *London Magazine*, 4:8 (November 1964).
46. *Eden*, p. 18.
47. Schmidt, p. 35.
48. Swigg, p. 229.
49. *Poetry Book Society Bulletin*, No. 75 (Christmas 1972).
50. *The Times Literary Supplement* (20 October 1972).
51. 'Movements VI: Written on Water' (CP p. 236).
52. CP p. 247.
53. A. Kingsley Weatherhead, 'Charles Tomlinson: With Respect to Flux', *Iowa Review*, 7:4 (Fall 1976), pp. 120–34.
54. CP p. 315.
55. 'The State of Poetry', *The Review*, 29–30 (Spring and Summer 1972), p. 50. Among phenomenologists Maurice Merleau-Ponty in particular has struck a chord with Tomlinson. In 'The Poet as Painter' (*Eden*) he quotes from Merleau-Ponty's essay 'Eye and Mind', collected in *The Primacy of Perception* (ed. James M. Edie, Evanston, IL: Northwestern University Press, 1964), and in 1975 told his interviewer that 'the little essay in it seemed to say all I'd wanted to say' about 'how we build our structures on the sensed and the given'. 'It says it for poetry and much more, and it makes us see how poetry is of a piece with other human activities.' ('An Interview with Charles Tomlinson', by Jed Rasula and Mike Erwin, *Contemporary Literature*, 16:4 [1975]). See also Ruth Grogan, 'Charles Tomlinson: The Way of his World', *Contemporary Literature*, 19 (1978).
56. CP p. 155.
57. 'Some Presences on the Scene', p. 217.
58. Schmidt, p. 37.

59. 'Some Presences on the Scene', p. 217.

60. *Essays in Criticism*, Second Series (1888): 'Thomas Gray'.

61. Peter Orr (ed.), *The Poet Speaks* (London: Routledge and Kegan Paul, 1964), pp. 252–53. He quotes from his essay 'Eye and Mind' collected in *The Primacy of Perception*.

62. *The Necklace*, pp. 67.

63. *Sewanee Review*, 70 (1962), p. 222.

64. *Ibid.*, p. 223.

65. Swigg, p. 231.

66. Doce, p. 25. See Ruth Grogan, 'Tomlinson, Ruskin and Moore: Facts and Fir Trees', *Twentieth Century Literature*, 35:2 (Summer 1989) and 'Tomlinson, Ruskin and Language Scepticism', *Essays in Literature*, 17:1 (1990). For a general account of the Objective Tradition in nineteenth-century writers see Patricia Ball, *Science of Aspects* (London: Athlone Press, 1971).

67. Ben Howard, *Prairie Schooner*, 63 (Summer 1989), p. 126. See Richard Swigg, *Tomlinson and the Objective Tradition* (London: Associated University Presses, 1994), and Alan Young, 'Rooted Horizon: Charles Tomlinson and American Modernism', *Critical Quarterly*, 24 (Winter 1982).

68. 'Movements V'.

69. *Poetry Book Society Bulletin*, No. 48 (April 1966).

70. *Eden* (CP p. 159).

71. 'The State of Poetry', *The Review*, 29–30 (Spring and Summer 1972), p. 50.

72. Swigg, p. 228.

73. 'Fate and the Image of Music: An Examination of Rosenberg's Plays', *Poetry Nation*, No. 3 (1974), pp. 64–65.

74. CP p. 227.

75. 'Yeats and the Practising Poet' in *An Honoured Guest*, ed. Denis Donoghue and J. R. Mulryne (London: Edward Arnold, 1965), pp. 1–7.

76. *Eden*, p. 15.

77. 'Yeats and the Practising Poet'.

78. *Eight Contemporary Poets*, p. 14.

Chapter One
An Ethic of Perception

In a chapter devoted to a closer examination of the landscape poems it is not enough to say, as I have said in my Introduction, that Tomlinson's verbal translations of sense experience invariably have an analogous human content: the relation between 'the analysis of sensation' (the phrase is Eliot's) and the discovery of human meaning calls for ampler and more particular definition. We may infer from a statement by the poet himself (quoted on the dust-cover of *Seeing is Believing*) that the relation is nearer to identity than to analogy. Tomlinson points to certain recurrent images in his previous volume, *The Necklace*—'the facets of cut glass . . . the shifting of light, the energizing weather which is the result of the combination of sun and frost', images of definition, of movement and change, of the interaction of contraries—and comments: 'these are the images of a certain mental climate, components of the moral landscape of my poetry in general', not exclusively of the nature poems. We must suppose, then, that looking and cognition are branches of the same mental activity of making the world intelligible, that both are forms of knowing. 'Perception' is one word, an important one in Tomlinson's vocabulary, that assumes their virtual identity—a close association certainly, which when we are reading Tomlinson we cannot easily forget. 'It is the mind sees': a sentence from the prose poem 'Skullshapes ' (CP p. 191) which expounds the thought-world of the painter, makes the point succinctly. Memory and expectation shape the meaning of what we see; mental temper and moral disposition humanize that meaning. For the same reasons that there is a natural communication between the physiological and the epistemological senses of 'perception' (therefore between the language of the painter and of the poet), for a poet-painter, but also for anyone who is attentive to what he sees, the physical world is inherently a human world.

These observations indicate the form of Tomlinson's interest in sense experience; they do not explain the interest itself, his preoccupation with the physical world. Why would a poet choose this particular method, the analysis of sensation, of interpreting and articulating meanings and values? The answer is in 'The Marl Pits' (CP p. 248), a poem of the 1970s. Recalling the blighted landscape of the industrial English Midlands in which he had spent his youth, he writes:

> It was a language of water, light and air
> I sought—to speak myself free of a world
> Whose stoic lethargy seemed the one reply
> To horizons and to streets that blocked them back
> In a monotone fume, a bloom of grey.

The nature to which the young artist turned for nourishment of the senses and enlargement of spirit was more than a theme: it was a language, a language of the elements; clear and exact, subtle and various, but above all concrete, particular, *objective*. Was Constable, he asks in 'A Meditation on John Constable' (CP p. 33), 'a descriptive painter'? (was nature, for him, an exterior to be copied?) and answers with a qualified yes, a definition of description that makes the thing described at once object and response (nature, in other words, was the painter's 'language'):

> If delight
> Describes, which wrings from the brush
>   The errors of a mind, so tempered,
> It can forgo all pathos; for what he saw
>   Discovered what he was, and the hand—unswayed
> By the dictation of a single sense—
>   Bodied the accurate and total knowledge
> In a calligraphy of present pleasure.

The submission of the thinking eye to the disciplines of observation and accurate transcription is, so to speak, a constitutional check upon the power of the self-regarding mind to make the world over into a reflection of itself. One must not, however, confuse impartiality and self-restraint with asceticism. Without the 'delight' and 'present pleasure' that humanize attention such 'exactness of art', in painter or in poet, would be an arid exercise: its purpose is not to suppress or confine feeling but, like a burning-glass, to focus sensibility and kindle feeling into knowledge.

Objectivism,[1] even as an artistic ideal, has no necessary connection with the painting of landscapes or the writing of nature poems. Although in much of Tomlinson's poetry it takes the latter form, it is more generally, for him as for others, an assumption about the sources of knowledge. The objectivist polemics of Eliot's early criticism proceed from that philosophical premise. It is, in fact, instructive to compare the terms of Tomlinson's early artistic manifesto, 'A Meditation on John Constable', with the case presented by Eliot for intellectual objectivity, 'the disinterested exercise of intelligence', in 'The Perfect Critic' (*The Sacred Wood*). In the field of vision an 'object' is material, but in the sphere of thought—and Eliot's theme in this essay, notwithstanding the title, is clear thinking in general—the word means anything that is regarded as external to the mind: which can be known by it, and is correlative to the thinking or knowing subject. Thinking may be concrete or abstract but, Eliot insists, it will not be exact unless, in one or other sense of the word, it 'deals with *objects*'. When it fails to do this it becomes mere 'verbalism', for there is a 'tendency of words to become indefinite emotions'; 'when we do not know enough, we tend always to substitute emotions for thoughts'. Aristotle is on this occasion Eliot's model for disinterested, analytic thought. Whereas Hegel dealt with 'his emotions as if they were definite objects which had arranged those emotions', Aristotle 'looked solely and steadfastly at the object'. In the *Posterior Analytics* 'he provides an eternal example ... of intelligence itself swiftly operating the analysis of sensation to the point of principle and definition'.[2] It would seem at first glance unlikely that the quality of a painter's attention to the phenomenal world and that of a philosopher to the contents of his mind have much in common, and yet plainly Tomlinson's Constable ('What he saw / Discovered what he was') and Eliot's Aristotle (who 'looked solely and steadfastly at the object') have, with regard to subjects and objects, the same priorities and related standards of mental discipline. They are priorities and standards which in the early 1920s Eliot labelled classical; thought that operates without a clear distinction between subject and object was, conversely, judged to be romantic. The 'verbalism' of nineteenth-century philosophy and early twentieth-century criticism was consequently diagnosed, in 'The Perfect Critic', as a symptom of romantic indefiniteness. These labels, counters of a debate revived in the early decades of this century, belong to an obsolete conception of literary history. Eliot's generic use of 'romantic' can be understood only if we remember that he was challenging a critical taste still largely fed by *late Victorian* romanticism. Tomlinson's objectivism—classical, in one sense of the word—was in the 1950s, like Eliot's, also part of a campaign against current 'neo-romantic' vices of thinking, feeling and style: the rigours of his early verse were those of a disciplined sensitivity, but one sharpened to a cutting edge by its resistance to the resurgent poetic romanticism of the 1940s. His art then and since, though no longer conspicuously armoured, has aimed at an objective clarity of both physical and mental vision.

'Skullshapes' (CP p. 191), the 'poem-in-prose' already cited, was first collected in *The Way of a World* (1969). An early product of the marriage of poet and painter that began in the late 1960s and lasted through most of the succeeding decade, it offers a compendious introduction to the perceptual world of Tomlinson's poetry. The title refers to a series of drawings executed in the latter part of 1968; the poem, at once concrete and abstract, crisply sensuous and analytic, translates into words the eye's knowledge of the surfaces and interiors of animal skulls, exemplifying in these particulars—in terms that make it as valid for poetry as for painting—an epistemology of art. It begins with 'the rural detritus of cattle skulls brought home by children'. Cleaned of soil and moss-stains and suspended from a nail, they each convey a simultaneous impression of 'weight' and 'a hanging fragility'; 'the two qualities fuse and the brush translates this fusion as wit, where leg-like appendages conclude the skulls' dangling mass'. This contemplation of the exhumed skulls and their translation into art is a prefigurative arrangement of the poem's central themes. The first part concerns the paradox of vision, which sees in the same object fact and possibility, what is and what seems, the literal (the thing itself indicated by its image) and the added meaning of analogy; the second part discusses art's repossession and extension of this dual reality. The argument has three stages: it considers first what the eye sees, looking at a skull; then what the mind brings to 'the art of vision'; and finally what art adds to 'the skull of nature'.

What the eye sees is a world of light and shadow. 'Flooded with light, the skull is at once' light and shadow, 'manifest surface and labyrinth of recesses'; 'shadow explores' cavities beyond the eyes' reach. As the world divides into light and shadow, so vision knows (by these different signs) both 'what lies in the eyes' possession' and 'what the eye cannot make out': light reveals visible fact, but equally shadow suggests or 'declares' invisible but imaginable fact. Reality presented to the eye is composed of exteriors and interiors. 'Skulls are a keen instance of this duality of the visible.'

'One sees. But not merely the passive mirrorings of the retinal mosaic.' 'It is the mind sees', and, if the eyes live in space, the mind lives in time: the mind brings to the instant of vision the contents of memory (a vision of the past, remembered images of, in Wallace Stevens's phrase, 'things as they are'[3]), and it brings the tribute and play of imagination (a vision of 'a future', of 'possibility', images of things as they might be or seem to be). Memory turns perception into 'conception': 'The senses, reminded by other seeings, bring to bear on the act of vision their pattern of images; they give point and place to an otherwise naked and homeless impression.' 'Place' is a position in relation to 'other seeings', and 'point' is the quality of relation, the reason for being there; the impression, grouped with others like it, is one of a kind and thus takes on identity and meaning. A visible world 'naked' of associations is 'clothed by comparison alone' (CP p. 26) and humanized by the seeing mind: sense experience is thereby made at 'home' in the country of the mind.

'Memory' is Tomlinson's word, 'imagination' is not. I use it for convenience, to mean perception of what is other than fact or, encouraged by a discerned likeness, of what goes beyond the fact.

The mind sees facts and possibilities, and as an explorer of possibilities imagination has an equal part with observation in 'the act of vision': 'the skulls of birds, *hard* to the touch, are [also] *delicate* to the eye' (my emphases). But, though transcending reality, imagination is not allowed by Tomlinson to belie or ignore it. Notwithstanding the suggestions of analogical meaning—egg-like or 'spherical' like blown glass—birds' skulls, for example, 'resist the eyes' imaginings with the blade of the beak which no lyrical admiration can attenuate to frailty'. Fact sets the limit to imagination's extension of fact. If seen and unseen, exterior and interior, are the two sides of fact, constituting 'the duality of the visible', memory and possibility are the two times of (past and future) meaning, and the mind's addition to the instantaneous 'retinal impression'. The two sides of fact and the two times of meaning comprise the space–time world of sensory experience.

Art works with and against the reality of the senses. Tomlinson first notes that even in its shaping of the visible, art follows nature. 'The skull of nature is recess and volume. The skull of art—of possibility—is recess, volume and also lines—lines of containment, lines of extension.' Although the lines are the artist's addition to the recess and volume of nature, brush and pen, in defining limits and exploring beyond them, merely imitate the dual actions of the eye and of the mind. The eye discovers 'borders' between what it can see and what it cannot; what is within the borders is *contained* by the eye, but also, even in the instantaneous act of vision, 'one *extends* the vertical impression, searchingly and instantaneously' (my emphasis), beyond edges and beneath surfaces. The mind adds to the three dimensions of space the dimension of time: memory contains reality by integrating the present impression into a previously formed whole of related images; imagination extends the impression 'beyond the instant' into 'a future', drawing the real into the possible.

'Skullshapes' is one of a group of poems in *The Way of a World* called 'Processes'. Another group is headed 'Instances', and there seems to me to be a connection, in Tomlinson's idea of the artwork as at once particular and general, concrete and abstract, between the 'instant' of time and an instance (in space and time) of a general principle or process. Just as instants of perception are mentally extended by remembered and imagined likenesses into the fullness of past and future time, so 'a cowskull', an instance of something, 'knived across by the challenge of a line', 'opens [in spatial metaphor] a visionary field, a play of universals'.

Possibility is an extension not a denial of reality. This is not to say, however, that the role of imagination is merely one of compliance. In the made world of art, reality is both rendered with minute fidelity and challenged by its opposite—'knived across by the challenge of a line, the raggedness of flaking bone countered by ruled, triangular facets'. The image of 'flaking bone' returns us to the opening words: 'Skulls. Finalities.' Skulls are instances of last things. In art, 'they emerge towards new beginnings from undergrowth' of death. Light and shadow are their literal selves, they are what the painter needs them to be; but notwithstanding the primacy of factual record and analysis, here, as elsewhere in Tomlinson's work, they are allowed to retain at the same time their figurative significance: they are 'the duality of the visible', but—uninsistent, stripped of intrusive emotion—they are still the natural metaphors for life and death. 'The skull is at once manifest surface and labyrinth of recesses', and in that labyrinth lurk rumours, foreshadowings, of death; shadow, which 'reaches down out of the world of helmeted cavities and declares it', hints at darknesses and underworlds (like the 'undergrowth' in which the skulls were buried) in a world of light. Against such images, such instances, of finality art opposes rule and measure ('ruled, triangular facets'), play ('a play of universals') and wit (as when the brush translates the simultaneous impression of skulls as 'weight' and 'fragility' into 'leg-like appendages'): it does not deny the fact but, confronting fact with an alternative vision, it refuses to be bound to it or silenced by it.

In this exposition of 'Skullshapes' are to be found, I believe, the essentials of Tomlinson's 'ethic of perception'. The ethic is also an aesthetic; 'perception' means both sensory and mental apprehension. Painting, for Constable, began with 'the labour of observation / In face of meteorological fact', and this is where Tomlinson's meditation, in *Seeing is Believing*, on the theory and practice of

Constable's art begins; for the establishment, measurement and definition of fact are the foundation of his poetry. The objectivist premise of 'Skullshapes' is already evident in the poem's initial posture of concentrated, analytic attention: the first word, and sentence, announces the object for study—'Skulls'; the second word, and sentence, sets a frame of meaning round it—'Finalities'. The dispassionate, professional language of the painter reinforces the objectivist message: 'retinal impression', 'recess and volume', 'shadow explores', the mind 'confronted' by its spatial environment. The human meaning of the eye's submission to the objective world is the mind's acknowledgement of natural limits, of conditionality.

The world is physical, impinging on the senses. It is also human, a world known to the mind. Objective truth and classical truth (the acknowledgement of limits) are preconditions for the 'improvement of truth'—'A Meditation on John Constable' (CP p. 33) concludes: 'The artist lies / For the improvement of truth. Believe him'—and the improvement consists in the humanization of sense experience:

> Facts. And what are they?
> He admired accidents, because governed by laws,
>   Representing them (since the illusion was not his end)
> As governed by feeling. The end is our approval
>   Freely accorded, the illusion persuading us
> That it exists as a human image.

Art imitates but at the same time it imbues observation with the quality of the artist's response: 'delight / Describes' in Constable's paintings, and the painter's hand 'Bodied the accurate and total knowledge' of what he saw 'In a calligraphy of present pleasure'; Tomlinson's drawings of birds' skulls are, it seems, touched with 'lyrical admiration'. The artist's appreciation is fused with his descriptions by connotation and metaphorical suggestion; the 'delicate' appearance of the birds' skulls is conveyed in the poem, and perhaps in the drawing, by comparison—'egg-like' and 'as if the spherical shape were the result of an act like glass-blowing'. The mind sees fact and its analogues; art translates fact and explores possibility, extensions beyond the fact. The world of perception is in one aspect limited and in another illimitable: the mind is contained by reality, the horizons of perception, but liberated and extended by imagination. As the eye registers the skull's surfaces and follows shadow into the 'labyrinth of recesses', so art answers to both reality and imagination, with 'lines of containment, lines of extension'. Like shadow, the prospecting imagination 'reaches *down* out of this world of helmeted cavities' (my emphasis), winding its way to the centre of the labyrinth, seeking knowledge of an interior reality; or in the exterior world it grasps for a total vision, opening *out* beyond the 'instantaneous impression' to 'a visionary field, a play of universals'.

Space and time are the coordinates of existence. Space is the realm of the eye, of instantaneous perception, an arena of light and shadow, of fact and conjecture. Time is a province of the mind, the means of extending perception 'beyond the instant' into the past of memory and into the future of imagination. The relation of fact and imagination is either complementary or contrary or simultaneously both. Fact extended into possibility composes a whole, harmonious world; challenged by an alternative vision, either it creates a tension of unresolved conflict or, as is the case in this poem, it creates a totality out of complementary opposites. The composite natural-human world postulated by Tomlinson's poetry is realized poem after poem in a dialectic of fact and imagination. There are, however, limits to what the mind can assimilate. The note heard once in 'Skullshapes'—'they resist the mind's imaginings with the blade of the beak which no lyrical admiration can attenuate to frailty'— sounds throughout Tomlinson's work and is more prominent in some poems than it is here: Cézanne's mountain is 'a presence / Which does not present itself', incomparable 'because irreducible' (CP p. 37). And yet the incomparable, the unhumanizable, is also part of his poetic world, a defining context. The desert landscape, in 'The Cavern', may be untranslatably 'inhuman' and 'this mountain-interior', the cavern itself, incommensurable with 'the mind's / hollow that would contain it'; nevertheless, to the mind that concedes and welcomes this it may still 'become / the self's unnameable and shaping home' (CP p. 119).

'Skullshapes' is, in Tomlinson's preferred nomenclature, 'a poem-in-prose'; the term discourages expectations of the 'poetical' liable to be aroused by the more familiar 'prose poem'. The poetry is in the concentration, the verbal spareness and tight syntax; its language is predominantly one of nouns and verbs, a few (definitive rather than descriptive) adjectives and fewer conjunctions; it is prose stripped, cultivating the virtues of good prose, a discipline that Pound and Eliot prescribed for themselves and recommended to their poetic contemporaries. By turns densely concrete and keenly conceptual, communicating with an impersonal energy and intensity, it is a poem *in prose* because it is a poetry of statement. Tomlinson has nearly always excluded the *'merely* personal'[4] from his poetry, but 'Skullshapes', though it speaks of 'lyrical admiration' as a constituent of art, does not allow even such indirectly personal feeling to influence its voice or rhythms. Many of his verse poems have the same 'philosophical' concern with the reality of the external world and the nature of the subject's knowledge of it, and are equally careful not to *impose* the self and its emotions on what the mind sees. This does not mean, however, that the feeling self is absent from them: personal, often passionate engagement with his material is as much their motive as (in Eliot's phrase) 'the analysis of sensation to the point of principle and definition'.

'Appearance', published three years later in *Written on Water* (1972; CP p. 221), announcing in its title a preoccupation it shares with 'Skullshapes', is a verse poem in which analysis and definition count for as much as they do in the poem-in-prose; but the 'philosophical' theme and the discursive component in his diction do not in this instance banish feeling from the poem.

> Snow brings into view the far hills:
>   The winter sun feels for their surfaces:
> Of the little we know of them, full half
>   Is in the rushing out to greet them, the restraint
> (Unfelt till then) melted at the look
>   That gathers them in, to a meeting of expectations
> With appearances. And what appears
>   Where the slant-sided lit arena opens

> Plane above plane, comes as neither
>   Question nor reply, but a glance
> Of fire, sizing our ignorance up,
>   As the image seizes on us, and we grasp
> For the ground that it delineates in a flight
>   Of distances, suddenly stilled: the cold
> Hills drawing us to a reciprocation,
>   Ask words of us, answering images
> To their range, their heights, held
>   By the sun and the snow, between pause and change.

The poem's images are supported by a discursive skeleton. It opens with a statement—something between an observation of fact and a proposition—that in the first two lines problematizes the nature of perception and in the next five frames that problem as an epistemological puzzle about subjective and objective knowledge, the 'meeting of expectations / With appearances'. The following sentence leaves the conundrum unsolved. The unasked but implied question, the very possibility of human enquiry, is serenely and summarily dismissed: 'what appears ... comes as neither / Question nor reply'. It comes as power—immediacy of revelation and unilateral action. In Tomlinson's next collection of poems (*The Way In*, 1974) he includes, under the title 'The Insistence of Things', some paragraphs from a journal, which provide an explanatory context:

> At the end of conversations, uncompleting all acts of thought, looms the insistence of things which, waiting on our recognition, face us with our own death, for they are so completely what we are not. And thus we go on trying to read them, as if they were signs, or the embodied message of oracles. We remember how Orpheus drew voices from the stones.

The world of things is 'what we are not', our opposite, our opponent—its 'glance of fire' and 'the cold / Hills' may, too, 'face us with our death'—except that in this 'arena' contest would be unthinkable. It is not subject to question and gives no answers: we are *its* subjects, of whom it requires nothing but service, our unquestioning 'reciprocation' of words and images to translate its reality. This is the firmly articulated argument. It negotiates its way through long, elaborately structured sentences of seven and twelve lines apiece, where punctuation and line-divisions guide the voice and map the logical and grammatical relations; where the colons, in particular, play a crucial part in signposting parallels, equivalences, expansions and consequences. Subtracted from the body of the poem, this argument serves as an 'abstract' of its meaning. But, of course, it is not really possible, without killing the poem, nor have I attempted, to separate the abstract from the concrete, the neutral tone of idea-statement from the voice of the engaged subject. Notice, for example, how the voice moves from the informative directness of 'the little we know of them', its quick syllables skipping away from the accentuated 'little', to the slowed-down spondee, feeling and appraising the fullness of the 'full half' of eager expectation, and then to the dam-burst of racing excitement in the rhythm of 'Is in the rushing out to greet them' and the enactment, by the delaying parenthesis, of the 'restraint' suddenly 'melted'. Matter of fact combines easily with 'lyrical admiration'; observation swiftly turns itself into delight, gratitude, celebration. This exhibits the 'sensuous abstraction' and the operation of 'passionate intellect' which Tomlinson has admired in French poetry.[5] The sensuous and the affective collaborate, as equal partners, with a crisp, confident cerebration. The intellect directs but, as the images crowd in, the concrete realization of the experience is only just held in check by the argument. Concreteness serves, but *pressurizes*, the conceptual containment of the poem.

Tomlinson's definition of objectivity in 'The Poet as Painter' provides a key to the intention of this poem. Its theme is not 'the purely imaginary and outmoded objectivity of nineteenth century positivistic science—the objectivity which supposed a complete division between the observer and the observed', but the objectivity he finds in Cézanne, which 'implied an outward gaze that would draw the sensuous world closer to the inner man and that would narrow the gap between abstraction and sensation, between intellect and things'.[6] Looking 'solely and steadfastly at the object' (in Eliot's words) distinguishes but does not separate the knower from the known: knowledge is 'a meeting of expectations / With appearances'. 'The winter sun *feels* for their surfaces', the snow-lit planes of 'the far hills', and light melts 'restraint' of *feeling* in the observer, or acts on his behalf. What we know of the world's 'surfaces' is composed about equally of what is 'there' and what we bring to them: delight, as the Constable poem also says, is part of our knowledge of it. 'Outward gaze' and 'inner man' combine in such a fashion that it is hard to tell whether 'the look / That gathers them in' and the 'glance / Of fire' are given or, mysteriously, received.

But the object is still primary, the eye subservient to what it sees. Things catch the eye before the eye seeks to possess them: it is 'The snow *brings* into view the far hills', and light on the snow not only delivers the scene clearly to the eye but comes as 'a glance / Of fire, sizing our ignorance up, / As the image *seizes* on us'. What we see discovers what we are, but the reversal indicates an expansion not a contraction of self; seizing, sizing—as the consonance persuades us to feel, the one presumes the other. There are limits to objective knowledge, to knowledge ('the *little* we know'), but, 'sizing us up', the view both measures our former ignorance and, with a punning literalness, enlarges us to its size, momentarily admitting us to a larger world in our increase of knowledge. Responsive feeling does not alter the object: the observed transforms the observer, and feeling is that of the incandescent self seized by the 'glance / Of fire'.

Object and subject are brought closer together, but there is a disparity between reality and our mental image of it which is intrinsic to perception. Art, moreover, exists at *two* removes from reality: there is first the perceptual image and then its translation into a pictorial or linguistic equivalent. 'The image seizes on us, and we grasp / For the ground it delineates'; what we grasp for is, concretely, the thing itself and, abstractly, something ultimate; we grasp for the ground, and catch instead from the ceaseless flow of appearances an image 'suddenly stilled' in the mind and stored in the memory. This is all we can do, but art, recording its gratitude for these intimations of reality, reciprocates with 'answering images'. A comment in 'The Poet as Painter', part of which was quoted in the Introduction, once again confirms the poem. 'Poems based', as are Tomlinson's landscape poems, 'on exposure to and observation of the fleeting moments of visual sensation ... endeavour to catch this fleeting freshness and unite it to a stable form where others may share in it';[7] 'the desire to seize on and stabilize momentary appearances'[8] is part of what he means by Cézanne's ethic of perception. Such poems seek definition and permanence in 'a world that must decay' (CP p. 233); they both welcome and resist time. To the seeing mind the world, 'between pause and change', is at once 'fleeting' and 'stable'; the 'answering images' of art, likewise, link change and permanence, time and the mind's stillness.

Art answers in two senses: its images respond and correspond to the perceptual images impressed upon the mind. The phenomenal world is a gift 'drawing us to a reciprocation' of signs *corresponding* to its full reality and *responding* to its grace. The quality of feeling is religious and the poem's interpretation of it is, it seems to me, metaphysical—'a sort of religion, a bringing of things to stand in the light of origin', is how Tomlinson explains the authority for him of Cézanne's artistic ethic.[9] The poem is a celebration, an act of thanksgiving. In celebrating a *reciprocal* relationship of man and landscape, it affirms, as Wordsworth's poems do, the existence of a human-natural world. Nature, as far as it will allow, is humanized by the self 'rushing out to greet' it, and self, given the freedom and scope of space, is naturalized—made, in a phrase of Edward Thomas's, a 'citizen of Earth'.[10] Cézanne's ethic is founded on the conviction that 'by trusting to sensation, we enter being, and experience its primal fulness on terms other than those we dictate';[11] 'being' is neither interior nor exterior but self-and-notself, self and its circumference of space. 'Song is being', said Rilke, but Tomlinson, retaining the distinction between art and experience, answers, in 'Melody' (CP p. 269): 'Song is the measure, rather, / Of being's spread and height'. The last phrase recalls the conclusion of the earlier poem: confronted by 'the cold / Hills', the poet makes images that answer 'to their range, their heights'. In the human-natural world of Tomlinson's poetry, 'you wear / The vestment of space' (CP p. 233): you 'enter being'.

'How great and incorruptible this objectivity of his gaze was'—

this is Rilke on Cézanne, quoted in 'The Poet as Painter'.[12] 'Cézanne at Aix' (*Seeing is Believing*, 1958; CP p. 37)—in the same essay Tomlinson calls it 'a kind of manifesto poem'—is a poetic realization of all that 'incorruptible' means in this connection. What did Cézanne see in the mountain at Aix and seek to transfer to his painting?— 'Immobile like fruit', yet, without human associations, 'Unlike, also / —Because irreducible'. It resists 'the eyes' imaginings', as does the blade-like beak of a bird's skull; likenesses convey nothing of its reality: fruit is 'a component of the delicious', and the mountain is not that. Neither is it self-conscious:

>   it is not
> Posed. It is. Untaught
> Unalterable, a stone bridgehead
> To that which is tangible
> Because unfelt before.

It is 'naked nature', and not even 'clothed by comparison alone', as the fugue's theme is by its developments in 'Glass Grain' (CP p. 26). Fugal 'inversions and divisions', 'apprehensions' by analogy of the core theme, are 'ways of knowledge' closed to the painter and the poet who would seek a relationship with the elemental. It cannot be contained: it can, however, be lived with, lived in, 'as if it were / A self one might inhabit' (CP p. 59). Greeting the non-human, feeling, I said, with reference to 'Appearance', does not alter its inhumanity: on the contrary, sensation links self to what is not self, and if the observer keeps the sensation clean of preconceptions and personal histrionics, he is transformed and extended by what he sees. Recalling this helps to explain 'untaught'. Initially a reinforcement of 'not / Posed', it has a different range of meaning, which includes an implication of its opposite: the mountain is itself a way of knowledge, 'a stone bridgehead to / That which is tangible'. The 'tangible' is the 'irreducible'. It is that which is impermeable by personal emotion, but which none the less exists to be felt, to be known in its 'unalterable' otherness; 'unfelt before' discloses that here in Cézanne's paintings— and in Tomlinson's poem—it is felt now.

Tomlinson's language has often a religious accent. I have quoted his remark from 'The Poet as Painter' that Cézanne's ethic of perception is 'a sort of religion' to him; and by way of defining it he himself quotes from Merleau-Ponty's essay, 'Eye and Mind', this: 'Quality, light, colour, depth which are there before us, are there only because they awaken an echo in our body and because the body welcomes them ... Things have an internal equivalent in me; they arouse in me a carnal formula of their presence'[13]—which is a *sort* of incarnation. I pointed out this quality of Tomlinson's language in 'Appearance', where the world is a gift *'drawing* us to a reciprocation', *asking* 'words of us'. And Cézanne's mountain is 'a presence', more in Merleau-Ponty's sense than Wordsworth's, 'a presence / Which does not present itself'. 'A Given Grace' (*American Scenes*, 1966; CP p. 115) in its title-phrase, repeated and elucidated in the poem, explicitly consecrates the physical world.

In the 1950s and 1960s—in *Seeing is Believing* (1958, 1960), *A Peopled Landscape* (1963) and *American Scenes* (1966)—Tomlinson developed and stabilized his repertoire of poetic forms. Most of his verse is written in accentual metre; the major division in his work is between the poem of four to five accents, like 'Appearance', and the poem of two to three accents, of which 'Cézanne at Aix' and 'A Given Grace' are examples. The longer line is needed for the reasoned syntax of the meditative poem, which sometimes combines with narrative; the short-line poem slows down and pauses over the unfolding sense. This can be observed in the opening lines of 'A Given Grace':

> Two cups,
> a given grace,
> afloat and white
> on the mahogany pool
> of table.

This is, as I said, accentual verse, but if we ignore the lineation in this and subsequent quotations from the poem we find we are listening to iambic metre with the usual quota of metrical substitutions. Each line is, however, a single rhythmical unit, with functional end-pauses of varying length, and only lines 2 and 3 rhythmically duplicate each other. The momentary retardation of the flow of sense and rhythmical differentiation of the lines concentrate attention upon their individual expressiveness at the same time as the overall approximation to an iambic norm gives weight and continuity to the poem.

In the course of the first four lines the cups pass from 'common ware' to 'rare reflections', though in the fifth the solidity of the cups at the head of the sentence meets solidity again in its tail—the floating grace in between steadied, as it were, by the density of substance ('table' without its definite article). This effect of ascent and descent is produced, in part, by the growing line of the verse, an expansion suddenly aborted by the sentence stop immediately upon entering the fifth line: the firmly planted accents of the initial spondee, followed by the pair of dimeters (the third line audibly as well as visually a fraction longer, though metrically equivalent to the second), and then the rush of syllables to the climactic stress on 'pool', bursting through the line-end to bump up against 'table'. The first three lines, end-stopped and metrically either parallel or the same, create a stillness, at once the stillness of something contemplated and the stillness of being, objects of which you can say only that they are there, they exist. The fourth line breaks the stillness, and the still cups become then active agents of transformation. The physical world is consecrated; the object takes precedence. The poem continues—

> They unclench
> the mind, filling it
> with themselves—

and concludes with the assurance that you are 'replenished by / those empty vessels'. A reminder from 'Skullshapes'—'One sees. But not merely the passive mirrorings of the retinal mosaic'—alerts one to an implication latent in the imagery, the not merely passive part played by the mind in this transaction:

> Though common ware,
> these rare reflections,
> coolness of brown
> so strengthens and refines

> the burning of their white,
> you would not wish
> them other than they are.

The reflections are also mental, for objects need the firmness and coolness of the containing mind to intensify their burning essence.

'White' is a word like 'tangible', though occurring more frequently in the poems, denoting a concentration of being—as though white were the essence, or substance, of a prismatic reality. The cups *are* as the mountain *is*. Once again, therefore, we approach the absolute, as we do with 'ground' in 'Appearance'. And once again we encounter an enigma; or is it a mystery? 'In both graphic and poetic art', writes Tomlinson, 'I like something lucid surrounded by something mysterious.'[14] Just as, in 'Appearance', the ownership of the 'look' and the 'glance' is elusive, so the givenness of the 'given grace' is questionable: how much of it is *in* the object and how much is contributed by human response? What gives the rareness to the reflections? What makes the white burn? These are questions not to be answered. In prose Tomlinson speaks of 'an outward gaze that would draw the sensuous world closer to the inner man', making do with the approximate language of prose; but the poem has entered *being*, which, if it is not mind, is not, simply, matter: the poem supposes a reality which eludes the measure of clumsy distinctions between object and subject. What is the point of the conundrum—*'empty* vessels' *'filling'* the mind 'with themselves'—unless it is by wit to announce a mystery?

It will be apparent from my interleaving of comment on one poem with quotation from others, of the same or a different period, that the poetry forms a tight web of intricate interconnections. Tomlinson's work is indeed remarkable for the continuity and coherence of its thinking. His successive remakings of his poetic world have involved no dismantling of the past. It is a major *body* of work, a continuous process of thought. The poems speak to each other, and each poem means more by its relation to the whole. What is also remarkable is how early in his career Tomlinson recognized the nature of his poetic temperament and arrived at his convictions. All his experiments are contained in his first pamphlet, *Relations and Contraries*, which he published at the age of 24 with the Hand and Flower Press in 1951. 'Except for the title and "Poem" ("Wakening with the window over fields")', he writes in the Preface to his *Collected Poems* (1985), 'there is little I wish to rescue from that collection. "Poem" stands in the present volume as a kind of prelude to what follows. I realized, when I wrote it, that I was approaching the sort of thing I wanted to do, where space represented possibility and where self would have to embrace that possibility somewhat self-forgetfully, putting aside the more possessive and violent claims of personality.'

'Poem', 'Aesthetic' and 'Venice', the last two from *The Necklace* (1955), stand together at the beginning of the *Collected Poems*. They speak to each other, as do all Tomlinson's poems, but I turn to them at this point because they also illustrate, in a striking fashion, the poet's early command of his themes. Clarity of sensory report is the first quality of 'Poem' (CP p. xix) to make its imprint on the mind. The early morning sound of a horse's hooves 'Breaks clean and frost-sharp on the unstopped ear' in an otherwise 'unawakened village'. The quotation from Ezra Pound—in 'E.P. Ode Pour L'Election de Son Sepulchre', the sirens' song that reminded Odysseus of the sufferings at Troy 'Caught in the unstopped ear'—signals a difference: while acknowledging a debt to the clean, taut line and crisp definition of *Mauberley*, it pledges itself to a different heroism, the ear daring to register not the sirens' song but the sharpness of sense experience.

Tomlinson has said that between 1948, after going down from Cambridge, and 1951, when this first pamphlet of verse, *Relations and Contraries*, appeared, he was searching for 'a good antidote to the effects of Dylan Thomas's romanticism'.[15] He was shortly to discover it in the modernism of certain American poets, but at this time his knowledge of them amounted to little more than the contents of the Sesame Books selection of Pound and a few poems of Marianne Moore and Stevens encountered in the anthologies, which, having something in common with the 'clean surfaces'[16] of Pound, he found congenial and suggestive. In the early 1950s he returned to Moore and Stevens, and a reading of their work was partly responsible for the new direction taken by his poetry in *The Necklace* (1955) and *Seeing is Believing* (1958, 1960); although Williams praised the latter, his influence was only first discernible in *A Peopled Landscape* (1963).[17] In Tomlinson's search for a contemporary style the example of these and other Americans was to be decisive, but in his pre-American period the antidote to Thomas was provided by Augustan poetry. Constable's aspiration, which is also Tomlinson's, was, we recall, to embody an 'accurate and total knowledge' in his transcription of sense experience. Accuracy, we may say, is the objectivist part; the insistence on totality is the Augustan demand for a *reasoned* objectivity, a proportionate and impartial view. The figure-ground organization of perception would seem to be a principal expression of the 'Augustan' aspect of his sensibility.

If 'Poem' exemplifies his meticulous rendering of sense experience, it also supplies the first instance in the *Collected Poems* of this structural principle. As the sound of the horse-drawn milk-float approaches and recedes, 'The hooves describe an arabesque on space',

> And space vibrates, enlarges with the sound;
> Though space is soundless, yet creates
> From very soundlessness a ground
> To counterstress the lifting hoof fall as it breaks.

As lines on paper can suggest volume, so the ear tracing a three-dimensional 'dotted line in sound', producing a sort of hologram, gives body and form to the space it apprehends. It occupies, it does not contain, space. Serving the imagination (the inward eye) no less than the organ of hearing, it enlarges—or seems to enlarge—the world of the senses: in reality, sensory consciousness has filled out to its size. Conversely, in the language of Gestalt psychology, the *ground* of space gives to the *figure* of 'the lifting hoof fall' not only a precise location but a sharper definition and (to use Hopkins's apt term) an 'instressed' intensity of life. Concentration on particulars opens up the general; having a place in space, the sensation becomes a part and a materialization of a whole. A *whole* world is built up out of and defined by its relations and its contraries: by the correspondence between sound and sight; by the 'counterstress' of sound and silence and the counterpoint of qualities—the steady attention of the alert senses and observing mind and the descant of imagination exhibited in 'arabesque' and 'lifting'. A poem, too, puts into tense relationship or complementary opposition fact and feeling and their stylistic counterparts, exactitude and excess. (The 'lilting' rhythm of a poem—this is perhaps the significance of the title—also defines itself against a 'ground' of 'soundlessness'.)

'Aesthetic' (CP p. 3), announcing its intention in its title and its placing at the head of *The Necklace*, provides the keynote to the collection.

> Reality is to be sought, not in concrete,
> But in space made articulate:
> The shore, for instance,
> Spreading between wall and wall;
> The sea-voice
> Tearing the silence from the silence.

During the war, and for some years after, England's beaches were divided by concrete walls extending from the promenade down into the sea. This is the primary sense here of 'concrete', but the poem's wit also brings into play its other sense, in which it is opposed to 'abstract'; 'space made articulate' means also, therefore, the universal concretized in individual things. Reality is not particulars, not even the sum of particulars, but the whole of *possible* sense experience, of which particulars are instances, and 'total knowledge' is speculative knowledge of the whole in and through its parts. One may conceive of this as a corrective to the kind of emphasis that the imagist poets or a critic like Leavis laid on concreteness in poetic language. The balance Tomlinson would strike is indicated by his praise for the 'sensuous abstraction' of French poetry.[18] The parts of the whole, of space, are represented as the objects of perception; in them the whole is focused and objectified into 'articles' (component parts) and, since 'articulate' is used in both its material and its aural sense, into vocables. The object is always, in the words of a poem-title in his next collection, *Seeing is Believing* (1958), the 'object in a setting' (CP p. 23).

The poem begins with a proposition: reality is in the whole—

concretions are subordinate, being articulations of the whole. But the relation between the object and its setting, in 'Aesthetic' as in 'Poem', is reciprocal: space is reified in objects, objects are defined by their relationship in space. The following demonstrations of the proposition take this further. The first instance, copying the syntax of the statement, repeats its emphasis: the real is the universal, the expanse of shore measured to the eye by the frame of walls (sea and promenade complete the rectangle); its infinity is merely given active presence by the concrete outline, at once accommodating itself to the set limits (filling the space marked out) and tacitly resisting its confinement ('spreading' also implies that it could spread *beyond*). The second instance, however, surprises—and therefore transforms theorem into poem—by not corresponding, by seeming actually to contradict the statement: reality, the syntax would suggest, is in the specific sound of the sea violently interrupting, in effect challenging, the general silence. Reality is not, then, simply in the subordination of the part to the whole, but in the dialectic between them. The concretions of space (and silence) have both a static and a dynamic relation to the universal: on the one hand they give form and utterance to it, on the other they assert themselves in contradistinction to it. In each case the relation is a relation of contraries.

'Poem' spells out, in reasoned analogy and antithesis, the prior reality of space, of the totality of sense experience; 'Aesthetic' epigrammatizes the same message. The opening stanza of 'Venice' (CP p. 3), by abruptly inverting the customary order of priorities—by direct attack upon mental inertia—startles into being a new consciousness of space.

> Cut into by doors
> The morning assumes night's burden,
> The houses assemble in tight cubes.

Morning and night are containers; doors and houses are their contents. Cut into, space is endowed with that solidity of objects which conventionally signifies the real. These are self-contained lines. The sharp, curt syllables of the initial spondee in the first line reinforce the image's dramatization of the inversion as an accomplished act. The effect is repeated in the following lines, with heavy accentuation closing the second and third. The parallel symmetries of these last two lines, supported by the duplicated prefix of the verbs and the rhyme of 'night' and 'tight', also mime the weight and mass of a world obeying the inescapable law of its existence.

Again, space is enlarged to include silence, matter to include sound.

> From the palace flanking the waterfront
> She is about to embark, but pauses.
> Her dress is a veil of sound
> Extended upon silence.

Sound is to silence as thing is to space—and, apparently, as land is to water. Space, silence and water are the unconcrete and uncontainable. The interchange between the senses effected by a systematic use of synaesthesia in each of these poems ('veil of sound', 'a dotted line in sound', 'space made articulate' palpably, visibly and audibly) generates a *sense* of the whole unavailable to the separate *senses*: in it perception transcends itself (as, in 'Skullshapes', 'the visible ... transcends itself with the suggestion of all that is there beside what lies within the eyes' possession'). The poem is a sequence of four vignettes. This is an image of adventure, 'held' (as in 'Appearance') 'between pause and change'. Movement—from one element, one reality, to another—is anticipated: the first clause, with the enjambement and its anapaestic spurts of expectation, threatens to break free from the formal constraints of the preceding stanza and the inescapable realities that frame our existence whose presence is dramatized in its imagery and the physicality of its language, but it is brought to a halt at 'embark'. Borders are indicated—between land and water, between movement and stillness, between a garment of sound and a body of silence—and the woman 'pauses', as the poem does, before crossing. Positioned in a known, precisely located concrete reality ('doors' and 'houses' culminate in 'palace'), she is on the threshold of the horizonless whole, the encompassing immeasurable silence, about to 'embark' upon the as yet unknown.

In the third vignette borders are retained, and then eliminated.

> Under the bridge,
> Contained by the reflected arc
> A tunnel of light
> Effaces walls, water, horizon.

Light, as in a Turner painting, melts and absorbs into itself the three-dimensional world—floor of water, sides of walls, extent of horizon—as if to show us the possibility of an unarticulated space, where a 'tunnel of light' might be an exit from appearances. I write 'as if' and 'might be' to register the impression left on the reader that in these lines imagination has taken over from observation, to *improve* truth, to extend perception beyond 'what lies within the eyes' possession'. Each vignette is a separate view and makes a distinct point, but it is set in suggestive juxtaposition with its sequel. The last, standing apart in its simple directness, makes a gesture of summary, but at the same time completes the (disguised) humanization of light.

> Floating upon its own image
> A cortège of boats idles through space.

Light creates the visible, but also in Tomlinson's poems it releases, or is an instrument of, feeling: it is, we might say, an objectification of subjectivity. As in 'A Given Grace', reflection ('the reflected arc' of the bridge), especially as it is repeated in the 'image' of the boats, intimates, without overt comparison, the mind's part in this 'act of vision'. Thing and its (also mental) image ride together in easy partnership, neither confused nor sharply divided, the disparity between mind and matter, subject and object, suspended by a grace of the moment; the 'cortège of boats *idles* through space' like imagination itself, in lordly possession, it would seem, of the limitless whole.

'Poem', 'Aesthetic' and 'Venice' are the earliest pieces in the *Collected Poems*. They are not a sequence but they are closely connected in image and idea, and each is made more significant by its relation to the others. There are more complex poems to come, in a variety of forms, but they will be ramifications and offshoots from one stem of thought; there is nothing in them that later developments in style or content will invalidate. They are separate crystallizations of a unitary process of exploratory thinking trained upon sense experience, and a composite realization of a physical world quickened with meaning and value.

The pleasures of attention, the keener life of the senses, are not only the originating impulse but frequently the theme of Tomlinson's poetry. When he chose from his first pamphlet of verse 'Poem' ('Wakening with the window over fields') to introduce both *Selected Poems 1951–1974* and the *Collected Poems*, the luck of that first word, 'wakening', was, no doubt, part of what constituted its fitness to be a prelude to his work. The alert posture of mind and senses, attentive specifically to a natural world, and the contrast drawn later between the awakened ('clean and frost-sharp') faculties and the 'unawakened' faculties of the sleeping village, acquire from the poem's position an emblematic force. To be awakened to a sharper consciousness of the physical world is at the same time to *give* it fullness and intensity of life, as if the awakening were reciprocal. Fifteen years later, in 'The Weathercocks' (*American Scenes*, 1966; CP p. 113), this thought is made explicit. It considers how the bronze weathercocks have been 'Bitten and burned into mirrors of thin gold' by wind and sun, and how light on these mirrors seems to penetrate 'pure metal' with 'consciousness', so that 'they / have their days of seeing as they / grind round on their swivels':

> As if the sole wish of the light
> were to harrow with mind matter, to shock
> wide the glance of the tree-knots and the stone-eyes
> the sun is bathing, to waken the weathercocks.

It is a recurrent theme, and where it is not a theme it is a constant implication of Tomlinson's poetry. It spans his work. Earlier in this chapter I grouped 'Poem' with work of the same period to illustrate an impressive unity of imaginative thinking at the start of his career. By setting the youthful 'Poem' with 'Focus', from *American Scenes* (1966), and 'Snow Signs', from *The Flood* (1981), a grouping that links examples of early, middle and later work, I want to show the poet returning to, and revolving the facets of, a theme that is basic to his preoccupation with sense experience.

'Focus', the last poem of a sequence entitled 'In Winter Woods' (CP p. 119), scrutinizes what Hardy might have called 'a commonplace day': an almost colourless, featureless winter day, of a uniform dead brown partly washed out by a grey mist, 'like a blue / dank bloom that hazes / a long-browned photograph'. Formally it resembles 'A Given Grace' in being a short-line poem of two or three accents to a line. The difference is that in this poem the verse is more fluent and limber. The line-divisions are more active in governing pace and signalling changes of pitch, picking out for the ear the contours of voice movement and the shapes of grammar and logic.

> Morning has gone
> before the day begins,
> leaving an aftermath
> of mist, a battleground
> burnt-out, still smoking.

Notice how in these opening lines myth, in a playfully hyperbolic evocation of a war in heaven, creeps into the factual record. Adapted to a different setting and preoccupation, the myth keeps only some of its meaning. The 'morning' that never was is a pristine dawn world known only in its absence. 'Eden'—the word is used later in the poem—names a quality of sense experience; it is the 'burning' brilliance and intensity of colour that is missing from a 'monotone' landscape. The picture also carries over from the story an acute sense of a categorical division between opposite conditions, without the quasi-historical explanation of it; in terms of the natural, visible world, it is the division between a 'burnt-out' grey-brown winter scene and hidden colours waiting to be found:

> under that monotone
> sleep ochres, reds,
> and (to the eye
> that sees) a burning
> of verdure at the vapour's edge
> seems to ignite
> those half-reluctant tones.

Other meanings embedded in the myth are set aside and, as it were, held in reserve by a light mockery of its epic grandeurs. No supernatural Fall has taken place. But passionately felt, directly revealed truth, not in its Christian sense but as distinguished from received truth, needs for its communication a language that stretches the truth. The truth is that this unfallen world—'Eden' is its nostalgic name—is not lost, but sleeps; it is there for 'the eye / that sees', which is 'the heart's eye'. *This* world of death and resurrection is the cycle of the seasons, the yearly suspense and rebirth of nature. Eden is immediate experience; it is lost only as a faded photograph, the dead record, of the past is lost. It is a world stirred into life by senses *awakened* to a rare purity of attention. It is at once what one sees with such clarity and the gift itself of clear seeing, which in a later poem, 'Eden' (CP p. 159), Tomlinson would call, with many poems like 'Focus' in previous collections to justify his choice of words, a 'clairvoyant gift'.

Winter is a 'monotone'—a monochrome, monotonous state; by implication it is also, generally, the world of daily appearance. It is a condition of being unawakened and, in a sense to be defined, unfocused. Characteristically, inner and outer are made to interpenetrate. Winter is, externally, the sleep of nature and, internally, the sleep of the senses; the 'grey contagion' of mist is a spreading affliction of the eye and spirit as much as it is an exhalation of damp. It is the unburning, unignited quotidian which is reality to the dull vision. A glint of 'green' in all this grey affords the one glimpse of a contrary condition; catching the attention, it 'leads the eye/ homewards' to a thread of moss vivid against the black of a cut beech log upended like 'a muddy anvil'—'an Eden / on whose emerald tinder . . . the heart's eye enkindles':

>   a moss
>   that runs with the grain-mark, whirled
>   like a river
>   over a scape of rapids
>   into a pool of mingling
>   vortices.

And thus

> the whole, gigantic
> aperture of the day
> shuts down to a single
> brilliant orifice.

Here too, in the image of 'focus', Tomlinson manages to transcend distinctions of subject and object: the focusing agent is by turns the eye of the observer and the 'burning' glaring green of moss on 'a black / cut block of fallen beech'. The 'eye that sees' joins with the eye of the day; interior and exterior remain themselves, but a kind of pun dangles the possibility of a whole subsisting without these categories. The full circle of the day is—by whatever agency—focused in this tiny concentration of its life.

The word 'orifice' turns the eye of the camera into a passage of entry, an interior day. As though colour, the 'emerald tinder' of moss, were an inner fire, this interior is the day's essential life. 'Eden' is what we call the contrary—for example, the opposite season to a colourless winter—when it is not literally there but by the leading of one slight clue is released to the imagination and made simultaneously present with its lack. The interior is the winter's contrary as life is the contrary of death, as the pristine world which (by Blake's assurance) would open to the 'cleansed' organs of perception is the contrary of the 'grey contagion' of a misted vision. It is the office of imagination to find and include the contrary, for that is, 'unabashed / by season', to see all round, or all through, time—in another sense to experience Eden. The seeing-seeking eye is *led*, and 'the heart's eye' is *enkindled*, by what it gratefully encounters, but eye and heart (mind and feeling) in turn lead and kindle, waken and focus, the Eden contrary dormant in the grey quotidian.

The organization of contraries into complementary relationship, invariable in Tomlinson's work, is an expression of his preoccupation with the integrity of mental experience. The difference between the torpid and the alert mind is not simply one between dullness and sharpness but that which distinguishes partial from whole vision. 'Awakening' is an image for the self's entry into the 'primal fulness' of 'being',[19] by which it becomes part of a living whole; I could be paraphrasing Wordsworth's line, 'An inmate of this active universe'.[20] Tomlinson has found means appropriate to a twentieth-century outlook, which must have due regard for facts as they present themselves to a detached observer, of articulating a sense of the world as it appears to the *participatory* consciousness, an achievement of the early Romantics. He has made available again, on his own terms, the insights of Blake, Wordsworth and Coleridge.

This lineage and at the same time the un-Wordsworthian rendering of a Wordsworthian theme are both clearest in 'Snow Signs' (CP p. 315), the third of the three poems under consideration. The opening poem of *The Flood* (1981), appearing fifteen years after 'Focus' and thirty years after 'Poem', it is as it were a re-ordering, prompted by the stimulus of new particulars, of a large portion of his visual experience. Contraries play a prominent part in the structuring of its thought. Snow that has retreated in thin lines and dots and, with 'Touched-in contour and chalk-followed fold', 'has left its own white geometry / To measure out for the eye the way / The land may lie', discovers what otherwise would be missed, 'the fortuitous / Full variety a hillside spreads for us'; the simplification of geometry sharpens the eye's sense of the scene's complexity, and the satisfaction of taking mental possession by a kind of geometrical sectioning of the field of vision enhances appreciation of what cannot be possessed, what measurement leaves out, the indefinable, unpredictable fullness and variety in what the eye sees. It is essentially the same surprising conjunction as we have already noted in 'A Meditation on John Constable', the cooperation of 'scientific' observation and delight. It seems a paradox that the analytic eye and the impartial mind should serve, as they do in 'Snow Signs', the Romantic motive of celebration.

It is the celebration of life reborn—in an accentual metre (referred to by Tomlinson, after Hopkins, as 'sprung rhythm'[21]) which has the sort of pulsing vigour and the modulation of tone and emphasis that characterize alliterative verse at its best. Looking discovers features previously unnoticed; in turn (as also happens in 'Poem' and 'Weathercocks') the act of discovering, which is a kind of wakening or regeneration, wakens us, the onlookers, to new life.

> Walking, we waken these at every turn,
> Waken ourselves, so that our walking seems
>   To rouse some massive sleeper out of winter dreams
> Whose stretching startles the whole land into life,
>   As if it were us the cold, keen signs were seeking
> To pleasure and remeasure, repossess
>   With a sense in the gathered coldness of heat and height.

The increase of alertness and awareness is an intensification and expansion of self. Tomlinson's images and word-play ('walking ... waken', and their inverted repetition in the second line) accentuate the reciprocal action of waking and being wakened. They convey at the same time a sense of almost overflowing profusion and variety, and an 'intense personal excitement'[22] that culminates in the end-rhymes 'seems' and 'dreams', and is supplemented, in 'pleasure and remeasure', by an incantation of internal rhymes. The next stage in the sequence is that, wakening and being wakened, we therefore *seem* to rouse a whole landscape from its winter sleep, and a few lines later the words 'transfigured' and 'resurrection' appear. But the poem leaves no doubt about the meaning of those words: the vocabulary of religion is used to signify the transformations of the imagination. As it does in 'Focus', imagination here brings to immediate perception an inner sense of its contrary; what is present is thereby complemented by what is absent, the visible by the invisible. Fact is completed by imagination to create a whole composed of what is and is not immediately perceptible. It is the theme of 'Skullshapes'.

When 'awakening', in a combination of its transitive and intransitive senses, is Tomlinson's theme, it may appear that he is sometimes betrayed into confusion or is guilty of deliberate equivocation. Does the eye, in 'Focus', focus the day or does colour, the 'green' of moss on the beech log that *'glares* up through' the grey mist? The answer would have to be both and neither; but it is the wrong question. This kind of language, in which the agents are seemingly interchangeable, expresses the peculiarity of all perceptual awareness: at the moment of perception subject and object are identical; they not only converge but occupy the same space. Coming awake, coming to a focus, is what this coinherence of inner and outer feels like when it becomes a process of *conscious* identification. It may seem to an artist, therefore, that he is not inventing, but discovering an already existent pattern; it is what Cézanne meant when he distinguished his artistic purpose from that of the old masters: 'They created pictures: we are attempting a piece of nature.' The painter who makes that his goal is seeking to participate in, belong to, a larger order than himself. Cézanne did not hesitate to say that nature is a 'perfect work of art', nor that 'the artist must conform' to it. John Berger in his excellent essay, 'The Sight of Man', unriddles these and similar statements by asking and answering a precise question: 'At what moment can art and nature converge and become the same? . . . The answer is: . . . at the moment when the subject of perception can admit no discontinuity between himself and the objects and space before him; at the moment at which he is an irremovable part of the totality of which he is conscious.'[23]

The interdependence of both motifs—of nature viewed as art and of nature wakening and being wakened by 'the sight of man'—is there for inspection in lines I have already quoted from 'Snow Signs'. Let me repeat and extend the quotation:

> Snow has left its own white geometry
> To measure out for the eye the way
> The land may lie where a too cursory reading
> Discovers only dip and incline leading
> To incline, dip.

Nature is here the teacher, educating the eye by diagram and book. The teacher's role is not separable from that of the (visual and verbal) artist in the next lines, when the landscape's 'fortuitous / Full variety' is said to be

> written here in sign and exclamation,
> Touched-in contour and chalk-followed fold,
> Lines and circles finding their completion
> In figures less certain, figures that yet take hold
> On features that would stay hidden but for them.

Revealing hidden features, nature the didactic artist wakens us to their existence; or 'Walking we waken these at every turn, / Waken ourselves'—it makes no difference which: an awakening takes place.

Tomlinson is close to the spirit of Cézanne's synthesis of art and nature again in 'Nocturnal' (CP p. 118), the third poem in the sequence entitled 'In Winter Woods' (of which 'Focus' is the fourth and last poem). But he approaches the painter's position by a private route. Nature is, it seems, both bad art and good art—that is our first impression; this changes, however, when we notice that nature is also, still, the 'teacher', and what it demonstrates is the *difference* between bad and good art. There are two scenes; the first, a twilight of blurred distinctions—'shade confounds shadow now', the 'wide view / dimming in shrinking vista', and 'the sun smearily edges / out of the west'—gives way to the second, the clarity restored correctively by moonlight:

> that light which seemed
> to have drawn out after it
> all space, melting in horizontals,
> must yield now
> to a new, tall beam,
> a single, judicious eye.

The poem shows that in nature, if not in the life of man, confusion of identities does not have the last word; the physical world reasserts itself in sharpened perspective of light and shadow:

> it will have
> roof behind roof once more, and these
> shadows of buildings
> must be blocked-in
> and ruled with black, and shadows
> of black iron must flow
> beneath the wrought-iron trees.

Dusk tells its 'tale of confusions' by enactment: the moon, refocusing, rebuilding the whole, tells it in the different mode of judgement. The language of artistic intention is, half-punningly, superimposed on nature's language of necessity; a statement of some intricacy is thus condensed. It might be paraphrased as follows: this is what nature does—which is to say, the eye interacts with what is external to it to this effect—and art must copy, and in copying, reproduce this act of perception. I say '*half*-punningly' because the pun on 'must' (in the nature of things and by an act of will) is not a witty disclaimer, advertising its duplicity, but Tomlinson's way of expressing the synthesis desiderated by Cézanne. Berger reports another conversation. To Bernard's question, 'But aren't nature and art different?', Cézanne replied: 'I want to make them the same';[24] the same by virtue, not of the law of identity, but of the law of participation (by the percipient in what is perceived).

'Reality', we remember from Tomlinson's first manifesto poem, 'Aesthetic', 'is to be sought ... in space made articulate'. The poems of visual sensation which have been the subject of this chapter have all, consistently with this definition, concentrated attention upon objects in space. But even 'Skullshapes', the poem-in-prose from which I drew my map of Tomlinson's perceptual world, and which is so strictly concerned with 'the act of vision' and the visible, sets the contemplated object in the contexts of both space and time, the twin coordinates of physical existence. In his essay on Tomlinson's graphics Octavio Paz said that Tomlinson is 'fascinated ... at the universal busyness, the continuous generation and degeneration of things'.[25] Tomlinson is fascinated by change because time, added to the three dimensions of space, completes the reality of the physical world.

Time is there by implication in most of Tomlinson's landscape poems. The nature of his preoccupation with it is best studied in poems where the action of time is the thematic focus.

In 'Farewell to Van Gogh' (*Seeing is Believing*, 1958; CP p. 36) the poet opposes to the subjective 'violence', the expressionist 'frenzy', of the painter both a classical sense of natural process, the imperturbable workings of necessity, and a correspondent voice of temperate reasonableness: 'The world does not end tonight / And the fruit that we shall pick tomorrow / Await us'. 'We have lived through apocalypse too long' is his reflection in a later poem, 'Prometheus'

(CP p. 56), on the turbulent consequences of a comparably violent revolutionary idealism; the gist of 'Farewell to Van Gogh' is that time is our element—we cannot live in a perpetual last-day of apocalypse.

> The quiet deepens. You will not persuade
>   One leaf of the accomplished, steady, darkening
> Chestnut-tower to displace itself
>   With more of violence than the air supplies
> When, gathering dusk, the pond brims evenly
>   And we must be content with stillness.

There is a *law* of nature; we feel it in the 'steady', deliberate, irresistible advance of the long sentence reproducing the process it describes. Ripeness is all, and time is its accomplishment; its fruit need no forcing—they are ours when time gives, not when we will, 'in the fullness of time' (the title of a later poem, addressed to Paz (CP p. 163); 'the pond brims', likewise, to an equable fullness. In this image—it brims *evenly*—we glimpse what it means to say that movement expects 'stillness', and 'the quiet' into which the scene 'deepens' is its essential reality. It all leads to this, the first sentence of the next stanza: 'Unhastening, daylight withdraws from us its shapes / Into their central calm'. 'Central calm' recalls 'the equitable core of peace' in 'Flute Music' (CP p. 9); the idea has a key position in the thought-pattern of Tomlinson's poetry. The point to make here is that the absorption of movement into stillness represented in these images of brimming pond, deepening quiet, daylight darkening into night is also accomplished by the one word 'steady', combining the two senses of fixed and moving 'evenly'. The images and the word suggest an unmovingness in an even ('unhastening' but also un-delaying) movement: the steadiness of law; as if the *law* of movement, its governing principle, is its stillness, its 'central calm'.

Discovering in the flow of time a stability and a permanence, Tomlinson has managed by this paradox to validate the feelings of satisfaction and trust in time conveyed by the poem. A full 'consent to time' (the phrase is from 'In the Fullness of Time'; CP p. 163)—obedience to the law of nature—is an implication of objectivism: if you accept the nature of *things*, you consent to the *nature* of things. 'You *will not* persuade' and 'we *must* be content' announce, as to a rebellious child, the conditions of existence; the manner of address implying that to him, the person addressed, they have the appearance of constraint: the poet's language carries a stronger counter-suggestion of largesse, both a completeness of giving and a graciousness in the giver, even as it recognizes, in the balanced opposition of 'accomplished' and 'darkening' (bridged by 'steady'), the duality of nature, the cycle of light and dark, ripening and decay, 'generation and degeneration' (Paz's phrase). The serenity of tone discloses in this acknowledgement of necessity the very contentment with its terms that 'we' are called upon to show. It is a sort of participation: the even-paced, 'unhastening' but inexorable, maturing of time's purposes, imitated in the movement and celebrated in the content of the lines, nourishes in the participating poetic voice a comparable maturity of tone—precision and largeness of understanding, firmness and dispassionateness of judgement.

In 'Farewell to Van Gogh' the emphasis on the homogeneity of nature—unquestionable, ungainsayable, unalterable—is a consequence of the corrective intention of the poem, to counter a romantic subjectivism by a classical objectivism. Movement is the theme—calm and steady movement as against the agitation of the painter's landscapes—and movement in the one dimension of time, or of space as a manifestation of time. Nature is depicted as a one-directional 'steady' force; 'generation and degeneration' are stages in one sequence. In 'The Way of a World' (the title-poem of a later collection, 1969; CP p. 165) there is no polemic, no refutation of mistaken, *immature* views; demonstration in its various instances of the single 'way of a world' is in itself the purpose of the poem. Memory having mislaid the image of 'a gull the autumn gust / Had pulled upwards and past / The window I watched from' and 'The ash-key, borne-by whirling / On the same surge of air', the poet recovers much later, 'in a changed mind', the whole scene:

> the bird,
> The seed, the windlines drawn in the sidelong
>   Sweep of leaves and branches that only

> The black and supple boughs restrained—
> All would have joined in the weightless anarchy
> Of air, but for that counterpoise.

This is in the first place an image of *spatial* movement, but the reminders of time in 'autumn gust' and 'seed', the strong suggestion specifically of time as a destructive power in 'weightless anarchy / Of air', become explicit analogy in a later phrase, 'these evanescences of daily air'. Space and time have equal reality here: the poem parallels the two kinds of movement. The 'way' of this space-time 'world' is not quiet or calm, it is not movement in one direction but a deadlock of conflicting forces; if there is a steadiness, it is imaged in the resistance of boughs, 'steadied / And masted' by deep-rooted trunks, to the 'weightless anarchy / Of air' in high wind—a *dynamic* equilibrium between forces of creation and destruction. To set against its 'evanescences', there is the *weight* of a world, what endures as well as what is fleeting,

In 'Farewell to Van Gogh', the idea of nature as a single, simple force is paralleled by the poet's unqualified 'consent to time': in 'The Way of a World', the tension between opposing forces has its counterpart in the resistance offered by human memory to the rule of time. Memory and a vision of possibility, we remember from 'Skullshapes', are what the artist 'adds' to immediate sensation. Memory gives 'point and place' to a present impression; a vision of possibility—what I choose to call 'imagination'—challenges the given reality by confronting it with its opposite. 'The Way of a World' appears in the same collection as 'Skullshapes'; once it is understood that the differences between the poems are differences of emphasis and terminology, the essential similarity in their conceptions of art's transaction with nature will be quickly recognized. The title-poem of the collection is not about present impressions: it is about memory as having value in itself. Memory rescues the past and it is further represented as counteracting the action of time; recovering along with the whole scene a 'worth' in it 'that outlasted its lost time', a worth which is its meaning as an image of 'the shapes of change'. Here memory serves the contrary purposes of art as they are defined in 'Skullshapes'—working both with and against nature: the poetic act is at once a flowing with and a countermovement to time. The mind that took the original imprint of the scene is not the same mind as the one that remembers; it too is subject to time: but in recovering this event, finding again this image of a world in ceaseless movement, the 'changed mind' also rediscovers a constant in this world of change. It is essentially the paradox of art as it is represented in 'The Poet as Painter' when Tomlinson, defining the aim of those of his poems that are based on 'exposure to and observation of the fleeting moments of visual sensation', writes that they 'endeavour to catch this fleeting freshness and unite it to a stable form'.[26] For if art embodies a tension between consent and resistance to time, it also partakes of what transcends the conflict, the stability of natural law. The value of this remembered event to the recollecting mind is, as I said, its meaning as an image of 'the shapes of change', and that is a phrase for the constants 'In all these evanescences of daily air': 'It is the shapes of change, and not the bare / Glancing vibrations, that vein and branch / Through the moving textures'.

Characteristically, Tomlinson's attention, beginning with the natural phenomena, moves through the facts to a kind of interior meaning: not the event or the individuals taking part in it but ultimately organic law itself is his theme. What I have called 'the law of nature' in the course of discussing 'Farewell to Van Gogh' is more explicitly a motif in 'The Way of a World'. In the former poem, however, the implications of tension in a view of nature as at once stable and mutable, fixed and moving, are minimized or made totally inactive, as I have shown, by such means as the conflation of the two ideas in the word 'steady': in 'The Way of a World' the paradox focused in the one phrase, 'the shapes of change', is on the contrary magnified. All that I mean by the word 'law' is contained in that characteristic phrase—as we shall see, there are others like it in Tomlinson's poetry: I want to combine in this one word the concepts of unity in multiplicity, continuity of form throughout its permutations, the inherence of the whole in each of its parts. 'Vein and branch', which together convey the notion of living change, express the action not of tree, seed and gull, organisms to which the verbs would apply literally, but of the whole moving scene, which includes the 'windlines' and the steadying 'counterpoise' of the tree; they express what Paz refers to as 'the universal busyness' in Tomlinson's poetic and pictorial images of reality.

* * * * *

With some exceptions Tomlinson's nature poems have a normative intention. The exceptions are important, and our understanding of the nature poetry is incomplete without a consideration of them. In these poems the disposition to seek in sense-experience a discipline not only of the senses but of the mind and heart encounters situations where the life of nature cannot be conceived as exemplary. What is to be learned, for example, from the bearing of the carrion-crow, 'all black assumption', displaying in flight 'an ease that's merciless'? 'Crow' (*A Peopled Landscape*, 1963; CP p. 68) is one of several poems in which predatory or scavenger birds are the means of dramatizing a confrontation between the two 'natures', the humanly assimilable and the humanly unacceptable. In another poetic context the 'steady' intentness of the crow's 'inspecting eye' and the 'will behind it' would be virtues and, without the consequences, it could be presented as exemplary; but

> Acting, it will be
> as faultless as its eye
> in a concerted drop
> on carrion

and as moral beings we must bear '*affronted* witness' (my emphasis) to such faultlessness. What appears, morally or aesthetically, admirable in its undeviating attention and concentrated purpose ceases to be so when translated into action. The movement that is action taken, the movement implicit in the sharpness and precision of the 'inspecting eye', is also a dimension of the nature of things, but this normality cannot be normative for human beings, and recognition of it is not so readily followed by assent.

Encounters between opposites are the rule, not the exception, in

Tomlinson's poetry; they do not necessarily challenge, as the confrontation between two evaluations of nature in 'Crow' challenges, the normative intention of a poem. But such poems as 'Icos', 'How Still the Hawk', 'Winter-Piece', and 'Translating the Birds', rather than making nature the standard, stress, like 'Crow', the disparity between the nature of nature and man's view of it. In 'Icos' (*Seeing is Believing*, 1958; CP p. 22), for example, there is a disturbing similarity between the nature that cleanses and sharpens the poet's vision and the nature that gives the eagle its pitilessly 'level gaze'. The eagle does not enter the poem until the last three lines, and when it does it is merely a hanging shape 'scanning the shore', but the tension between the two images of perception is no less palpable for the poem's reticence about the bird's purpose. 'Icos' describes a Mediterranean land- and sea-scape of gleaming clarity, dominated by white—a white shingled path, olives dusted white, 'houses, whiter / Than either dust or shingle', and a white line of surf—and provides at the same time a hilltop view of the whole scene, one which, 'unsoftened by distance', is as sharp as a nearer view. The view composes a picture, which lacks for its completion only one speck of white 'piercing the empty blue' of sky, a patch of whiteness that a gull (say) could provide. But there is no gull, only the dark shape of the eagle. The poem is about perception, and is linked together by a chain of images for the act of vision. The sequence is a progression. The first image is a metaphor for the brilliance of Mediterranean light: the path climbs 'To where at the hill-crest / Stare houses', as though the white houses are a concentration of all the white in the landscape. But the stare is blank and unfocused. The intensity of light, however, promotes, or becomes, then a lucidity of human vision:

> The view, held from this vantage
> Unsoftened by distance, because
> Scoured by a full light,
> Draws lucid across its depth
> The willing eye.

Again, the lucidity lacks something. Though the view is 'scoured by a full light', the eye is merely receptive to what is given. The progression culminates in the eagle's 'piercing' scrutiny of the scene from a yet higher vantage-point:

> But, there, scanning the shore,
> Hangs only the eagle, depth
> Measured within its level gaze.

Measuring and, as it were, taking possession of the dimension of depth, the predatory eye at the same time supplies a missing dimension of meaning to the brilliant stare of the houses and the sharp clarity of the view.

It is interesting to compare the concentrated vigilance of the eagle with that of the two figures whose still, but not at all predatory, gaze is admired in 'Ponte Veneziano' (*Seeing is Believing*, 1958; CP p. 19).

> Tight-socketed in space, they watch
> Drawn by a single glance,
> Stripping the vista to its depth.

An orange canopy 'Flares from the line through which they gaze', but

> They do not see it, or,
> Seeing, relegate the glow
> To that point which it must occupy.

They are untempted, hardly noticing or coolly disregarding all diversion from the straight and narrow. 'Undistracted', 'Their glance channels itself' down the vista and under the vault of a bridge to where 'It broods on the further light'.

> They do not exclaim,
> But, bound to that distance,
> Transmit without gesture
> Their stillness into its ringed centre.

'Tight-socketed', the figures are seen, and perhaps feel themselves, to be an integral part of space. They are stretched along a line of vision that binds viewpoint to focus; they belong to space as subject belongs to the object of attention. '*Drawn* by a single glance' and '*bound* to that distance', they do what they have to do; their fixed gaze transmits the inner 'stillness' of the watchers, which is in part a sense of necessity. They belong to what they see by virtue not merely of being but doing: 'stripping' is an action, and theirs is an *act* of attention, which is more than receiving impressions. By their trenchant gaze they seem to *create* the dimension of depth. Tunnelling into space is a metaphor for penetrating deeply into reality. The resemblance between this act of vision and that of the predatory bird in 'Icos' is remarkably close. The still watch of the two figures is at the core of the Venetian scene: not witnesses of a spectacle but inhabitants of a world, helping to shape their perceptual environment, they transmit 'Their stillness into its ringed centre'. The Mediterranean scene likewise is presented in sharpest focus, receives its final meaning, in the 'level gaze' of the eagle: not only a necessary part, it is the point of the picture. Although the painter's first thought is that 'A gull would convey whiteness / Through the sole space that lacks it', the picture is truly completed by the eagle's insertion of the third dimension, and by implication the dynamics, of life. Depth is already there in the view from the hilltop, but the eye responds passively to what it sees, travelling *across* but not entering it. The word 'through'—'convey whiteness / Through…'—hints at what is needed, which it is left to the calculating, steady eye of the eagle to provide. Measuring 'depth', its gaze, like the glance of the Venetian figures, 'channels itself' through a seemingly solid medium, realizing space by plotting the path of penetration. Each act of vision mines reality; to each the concluding lines of 'How it happened' (the last of 'Four Kantian Lyrics'; CP p. 77) are equally applicable:

> no absolute of eye can tell
> the utmost, but the glance
> goes shafted from us like a well.

Comparison of the 'undistracted' stare in 'Ponte Veneziano' with the unwinking 'level gaze' of the eagle in 'Icos' draws out the latent suggestion of aquiline singlemindedness in the 'single glance' of the watchers; the verbs of imperious action or imperative mood— 'stripping', 'relegate', 'channels', 'must occupy'—improve the likeness by reminding one further of the ruthlessness with which the eagle rules its kingdom. The two acts of vision are indeed almost identical, yet the fact is that, notwithstanding the closeness of the parallels, morally the two poems are very nearly contradictions of each other. The normative intention of 'Ponte Veneziano' is never in doubt; the last line is implicit in the first. This is not true of 'Icos'. The discipline and vigilance of eye with which the two figures command the Venetian scene, which are admirable and exemplary in them, elicit admiration too when exercised by the eagle; but, if a retrospective view of 'Icos' discovers an imaginative logic in the transition from the blank stare of the houses through the lucid absorption of the surveying eye to the armed and aimed vision of the predator, nevertheless the dark spot and its dark purpose also jar with the scene. Knowing its, as yet undeclared, purpose, we must bear 'affronted witness' to its poised assurance, its precisely gauged aim and penetration, as to the merciless ease of the carrion-crow.

The eagle's 'level gaze' suggests stillness. In 'How Still the Hawk' (CP p. 23), the poem that follows 'Icos' in *Seeing is Believing*, the quality is named, and the mutually incompatible implications of the word, in this context, are used to expose the paradox of a nature that is at once an image of what is right and fitting and of what is alien and unacceptable.

> How still the hawk
> Hangs innocent above
> Its native wood.

Its innocence is not a masquerade: in the sense that there is no crime in being what it is and doing what it has to do, it *is* innocent. And it has a right, too, to be *where* it is: it is no more and no less 'native' than the animal it hunts. The interaction of 'native' with 'innocent' generates, indeed, a teasing hint of Eden, as it were an Eden of *fallen* nature. The stillness of the hawk becomes, then, the visible expression of being oneself and of being, and having the right to be, where one belongs. Like the Venetian figures, it is an integral part of the scene; its stillness has the same meaning as theirs. Doing what they have to do—an image of unflinching assent—they find, or create, a still centre in themselves and in their field of vision: the hawk

An Ethic of Perception

not only belongs to its native wood, but is at peace with itself and at one with nature. 'Innocent' means what it says, though it invites rebuttal. The next lines seem to provide it:

> Distance, that purifies the act
> Of all intent, has graced
> Intent with beauty—

only to the spectator, that is, who is outside 'The shrivelled circle / Of magnetic fear' enclosing predator and prey, is the hawk's drop 'Plummet of peace'. Distance lends enchantment to the view? Hardly: the beauty is grace more than illusion, and given not lent. 'Beauty must lie', it is true, when the distanced view that bestows beauty conceals intent. Nevertheless beauty *is* not, in itself, a lie. The fact of the act does not invalidate the grace of the appearance. Nor is it merely appearance: 'beauty' marks the spectator's approval of what he sees, but also of what it means to him—in this case, naturalness. The poem persuades us that 'beauty' and 'innocence' are appropriate, if surprising, words for the hawk, but the motive for doing so is not to deny the paradox. Not only must beauty lie, but such 'innocence must harm': like the stormy Atlantic in Yeats's 'A Prayer for my Daughter', the hawk has a 'murderous innocence'. There is an irreconcilable contradiction for the human observer between the *stillness* of being, the 'peace' of being completely what one does, and the vigilant *stillness* of an intent to kill, although the word, applying equally to both, makes them in the hawk inseparable.

The nature of 'Winter-Piece' (*A Peopled Landscape*, 1963; CP p. 62), which metaphorically feeds the poet's mind, is the same nature that literally starves the rooks.

> You wake, all windows blind—embattled sprays
> grained on the medieval glass.
> Gates snap like gunshot
> as you handle them. Five-barred fragility
> sets flying fifteen rooks who go together
> silently ravenous above this winter-piece
> that will not feed them.

As in the early 'Poem', this wakening is a cleansing of the senses, a sharpening of perception, imparting to the world a hard superclarity; but where in the former the atmosphere has a comparatively genial 'clean and frost-sharp' crispness, here it is 'the bladed atmosphere, the white resistance' of a pitiless opponent, an enemy of life. Yet it sustains the poet by instructing the eye—in iron-hard ruts 'you discern once more / oak-leaf by hawthorn, for the frost / rewhets their edges'—and by invigorating the will: the bladed mind, confronting (say) the spider still clinging to 'a perfect web' 'death-masked in cold', matches itself against the 'bladed atmosphere' of winter. Responding to a common criticism of his poetry, Tomlinson has said that, while he aims at a linguistic balance of the kind indicated by his phrase 'sensuous abstraction',[27] his verse is nonetheless very 'physical'. These lines bear him out. Hard consonants, the emphases of assonance and alliteration, the violent energy—bursts and jolts—of rhythm enact not only the relentlessness of winter but also a kind of relish in the *human* response to its challenge (avoiding the 'I', 'you' generalizes the subjective presence).

The 'medieval glass' of the opening lines adds a temporal dimension to the scene, reminding us that generations of endurance have shaped the grain of human character. There are similarly human implications in the closing descriptions of the windows:

> Returning
> you see the house glint-out behind
> its holed and ragged glaze,
> frost-fronds all streaming.

These descriptions frame the poem, picturing the house as a scarred veteran of 'embattled' centuries. Because of this I hear echoes of the 'looped and windowed raggedness' of poverty in Lear's prayer (*King Lear* III, iv). It is highly unlikely that Tomlinson intends any such allusion to the suffering of the 'poor naked wretches / That bide the pelting of this pitiless storm' whom Lear addressed with that cry of immoderate pity. But the contrast between these passages is nevertheless instructive. Tomlinson's image simply recognizes the fact, the reality of the inhuman, of what is presented here as anti-life:

An Ethic of Perception

his lines do not cry out with or against it. It is assimilated and at the same time resisted—a resistance that meets the force of death's own 'white resistance': in acknowledging the cost of a complete realism, the poem neither accepts nor rejects the mercilessness of nature. The disparity between the human and the non-human view remains stark and unresolved. For the rooks it is relentless winter: for the poet it is a 'winter-piece', a picture. It brings nourishment to the poet and his readers, but not to the birds.

The difference between a nature that is and is not conceived as exemplary is presented in 'Translating the Birds' (*The Shaft*, 1978; CP p. 310), too, as the difference between distance and nearness, the contrary views of spectator and actor. We admire the buzzard as 'It veers a haughty circle with sun-caught breast', but the small birds 'do not linger to admire the sight . . . Beauty does not stir them, realists to a man'. In this late poem, however, the distinction includes more than this: finally, it is made to define the disparity between the world of language, one that is made intelligible to human understanding, and a world 'beyond the clasp of words', a world of power and fear, mastered not by the mind but by the 'supply pulsing' wings of the buzzard. The distinction entails incompatible views, a positive and an ironic view, of verbal art. According to which view you take, art's command of reality is either imperial or imperious. Although irreconcilable, both views are present in the poem. To our ears 'the buzzard's two-note cry' sounds plaintive, a cry that seems to hesitate between 'A mewing, a regret, a plangent plea', or, the poet adds, 'so we must translate it who have never / Hung with the buzzard or above the sea'. Translation is the act of taking possession by the exercise of eloquence, and when nature is thought of as compatible with the human interpretation of it, art, admiring what it has perceived and incorporated, is seen as taking rightful *imperial* possession of that reality. But when nature is thought of as resisting words, art is seen to act *imperiously* in giving semantic shape to its perception of reality: 'eager always for the intelligible', listening to the songs of small birds we hasten to 'Instruct those throats what meanings they must tell'. Art's celebration of nature finds the word 'empery' for the buzzard's absolute dominion—'The flash of empery that solar fire / Lends to the predatory ease of flight'—and, employing in those lines a language of *artistic* empery, a poetic opulence that parades the artifice of art, it sees its own lordliness reflected in the bird's mastery of the air and aloof view of its subjects. But irony has an equal part with celebration in those lines; irony notes the momentariness of the 'flash' and the temporariness of 'lends'. If we remember from the previous line the small birds that 'do not linger to admire the sight', then we give more emphasis to 'predatory', and regard with scepticism the aggrandizement upon which for one line 'haughty' buzzard and admiring poet agree.

* * * * *

At the beginning of this chapter I quoted the opening lines of 'The Marl Pits': 'It was a language of water, light and air' he sought to 'speak [himself] free' from conditions and attitudes that stunted spiritual growth. The enlargement of spirit that the young artist coveted was to be dependent upon a discipline of attention that transcends, not the personal, but the *merely* personal focus. The language of the elements is a language that seeks relationship with the permanencies of being. The focus, that is to say, is metaphysical. A poem written early in his career, published in *Seeing is Believing* (1958; CP p. 37), has the title 'In Defence of Metaphysics'. He asks 'What is the language / Of stones?' and answers: 'Stones are like deaths. / They uncover limits.' To *uncover* limits is to experience that 'primal fulness' of 'being' which Tomlinson has associated with Cézanne's 'ethic of perception'.

NOTES

1. There was an 'Objectivist' movement in American poetry, which for a time, in the early 1930s, was associated with the names of Louis Zukofsky, Charles Reznikoff and Charles Oppen. The term was vaguely defined; whatever it meant, it was not, as David Perkins has pointed out in the second volume of *A History of Modern Poetry*, 'in any simple sense, a concrete representation of objects'. Although

Tomlinson has taken an interest in these poets, writing about them in *Some Americans* and editing a selection of Oppen's poems, they had ceased to appear as a group and the term has lost whatever significance it had. With the word 'objectivism' I am identifying that aspect of his work which Richard Swigg examines in *Charles Tomlinson and the Objective Tradition*. See also Denis Donoghue, 'The Proper Plenitude of Fact' in *The Ordinary Universe* (London: Faber and Faber; New York: Macmillan, 1968) and, for a general account of the Objective Tradition in nineteenth-century writers, Patricia Ball, *Science of Aspects*.

2. T. S. Eliot, *The Sacred Wood: Essays on Poetry and Criticism* (7th edn, London: Faber and Faber, 1950), pp. 9–12.

3. Wallace Stevens, 'The Man with the Blue Guitar', *The Collected Poems of Wallace Stevens* (New York: Knopf, 1974), p. 165.

4. *Eden*, p. 13; my emphasis.

5. *PN Review*, 5:1 (1977), p. 37.

6. *Eden*, p. 14.

7. *Ibid.*, p. 13.

8. *Ibid.*, p. 16.

9. *Ibid.*, p. 14.

10. Edward Thomas, *A Literary Pilgrim in England* (London: Jonathan Cape, 1917, repr. 1937), p. 54.

11. *Eden*, p. 14.

12. *Ibid.*, p. 14.

13. *Ibid.*

14. *Ibid.*, p. 20.

15. *Some Americans*, p. 6; an account of 'the way certain American poets, together with a painter, helped an English poet to find himself', and a record of his meetings with them.

16. *Ibid.*, p. 3.

17. See Tomlinson's *Some Americans* (1981). He has also edited *Marianne Moore: A Collection of Critical Essays* (1969), *William Carlos Williams: Selected Poems* (1983) and *William Carlos Williams: A Critical Anthology* (1972); see his Introductions to the first two and his Introduction and interspersed commentaries in the last. See Richard Swigg, *Charles Tomlinson and the Objective Tradition* (London: Associated University Presses, 1994) and Paul Mariani, 'Tomlinson's Use of the Williams Triad', *Contemporary Literature*, 18 (1977).

18. *PN Review*, 5:1 (1977), p. 37.

19. *Eden*, p. 14.

20. *The Prelude* (1850), Book II, 254.

21. *PN Review*, 5:1 (1977), p. 36.

22. Tomlinson praises Williams for being able to convey 'intense personal excitement...without heavyweight expressionist insistence' in *On Modern Poetry:*

Essays Presented to Donald Davie (Nashville: University of Vanderbilt Press, 1988), p. 222.

23. John Berger, 'The Sight of Man', *Selected Essays and Articles: The Look of Things*, p. 194

24. *Ibid.*

25. Octavio Paz, 'The Graphics of Charles Tomlinson'; reprinted in *Charles Tomlinson: Man and Artist* (ed. Kathleen O'Gorman), p. 194.

26. *Eden*, p. 13.

27. *PN Review*, 5:1 (1977), p. 37.

Chapter Two
One World

There are poems of the natural world, but with human implications, and there are poems with an explicit human content. In considering Tomlinson's work, the distinction, thus qualified, is a useful one. The terms may vary, however, to emphasize different aspects of the antithesis: sometimes the distinction we need to draw is not between the natural and the human, but between poems of perception or stillness or fixed relations in space and poems of process or movement or shifting relations in time. But whatever the subject-matter, the experiences treated in Tomlinson's poems belong, conspicuously and emphatically, to one world, irreduceably various but still one world, a natural-human world. The categories of thought by which he organizes his understanding and moral discrimination of human being and action are the same as, or extensions of, those by which he organizes visual experience in his landscape poems.

One way of demonstrating this unity is to bring together several 'natural' and 'human' poems governed by the same patterns of thought. I have grouped them by motif. Selecting three image-ideas pervasive and fundamental in Tomlinson's work, under each heading—'Meetings and Encounters', 'Prospects' and 'Perfections'—I have collected for comparison poems dissimilar in subject-matter but connected by belonging to a common frame of thought.

Before proceeding to the first of these groupings, however, I want to look closely at one poem, 'The Atlantic' (*Seeing is Believing*, 1958; CP p. 17) which in the *degree* of emphasis laid on the human content stands somewhere between the poems of perception and those that delineate the human scene. It provides a very clear demonstration, on the one hand, of the separate existence of natural processes and human actions and, on the other, of the unity that overrides those differences.

'The Atlantic' is a visual and kinaesthetic image of the incoming tide as an assault launched against an immovable object, a perpetual re-enactment of force gathered and expended. As if it were a demonstration of the physical laws governing its motion, in regulated, invariable sequence the wave lifts, hangs and then 'drops ... over and shorewards'. Nor has the sequence finished when the wave collapses:

> The beach receives it,
> A whitening line, collapsing
> Powdering-off down its broken length;
> Then, curded, shallow, heavy
> With clustering bubbles, it nears
> In a slow sheet that must climb
> Relinquishing its power, upward
> Across tilted sand.

Throughout the poem but especially in these lines we have an obscure sense of human meanings stirring in these words. The human correspondences we discern in nature, being intrinsic to the way the mind works when it takes linguistic possession of the non-human world, are embedded in the language we use to record them. The minutely accurate description and close enactment of the natural sequence, give us immediate, inner experience of its human analogue. 'Launched into an opposing wind' (the poem begins), the wave 'hangs / Grappled beneath the onrush'—an image of asserted power—and after its collapse, compelled forward by its continuing momentum, it '*must* climb' the beach even as it must eventually relinquish its power. Likewise, human assertion in the face of opposition and ultimate surrender to inevitable defeat are, in the poem, equal and contending imperatives.

'The Atlantic' is indisputably a nature poem, a translation of sense experience. It is also by analogy, as we have seen, a poem of human meanings. What distinguishes it significantly from some other nature poems by Tomlinson, however—'Poem' (CP p. xix) and 'Venice' (CP p. 3), for example—is that by adding movement, a dimension of time and action, the image in 'The Atlantic' makes possible a more inclusive metaphor for human reality. 'Poem' and 'Venice' ask the reader to be a spectator or an auditor; 'The Atlantic' engages him or her as a participant. There are other differences, but all stem from this radical contrast. Because the differences are conspicuous, their obviousness may obscure the no less striking resemblances; but the latter go deeper and, revealing as they do a strong continuity of thought, prove to be the more important.

'Venice' charts the relations and contraries, the geometry, of a still, or stilled, scene; a world is plotted and demarcated, defined and *contained*. 'The Atlantic', too, depicts a natural world of known qualities and limits, obeying fixed laws, defined by its relations and its contraries. Although the contrary elements are in *active*, or transactional, relation to each other, the energies of 'The Atlantic' are none the less tightly ordered and its action swings between earth and water, the conditions of solidity and fluidity.

This is not, however, a complete account of either poem—not of 'Venice', as we saw in Chapter 1, nor, as I am about to propose, of 'The Atlantic'. Each creates a contained world, but each also includes a moment of release from law and limit, suggesting thereby a world without divisions, a reality that exceeds what is immediately present to the senses. In that moment contraries commune. In 'Venice' there is a still pause: 'From the palace flanking the waterfront / She is about to embark, but pauses'. Movement is frozen for an instant, the woman suspended between two states at the borderline dividing land from water. During the pause there is heard the rustle of her dress— 'Her dress is a veil of sound / Extended upon silence'—and juxtaposition of this image with the preceding spatial image implies a relation between sound and silence that parallels the relation between land and water. In that meeting of contraries, which is also a joining of part to whole, it is as if sound and silence, known and unknown, appearance and reality settle their differences. In 'The Atlantic' the sea, losing its turbulence as its movement up the slope of beach slows to a halt, becomes a 'lucid pane' of water and, in the interlude between the sea's advance and its return, creates a moment of rest.

> The sun rocks there, as the netted ripple
> Into whose skeins the motion threads it
> Glances athwart a bed, honey-combed
> By heaving stones.

It is a pause but not a still pause: there is a continuous gentle motion, the motion of the universe interweaving sea, sun and pebbles. It is a pause generated by encounter, when contraries interpenetrate, and outer and inner (imaged as incoming tide and receiving beach) dance together.

The virtual identity of the patterns of thought in poems of observation such as 'Poem' and 'Venice' and in a transactional poem like 'The Atlantic' may be illustrated further by approaching the question of similarity and difference from another angle. In his poetry of observation the object is primary, the subject is discovered in what he sees: 'the image seizes on us ... drawing us to a reciprocation' (CP p. 221). When it is objective, 'Style speaks what is seen'; when it is subjective, 'it conceals the observation / Behind the observer: A voice / Wearing a ruff' (CP p. 11). In 'The Atlantic', which enacts the encounter of self and not-self, *encounter* is the activation in time of the *division* in the field of perception between subject and object. The still world of observation is transformed into a world in movement and a human image of moral action. The ethic of perception is thus extended to encompass an ethic of behaviour, the basis of which is that, as the body is nourished and sustained by its natural environment, so is the self dependent for renewal on all that is not self; we must 'embrace' the world 'somewhat self-forgetfully'[1] if we would experience personal growth. In the perceptual world the whole takes precedence over the part, the general over the individual. In the field of action self is the individual, conditionality the general. Conditionality determines the bounds of possibility; the final posture of self is that of subservience, as of the part to the whole.

Meetings and Encounters

Discussion of 'Venice' and 'The Atlantic' would have been almost impossible without the words 'meeting' and 'encounter' or their equivalents. They translate into action the static properties denoted by that other pair of words, 'relations' and 'contraries', terms which are equally necessary in any discussion of the poetry. 'Venice', I said, charts the relations and contraries, the geometry, of a still-life world; and I compared this geometry with the system of oppositions and momentary accords—encounters and meetings—that constitutes the dynamic world of 'The Atlantic'.

These poems have in common the belief, expressed in 'Aesthetic' (CP p. 3), that reality is 'space made articulate'; that is, a whole concretized in its parts, a whole that may be thought of as static or dynamic. This belief has influenced the organization of experience in many of Tomlinson's poems. It has an obvious affinity with the perceptual theories of Gestalt psychology. I mentioned this in the previous chapter, where I drew attention to 'the figure-ground organization of perception' in 'Poem' and observed that it is a characteristic structural principle in Tomlinson's verse. Other poems in this volume are similarly concerned to establish a proportionate, impartial and un-partial view. In 'At Delft' (CP p. 32), a witty but admiring epitome of the civilized values embodied in Vermeer's images, the human is *placed* in its context, defined as what it is and is not by what stands with it and what stands against it: 'All that is human here stands clarified / By all that accompanies and bounds'. Another statement in this poem, 'For if one dances / One does so to a measure'—which is about the relation of part to whole, and applies to poetry as much as to its ostensible subject, the separate but simultaneous chimes of the civic clocks—balances the values of individuality and pattern, freedom and order. In 'Ponte Veneziano' (CP p. 19), the orange of a canopy shading a boat in a Venetian vista, making its flamboyant gesture of independence, is given due appreciation before perspective is restored by the watching figures, who, refusing to be distracted, 'relegate the glow / To that point which it must occupy'.

As the relations and contraries of a scene comprise its geometry, so meetings and encounters are dynamic expressions of a system: they constitute, respectively, the spatial and the temporal languages of a coherent world, a world of given attributes and powers, regulated by immutable laws. *Relations and Contraries* is the title Tomlinson chose, clairvoyantly, for his first pamphlet of verse. The ideas indicated by the terms are fundamental to his work, but the terms themselves are perhaps too abstract to be used very frequently. 'Meetings' and 'encounters' and their approximate synonyms, however, occur more often, both in the poems and in their titles, possibly because Tomlinson is more interested, as Octavio Paz has said, in 'the world as event' than in 'the world-as-spectacle'.[2] Among poem-titles, for example, we have 'Encounter' (CP p. 47) in *Seeing is Believing* (1960) and 'Oppositions' (CP p. 189) in *The Way of a World* (1969), 'The Meeting' (CP p. 117) in *American Scenes* (1966) and 'The Greeting' (CP p. 260) in *The Way In* (1974). I list them not to demonstrate the obvious, but to note the presence of these motifs in a poem not yet mentioned, 'One World' (CP p. 112), (*American Scenes*); for here the underlying metaphors of meeting and greeting, encounter and opposition are enactments of the poet's belief that reality is a whole concretized in its parts. The poem is in the first place an ironic consideration of the title-phrase, used by a companion in appreciation of the autumn weather: 'One world you say / eyeing the way the air / inherits it'. The confident declaration, expressing no more than the contentment of the speaker, is then confronted with the facts of seasonal change. Not only is winter clearly on the way, but late autumn is itself a time of contradictions:

>   The year
> is dying and the grass
> dead that the sunlight burnishes
> and breeds distinctions in. Against
> its withered grain the shadow
> pits and threads it, and your one
> lies tracked and tussocked, disparate,
> abiding in, yet not obedient
> to your whim.

The coincidence of dying and breeding calls for 'distinctions' to be made; yet, we observe, his companion's statement needs to be qualified rather than abandoned. The whole is implicit but not always apparent in its 'disparate' parts. The poet asks his companion, and his readers, to pay equal attention to both diversity and unity, conflict and harmony, accident and law—encounters and meetings. This is also the implication of his conclusion: 'The breath of circumstance / is warm, a greeting in their going [the dying of the leaves] / and under each death, a birth'.

The Way of a World (1969) took its title from that of one of its poems (CP p. 165), and did so, evidently, because it conveyed a message: *this is my perception of the world and the way it behaves*. Part of the poem's message is that the world is a place of *encounter*, where life is a contest between the forces, the centripetal and centrifugal forces respectively, of generation and destruction:

>   we grasp
> The way of a world in the seed, the gull
> Swayed toiling against the two
> Gravities that root and uproot the trees.

The other part of the message is that it is nevertheless *one* world, a place of *meetings* where contraries sometimes settle their differences: 'In all these evanescences of daily air' there are 'shapes of change' (a paradox which suggests that the idea of spatial pattern and temporal movement are not incompatible with each other), permanencies at once found and made by the perceiver.

This poem is primarily about the natural world, the struggle between 'the weightless anarchy / Of air' seeking to uproot trees and the weight and steadiness of rooted things. 'Anarchy' tells us, however, that the poem is not without human content. The resistance offered by the creative force to the winds of destruction is paralleled in the human world by memory's accumulation of images rescued from the flow of time and by the mind's discovery of enduring forms—the way of a world—in all this evanescence. The struggle *in* nature is also the struggle *of* nature, it is the law of its being. The encounter between the retentive mind and transience, on the other hand, does not bring into action the whole man; we may think of the human analogue therefore as a secondary theme. Even so, the poem exemplifies the way of a composite world, nature and humanity activated by the same powers, a human-natural world polarized between the 'two gravities' that make and unmake life, work with and against time. As always in Tomlinson's poetry, the language used, merely by staying true to the facts of perception, corresponds with equal accuracy to natural and human realities, keeping us aware of the identity without anthropomorphic transformations. The 'shapes of change' are at the same time abstract and organic, formations of the mind which yet 'vein and branch / Through the moving textures' of the wind-swept and therefore seemingly animated scene. When 'the ash-key, borne-by whirling / On the same surge of air' as the gull, is given the appearance in consequence of 'an animate thing', the wind and the poet's eye have cooperated to produce that appearance, that meaning; together they have made the seed seem to have the same kind of life as the gull, so that both may be represented as 'toiling' in the grip of opposing forces. The scene recovered by memory was inseparable—took its form—from its 'value' to the poet, its disclosure of a life-pattern, and so when it came back to mind 'it came / With its worth' as an embodiment of meaning.

It has been my contention that the words 'meeting' and 'encounter' have almost the status of technical terms in Tomlinson's vocabulary, and I have used them as such in my exposition of the poems. It is time to concede, however, that they are not in fact technical terms. Although the words are far from being interchangeable in Tomlinson's usage, the meanings they carry are determined by the poetic contexts in which they occur, and the operative distinction between them is not always identical with mine or as clear-cut. It is true also that, with a poem like 'Winter Encounters' (CP p. 17) in *Seeing is Believing* (1960), there is no reason to maintain a strict separation between the two sets of antitheses, relations and contraries on the one hand and meetings and encounters on the other: the languages of space and time, which I have carefully differentiated, cannot be regarded as mutually exclusive when one is discussing a Tomlinson poem.

Notwithstanding the title, 'Winter Encounters', in this early poem there are meetings as well as encounters (both words are used)—here it makes little difference, either, if one prefers to call them relations and contraries. As we should expect, however, the emphasis is certainly on encounters, or contraries. The word 'encounter' bridges opposite kinds of awareness—awareness of crowded, diverse particularities and a simultaneous awareness of order and pattern; it describes the way things are connected, as parts of a fluid whole, without forfeiting their separate identities. As in 'The Way of a World', these opposites are the polarities—the complementary opposites, one might say—of a single world. Since this world exists in space and time, it can be experienced as at once a static geometry and a system of interacting parts.

> House and hollow; village and valley-side:
>   The ceaseless pairings, the interchange
> In which the properties are constant
>   Resumes its winter starkness. The hedges' barbs
> Are bared. Lengthened shadows
>   Intersecting, the fields seem parcelled smaller
> As if by hedgerow within hedgerow. Meshed
>   Into neighbourhood by such shifting ties,
> The house reposes, squarely upon its acre
>   Yet with softened angles, the responsive stone
> Changeful beneath the changing light:
>   There is a riding-forth, a voyage impending
> In this ruffled air, where all moves
>   Towards encounter.

In this passage, the first half of the poem, despite certain human associations and implications of the diction, the field of reference is predominantly perceptual. The achievement of these lines is to convey precisely and vigorously a reality that is, in spatial terms, at once simple and complex, single and multiple (a single 'all' that moves, in singular number, 'towards encounter'), and is, in temporal terms, at the same time constant and in ceaseless change. The theme is, again, the way of a world, but the poem presents it as both fact and possibility: this, it says, is how the mind organizes what it perceives, how the world appears to the eye that sees clearly; but, since clear seeing is rare, we are also invited to recognize in these observations an interpreted paradigm, and to share the poet's experience, of a world ungraspably various and yet made to cohere. Tomlinson's language—sensuous and abstract, particular and general, mimetic and conceptual—reflects the polarities of his vision: a hard-edged denotative vocabulary and a firm structure of logical and analogical relations are matched by a forceful rendering in word-sound, syntax and rhythm of a densely physical world—solid, 'changeful' and various; tension is expressed in paradox—'shifting ties'—and in such precisions as 'ceaseless pairings', which identifies a state of fluctuant constancy; a state of complementary opposition—difference and resemblance—is embodied in the balances, chimes and transitions of the first line.

In the sequel to this passage the human correspondences are made explicit and given more prominence than in 'The Way of a World'. The inter-relations and activities of nature and of man are assimilated in a common terminology by which they are referred, as it were, to the same law of being. This dimension of Tomlinson's theme is to be glimpsed earlier in such words as 'interchange', 'neighbourhood', 'responsive', the primary associations of which are human but which without violation to the literal sense can be stretched to include relationships seen by the eye. There is no imposing of a metaphysical connection: correspondences are discovered that already exist and are reflected in the language. The phenomenal world is inevitably a human world, for eye and mind involuntarily organize what they perceive into shapes and categories. To acknowledge this is to discard the notion of man as a misfit in the universe.

> Inanimate or human,
> The distinction fails in these brisk exchanges—
> Say, merely, that the roof greets the cloud,
> Or by the wall, sheltering its knot of talkers,
> Encounter enacts itself in the conversation
> On customary subjects, where the mind
> May lean at ease, weighing the prospect
> Of another's presence.

The language systematically demonstrates an interchange of qualities between the human and the inanimate and between mind and body. Opposition and agreement constitute the double principle governing what the eye sees, the relation of man to nature, and—a further extension of his theme—the social encounters of man and man in his dual capacity as an individual and the inheritor of a common tradition (the *separate* strands *meet* in a 'knot', the talkers *exchange* views but on '*customary*' subjects').

All in this winter scene moves 'towards encounter', the transitory conjunctions arranged by light and perspective, in which, however, 'the properties are constant'. But the note of celebration sounded in the lines beginning 'There is a riding-forth', the rhetoric of aroused expectancy, responds to something beyond the encounter of known quantities; we are first made aware of it by the unexpectedness of the word 'prospect'. 'Presence' points also to what is undisclosed: in conversation individuals meet without merging, but in doing so a further prospect opens and 'one meets with more / Than the words can witness'. Beyond the known and definable lie future possibilities undefined (the abstract sense of 'prospect') and (in the physical sense) a fuller, conceivably unbounded view.

In 'Winter Encounters' the ways of nature and the ways of man are presented as separate manifestations of a common pattern of behaviour: they are in a correspondent relation to each other. On the other hand, 'Flute Music' (*The Necklace*, 1955; CP p. 9), 'On a Landscape by Li Ch'eng' (*Seeing is Believing*, 1958; CP p. 29) and, as we saw in the previous chapter, 'Appearance' (*Written On Water*, 1972; CP p. 221) put man and nature into a reciprocal relation, each acting upon the other: not illustrating, but in process of creating, one world. In 'Appearance', for example, perception is depicted both as an exterior 'image' seizing our attention and as 'a meeting of expectations / With appearances', a meeting which is an impetuous 'rushing out to greet them'.

The recognition in this poem of two facts of perception, that subject and object exist separately and yet have moments of identity, also informs the aesthetic discussed in 'Flute Music'. Many of the poems in *The Necklace* are about art; 'Flute Music' compares the arts of painting and music. It begins by acknowledging division. 'There is a moment for speech and for silence'—man's speech and the silence of nature, the silence viewed and framed by the painter. But Tomlinson tries to imagine a transcendence of division which is not a denial of difference. Nature may resist *translation* into human terms 'yet still bear the *exegesis* of music', the flute's music which is here an image for his poetic ideal. Seeking a harmony but not 'a forced harmony', he creates instead an accord which is not an agreement simply, but an agreement to differ; exegesis parallels, it does not replace, the text—it is different and the same. Thus the poetry of the flute is 'reason's song / Riding the ungovernable wave', riding (say) as the surfer rides—in unison with the element in that he takes his motion from it; not pretending to rule the unruly but tracing its outline, marking its boundaries.

'Flute Music' partly dissolves the distinction between encounter and meeting. The aesthetic expounded, a not 'forced harmony' between man and nature, is less a reconciliation than a negotiated agreement to live together in difference. 'On a Landscape by Li Ch'eng' shows, rather, the interdependence of meeting and encounter: encounter prepares for meeting and meeting is nourished by encounter. The encounter in Li Ch'eng's painting is, in the first place, between the human and the non-human: a tiny band of men on the one hand, and featureless white and grey expanses of nature on the other—travellers dwarfed by their barren setting. It is also an encounter between contraries in nature—snow which extends down to the coast, and sea 'Grey among capes / Like an unvaried sky'. By adding sky the simile makes of snow and sea the opposite poles of one world; contraries which 'meet' in the experience of the travellers, who carefully 'skirt between' them as they thread their way along the coastal rim. The 'meeting' suggested visually by the design gives rise to a literary development of the pictorial theme:

> Minute, furtive and exposed,
> Their solitude is unchosen and will end
> In comity, in talk
> So seasoned by these extremes
> It will recall stored fruits
> Bitten by a winter fire.

The inhuman wastes and solitude are neither chosen, in wilful withdrawal from others, nor shunned; one does not seek 'extremes' but one's assent to them as part of the seasonal rotation contributes to the value and significance, and intensifies the experience itself, of 'comity', the mutual consideration that constitutes civil relations. 'Comity' is one of a group of words in Tomlinson's vocabulary (e.g. 'truce', 'treaty', 'negotiation') in which it is assumed that a human world is built on respect for rather than avoidance of difference; it is a notion of inclusion—on terms that safeguard individuality—not of fusion. When the experience of solitude thus vitalizes social intercourse, encounters, we may say, are subsequently composed into meetings.

Not until the end of the poem are the human figures in the landscape precisely identified: 'The title, without disapprobation, says "Merchants"'. Crossers of boundaries, intermediaries between distinct but complementary interests, agents of interchange—merchants are named by the painter and, with a challenging emphasis, by the poet as worthy representatives of humanity in its self-defining enterprise of civilization. The poem, like the painting, is about merchants, but it is also about merchants in a painting, about art itself. The 'comity' in which their experience of extremes is consummated and concluded corresponds to the ordering and balancing activity of the artist: seeking, like them, a not 'forced harmony', he not only conveys by the title his approval but duplicates in his composition their composure. 'Look down', the poem begins, and with these words we are invited to share the high and distanced viewpoint of the painter. Soon we are also taking part in the construction of his perspective: we look down and find snow, and 'Where the snow ends / Sea, and where the sea enters', grey among snow-covered capes, 'lapping / From finger to finger / Of a raised hand', we come upon the travellers—the raised hand, besides being a simile for the headland jutting into the sea, is the hand of the artist measuring and assimilating his subject.

In 'Flute Music' and 'On a Landscape by Li Ch'eng' opposites are in complementary relation: meetings and encounters are not mutually exclusive. There are many poems in Tomlinson's work, however, in which the encounters between man and nature are depicted as taking place between irreconcilable and uncompromising antagonists. As some of the titles reveal—for example, 'Winter-Piece', 'The Snow Fences', 'Arizona Desert'—nature is present in these poems as a relentless, unremitting enemy of human endeavour, permitting no accommodations, resisting any mitigations of its powers; man's part is to stand his ground. In this everlasting war between life and death there are no final victories: what humanity wins will be lost and recovered again and again; what is established must decay but must therefore be rebuilt, renewed. On the other hand, this is not a poetry of resignation: these are energizing encounters, having a tonic effect on the human constitution—clearing the mind, strengthening the will, quickening sense and feeling. Some of this may be substantiated by a reference back to my discussion of 'Winter-Piece' (CP pp. 116–19) in the previous chapter. It will be recalled that for the rooks winter is nothing but a 'bladed atmosphere, the white resistance' of life's antithesis. Yet if it does not feed the birds, it feeds the eye of the poet, on whom the effect of this encounter is invigorating. It sharpens the senses, 'for the frost / rewhets their edges' as it does the outlines of oak-leaf and hawthorn in the wheel-ruts of the frozen ground, and it gives a kind of etched permanence to the fleeting pleasures of the eye, such as frost-patterns on the windows like 'embattled sprays / grained on the medieval glass'.

In 'The Snow Fences' (*American Scenes*, 1966; CP p. 108) encounter is a moral stand taken by the human participant confronting winter and death. It defines the heroism of being human. The struggle against wind and cold as you climb the hill to a view of 'the church's dead-white / limewash' and a graveyard with 'its ill-kept memorials' is an image and an instance —it makes comparable moral and physical demands—of man's struggle against time and nature. The conditions of life are the same here as when the Saxons 'chose / these airy and woodless spaces / and froze here before they fed / the unsuperseded burial ground'. 'Fencing the upland against / the drifts' is an activity characteristic of man's determination to hold off the inevitable.

> The bitter darkness drives you
> back valleywards, and again you bend
> joint and tendon to encounter
> the wind's force and leave behind
> the nameless stones, the snow-shrouds
> of a waste season: they are fencing
> the upland against those years, those clouds.

The 'frosts have scaled' the grave stones of their names, as time has erased signs of human occupation, but the verse here, in the last stanza, continues to make its unflinching gesture of resistance to final defeat. The scene is as bleak as any to be found in Tomlinson, yet the poem is an act of human assertion; its effect is invigorating, rallying the forces of will and courage in the reader. The mood is more positive than stoicism, as these lines, in paying tribute to man's opponent, reveal:

> brow and bone
> know already that levelling zero
> as you go, an aching skeleton,
> in the breathtaking rareness of winter air.

Death the leveller strips you to the skeleton but 'breathtaking rareness' means both life-taking and life-giving—the phrase combines the extremes of danger and privilege. Fencing against the devastations of winter and time is not the same as fencing *out* the non-human: fences maintain separateness (until death drags them down) but do not prevent encounter, and, though the struggle is grim and necessary, even more it is bracing and exhilarating.

Man is pitted against nature, again, in 'Arizona Desert' (*American Scenes*; CP p. 121). This struggle is the basic humanizing enterprise of civilization, celebrated in both poems. The wider the gulf between the human and non-human—and the disparities in 'The Snow Fences' and 'Arizona Desert' are extreme—the more invigorative the encounter. The otherness of the outer world is always in Tomlinson's poems a source of inner nourishment. The upland spaces of 'The Snow Fences' are ruled by the 'levelling zero' of a winter cold that would reduce life and matter to the one cipher: the Arizona landscape is ruled by 'the levelling light' of a desert sun, *'imageless* arbiter' of a world emptied of consciousness. Yet, ironically, man's imaginative defiance of the poverty of nature feeds on that very poverty—the aridity, for instance, of a parched land. Even the desert flowers to the *eye*. It flowers only in ironic metaphor, it is true, but the irony, conceding the illusion, nevertheless enforces another point: the eye, animating what it sees, makes us denizens of a country not ours.

> Eye
> drinks the dry orange ground,
> the cowskull
> bound to it by shade:
> sun-warped, the layers
> of flaked and broken bone
> unclench into petals,
> into eyelids of limestone.

'Eye / drinks': the satisfaction of sight, the quenching of a visual thirst, is enacted in the surprise of the synaesthesia and the line-division's protraction and enhancement of that surprise. The weaving of alliteration, assonance and rhyme, especially internal rhyme, reflects, as often in Tomlinson's verse, the 'shifting ties' (CP p. 19) between things and the interpenetration of inner and outer. *Actual* occupation, however, of this barren land, signs of which are noted in the concluding stanza, is mentioned merely to extend the ironic message:

> Villages
> from mud and stone
> parch back
> to the dust they humanize
> and mean
> marriage, a loving lease
> on sand, sun, rock and
> Hopi
> means peace.

The thought echoes Wordsworth; unexpectedly, since the ironic limitation placed on the ideas of 'marriage' and 'peace'—the hope and aim of the civilizing enterprise—by the challenging insertion of these words into a description of a literal waste land, the site of 'unceasing unspoken war' between the forces of creation and destruction, is not at all typical of Wordsworth. Tomlinson has succeeded in reclaiming for the modern *sceptical* intelligence Wordsworth's theme, man in nature, tempering and qualifying rather than subverting the Romantic affirmation of the relationship. Wordsworth contends, in his Prospectus to *The Excursion*, that 'Paradise, and groves Elysian, Fortunate Fields' were not 'a mere fiction':

> For the discerning intellect of Man,
> When wedded to this goodly universe
> In love and holy passion, shall find these
> A simple produce of the common day.

(He also notes 'how exquisitely... The external World is fitted to the Mind'.) In Tomlinson's modification of the theme, 'peace' is temporal and temporary; 'Hopi means peace' exactly as extinct villages 'mean marriage'—it is an aspiration in ironic contradiction of the reality, the state of truceless war evidenced in the landscape; therefore it is not the 'produce' of holy simplicity but of unremitting labour. Death, as also toil, is conspicuous in—and necessary to—Tomlinson's paradise. The distinctions between the human and the non-human and between 'the purgatories possible / to us and / impossible' are sharp; words have sharp edges—there is no Romantic blurring of their semantic outlines. For the poem celebrates not myth but the fact of human resilience, patience, tenacity: the dust is transformed but by human effort not miracle. The verse has nothing of Wordsworth's exaltation —it is hard and spare—but its affirmation, though not absolute, is unequivocal.

In the last stanza of 'Arizona Desert', quoted above, the encounter between man the builder and his natural setting is described in the language of meeting, but this is not a dissolution of the distinction; it is not even that 'comity' predicted for the travellers in 'On a Landscape by Li Ch'eng', the special virtue of which is that it is a coming-together made more welcome and meaningful by the experience of its opposite. Encounters in 'Arizona Desert' are not so much composed as yoked into meetings: razed villages mean marriage by their intention and despite a history of failure. It is characteristic of Tomlinson to wrest a positive meaning out of a negative condition.

Meeting and encounter, greeting and confrontation, agreement and opposition; relations and contraries, union and division, pattern and diversity, law and chance—these antitheses serve to identify the dialectic of Tomlinson's poetic thinking. Such formulations as 'complementary opposition', 'meeting of opposites' and 'agreement to differ' are no more than pointers to the nature of that complex dynamic poise—the protean form, the diversified unity, the shifting coherence—which repeatedly Tomlinson discovers in his experience and exemplifies in his art. Insomuch as it entails a refusal of extravagance and excess it is the poise perhaps of classicism, a classicism exercised in the interests of vital, concentrated centrality; not judicious restraint but intensity and tension, a tension of competing energies, are the key qualities. Classicism is in this case synonymous with a passionate, strenuous occupation of the here-and-now. This is one conclusion we may draw from a reading of 'Wind' (*American Scenes*; CP p. 111). Wind is an extreme phenomenon, an enemy of centrality; to which, however, one is tempted to give the inflated significance that 'the airs' commotion' would seem to arrogate ('The woods shook, as though it were the day / of wrath'): but, stripped of apocalyptic rhetoric, it means simply that 'time was in mid-career / streaming through space'. The chances, the hurly-burly, of time (motion agitated into 'commotion') and the still certainty of death are the opposite poles, the upper and lower extremes, of existence; one's position is at a mid-point between these 'two gravities' (as he will call them in 'The Way of a World' (CP p. 165)).

> The noise above, and the rooted silence
> under it, poised one in place,
> and time said: 'I rescind
> the centuries with now', and space

banishing one from there to here:
'You are not God. You are not the wind'.

Prospects

Relations and contraries, meetings and encounters are names for, respectively, the properties and the dynamics of a human-natural world; they identify qualities and actions as particular manifestations of general principles. Tomlinson is always seeking, through sense experience, for a concrete-abstract sense of the whole: things and events, having both an individual and a generic reality, are realized equally as separate identities and as concrete articulations of space and time. 'Song is being', said Rilke; Tomlinson, restoring the distinction between life and art, gives his own version of this dictum in 'Melody': 'Song is the measure, rather, / Of being's spread and height' (CP p. 269). His predilection for the high or distanced view is a characteristic expression of this belief. It may be the spatial perspective of the eagle in 'Icos' (CP p. 22), 'depth / Measured within its level gaze', or it may be the temporal superimposed upon a spatial perspective, as in 'A Sense of Distance' (*The Way of a World*, 1969; CP p. 175), where the poet, in England, recalls, at 'a later distance', a scene from his stay in New Mexico—'the red rider' crossing 'the canyon floor / under a thousand feet of air'. It is clear that these are the perspectives of an extended and expanded *mental* vision:

> For I am in England,
> and the mind's embrace
> catches-up this English
> and that horizonless desert space
> into its own, and the three there
> concentrically fill a single sphere.

Invariably the emphasis falls less on the possession of an inclusive vision than on the activity of seeking: 'the glance / goes shafted from us like a well'. The force of the verb here and, as we shall see, the images in this, the conclusion to the last of 'Four Kantian Lyrics'

(*A Peopled Landscape*, 1963; CP p. 77), typically inject an energy of will and desire into the language of 'heights and distances' (CP p. 57). Meetings and encounters describe the behaviour of a known world: the sinking of shafts and wells represents the mind's penetration into what is not yet known. The last lines of 'A Sense of Distance' envisage entry into boundless space, 'where all / the kingdoms of possibilities shone / like sandgrains crystalline in the mind's own sun'. I have yet to introduce the word which, rather than 'heights' or 'distances', 'shafts' or 'wells', identifies the theme of this section. It appears, for example, in the first of the poems called 'Movements' (CP p. 233): 'I want that height and *prospect* such as music / Brings one to—music or memory'. I have chosen 'prospect' as my title for this portion of the chapter because it allows me to take advantage of the special verbal sense, as applied to mining engineering, and to speak not only, passively, of prospects as (literally or figuratively) extensive views but also, actively, of *the prospecting imagination* seeking beyond the known horizon further lengths and breadths of vision. The search beyond encounter—signalled in 'Winter Encounters', as noted in my earlier discussion of the poem, by the unexpected appearance of the word 'prospect'—is a movement beyond ascertainable facts to unknown but imaginable possibilities. Two kinds of meeting are differentiated: audible and visible, in the 'knot of talkers' and their exchange of views 'on customary subjects'; silent and speculative, in the meeting of the reflective 'mind'—'weighing the prospect of another's presence'—with '*more* / Than the words can witness' (my emphasis).

In this section, as in the last, I am concerned first of all to show that in Tomlinson's work 'nature' poems and 'human' poems are governed by the same patterns of thought and share a common language. In the fourth Kantian Lyric, cited above, although the subject is sense experience, the theme is Wordsworth's, the marriage of 'the discerning intellect of Man' with 'this goodly universe' which is the content of its experience:

> It happened like this: I heard
> from the farm beyond, a grounded
> churn go down. The sound

One World

>chimed for the wedding of the mind
>with what one could not see,
>the further fields, the seamless
>spread of space.

The words draw out the human significance of this 'event': this 'wedding' affirms the possibility of a human-natural world. In the satisfaction of discovering through the ear ranges of perception beyond the visible the poem, at the same time, exemplifies and celebrates the compass and grandeur of human identity:

>the sound
>that brings all space in
>for its sound, when self is clear
>as what we keenest see and hear.

This 'whole / event' is at once an instance and an image of the 'seamless' unity of sensory and mental experience; or, more precisely, it expresses the poet's urge to discover such a unity in his experience. As, in 'Winter Encounters', the 'prospect' contemplated by the talker stretches behind the surface impression of 'another's presence' and 'one meets with *more* / Than the words can witness', so in this poem the prospect opened to the ear adds to the circle of the visible the wider circle of 'what one could not see, / the *further* fields'. This, with the poem's conclusion already quoted ('the glance / goes shafted from us like a well'), takes us back to the 'glance' of the two figures in 'Ponte Veneziano' (CP p. 19), which 'channels itself' beneath and beyond the bridge to where 'It broods on the further light'. In all three poems the prospecting imagination is represented as searching out those 'kingdoms of possibilities' (CP p. 176) suggested by but extending beyond the immediate experience.

The image in 'Ponte Veneziano' (*Seeing is Believing*, 1958; CP p. 19), however, invites a closer examination. 'Further light' has a mystery that 'further fields' lacks: it seems to promise release from the ordinary constrictions of vision, making it not just quantitatively more but qualitatively different. On a first impression, indeed, the resonance of the phrase and the expansive gesture of the line would appear to be inconsonant with the classical temper of the whole poem, celebrating as it does an aesthetic and moral discipline which consists equally in the exercise of will—the intent concentration of 'a single glance / stripping the vista to its depth'—and in the stoic acknowledgement of and obedience to necessity:

> They do not exclaim,
> But, bound to that distance,
> Transmit without gesture
> Their stillness into its ringed centre.

The poem imagines undoubtedly an intensive rather than an extensive vision, a conditioned rather than an unbounded freedom, and yet, if our first impression was that the contemplation of a 'further light' beyond the closure of the bridge has no connection in what it signifies with the rest of the poem, we should be mistaken. The 'stillness' of the watchers is overtly an expression of their willing subjection to conditionality, but there is also a tacit correspondence between the undemonstrative stillness of the human figures and the reticence of that 'further' reality; eye and light, as it were, meet in one still 'centre'. Similarly, the striking image which introduces the watching figures—'Tight-socketed in space, they watch'—suggests that their consciousness is an integral part of what it is conscious of, fits into space as the eye into its socket, even as it also suggests that their fixity is the result of external constraint. The image reconciles these apparently contradictory suggestions: they are indeed constrained to be in one place, occupy one point of view, but accepting their finitude is the *condition* of their (limited) freedom as citizens of space. The implications of freedom in the imagery of light are brought out more fully in the earlier 'Venice' (CP p. 3), discussed in the previous chapter. 'Contained by the reflected arc' of a bridge, 'A tunnel of light / Effaces walls, water, horizon'; it is as if light, tunnelling through the concretions of space, has penetrated into the dimensionless reality of space itself. As a possible consequence of this dissolution of boundaries, in the succeeding (and final) stanza imagination, no longer 'contained', no longer merely prospective, *'idles'* like the boats on the water, in a suspended state where thing and image (matter and mind) ride together in undifferentiated equality: 'Floating upon its own image / A cortège of boats idles through space'.

'The glance / goes shafted from us like a well'; much of the meaning accumulated by the series of images that started with the 'tunnel of light' in 'Venice' on the very first page of *The Necklace*, in 1955, was gathered and compressed into this terse closing sentence of 'How It Happened' (CP p. 77) in *A Peopled Landscape* eight years later. It was only a matter of time, one might have speculated, before Tomlinson should feel the need, or find the occasion, to devote whole poems to further exploration of these two image-ideas and name them, simply, 'The Well' and 'The Shaft'. 'The Well' (CP p. 142) appeared in his next volume of poems, *American Scenes* (1966); 'The Shaft' (CP p. 306) is the title-poem of a collection published in 1978. Both exhibit the activity of the *prospective* imagination. Each is remarkable, however—and this is my reason for introducing them at this stage—for the range of human experience organized and given significance by its ruling image.

The prospective imagination pursues an inclusive vision, seeking to incorporate in a 'single sphere' (CP p. 176) of consciousness both what is immediately perceptible to the senses and what is present only to the inward eye and ear. 'The Well' is an outstanding example of this poet's ability to give compact yet limpid, at the same time elegant and relaxed expression to such a vision. The landscapes referred to as 'American Scenes' are situated mainly in the south-west of the United States and in Mexico; the well, in this poem, is in the grounds of a Mexican convent damaged by the revolution. Apart from the central image itself, three grammatical devices facilitate that interweaving of sensations, times and places which is Tomlinson's means of integrating disparate perceptions: the avoidance of the singular personal pronoun, the conspicuous structural use of present participles, the omission of periods. Usually, the 'I' having no necessary place in his poems, its absence goes unnoticed, but here, in a poem that is one long utterance strung together on a thread of four present participles and a predicative adjective, the absence of an agent draws attention to itself.

> Listening down
> the long, dark
> sheath through which the standing
> shaft of water
> sends its echoings up
> Catching, as it stirs
> the steady seethings
> that mount and mingle
> with surrounding sounds
> from the neighbouring
> barrack-yard: soldiery...
> strollers in khaki
> with their girls Aware
> of a well-like
> cool throughout
> the entire, clear
> sunlit ruin, ...
> Hearing the tide
> of insurrection
> subside through time
> under the still-
> painted slogans...

The unspecified agent could equally be first, second or third person. Which it is, however, is immaterial, for it is all and none of these: this particular sequence of actions—attending, remembering, relating and identifying—is perception itself, registering, ordering and interpreting. It is anyone's and everyone's, an awareness that grammatically transcends the individual. Another consequence of the omitted pronoun is that there is no separation of subject from object: the organ of perception and the thing perceived are together, indistinguishably, in the verb. Liberated on the one hand, then, from the exclusiveness of the single point of view (mine, yours, his or hers) and on the other from the subjectivity of the perceiver, perception implies the existence of a seamless whole, of a world simultaneously personal and transpersonal, human and natural. The circle of inclusion is enlarged by the omission of periods, which gives an impression of simultaneity to seemingly distinct stages in the operation of the poet's attention, marked by the capitalization of the participles, but is, in fact, the sequential arrangement of what may be seen as the vertical stratification of an indivisible experience. In the participial form of the verb the act of perception becomes, moreover, a continuous process of attention given and impressions received, the mind a conduit for the multiple, mingled, inflowing world of images and sensations. Contraries flow into and mingle with each other: place and time, past and present, near and far, war and peace, movement and stillness, sunlight and the dark, cool well. A spatial image figures a temporal perspective—the well, like an archaeological shaft, yielding up mementoes of revolutionary times; 'then' flows into 'now', the historical imagination and the senses working together; 'here' in the ruined convent mingles with 'there' in the barrack-yard; a past turbulence becomes the tranquil present. The poem aims at an effect of fusion, but not diffusion or confusion. Here-and-now is centred on the well—a coolness in the heat of events, a shaft of darkness in the sunlight, a stillness at the core of sound and movement and the vicissitudes of history. Cool, dark and still, the well is an image for the reflective mind, which in the continuous present of attention imbues time with a quality of eternity, a 'steady' sense of what always is. 'The tide of insurrection' subsides and is effectively absorbed into the stillness of 'the standing / shaft of water'; insurrection being, so to speak, an eccentricity of time which *through* time is re-centred and restored to the peaceful round of a normality that time, not in its divisions but in its fullness,[3] creates. The 'well-like / cool' spreads *like* thought through the 'clear / sunlit ruin' and as its coolness seems to permeate and embrace the sun's warmth, so the 'long, dark / sheath' of the well contains within its still depths the 'seethings'—they are precisely, therefore, 'steady seethings'—of earlier troubled times.

In my observations on 'Venice', 'Ponte Veneziano' and 'How It Happened' my purpose was to show how natural and human phenomena are integrated by a common descriptive language into a single system of meaning. 'The Well' and 'The Shaft' could have illustrated no less aptly this unity of sensory and mental experience; but, more ambitious than their predecessors, these two poems serve better to exhibit the compass and diversity of human experience constellated by means of such images. The most striking thing about 'The Shaft', however, if considered as a late product of long and continuous reflection, is that here the image is made to express meanings and values which at first glance seem totally unrelated to those embodied in the earlier poems and even to contradict them. Recurrent images in a poet's work are not obliged to carry the same meanings and values and frequently don't; but usually, if they bear the imprint of exact feeling and concentrated thought, the differences are not arbitrary but, rather, variations upon a theme. So it is, I would suggest, with this poem. The difference between the image-idea as used in 'The Shaft' and as used previously is one that reveals new aspects and new relations of the experience common to all the poems, and in doing so amplifies and elaborates its significance.

The extensions of meaning latent and waiting to be used in the imagery of tunnels, channels and shafts—even, as I have proposed, in the word 'prospect'—are opened up in this poem about an abandoned mine shaft. Let me recall once more the concluding words of 'How It Happened': 'the glance / goes *shafted* from us like a well'; with the translation of metaphorical shaft into an actual scene of mining and excavation the motif of prospecting—of sinking or driving shafts through reality—undergoes a mutation. The penetrant eye in 'How It Happened' is the *prospective* imagination, annexing 'further fields', craving something 'more'—'more-than-earth' (CP p. 39), 'more-than-bread' (CP p. 60), 'more / Than the words can witness' (CP p. 18), claiming its inheritance, 'kingdoms of possibilities' (CP p. 176). The phrases magnify (in the biblical sense) the life and power of the imagination. They do not, however, thrill with quite that vibrancy of emotion which, by detaching them from their poetic matrices, I have managed to suggest. They combine ringing celebration of the imagination's transformative power with a sure sense of the limits of that power, a precise estimation of where the boundary lies between the passionate pursuit of the possible and the indulgence of an inordinate idealism. Yet the danger that a loose romanticism—or, as 'The Shaft' will instruct us, the more sinister thing it may lead to—should divert that passion from its proper end is indeed inherent in Tomlinson's metaphors. Introduction of the facts and analogues of mining, in 'The Shaft', is the means of redirecting our attention to focus not on the heroism but on the exorbitance of imagination—in this instance the greed and violence of religious aspiration in some of its expressions, the coveting by religion of what it imagines to be 'out of nature'.[4] In this, the latest revelation of its character, it is *not* celebrated: on the contrary, without any minimizing of its fascination, it is treated with wary and apprehensive scepticism.

It is, I think, one of Tomlinson's finest poems, and I quote it in full.

> The shaft seemed like a place of sacrifice:
>   You climbed where spoil heaps from the hill
> Spilled out into a wood, the slate
>   Tinkling underfoot like shards, and then
> You bent to enter: a passageway:
>   Cervix of stone: the tick of waterdrops,
> A clear clepsydra: and squeezing through
>   Emerged into cathedral space, held-up
> By a single rocksheaf, a gerbe
>   Buttressing-back the roof. The shaft
> Opened beneath it, all its levels
>   Lost in a hundred feet of water.
> Those miners—dust, beards, mattocks—
>   They photographed seventy years ago,
> Might well have gone to ground here, pharaohs
>   Awaiting excavation, their drowned equipment
> Laid-out beside them. All you could see
>   Was rock reflections tunneling the floor
> That water covered, a vertical unfathomed,
>   A vertigo that dropped through centuries
> To the first who broke into these fells:
>   The shaft was not a place to stare into
> Or not for long: the adit you entered by

> Filtered a leaf-light, a phosphorescence,
> Doubled by water to a tremulous fire
>   And signalling you back to the moist door
> Into whose darkness you had turned aside
>   Out of the sun of an unfinished summer.

Running through the poem is an opposition between seasonal time and the illusion of life out of time. This illusion is, to stay close to the poem's images, that which lures one to places that recall the beginning of personal time, the womb—a chthonic womb imaged also as a 'cathedral space' awaiting whoever journeys back through the passageway's 'cervix of stone' to the earth's interior world—and the end of personal time, the tomb. The 'tinkling underfoot of shards', fragments of the past, is, like 'the tick of waterdrops, / A clear clepsydra' (water-clock), the sound of time. The 'cathedral' cave, on the other hand, is a space that (in the archaic sense, but here with a kind of literalness too) *magnifies* the eternal. Yet *this* space for eternity, this cave of the spirit, like any man-made cathedral exists by the grace of physics, sustained by a stone prop; not merely that, but a 'single rock*sheaf*, a *gerbe* / Buttressing-back the roof'—heraldic emblem of the harvest of natural life. Other, more intricate ironies are engendered by this interaction of the natural with the supernatural. The bodies of the *excavating* miners 'might well have been' the mummified remains of pharaohs *excavated* by the archaeologists—as if the miners were what they were labouring to unearth; not a passing flippancy, but an ironic contemplation of the generic relation between the material rapacity in the service of which the miners had died and the otherworldly aspirations that had built the dynastic tombs. For—another irony—the pharaohs were certainly not, in any active sense, 'awaiting excavation' as dead relics of the past in a future age: on the contrary, they awaited—went to inordinate lengths to ensure—resurrection to a future life.

We may be reminded of a phrase in 'Prometheus' (*The Way of a World*, 1969; CP p. 156), a poem about the Russian Revolution. A note informs us that the title refers to the tone-poem of the Russian composer Scriabin, whose 'hope of transforming the world by music and rite' is seen as providing an anticipatory sanction—it was composed in 1909–10—for the ensuing political terror; for out of Lenin's 'merciless patience grew / The daily prose such poetry prepares for'. The phrase we remember as we read 'The Shaft' is one that gives this apocalyptic romanticism its mythic name. It comes at the end of the fifth stanza, from which I quote the closing lines:

> Each sense was to have been reborn
> > Out of a storm of perfumes and light
> To a white world, an *in-the-beginning*.

These images carry their own refutation; it is the facts of history, however, that carve the poet's immediate rejoinder into a line of marble judgement: 'In the beginning, the strong man reigns'. The mythic concept, though not the phrase itself, is active in the later poem. The shaft, like an archaeological shaft, goes back 'through centuries' to a first time, linking the exploring poet to 'The first who broke into these fells'. This initial act of violation was not itself an 'in-the-beginning', which in the language of time names a condition of timelessness; but it was the first attempt to break through nature into that inner sanctum, that dark—womb-like, tomb-like—interior reality. A connection is insinuated between the prospecting of those miners and the pursuit by an insatiable imagination of forbidden treasure, the primal mystery. The miners had lost their lives in the attempt, and now the shaft, flooded from some deeper, inaccessible source, 'all its levels / Lost in a hundred feet of water', has been rendered impenetrable. The image of that first time, and of what lies beyond it, is given a moment's thought, but imagination is not tempted to pursue it: 'The shaft was not a place to stare into'; the poet is content that it should be 'a vertical unfathomed'. For it is unfathomable. Its depths are impenetrable to the eye too: all you see are reflections of the world above it, your own world, 'tunneling the floor' with images of itself. 'Doubled by water to a tremulous fire', the 'leaf-light' of nature by which you entered becomes the 'phosphorescence ' of a delusive *ignis fatuus*, tempting the fascinated seeker to self-destruction. To the wary and undeluded poet the light of jack o'lantern signals danger, and nature beckons him back through the womb-adit door out of interior darkness into the common day of 'an unfinished summer'. The summer of this life is not unending, but its invitation is warmer and more dependable than that tendered by the cold, intermittent false lights of an imagined other life. Not until the last words of the poem have been carefully weighed does the arresting first line yield its full significance. 'The shaft seemed like a place of sacrifice' because mining is, literally and figuratively, a sacrifice of visible nature—the light and warmth of 'an unfinished summer', for instance—to a desire either for what lies hidden within it or, by analogy, for what supposedly lies behind it, a more-than-nature masked by material appearance. In other instances the prospective imagination is represented by Tomlinson as directing its search not inward, as in this poem, to a source or centre, but outward, as in 'How It Happened', to the furthest horizon.

Imagination is, for Tomlinson, a creative counterforce to the forces of destructive time. But it has strict limits, and Tomlinson is as positive in his observation of those limits as he is a passionate advocate for an active, metamorphic imagination against that species of 'realism' which is nothing but the passive record of what happens to a receptive mind. Imagination *is* reality, that is, the actual stretched to the furthest extent of the possible, no less and no more; it is in this sense that 'The artist lies / For the improvement of truth', and why, in the corollary to that statement in 'A Meditation on John Constable' (CP p. 33), the poet exhorts the reader to 'Believe him'. If his experience tells him that imagination may afford momentary glimpses of a core reality, a pristine source, it also gives him reasons to distrust the same faculty when it presents itself not as an auxiliary to reality but as an enemy of it. It may infuse time with a quality of eternity—I have suggested that it does so in 'The Well'—and may be said therefore to transcend time: transcending it, it cannot, however, usurp or defeat time. The cautiously exploring poet knows this and is proof against the enticements that had betrayed miners to their death and pharaohs to immoderate expectations. Having penetrated as far as the antechamber of the shaft and stared—but 'not for long'—into its taciturn depths, and having felt the sinister pull of 'vertigo', *his* realism—which is the sum of recognitions won by following to its limits, not avoiding, the path of imagination—willingly acknowledges the wisdom of return. Time, offering another kind of completion, 'the fullness of time' which is time greeted and complemented by 'our consent to time' (CP p. 163), calls us back from such treacherous perspectives. Imagination pursues something more but not something intrinsically other than the immediate fact; it aims to suggest a totality—comprehending the actual and the possible, the near and the far, the visible and the invisible, the known and the unknown—a totality that is still, nevertheless, the world of nature, not its substitute. It aspires to be the completion of the natural. The mental refuge from the unblinkable glare of fact to which at times it must resort is not permanent and may not be portrayed as such. The country church to which, in 'Las Trampas U.S.A.' (*American Scenes*, 1966; CP p. 124), the poet seeks admittance is no 'cathedral space', no temple for the eternal: it is a modest 'place / of coolness out / of the August sun', offering no more than a respite, a temporary and temporal solace for the exposed traveller.

'The Shaft' and 'The Well' are linked, of course, by their central images; but they are connected also by other common features, words and images which, in turn, relate both poems to 'In Arden' (CP p. 305), from the same volume as 'The Shaft'. The principal shared features are a second common image and a recurring motif. The image is that of water: 'In Arden' has an underground river running from Eden to its 'rhyme', or half-rhyme, Arden in the world outside, but in 'The Shaft' as in 'The Well', it is a 'standing / shaft of water'. The recurring motif is the idea of vicarious communication between inside and outside, depths and surface. Adam is banished but 'the depths of Arden's springs / convey echoic waters'—the Arden of art—from their source in Eden:

>   voices
> Of the place that rises through this place
> Overflowing, as it brims the surface
>   In runes and hidden rhymes, in chords and keys
> Where Adam, Eden, Arden run together
>   And time itself must beat to the cadence of this river.

In 'The Well', the mind's relation to an imagined historic past is expressed by the same image—'the standing / shaft of water / sends its *echoings* up'—as is used by 'In Arden' for the mind's relation to a mythic past. 'Echoings' and 'echoic waters' are images for an intermediary connection between the here-and-now and some not directly accessible source, a mythic or historic dimension of meaning to be incorporated by the imagination into present experience. The imagination that 'somewhat self-forgetfully',[5] with an alert readiness, attends upon the generosity of the moment is rewarded with not actual possession, but reflections, of an enlarged experience. An image in a later poem, 'Hill Walk' (CP p. 257), makes the vision of perfection dependent upon an unpredatory gratitude:

> The unseizable citadel glimmering back at us,
>   We contemplated no assault, no easy victory:
> Fragility seemed sufficiency that day.

The poet's temperate recognition that there is no *storming* of this citadel separates his 'will to wish back Eden' (CP p. 159) from the apocalyptic imaginings of Scriabin and the Utopian dreams of the revolutionary idealists arraigned in 'Prometheus', who, mistaking usurpation for rebirth, would 'Out of a storm of perfumes and light', create, rather than restore, Eden—'a white world, an in-the-beginning'—as a *tabula rasa* on which they could rewrite history.

The image of water and the motif of vicarious communication have the same centrality in 'The Shaft' as they have in 'The Well' and 'In Arden', but the meanings they carry in 'The Shaft' are not merely different from but contradictions of their meanings in the other two poems. The contradictions stand, however, in a relation of complementary opposition: the two sets of meanings are obverse and reverse of the same coin. The water in the mine-shaft is not, as it is in the well, a transmitter of messages between friendly powers: it is an inhospitable element, an uncrossable frontier, a 'vertical unfathomed' and, we are to understand, unfathomable. The theme of communication is sounded, briefly, in the archaeological analogy between broken 'slate' and 'shards', but with a different intention. The echoes from the past are not in this instance living, flowing reverberations: they are dead relics of a lost connection—strictly speaking, not echoes at all. The difference between the use of these images here and in the other two poems could be expressed in terms of civility or courtesy. Depending on the decorum of the seeker, water is either a medium of or a barrier to intercourse between first things and the mind. The source gives out echoes of itself only to an imagination that is finely attentive and can read the faintest signs: it cannot be forced, gives nothing to the imperious imagination of unrestrained appetite.

If it is a poet's intention to contrast two uses of the prospective imagination, as they are contrasted in 'In Arden' and 'The Shaft', distinguishing the realistically continent from the unrestrained exercise of that faculty, it would seem at first glance a paradox that he should choose to exemplify realism with a poem about 'Adam, Eden, Arden' and the confluence of time and eternity. For Eden is necessarily an image of perfection, another place than where we live: it is an elsewhere or, as he phrases it in 'Canal' (CP p. 64), a 'something else' of the imagination; the 'discriminating swans', as they 'go by in grace / a world of objects', are depicted as seeking—like the poet— for 'something else' than the repetitions of the industrial manscapes they sail past. The fact is, however, that the Eden celebrated by Tomlinson is not the Eden of myth: the theme of these poems is the power of art, not to substitute the imaginary for the real, but to view the real in the light of a *possible* perfection; which is the light of imagination that the artist brings to memory. The thought and the metaphor are Wordsworth's. In 'Elegiac Stanzas', remembering 'four summer weeks' of halcyon weather spent by a sea of 'glassy' calm, he declares—in words recalled by Tomlinson in 'The Weathercocks' (CP p. 113)—that to convey the magic, the seeming permanence of that 'perfect time', a painter—Wordsworth if he had been a painter— would need to 'add the gleam, / The light that never was, on sea or land'. The perfection of those weeks was *as if* permanent; the possibility had been glimpsed, and to express that double vision the painter or the poet must, in his rendering of the experience, *add* to the actual the aura of the possible. For Tomlinson, as for Wordsworth, imagination is an auxiliary to, not an enemy of, reality.

Perfections

In my introductory remarks to the second section of this chapter I noted that a study of the meetings and encounters characteristic of the known world leads naturally to a consideration of the prospective imagination, which seeks to expand the boundaries of the known. Similarly, in a sampling of the prospective imagination at work in Tomlinson's poems, it has seemed both natural and necessary to show its connection with the poet's idea of Eden. The three themes of this chapter—Meetings and Encounters, Prospects, and Perfections—are not only inter-related but, in this order, constitute the beginning, the middle and the end of a single thought-process: encounters frequently end in meetings, meetings sometimes open prospects, and those prospects have in view images of perfection.

'An Insufficiency of Earth' (CP p. 77), the third of 'Four Kantian Lyrics' (*A Peopled Landscape*, 1963), opposes the beginning and the end of this process:

> We cannot pitch
> our paradise in such a changeful
> nameless place and our encounters
> with it. An insufficiency of earth
> denies our constancy.

'Encounter' is the language of time and place—time the agent of change, place that will not take an indelible imprint of human meaning. Paradise is the imagination's humanizing of the non-human in an act of linguistic colonization, represented in Genesis by Adam's naming of the creatures. It also symbolizes man's 'constancy', an ability to stay firm and keep faith that seeks an object of corresponding stability and trustworthiness. The temper of the two statements quoted is realistic if regretful; it would certainly be mistaking the poet's intention if we read the antithesis between change and constancy as simply sceptical. For if 'an insufficiency of earth / *denies* our constancy', 'constancy', an admiring word, does not cease to be a virtue: 'our constancy'—a will to believe and a craving for something to believe in—contradicts change and would *deny* mortality.

In 'Winter Encounters' (CP p. 17), notwithstanding the title, all three stages of the thought-process are present. *Encounter*, whether 'inanimate or human', revealed in the movements of nature or that which 'enacts itself in the conversation' of men, may easily suggest the possibility of a place, or reality, beyond encounter—in talk, for example, 'weighing the *prospect* / Of another's presence, . . . one meets with more / Than the words can witness'. Insomuch as these encounters are a matter of 'interchange' and 'brisk exchanges', they express the 'ceaseless pairings' of a 'changeful' world; but they also signify relationship, something established: 'Meshed / Into neighbourhood by such shifting ties', though subject to the 'changing light', 'The house reposes, squarely upon its acre'. Though change is 'ceaseless', 'the properties [interchanged] are constant'. The constancy of the properties corresponds to a constancy in man; the combination of this correspondence, between a perceived stability and human fidelity, with the transience of things prompts the search for permanencies. The hidden interior world one senses in the talkers' casual, unrevealing 'conversation / On customary subjects'—'more / Than the words can witness'—is a glimpsed *perfection*: 'One feels behind / Into the intensity that bodies through them / Calmness within the wind, the warmth in cold'. It is not merely that the complementary opposition of sense experience and imagination, of the actual and the possible, creates an image of wholeness: it is a more mysterious perfection. 'Calmness' and 'warmth' are related to 'wind' and 'cold' not simply as contraries, but as the inside of the outside, as if there were a stillness within movement, an ease in adversity.

Eden is frequently the name given by Tomlinson to his 'images of perfection' (a poem-title in *The Shaft*, 1978). The word itself appears first in *Seeing is Believing*, but the notion of a core reality—the inside of the outside—expressed in the closing sentence of 'Winter Encounters' (CP p. 17), one of the meanings of Eden in the poetry, occurs earlier, in *The Necklace* (1955). In 'Flute Music' (CP p. 9), 'The flute speaks (reason's song. . .) / The bound of passion / Out of the equitable core of peace'. 'Farewell to Van Gogh' (CP p. 36), in *Seeing is Believing* (1958), makes a comparable distinction between the expressionist 'rhetoric' of this painter's art and the 'central calm' of nature.

'Inanimate or human, / The distinction fails'—not only in the instances presented by 'Winter Encounters', but also in 'Flute Music' and 'Farewell to Van Gogh'. Poems as much about the act of perception as about the thing perceived, 'the equitable core of peace' in 'Flute Music' and even 'the central calm' of nature in 'Farewell to Van Gogh' (whipped into 'frenzy' only by the emotions of the painter) are expressions which choose to ignore the boundaries between metaphysics and psychology. 'Before the Dance' (*The Way of a World*, 1969; CP p. 174) has for its theme a definitely *human* occasion—the look and posture of the Indian performers waiting tranquilly for the ritual dance to begin—but the occasion acquires other-than-human implications. Waiting, they give 'to the moment' a quality of eternity 'by their refusal / to measure it': 'the moment / is expansible'; and like the burning bush in which God appeared to Moses, 'it burns / unconsumed'. Equally,

> the Navajo faces
> wear
> the aridity of the landscape
> and 'the movement
> with the wind
> of the Orient and
> the movement against
> the wind
> of the Occident'
> meet
> in their wrinkles.

At the still centre of time they find a condition of timelessness; at the core of space, where contraries meet, escaping its limits they become all space, the total landscape written in their faces.

The notion of a core, or still centre, is related in Tomlinson's thinking to the idea of form, an essential shape. They come together, notably, in the phrase 'its shapely self', which appears in 'Glass Grain' (*Seeing is Believing*, 1958; CP p. 26). Here, too—in a poem that reveals quite clearly the relationship of Tomlinson's concerns and sensibility to those of Hopkins—we have the first occurrence of the word

'Eden', meaning what Hopkins meant by *inscape*, an inner form that constitutes the sharply individuated 'self' of a thing. The poem is about analogical thought. A poet approaches his subject by way of comparisons, and in this he is not unlike the composer of a fugue, who explores the possibilities of his theme by way of 'inversions and divisions'. Comparisons and variations are, however, *'ways* of knowledge' only, and we wait for the return of the theme, the thing itself, as we might look for the return of Eden—'Eden comes round again, the motive dips / Back to its shapely self, its naked nature / Clothed by comparison alone—related'. The ideas of inner form and core reality are associated, again, in the opening lines of 'At Holwell Farm' (*Seeing is Believing*, 1960; CP p. 39):

> It is a quality of air, a temperate sharpness
>   Causes an autumn fire to burn compact,
> To cast from a shapely and unrifted core
>   Its steady brightness.

It is a recurrent thought in Tomlinson's poetry that a world is the union of its opposites. A special sort of 'steady' burning, a 'temperate sharpness', by which 'sharp disparities' are fused into 'a single glow', distinguishes the autumn meeting and interpenetration of summer and winter: a consciousness of time not as sequence but as a single whole, of time *perfected*, brought to its fullness, ripens, so to speak, in autumn, in which season we are granted a vision of time as simultaneously seed and fruit, as the core, the essence of the year's cycle. When the year is thus condensed, the outer shape of 'an autumn fire' (say) will express its inner form. When, in 'Eden', to justify his opening statement, 'I have seen Eden' (CP p. 159), he writes that 'the gift / Of forms constellates'—brings order and pattern to—'cliff and stones', we learn from the preceding parallel images that the word 'form' is used to mean both outer shape and inner principle: for Eden is also 'a light of place / As much as the place itself; not a face / Only but the *expression* on that face'. 'Shapes of change', the striking phrase I have quoted before from 'The Way of a World' (CP p. 165), sharpens to the point of paradox—the same paradox as 'a geometry of water' in 'Swimming Chenango Lake' (CP p. 155)—the assertion of an identity between inner and outer, of the one with its many appearances.

The idea of perfection—what moves Tomlinson, for example, to label an experience as Edenic—changes from poem to poem, but the several 'perfections' and the various meanings of 'Eden' in his work are, of course, related. Nor are they neatly distinguishable. The preceding discussion of 'Winter Encounters', 'Before the Dance' and 'At Holwell Farm' has already demonstrated the impossibility of separating the notion of Eden as a core reality or *inscape* from its apparent antithesis, Eden as an image of wholeness. Thus, in the last of these poems, the sharply focused consciousness of time as an autumnal *essence* distilled from the blended opposition of summer and winter is by the same token the expanded consciousness of time as a single whole, as simultaneously beginning and end. Moreover, the presence of this total view in a poem may also be—indeed usually is—associated with yet other aspects of the 'Eden image'; other kinds of perfection which can be named separately but, as we shall see, rarely exist separately in Tomlinson's poems.

Wholeness is a frequent motif and one that has been noted several times already in this and the previous chapter; I need only glance briefly at some examples in the light of my present theme. In 'The Greeting' (*The Way In*, 1974; CP p. 260), for instance, the mind is granted a momentary vision of all 'space and its Eden / of green and blue'—and not only space:

> one instant of morning
> rendered him time
> and opened him space,
> one whole without seam.

The appeal to Tomlinson of the long perspective is that it enables the poet to present what it reveals as a total vision, a seamless whole; invariably the glance that tunnels into space is seeking such a vision. In 'A Sense of Distance' the poet's memory of the high view from the cliff top of 'the red river' crossing 'the canyon floor' is absorbed into the much longer perspective in which the poet, back in England, views from there his mental image of the same desert scene; what he 'sees' is seen, moreover, from the retrospective vantage-point of 'a *later* distance'—with the addition to the dimensions of space of a temporal dimension the perspective deepens. The metaphor used by Tomlinson is that of widening circles. The first two circles are the 'near' of England and the 'far' of the American Southwest—which are at once different places and different times, a here-now and a there-then. The third and largest circle is the 'single sphere' of the containing mind. As the perspective deepens the circles widen, the self embracing more and more of an expanding world. The poem's climax is an entranced vision of circle outside circle extending beyond the known into the knowable, 'all / the kingdoms of possibilities' to be ruled imperially by 'the mind's own sun'. This *would* be Eden: to dwell in a reality endlessly open to further and further possibilities, an ever-growing totality. It is, to use Wordsworth's (ultimately Biblical) image, like entering into 'an inheritance, new-fallen' by 'one / Who thither comes to find in it his home'.[6]

Such a reality is, however, a hope not a habitat. To know it in imagination only—this too is Eden. For Eden is a landscape of the mind—a state of mind, sometimes an ambiguous state of mind. The metamorphoses of imagination are momentary—recurrent but fleeting glimpses of permanence. Whether they are to be regarded as intimations of truth or deceptive appearances is an unavoidable question; but it is the wrong question, since the *as if*s of Tomlinson's poetry are at once less than fact and more than illusion. Even the last stanza of 'A Sense of Distance', which envisages a door 'flung wide' for the poet upon 'kingdoms of possibilities', begins none the less on a note of caution: 'And it seems as if . . .' The effect of these words of reservation, however, is not at all to subdue or qualify the exultant mood of the stanza. In 'Snow Sequence', on the other hand, the first of four poems grouped under the general title 'In Winter Woods' (*American Scenes*, 1966; CP p. 157), the ambiguities of Eden are at the centre of the poem. 'A just-on-the-brink-of-snow feel, / a not-quite-real / access of late daylight'. It is an early evening 'stillness', a seeming 'pause' in time when nothing moves. Time suspended, sequence brought to a standstill, is time extended into a quasi-eternity; but 'access', a word of spatial rather than temporal reference, implies enlargement as much as a lengthening of the day: the true blessing of the moment is that it opens a larger day, a larger whole. This suggestion of a spatial parallel is reinforced by what follows:

> I tread
> the puddles' hardness: rents
> spread into yard-long splinters–
> galactic explosions, outwards
> from the stark, amoebic
> shapes that air has pocketed
> under ice.

The sudden 'spread' of air bubbles 'outwards' into galaxies is a fantastic instance of the rapidly expanding whole, from the smallest unit to the largest whole conceivable. It is a growth that not only encompasses but harmonizes all: angles are softened by mist and 'Even the sky / marbles to accord with grass / and frosted tree'. Nevertheless, as we were warned, there is something 'not-quite-real' in all this; the Eden image—satisfying, compellingly 'real' in one sense—is not presented simply for our implicit acceptance. The metaphors of the second sentence—'rents', 'explosions'—advertise the violence of their transformations, speaking of 'accord' in the language of discord. Our pleasure in the moment must include the recognition that in this instance imagination has forcibly converted reality into an eternity and infinity of the mind. Grace or illusion, truth or seeming? The poem neither asks nor implies an answer to such a question. What matters is the experience itself—and our gratitude for it. In its conclusion, 'Snow Sequence' greets the dissolution of this momentary 'accord' with equal gratitude. As 'the sun began / to slide from this precipice, this pause', so

> first flakes simultaneously
> undid the stillness, scattering
> across the disk
> that hung, then dropped,
> a collapsing bale-fire-red
> behind the rimed, now snow-spanned
> depth of a disappearing woodland.

The movements of *setting* sun and *winter* snow-fall in combination reintroduce the real, a three-dimensional world—sequence, change, mortality, but also the 'depth' hidden within the marbled, misted sameness of a grey-white landscape.

Most of Tomlinson's images of perfection are the bounty of exceptional moments. Such moments of glimpsed perfection have been noticed already in 'Before the Dance', 'The Greeting', 'A Sense of Distance' and 'Snow Sequence'. In my examination of those poems, however, I concentrated on special meanings of the Eden image. Of some poems, however, one wants to say, not that they display this or that facet of perfection, but that, in part or wholly, they are about perfection itself.

In my analysis of 'The Atlantic' in the opening pages of this chapter I focused on the motif of encounter, but I also gave some attention to the brief 'instant', quickly superseded, during which the oppositions of wind and wave, sea and land are suspended in momentary truce. The advancing tide, having climbed the beach and reached its turning-point, has thinned and subsided to a gently rippling 'sheet', a 'lucid pane', of water, and there is a restless pause:

> The sun rocks there, as the netted ripple
>   Into whose skeins the motion threads it
> Glances athwart a bed, honey-combed
>   By heaving stones.

The laws of time are as if in temporary abeyance. The sun, as it were time itself, is held and gently cradled in the moving waters of time— that which is unchanging contained within, and reconciled with, the element of change. Equally, the laws of space are apparently transcended: the exterior world, the power of the universe, is woven into the interior mirror-world of water, the reflective power of the mind.

'As if', 'as it were', 'apparently'—such expressions in the above discussion of 'The Atlantic' are perhaps unnecessarily insistent reminders that these are indeed '*images* of perfection'. The phrase itself occurs in 'Departure' (CP p. 289), and it supplies both title and theme to the poem that succeeds it in *The Shaft* (1978), where both poems first appeared. The explicitness of the phrase is one of many indications that a poetic self-consciousness has entered into Tomlinson's later work; by which I mean that questions about the poetic act, the transformations of art, accompany tacitly, and sometimes expressly, the image-exploration of his themes. What is imagined comes now with a sense of the enigma of imagination.

In 'Departure' the poet speaks to his recently departed guests of 'that stream / Which bestows a flowing benediction and a name / On our house of stone'; speaks of liking best a place

> where the waters disappear
> Under the bridge-arch, shelving through coolness,
> Thought, halted at an image of perfection
> Between gloom and gold, in momentary
> Stay, place of perpetual threshold.

There are no overt questions here or elsewhere in the poem, yet the manner in which the key phrase is introduced seems to hedge it around with reservations. That 'an image of perfection' belongs, syntactically, to a parenthesis within a parenthesis within a subordinate clause removes attention to some extent from the claims it makes. Furthermore, the informal, unassuming mildness of the statement that prefaces the lines quoted—'it is here / That I like best'—gives a tone of modesty to the words and sets a tone for the whole passage that tempers the splendour of phrasing in some of the following lines: the poet, it seems to say, is describing one person's preference only, the satisfactions of 'thought', no more and no less; he neither claims nor disclaims objective truth for what the mind contemplates. An image of perfection is caught from the flux and, as an object of 'thought', it comes as a transient promise, endlessly repeated, of form and meaning; endlessly repeated but by the same token lost again and again in the rush of waters: it makes no more than a 'momentary / Stay'. It is a mental stillness in *the midst of* movement, the one a gift of the other. The poem emphasizes and values at least as much as the reflected image, the imageless element in which it is reflected, the stream of life that, for example, 'bestows a *flowing* benediction' on the human meanings fastened in a 'house of stone'. Where thought is halted is a 'place of perpetual threshold', endless possibility, but we are not more blessed in the reflected image than in its sequel, when 'all flashes out again and on / Tasseling and torn, reflecting nothing but the sun'. Perfection belongs with imperfection; it follows that Eden-watchers must also pay attention to the common stream. The appropriate attitude—a finely hesitant vigilance, at once narrowly focused and broadly receptive—is implied in the contrast between the brutally simple and direct passage of the jet-plane carrying his guests to their destination, 'scoring the zenith / Somewhere'—the perfection of the machine perhaps—and the poet hovering 'by the brink once more', not vaguely 'somewhere' but here, intensely absorbed in the particular features of one particular scene. What the poet sees has already been described in the preceding lines, the clumsily sensitive movements of the stream, enacted in the verse—'pooling, then pushing / Over the fall, to sidle a rock or two / Before it was through the confine'; accommodating itself in its quest for freedom, a way out, to the specific conditions of time and place: only now do we recognize in this description an image for the mind, moving diffidently and delicately, negotiating not forcing a way towards a prospect of those perfections it attended upon.

By promoting a merely descriptive phrase from the body of one poem to be title or theme of another, 'Images of Perfection' (CP p. 289) turns it into a subject for investigation. The question about imagination, in the margins of 'Departure' and at the centre of its sequel, originates in the same doubt that contributed a note of scepticism to 'Snow Sequence': is the imagined real or 'not-quite-real', truth or seeming? Yet in the later poem we have not scepticism so much as an open question which the poet is content to leave unanswered, and we have too a slight shift of emphasis. There are 'rarenesses' of visual experience—the poem starts from this imagined premise—'rarenesses / That are [in some sense] right', such as the surreal cloud-shapes, 'Mare's tails riding past mountainous anvils' noticed in 'yesterday's sky', a sky which in consequence, without ceasing to be itself, became something more-than-sky: 'you felt in the air the sway / Of sudden apocalypse, complete revelation'. But questions remain: wherein does perfection lie and what is its source?

The poem makes no attempt at a conclusive answer but, in the last lines, hangs balanced between opposite possibilities:

> Did Eden
> Greet us ungated? Or was that marrying
> Purely imaginary and, if it were,
> What do we see in the perfect thing?

It *'felt'* like 'complete revelation: *But what it came to was* a lingering / At the edge of time, a perfect neighbouring' (my emphases). The perfection now pertains not to the Eden image itself but to the delicately poised relationship, in the poet's mind, *between* world and Eden, real and possible, fact and image, the creatures of time and their visions. 'Neighbouring' is a tenderly human word, a human-social word moreover, for that felt interdependence, in 'Departure', of movement and stillness. The connection between the poems is marked by a similarity of demeanour—a sensitive hesitancy, an unprecipitateness of approach, combined with a finely precise awareness of borders. The poet who in 'Departure' is 'by the *brink* of the stream' (the sound of the word adds to the meaning a sense of *sharp* differentiation between land and water), catching his images, is here 'lingering at the edge of time', aware simultaneously of a sky that is the atmosphere of earth ('Every variety of cloud accompanied earth') and of a sky that is extravagantly unearthly. There is no urge in the poem, and no need, to answer the questions posed in its closing lines: 'Where was the meaning, then?' Was Eden real or imaginary? Whatever its status, 'the perfect thing' exists to be questioned. The important question, moreover, is the one not asked—since 'rarenesses' exist, how should one take them, live with them?—and the answer inheres in the word 'neighbouring'. 'A perfect neighbouring' is not the knowledge or possession of Eden but an association based on an acceptance of the facts ('But what it came to was . . .'), an ease in not knowing, not possessing—a relation of mutuality: in return for the visual gift, a giving, a surrendering, of oneself to the sight (the cloud-shadows 'expunge our own' shadows).

'Eden' as a name for a kind of perfection occurs first, as we have seen, in 'Glass Grain' (CP p. 26), a poem to be found first in the

American edition of *Seeing is Believing* (1958); there it means unmediated nature, the core or 'self' of a thing. The second occurrence of the word is in one of the new poems added to the second edition of that volume published two years later in England; here, in 'At Holwell Farm' (CP p. 39), 'Eden' names a human value. The poem's premise is that we live in one world, at once natural and human; its theme and a key image is maturation, regarded as a principle of being that is common to the animate and the inanimate world. Ripeness is the fruit of oppositions meeting, mating and bearing, as autumn is the interaction of summer and winter. There are three kinds of ripeness referred to in the poem: the literal ripeness of 'pears by the wall'; what might be termed the literal-metaphorical ripeness of old stone, weathered by time, giving us 'stone as ripe as pears'; and the purely metaphorical ripeness, the 'fruit' of civilization, that results from the marrying of physical fact and human intention. The poem celebrates specifically the interplay of complementary oppositions responsible for the perfection which is Holwell Farm:

> this farm
> Also a house, this house a dwelling.
> Rooted in more than earth, to dwell
>   Is to discern the Eden image, to grasp
> In a given place and guard it well
>   Shielded in stone.

There are implications in these lines, not spelt out by the poet, regarding the relation of mind and matter; they may be defined with equal aptness in opposed (but complementary) formulations. 'To discern the Eden image' is either, since one is 'rooted in *more* than earth', to fill the 'given place' with human meaning, to add to the three dimensions apprehended by the senses a symbolic dimension, or, as 'discern' implies, to discover what is already there immanent, if not rooted, in earth. The keyword is 'grasp'; in either formulation, 'to dwell', in this sense, is to live by what James in a famous letter called 'the grasping imagination'.

The epistemological ambiguity buried in these few lines of 'At Holwell Farm' is exposed to question in the opening lines of the poem entitled 'Eden', which appeared a decade later, in *The Way of a World* (1969; CP p.159), at a time when the theme was also a preoccupation of his painting:

> I have seen Eden. It is a light of place
>   As much as the place itself; not a face
> Only, but the expression on that face: a gift
>   Of forms constellates cliff and stones.

The word-play and insistent chime of internal and external rhyme, characteristic of Tomlinson's verse and so conspicuous here, reflect his sense of the intricate ties between things and the interpenetration of interior and exterior worlds. But the repetition of 'place' and 'face' in these lines has a specific resemblance to the riddle and the charm, expressing wonder and a sense of mystery. The riddle inheres in the creation of a parallel relationship between 'light', 'expression' and 'forms'. A visible *expression* transmits an invisible 'self': which is to claim that meaning is immanent in a material world. 'Light *of* place', suggesting that the place is self-illuminating, would seem to make the same point, except that, framed as a paradox, it reminds us that the light *in* a landscape has its source elsewhere. The expression is intentionally mysterious and questionable. The next phrase, 'the gift / Of forms', invites an obvious question: who or what is the giver, the physical universe or the human observer? The second alternative, the part played by subjectivity, provides the necessary clue. If form may be in the eye of the beholder, it is arguable too that expression exists only as it is interpreted by the observer. Returning now to 'light of place' and noting that it corresponds to 'the expression on that face', we are struck by the possibility that light, too, may serve the subjectivity of human perception: as perception reads the expression and perhaps creates forms, so it can make of light a metaphor for the illumination shed by thought. Each word has, of course, both a subjective and an objective reference. The mystery of Eden is that it is either or both or it transcends the distinction between subject and object.

If even landscapes can take the imprint of human aspiration and shadow forth man's image of Eden, it is certain that his dwellings and his cities are, intentionally or unwittingly, expressions of human perfectionism. There is evidence that in Tomlinson's mind no essential difference—no difference in, so to speak, their primary qualities—separates natural from civic Edens. In the poem 'Eden' the poet's 'clairvoyant' vision of the place is succeeded by reflections upon its loss and our resultant sense of 'dispossession'. Reflecting upon its loss five years later in a poem about manscapes rather than landscapes, 'The Way In' (CP p. 241), he returns to the conceits, the very images and rhyme-words, of the earlier poem to convey the experience of both possession and dispossession, of Eden and what that poem calls 'despair of Eden'. But in the fallen world of the modern city the gradation from 'place' to 'face' to 'grace' communicates not the confidence of a vision but a wistful tenderness for a vision betrayed:

> I thought I knew this place, this face
>   A little worn, a little homely.
> But the look that shadows softened
>   And the light could grace, keeps flowing away from me
> In daily change; its features, rendered down,
>   Collapse expressionless ...

'This place'—it might be almost any city in post-war Britain—is in fact Bristol. The poem is in effect a lament for the loss of 'civility' entailed by the demolition of urban working-class neighbourhoods to make room for 'mannerless high risers', buildings 'not built for them', the dispossessed inhabitants. Civility (a word which in its earlier senses carried most of the meanings borne in later centuries by 'civilization'), 'that civility I can only miss'—the modest instance of it here commemorated—is the name for the human principle in human relations; in this poem it is the interior reality, the human expression, of buildings which by habitation, 'daily contact', and the action of time have gradually become more than their function as *machines for living in*. 'Place' and 'face' in this stanza have the same sort of relation to 'light' and 'expression' as they have in 'Eden'; the precise verbal reminiscences establish 'civility' as the form in which, for Tomlinson, the Eden image reveals itself in human society. Light and expression 'grace' brick and mortar with human meaning; light and shadow add to bare fact the kindness and softness of human feeling. 'A little worn, a little homely'—shabby and plain—these mean streets may be, but we are asked at the same time to concede the 'home', the human identity, in the homeliness, the accretion of human interest in things that (like the stone of Holwell Farm) wear the patina of time. 'Mannerless', echoing 'expressionless', interprets and evaluates the absence of human association from the new high-rise towers. The pun in 'mannerless high-risers'—the high buildings housing the 'upwardly mobile' classes—gives a new definition to social climbing, since, rather than manners, it is manner they lack, expression of a mode of living formed by custom, equated later in the poem with the expression that is 'style', specifically architectural style.

In 'Eden' and 'The Way In' the paradox of Tomlinson's demythologized Eden is focused in the epistemological ambiguity rendered by the word 'expression'. In 'Adam' (CP p. 160), the poem that follows 'Eden' in *The Way of a World*, he uses the story of Adam's naming of the creatures to probe more deeply into the paradox of an Eden state that has at once an objective and a subjective reality.

> Adam, on such a morning, named the beasts.
> It was before the sin. It is again.
> An openwork world of lights and ledges
> Stretches to the eyes' lip its cup.

Eden is first of all the given, 'such a morning', the gift of 'an openwork world'—the cup that runneth over, the wine of (nature's) everlasting life: Eden was there before the naming. But Eden is also where language has made a home for us. Language humanizes, adding to, the given; in that sense it generates the world we live in: 'we tell them over', the 'beasts' of the exterior world, having named them—

>   surround them
> In a world of sounds, and they are heard
> Not drowned in them; we lay a hand
>   Along the snakeshead, take up
> The nameless muzzle, to assign its vocable
>   And meaning.

The creatures, things, qualities and abstractions 'are heard...*in*' the sounds that identify them. The act of naming is an act of identification—identifying what is already there—but it is also an act of appropriation: when we 'assign its vocable', we assign its 'meaning'. The act determines the identity of a thing, but does it not also *create* that identity? This question is assumed in the question Tomlinson actually asks:

> Are we the lords or limits
> Of this teeming horde? We bring
>   To a kind of birth all we can name
>   And, named, it echoes in us our being.

Adam's naming of the creatures stands for the humanizing of nature, man's incorporation of nature into himself by its translation into significant sound; but this subjectivity begins a process of creation which then, in transcending its creator, begets another kind of otherness. We are not 'the lords or limits' of even this human world, for 'all we can name', once named, 'echoes in us our being' as a child echoes its parent, resembling but not reproducing it: the named thing is at once ours and not ours, ourselves and not ourselves, the same yet different. 'Our being' is both the object humanized and the subject extended into nature, a world of named objects.

In 'At Holwell Farm', 'Eden', 'The Way In' and 'Adam', Eden, named or unnamed, denotes a human value. They are poems of place in which the spatial world is given a human meaning. Most of Tomlinson's poems are poems of place and the two examples of the Eden motif, a discussion of which will conclude this chapter, 'In the Fullness of Time' (*The Way of a World*, 1969; CP p. 163) and 'Hill Walk' (*The Way In*, 1972; CP p. 257), are not exceptions; but in these the aspect of the physical world brought into relation with the human world is not space but time. Humanization of the world of space and time does not mean either the transformation or the suppression of their realities: the relation between man and his physical condition is, so to speak, reciprocal, negotiable. There is no assertion of human meanings and values in Tomlinson's poetry which does not willingly grant the premises of time.

'In the Fullness of Time' is in the form of a letter to the poet's friend Octavio Paz; it opposes to Paz's notion of time transcended an unmystical alternative: 'a truce in time', an image of time as 'putting its terrors by' without changing its nature. 'You tell us', he writes, addressing Paz, of 'imminent innocence, / Moment without movement'; Tomlinson would rather hear a different message:

> Tell us, too, the way
> Time, in its fullness, fills us
> As it flows: tell us the beauty of succession
> That Breton denied: the day goes
> Down, but there is time before it goes
> To negotiate a truce in time.

The poem, recalling the circumstances of their meeting in Rome ('a place / Of confusions, cases and telephones') and their train-journey together, discovers then in the scene of their arrival an *image* of 'time in its fullness' and an intimation of the sort of 'truce' we may 'negotiate' 'in [and with] time'. The train, he recalls, slowed, 'curving towards the station', and paused, the crescent shape of its length bringing the windows of the head and of the tail within sight of each other; the lights in the front 'flung / A flash' of greeting to the travellers in the rear where the poet and his companion were waiting for their carriages to reach the platform:

> the future
> That had invited, waited for us there
> Where the first carriages were. The hesitant arc
> We must complete by our consent to time—
> Segment to circle, chance into event:
> And how should we not consent? For time
> Putting its terrors by, it was as if
> The unhurried sunset were itself a courtesy.

The future *invites* the present, waiting with the courtesy of a host welcoming a guest. Time plays its part and we, the guests of time, accepting both its gifts and its limiting conditions, must play our parts, reciprocating with a matching civility; it is unthinkable that we should deny 'our consent to time' when the undeniable comports itself with such winning grace that death itself ('the unhurried sunset') would seem but the ceremonious close of an ordered sequence ('the beauty of succession'). We could say, applying a different terminology, that this is an exhortation to turn an *encounter* into a *meeting*. If time 'meets' us by inviting our expectations and receiving us graciously, it is fitting that we 'meet' time by agreeing to its conditions and by participating fully in its undertakings. In cooperating with time we decide that what happens to us ('chance') shall be what we choose to happen ('event'). Time fills us with experience—happenings that are not merely happenings—so that time's fullness is the imagined completion of experience when it loses the appearance of randomness and reveals itself as the significance of a life; by giving 'our consent to time' at a particular moment we give it human significance and ('segment to circle') make that moment and occasion part of a whole meaning.

'Hill Walk' commemorates a day spent with friends in the Provençal countryside, a terraced landscape that in 'outworks, ruinous and overgrown', bears all the marks of a long history of human habitation. It, too, records a *meeting*—a meeting, in this instance, of man and history (time) and of man and nature (space). The truce in and with time and space composes, in the later poem, a momentary, fragile harmony, but one which is nevertheless a kind of Eden, for 'Fragility seemed sufficiency that day'. Looking back from a plateau, a temporary resting-place, to 'the place we had started from' and tracing with the eye the 'territory travelled'—a day's journey imitating a life—the travellers are given a vision of how individual lives join the measureless life of time and space: 'All stretched to the first fold / Of an unending landscape ... Where space on space has labyrinthed past time'.

> Innumerable and unnameable, foreign flowers
>   Of a reluctant April climbed the slopes
> Beside us. Among them, rosemary and thyme
>   Assuaged the coldness of the air, their fragrance
> So intense, it seemed as if the thought
>   Of that day's rarity had sharpened sense, as now

> It sharpens memory. And yet such pungencies
>   Are there an affair of every day—Provençal
> Commonplaces, like the walls, recalling
>   In their broken sinuousness, our own
> Limestone barriers, half undone
>   By time, and patched against its sure effacement
> To retain the lineaments of a place.
>   In our walk, time used us well that rhymed
> With its own herbs.

These spring flowers of a French province are not merely unknown to the English visitor but represent a nature that is ultimately unknowable, not accidentally but intrinsically foreign and 'unnameable'. The day's perfection is that nature's otherness briefly, if reluctantly, accommodates itself to the human image of it; for a moment the natural and the human worlds coincide. Among the nameable flowers, rosemary and thyme demonstrate the fragility of this coincidence—the playful conceit of 'rhymes' draws attention to it: for the conjunction depends on the arbitrary verbal correspondence of rosemary with its half-rhyme 'memory' (its meaning in the language of flowers) and of 'thyme' with its homonym.

   This sort of poem is at the opposite end of the linguistic spectrum from, say, 'Winter-Piece' (discussed in the last chapter). It names but on the whole does not attempt verbal reproduction of sensation. Its keywords are resonant abstractions—for example, 'assuaged', 'fragrance', 'pungencies', 'effacement'—words chiefly of Latin or Old and Medieval French derivation, given prominence by their placing, frequently at the end of a line. This is accentual verse in which the accents are unemphatic, the rhythms supple but unruffled, not impeding or interrupting the reflective tenor and pace, the smooth transitions, of the argument as it moves through and across the lines with the easy elegance of courteous conversation. There are hints in these lines of the host-and-guest metaphor for the natural world's courteous relationship with its human tenantry that was developed more explicitly in 'In the Fullness of Time'. The poem celebrates not just the physical experience of a day's walking but the *sharing* of its pleasure with friends and, we are to believe, with time and nature: time, that 'used us well', and herbs, that '*assuaged* the coldness of the air', are equally, it seems, considerate companions. The language of relationship is that of civil decorum, and this civil language, by assuming as it does the possibility of agreement between man and nature, qualifies itself as the language of Eden. The 'truce in time' imaged in the earlier poem is not so named in 'Hill Walk' but the idea is partly explicit and partly inherent in the description of the occasion: the accord commemorated *specifies* time's part—to mitigate its exigencies—and *presupposes* the walkers' 'consent to time', both their acceptance of its eventual victory, its 'sure effacement' of man's works, and gratitude meanwhile for such gifts as the pungent 'fragrance' of its April herbs.

NOTES

1. 'Preface', *Collected Poems*, p. vii.
2. Octavio Paz, 'The Graphics of Charles Tomlinson'; reprinted in *Charles Tomlinson: Man and Artist* (ed. Kathleen O'Gorman), p. 194.
3. See 'In the Fullness of Time', CP p. 163.
4. See Yeats's 'Sailing to Byzantium'.
5. 'Preface', *Collected Poems*, p. vii.
6. *The Prelude* (1850), Book XI, 145–48.

Chapter Three
Manscapes 1958–1966

'Manscapes' is a heading in *The Way In* (1974) under which Tomlinson has grouped a series of poems chiefly about the industrial English Midlands in which he spent his youth and generally about the urban universe of the twentieth century; the coinage implies an opposition between manscapes—these manscapes—and landscapes. In using the term as my title for this and the next chapter I am broadening its application. The subject of these chapters is Tomlinson's treatment of human experience. During the twenty-year period covered, from 1958 to 1978, there is a notable development of interests, which is best presented chronologically: in each collection the poet turns to new areas of human experience and introduces new themes and emphases, changes of attitude and focus.

Insomuch as the ethic of perception is operative in these poems as in the rest of Tomlinson's work, governing his outlook, providing the terms of signification and judgement, they too testify to the existence of that 'one world' which in the previous chapter I chose to demonstrate by tracing a line of continuity from nature poem to human poem. These chapters, however, emphasize not the thematic connection between the two kinds of poem but the manner in which perceptual categories are used to interpret the human content of the poems.

The title of his second collection, *Seeing is Believing* (1958), announced the conviction informing all his work. When he called his next collection *A Peopled Landscape* (1963) his intention was, no doubt, to reaffirm this conviction as much as to indicate what was new in it. The nature poems in the early collections are also, in at least two senses, human-nature poems: their theme is always the relation of the observer to the world of his sense experience, and frequently landscapes and objects have human associations. The novelty advertised by the title *A Peopled Landscape* is, rather, that the human meaning is no longer an implication but in many of the poems an overt theme; the human figure moves to the centre and the physical or social context takes an ancillary position. This, of course, overstates the difference. These were not actually the first pieces to reveal Tomlinson's interest in, and ability to make poems out of, explicitly human subjects: *Seeing is Believing*, the first of his collections to suggest the full range of his interests and poetic abilities, furnished sufficient evidence in 'The Crane' (CP p. 29), 'At Delft' (CP p. 32), 'At Holwell Farm' (CP p. 39), 'On the Hall at Stowey' (CP p. 40), 'The Castle' (CP p. 43), 'The Ruin' (CP p. 46) and the sequence 'Antecedents' (CP p. 49). Beginning, then, with *Seeing is Believing* and ending with *The Shaft* (1978), these two chapters survey in chronological order, with one exception, Tomlinson's rendering of the human world, in its social, cultural, historical and political aspects.

It may seem paradoxical to begin the exploration of Tomlinson's human world with 'Oxen: Ploughing at Fiesole' (*Seeing is Believing*, 1958; CP p. 19); yet it is clear that the motivation imputed to the ploughing oxen is human rather than animal and the poem translates the physical bearing of the oxen into the language of moral consciousness. This is so even in the opening lines of literal description:

> The heads, impenetrable
> And the slow bulk
> Soundless and stooping,
> A white darkness—burdened
> Only by sun, and not
> By the matchwood yoke—
> They groove in ease
> The meadow through which they pace
> Tractable.

The process of translation becomes perceptible towards the end of this sentence; it is conspicuous in the playful fiction of 'matchwood yoke'—*as if* the beasts were not in reality subject to man and his contraptions but had chosen to appear so. The 'as if' becomes explicit in the second sentence, which introduces an analogy with possible human attitudes and behaviour that is maintained to the end of the poem: 'It is as if / Fresh from the escape, / They consent to submission'. And what seems human in the look and motion of the oxen seems at last to deliver a message to the ploughman, who has fastened the yoke but whose position is *behind* the plough: 'now / Follow us for your improvement / And at our pace'.

In the humour of this conceit is the poet's light acknowledgement—and this is part of the potentially 'improving' message—that as *common* subjects of necessity the man and his animals are equal—the oxen 'burdened', or yoked, not at all by man's rule but by the sun, the rule of the universe. The 'even confidence' figured in their slow unvarying pace suggests that they *freely* 'submit' to this yoke—

> 'Giving and not conceding
> Your premises. Work
> Is necessary, therefore . . .
> We will be useful'.

The moral theme is that service given willingly (willed, not conceded) is not 'captivity' but freedom; for freedom results from consent to the terms of existence, one of which is the necessity of work—Adam's fate, as it were chosen rather than accepted, is thus freed of its curse. In the margins of the poem are the axioms of religious submission—'whose yoke is easy', 'whose service is perfect freedom'.

That quality in the poem which invites the description 'religious'—an acceptance of life that embraces its limiting conditions—can also be termed 'classical'. The summary expression of the moral qualities embodied in the oxen which begins the concluding sentence—'This calm / Bred from this strength'—is reminiscent, not only in its form of balanced oppositions but also in its substance, of the couplet in Denham's *Cooper's Hill* made famous by Dr Johnson's praise: 'Though deep, yet clear, though gentle, yet not dull; / Strong without rage, without overflowing full' (*Lives of the Poets*). The syntactical symmetries reflect and celebrate, as does Tomlinson's complementary opposition of 'calm' and 'strength', a state of equipoise, a balance and proportion of energies.

Strength that yokes *itself* breeds an inner calm, the calm of being at one with the conditions of life, a calm of *bearing* which is clearly in touch with the (metaphysical) 'central calm' of *being* invoked in 'Farewell to Van Gogh' (CP p. 36). Not to kick against the pricks, not to strain beyond the possible, is to be rooted in the reality of one's own being, and therefore to be grounded in being. Two images reinforce these connections: 'the heads, impenetrable' and 'a white darkness' imply an interior citadel, impregnable, inaccessible, a 'core of peace' (CP p. 9) and freedom which is at the same time the core of existence. The connections are tightened into a knot by a punning conclusion. The oxen have seemed to deliver a message, ' "Follow us for your improvement" '; what is there to be communicated, however, is not only not communicated in words but is beyond the reach of words: posture and carriage *present*, wordlessly, what is unspeakable, simply *the way things are*:

> the reality
> Broaching no such discussion,
> The man will follow, each
> As the other's servant
> Content to remain content.

The rhetoric of the last line brings to bear several senses and implications of the word 'content'. To the obvious sense, 'content to remain contented', the context adds another: since the theme is how oxen may be yoked and yet remain unsubjugated, the second 'content' must also mean 'contained'. The poem is a series of images for potency, power held in reserve; content to remain contented or contained, contented with containment—by the word-play we are made aware, ungrammatically, subliminally, that this contentment is full of content (with the accent on the first syllable). 'This calm' is the being contented with containment, a fullness of content (contentment and substance), a concentration of being which is power unexpended, always potential.

'Oxen: Ploughing at Fiesole' may be represented as a poem that stands midway between the poems of perception—for example, 'Venice' (CP p. 3)—and the human portraits in *A Peopled Landscape* (1963). It provides a convenient opportunity, therefore, to study the thought-process that transforms an ethic of perception into an ethic of attitude and action. The images in 'Venice' demonstrate for us the ways of a 'contained' world and imply an ideal of perception. The poem infers from the definiteness of 'doors' and 'houses' the finiteness of the natural world:

> Cut into by doors
> The morning assumes night's burden,
> The houses assemble in tight cubes.

An object, in its finiteness and definiteness, is limited by its shape and mass to what it is as against what it is not; these are the terms of its existence, its conditionality. Perception is bound by the same laws that bind the things perceived. Right perception is the recognition of these intrinsic defining limits of things. The idea of containment links the ideal of perception to the ideal of behaviour embodied in the ploughing oxen. In 'Ponte Veneziano' (*Seeing is Believing*, 1958; CP p. 19) we may observe the movement between the ethic of perception and the ethic of attitude and behaviour taking place in the same poem. First of all, it is explicit about the conditionality of perception: the watching figures are 'bound to that distance' which separates their viewpoint from the thing viewed. The next stage is an expansion: perception here includes mentality; their watching is also a kind of intellectual, or artistic, vigilance—the gestalt of perception serving as a paradigm of the conscious, deliberate ordering of art. That 'they do not exclaim' adds then a moral dimension: it indicates that, like the oxen, they 'consent to submission'; the 'stillness' of their watch implies, furthermore, not only acceptance but, like the 'calm' of the oxen, a firm, undistractable will-power and a centredness. This progression brings us, as it were, to the threshold of 'Oxen: Ploughing at Fiesole' (in fact, 'Ponte Veneziano' immediately precedes it in *Seeing is Believing*); where one poem ends the other begins; it begins, as I have said, with the oxen in full possession of a human, moral consciousness. But the relation to the human world is more than analogical: being what they are and acting as they do, the oxen are in a moral position to instruct man in the nature of service and freedom and to recommend to him assent and obedience to necessity; the poem makes a bridge between the landscape poems and the full human portraits of, for example, 'John Maydew' and the farmer's widow in 'Return to Hinton' (CP p. 59). I shall be discussing these poems later. Meanwhile, the nature and the closeness of the connection between 'Oxen' and the poems of *A Peopled Landscape* can be demonstrated simply and briefly—indeed they demonstrate themselves—in the following quotation from 'The Hand at Callow Hill Farm' (CP p. 73). The subject for investigation is a man's taciturnity; the theme is 'silence', interpreted not as absence but possession of something, self-possession, a self-containment like that of the oxen—a strength, it will be seen, that likewise generates 'calm':

> It shut him round
> Even at outdoor tasks, his speech
> Following upon a pause, as though
> A hesitance to comply had checked it–
> Yet comply he did, and willingly:
> Pause and silence: both
> Were essential graces, a reticence
> Of the blood, whose calm concealed
> The tutelary of that upland field.

Thus we have an expanding pattern of thought taking us from 'Venice' in *The Necklace*, through 'Ponte Veneziano' and 'Oxen: Ploughing at Fiesole' in *Seeing is Believing*, to the portrait of the farm labourer, 'The Hand at Callow Hill Farm', in *A Peopled Landscape*.

In several of the poems in *Seeing is Believing*, if we accept the rough distinction between nature poem and human poem, the 'human' content is large; I begin my discussion of Tomlinson's manscapes with 'At Delft', one of the poems added to the expanded edition of that collection in 1960. I choose 'At Delft' because, on the one hand, it is one of the first poems in which the theme of 'civility', an important one in Tomlinson's work, receives full treatment, and, on the other, it shares with 'Ponte Veneziano', 'Oxen . . .' and 'Farewell to Van Gogh', in the same collection, that fundamental preoccupation with calm and stillness.

'At Delft' (CP p. 32) bears the inscription *Johannes Vermeer, 1632–75*; it describes the exteriors and interiors of a seventeenth-century city that lives chiefly in the images of its most famous painter. Interpreting and reinforcing Vermeer's visual images, Tomlinson has added sound and movement to *his* 'picture' of the city. The word 'civility' does not appear in the poem (though 'civic' does), but it summarizes—as well as a single word and an abstraction can—what the poem is about. 'Venice' analyses sense impressions; 'Oxen', humanizing its subject, introduces a moral dimension; 'At Delft' enters by its images into a social world. 'Venice' implies an ideal of perception, 'Oxen' an ideal of conduct, 'At Delft' an ideal of civility.

> The clocks begin, civicly simultaneous.
>   And the day's admitted. It shines to show
> How promptness is poverty, unless
>   Poetry be the result of it. The chimes
> Stumble asunder, intricate and dense,
>   Then mass at the hour, their stroke
> In turn a reminder: for if one dances
>   One does so to a measure. And this
> Is a staid but dancing town, each street
>   Its neighbour's parallel, each house
> A displacement in that mathematic, yet
>   Built of a common brick. Within
> The key is changed: the variant recurs
>   In the invariable tessellation of washed floors,
> As cool as the stuffs are warm, as ordered
>   As they are opulent. White earthenware,
> A salver, stippled at its lip by light,
>   The light itself, diffused and indiscriminate
> On face and floor, usher us in,
>   The guests of objects: as in a landscape,
> All that is human here stands clarified
>   By all that accompanies and bounds. The clocks
> Chime muted underneath domestic calm.

What links 'Venice' and 'Oxen: Ploughing at Fiesole', is the idea of containment, acknowledgement of limits. This statement is, however, incomplete, for, as I have remarked in my previous discussion of these poems, the antithesis of this idea is also present. In 'Venice' there is 'A tunnel of light', accomplice of imagination, that seems to dissolve the boundaries between things when it 'Effaces walls, water, horizon' and to release them into illimitable space. 'Oxen', though it teaches submission, also represents the animals' 'consent to submission' as an act of free will; yoked but unsubjugated, leading the plough, dictating the pace, they are at once bound and not bound: 'They groove in ease / The meadow through which they pace / Tractable'. Containment and (limited or unlimited) freedom are treated in these poems not simply as opposites but, in a phrase that has occurred frequently in these pages, complementary opposites. The ideal of perception in 'Venice', of conduct in 'Oxen...', of civility in 'At Delft' is in each case represented as a desirable state of complementary opposition. The concept and its expression I have derived from a formulation in 'At Holwell Farm' (CP p. 39). The poem celebrates a way of life, one associated with the age and architecture of the building; its accomplishment is to have created a fruitful relation between the given (the physical world) and the added (human will):

> Crude stone
> By a canopy of shell, each complements
>   In opposition, each is bound
> Into a pattern of utilities—this farm
>   Also a house, this house a dwelling.

Finally, to define 'dwelling', the antithesis is framed in terms of (given) fact and (auxiliary) imagination: 'Rooted in more than earth, to dwell / Is to discern the Eden image'. It is evident that fact ('earth') corresponds to the doors, houses, bridge, walls—objectifications of space—that comprise the contained world of 'Venice', and to necessity in 'Oxen: Ploughing at Fiesole' ('Work / Is necessary, therefore...'); it is clear, too, that 'the Eden image' in 'At Holwell Farm' is related to the imagination that is licensed and empowered, so to speak, by the miracle of light in the last stanza of 'Venice' ('Floating upon its own image / A cortège of boats idles through space'), and related also to that inner freedom ('rooted in *more* than earth') which, belying the story of constraint, gives an 'ease' and an 'even confidence' to the stride of the oxen.

When we turn to 'At Delft' we find the same procedure: the definition and exemplification of civility as an interdependence of contrary principles. They are uniformity and diversity ('the clocks... civicly simultaneous' and the chimes that 'Stumble asunder'), restraint and vivacity ('for if one dances one does so to a measure'), geometry or order and flow, profusion, confusion, diffusion. In their specific application to bourgeois Delft, they are collectivity and individuality. The 'common' identity of the society is expressed in the regulation and conformity of its life. The individual citizen, on the other hand, is responsible for the 'variant' pattern in the mosaic floors and for the *love* that has brought warmth and opulence to these ordered interiors; it is love, too, that guides the brush of the painter, a fellow citizen, to touch the 'lip' of the salver with light; an *anarchy* of individuals is imaged in the confusion of the chimes until they meet in a combined 'stroke' at the hour. All are versions of the fixed and the free, which, like Tomlinson's 'invariable' and 'variant', are terms that disclose the complementarity of these principles: each logically necessitates and is partly defined by its opposite. The measure gives form to the dance; the dance is the 'poetry' of measured movement: they imply each other. Similarly, in 'Snow Signs (CP p. 315), without the 'white geometry', the contour lines, of the receding snow the eye would miss 'the fortuitous/Full variety' of the landscape; it is as if 'Snow has left its own white geometry / To measure out for the eye the way / The land may lie'.

When dance and music are in question, 'measure' must mean measured time. But in the total context of the poem, under the influence also of the sound of the word, other historic senses are brought to bear, rounding out the strict meaning with suggestions not only of symmetry and proportion, but also of moderation, of *gently* applied controls. The full meaning of the word then radiates out into the rest of the poem. For 'measure' as it pertains to the whole poem includes the idea of civility, though it is not simply an equivalent for it. In its widest application the word describes a less specialized ideal of living—living in the sense of dwelling or making a home in a particular place. Measure holds all the contraries together; it is the fulcrum of balance. It gives form to the flow of life—as we have seen in such phrases as 'geometry of water' and 'shapes of change', the paradox is a preoccupation of Tomlinson's. It binds freedom to law, but in the process saves freedom from anarchy and thus makes it possible. As in its poetic sense, measure is at once exacting and permissive; and this sense is covertly at work behind the overt themes, shadowing a parallel between the ideal of civility and a poetic ideal.

The argument of the poem divides at exactly the half-way point, the two halves corresponding to the exterior and the interior scenes of Vermeer's pictures. The first half, which takes us into the twelfth line, is about the public life of the city; the second half deals with the private life of the citizens. The dialectic of the fixed and the free operates in both areas; there is no contradiction between the public and the private life, but the poem nevertheless uses the contrast between the 'civic' and the 'domestic' to mark a distinction between them. Civility is a suppler, warmer, richer thing in these still rooms than in the streets. Depicting the 'invariable' part of the complementary opposition in his reflections on the town's civic life, the poet seems to emphasize a certain stiffness in its punctuality and, as it were, an enforced regimentation in its *massed* chimes and the *stroke* at the hour. It may be a 'dancing town' but there is just a hint that this is despite its staidness rather than because of its orderliness—the 'poetry' is provided not by the town but by the 'admitted' daylight. In the outer world, then, the balance between fixed and free is not quite equal. 'Within', however, 'the key is changed'. 'Ordered' and 'opulent' are words of equal weight and worth, the balance simulated in the alliteration and the symmetry of the comparative form. Indoors the dialectic engenders 'domestic calm', and 'domestic', as a word intended to epitomize the meaning of the private life, names a deeper, firmer foundation of stability. It is in touch—like the 'ease' of the oxen—with a 'central calm'.

At this point the idea of civility is better described as an ideal of dwelling. For the deepest source of the mysterious calm of Vermeer's interiors, it is intimated, is the symbiotic relation between the human and the physical in his paintings. The simple elegance of white earthenware and the salver expresses the intention of hospitality—the painter's placing of light on the salver adds a humanizing 'poetry' to its gracious gesture. But the beauty of the domestic objects lies only partly in their human meaning. It is not merely the placing of the light that is important but the 'light itself', the very nature of light, 'diffused and indiscriminate / On face and floor': by the operation of light, whether we reckon it as generosity or indifference, the human and the non-human are drawn into one circle, seen to belong to one, larger meaning. The civil relationship described, where objects play the host and we are 'the guests of objects', would seem to give a predominantly human character to the scene: but the comparison with landscape that follows that phrase effects a reversal of emphasis. Objects, which indoors unavoidably have human associations, are also, 'as in a landscape', simply objects, as light is simply 'itself'; they accompany the human, attached but separate, and they mark the boundaries of the human domain. 'To dwell', we recall, is an act of adjustment: it is 'to discern the Eden image, to grasp / In a given place and guard it well'. Place is the given; the transforming image is, of course, the addition of imagination. The art of dwelling is to join the human idea to the material fact, but not to confuse the two. Light, because it is 'indiscriminate', does in a sense confuse them, by humanizing objects and naturalizing the human figures: on the one hand, a room, a floor, utensils are touched with feeling; on the other, a face singled out by the light is a thing exposed to the coolly objective inspecting eye. Light creates a common world, more inclusive than the 'common brick' that bonds society, but the distinctions between man and thing are not thereby dissolved: light clarifies both what connects them and what keeps them separate.

The images of civic order in the first part of 'At Delft' give way to a picture of what I have called civility—a form of life finely poised between regulation and freedom, conformity and individuality; this is in turn absorbed into a broader conception of living, which sets man in proper relation to the natural order. In that context the 'human' stands fully revealed, in the sharpest possible clarity. This ideal of civility, enlarged and reconstituted as an ideal of dwelling, is the basis for angry reflections in 'On the Hall at Stowey' (CP p. 40) later in the same collection. For the now derelict Hall was once the living embodiment of a social order motivated by such an ideal; the anger is occasioned by the evidence, in the 'barbarous' refurbishment of the house to suit the meaner standards of recent generations and its subsequent neglect, that in the twentieth century this order of life is neither valued nor understood. The art of dwelling expressed in the life of a society and its characteristic artefacts and in a form maintained over a period of time is what we know as civilization: civilization is the civility of a whole society. The poem is set up as a contrast between past accomplishment and present decay—that is to say, between civilization and the barbarism of times that are indifferent to its destruction and betray a shameless, blank ignorance of the distinction and meaning of what is lost.

The Hall—a chance discovery made by the poet while 'walking by map' in unfamiliar country—recalls in one or two details the Country House of literary tradition, notably as celebrated by Jonson and Pope. The first building to catch his eye is the grange—

> That jutted beyond, lengthening-down
> The house line, tall as it was,
>   By tying it to the earth, trying its pride
> (Which submitted) under a nest of barns.

In the language of 'At Holwell Farm', this is to be tied to earth and yet 'rooted in more than earth'; 'pride' co-exists with the acknowledgement of function. (Pope's Earl of Burlington was similarly praised for showing that 'Rome was glorious, not profuse, / And pompous buildings once were things of use'.[1]) The same combination is reproduced in the house's architectural ornament, where the high aims and high spirits of human self-affirmation are ballasted once again by a counter-affirmation of the farming function:

> Five centuries—here were (at the least) five—
>   In linked love, eager excrescence
> Where the door, arched, crowned with acanthus,
>   Aimed at a civil elegance, but hit

> This sturdier compromise, neither Greek, Gothic
>   Nor Strawberry, clumped from the arching-point
> And swathing down, like a fist of wheat,
>   The unconscious emblem for the house's worth.

The opening lines of Jonson's 'To Penshurst' may come to mind: 'Thou are not, Penshurst, built to envious show / Of touch or marble'. Certainly its conclusion has a bearing on Tomlinson's concerns: Jonson writes that when people compare Sidney's Penshurst with the 'proud ambitious heaps' of others, then 'They may say, their Lords have built, but thy Lord dwells'. For the superiority to a mere 'civil elegance' of the Hall's 'sturdier compromise' lies in its apparent self-dedication to a more inclusive idea of dwelling.

Civilization is the social, moral and physical realization of an idea of complete human being. This is associated in Tomlinson's imagery and diction with the virtue of clarity: civilization is the emergence of a clear idea of living and its clear expression in every aspect of its life. Its clarity is partly exemplified, partly symbolized in a sample of its lapidary art found among the flagstones, a 'gravestone's fragment' carrying an incomplete inscription: the engraving is 'still keen', though all that remains of the original is

>   a fragile stem
>   A stave, a broken circlet, as
> (Unintelligibly clear, craft in the sharp decrepitude)
>   A pothook grooved its firm memorial.

The carved stone bears the clear, sharp, firm mark of 'a careful century'; it confronts our careless 'prodigal time' with an image of 'all that we cannot be'. Because that century believed in what it built for, its masons, aiming at permanence, built to withstand the ravages of nature, to resist time; the stone with which they worked, 'Cut, piled, mortared, is patience's presence'. But this is not all; the symbolism spreads a wider net. The circlet is firm but 'broken', the pothook '*unintelligibly* clear'—images of severance and a lost meaning: these not merely illegible but unintelligible strokes are, as it were, runes of a vanished civilization.

Clarity is a keyword from Tomlinson's moral-visual vocabulary; his ethic of perception and the value-system by which he distinguishes a civilized from a barbarous mentality share a common language. As in 'At Delft', the notion of clarity in this poem is associated with an imagery of light. The discovery of the Hall comes with the last light of day and the approach of 'the dimming night'; the season is towards the end of 'the exhausted year'; house and grounds bear the signs of 'conclusion'. The metaphorical implications are not obscure. The last light through which the poet and his readers approach this relic of another age is, appropriately for a century that lacks the confidence and sure direction of that age, a 'doubtful light, more of a mist than light'. The 'final glare' that 'burst' through the mist 'to concentrate / Sharp saffron', pouring all that remained of 'its yellow strength' down the path taken to reveal the house and admit the poet to its presence—this is the last light of an 'exhausted' civilization bequeathing a revelation of itself. Its bequest to the poet is a clear image of full humanity, an ideal of dwelling embodied in the social and architectural forms of a particular period; all this we may infer from the description of his departure, when, 'angered' by what he has seen, the poet turns once more to his path and makes his way through what now appears to him, in the aftermath of his discovery, as an *'inhuman*' light, light that a fish might swim / Stained by the greyness of the smoking fields'. If, in the words of 'Skullshapes', 'it is the mind sees', then an 'inhuman light' is a light that does not afford mental clarity, a grey sameness ('more of a mist than a light') that stains mind-sight, shuts down what the poet-painter of 'Skullshapes' will call the 'visionary field' of human thought and action. The civilizing enterprise brings to bear a full view of human potential; 'inhuman', therefore, is 'barbarous', the shrunken view of the unillumined mind. The changes made to the house by later generations are a melancholy instance:

> Each hearth refitted
> For a suburban whim, each room
>   Denied what it was, diminished thus
> To a barbarous mean, had comforted (but for a time)
>   Its latest tenant.

This is the language of anger not arrogance. To read it as 'élitist' disdain is to mis-hear its tones, and to miss the precision of 'suburban', its careful placing in the thought-pattern of the poem. A choice prompted by 'a suburban whim' is a merely personal, momentary and irresponsible decision—one made without reference to or knowledge of a *central* standard, in the interests of no larger, long-term, general human purpose.

The imagery of light has a comparable meaning and is used to express the same values as when it occurs in poems of perception. In a passage quoted on the dust-jacket of *Seeing is Believing*, Tomlinson writes of his own work that the phenomena of light and weather described in his poems 'are the images for a certain mental climate, components of the moral landscape of my poetry *in general*' (my emphasis). 'Northern Spring' (CP p. 28) features the weather and light of Northern Italy, but, in confirmation of this statement, the visual interest shown has a moral bias (it begins: 'Nor is this the setting for extravagance') and its images are the means of dramatizing and discussing the moods of a 'mental climate'. 'Spring lours': 'Trees / Fight with the wind', and cloud-shadow 'muffles the sun', 'quenching' the brightness of grass and draining blue from the sky; the poet asks us then to consider the contrast between this 'confusion' and, in a moment of 'broken calm, as the sun emerges', the transient 'promise of a more stable tone'. Calm of weather, stability of light constitute a normative condition by which all other conditions of weather and light are measured and judged. The inconsistencies and uncertainties of spring are to be understood, therefore, as deviations from that norm; a '*broken* calm', the epithet implies, is a calm waiting to be restored—as perhaps the 'broken circlet' of the lapidary script, in 'The Hall at Stowey', waits to be completed, waits for its lost meaning to be made once more intelligible to a dispossessed people. The analogy established in the light imagery of 'On the Hall at Stowey', between clarity or unclarity of view and clarity or unclarity of mind, is also explicit in 'Northern Spring':

> Spring lours. Neither will the summer achieve
> That Roman season of an equable province

> Where the sun is its own witness and the shadow
> Measures its ardour with the impartiality
> Of the just.

The 'stable tone', now sealed into permanence, is boldly translated into the language of politics: a Roman summer, where there is only the sun and its attendant shadow, burning light and sharp distinctions, is the imperium at its height; there civilization, uncompromised, superbly self-assured, without intermediary or outside interference dispenses the unchanging, impartial rule of law. Such a civilization, if it ever existed, would match the constitutions praised by the poet, in this poem's companion-piece 'Tramontana at Lerici', 'For the strictness of their equity, the moderation of their pity' (CP p. 27).

The ideal of dwelling that informs 'At Delft' and 'On the Hall at Stowey' is, as I have said, an ideal of the complete human being. It is expressed architecturally in the latter poem as a tension between idealism and realism, man's pursuit of the Eden image necessarily adjusted to the conditions of its attainment. It brings into play the forces of love and patience: 'the love' that motivates the civilizing enterprise, the 'patience' exemplified in the work of mason and craftsman; 'a careful century' is one in which love and patience, 'care' in each of its senses, are recognized as correlatives. These complementary opposites correspond to others in Tomlinson's dialectic of objective and subjective principles. Constable's art is represented, in 'A Meditation on John Constable' (CP p. 33), also from *Seeing is Believing*, as a fusion of observation and passion. In his Preface to the *Collected Poems* Tomlinson points out the same dialectic in his own work, when he notes that in his poems space represents possibility and 'self [has] to embrace that possibility somewhat self-forgetfully, putting aside the more possessive and violent claims of personality', but adds: 'the embrace [is], all the same, a passionate one'. The ideal of dwelling is one that transcends the personal: it is an ideal for a whole society, embracing a general humanity. For this ideal to take form in a social order and become a civilization, however, one other factor is needed: the generative love must become the '*linked* love' of a tradition; 'Five centuries—here were (at the least) five—/ In linked love'. The City of Man spans space and time; it is, by intention, as if for all men and all time.

Civilization in its aftermath remains a preoccupation in *A Peopled Landscape* (1963), principally as it survives in vestiges of rural tradition. In 'Return to Hinton' (CP p. 59), one of several poems in this collection written in the flowing, measured speech rhythms of William Carlos Williams's three-part line, Tomlinson turns his attention to the life of the Gloucestershire countryside in which he had settled after joining the Department of English at the University of Bristol. The poem opens with a question about this archaic 'order' of life witnessed in the character of a local farmhouse and its owner, the farmer's widow:

> Ten years
>   and will you be
>   a footnote, merely,
> England
>   of the Bible
>   open at Genesis
> on the parlour table?
> 'God
>   saw the light
> that it was good'.

'England of the Bible' is English civilization in its prime, a meagre remnant of which, we are to believe, is still discernible in the widow's life and home. In the field of literary and general culture, perhaps its major achievement was the development of a written language of great simplicity and resonance, emotional depth and moral and intellectual power: it is a commonplace that the works of Shakespeare and the composite creation by a succession of translators of a vernacular Bible are the supreme monuments of this linguistic achievement. The most obvious intention of the phrase, emphasizing as it does the literary and religious aspects of this almost spent tradition, is to signify the identity of the language and the character of a culture, presenting the qualities of its language as at the same time the qualities of its moral sensibility. The choice of the King

James Bible to symbolize the cultural legacy of the English Renaissance has other advantages for the poem. One that is immediately evident is the opportunity afforded by the quotation from Genesis; another advantage is that it facilitates a natural transition from consideration of the social and moral inheritance to the question of the linguistic inheritance and its poetic trustees.

Following the opening lines the poem examines and ponders signs of that social and moral inheritance. What survives visibly of a civilized mentality is modestly exemplified here, as more grandly by the Hall at Stowey, in the combination of 'pride' and function, the celebration of life being almost literally the shine on the practical performance of life. Although the 'television box' reveals the presence of the modern world,

> the mullions and flagged floor
>   of the kitchen
> through an open door
>   witness a second
>   world in which
> beside the hob
>   the enormous kettles'
>   blackened bellies ride—
> as much the tokens of an order as
>   the burnished brass.

The creation of light was the first action of the divine spirit; it revealed the depth and beat back darkness and led to the creation of order. The good that is 'light' and the good that is 'order' come together, without intrusive explication, in Tomlinson's text. From this association 'the burnished brass' catches an extra gleam of meaning: the burnish attracts, to use biblical language, the light of the spirit's action in the world, which, adapted to the theme of the poem, is the inspiring, driving idea that makes 'an order' of man's life on earth. Praising the widow's resilience in adversity, but avoiding some of the associations of 'spirit', Tomlinson prefers to speak of 'that more than bread / that leaves you undisquieted'. If 'the *burnished* brass' betokens life celebrated, the '*blackened* bellies' of the kitchen kettles, which 'ride' in no less triumph than the brass shines with pride, represent life unembellished, solidly founded, almost grossly functional. We may set out these oppositions—once again, complementary oppositions—schematically. A civilized order consists, then, in the balance of light and dark, shine and use, idea and function, the more-than-bread of spirit and the bread and belly of necessity. All may be subsumed under one other pair, word and work; word being, not indeed the Word of God, but the word of tradition and of its book, the word of its beliefs and values, and the word generally of sources, beginnings ('open at Genesis', open to the original light).

The television in the parlour is, says the poem, the world—or *a* world—we live in, and that would be a facile identification if it were the only image or instance of the contemporary provided by the poem, or if in this one mention it lacked a significant context. In fact there are other images, and this image receives surprising enrichment from its juxtaposition with the counter-reality of the farmhouse kitchen. The 'television *box*' invites comparison with the squares and rectangles of the other world revealed to the visitor 'through an open door'. The exploitation of a geometrical accident has the quality of a conceit, giving a witty, sharp clarity to the contrast between the featureless, impersonal shape and instant shadow-world of the one and the robust, human world of the other: the detailed craft of mullioned windows, the 'flagged floor' where stone is as much a symbol of the familiar and long-lasting as it is in the walls of the Hall at Stowey, and the door itself opening on to the solid 'tokens of an order'. This order lives in locality—in the concrete, individual difference of locality; it is under threat from the creeping 'death' of modern centralized utilitarianism. The 'generous / rich and nervous land', which has yielded to hard work nourishment for countless generations, is to be 'buried by the soft oppression of prosperity', to serve which

>   locality's mere grist
>   to build
>   the even bed
>   of roads that will not rest

>   until they lead
>   to a common future
>   rational
>   and secure
>   that we must speed
>   by means that are not either.

The modern is in one aspect the easy, rootless convenience world of television, and that, we see, is a representative instance of the general 'soft oppression', mental and moral debilitation by a prosperity that is given rather than 'earned'. It is also the 'even' uniformity and 'common' conformity of materialist, utilitarian purpose, the blueprint Utopia of the social planner's instant future.

The widow is the heir of that 'second world' which the visiting poet does not enter but must view from the vantage-point of the parlour. She is its sole survivor, bearer of its word, exemplar of its spiritual 'qualities'. She lives between two worlds, the world symbolized by the television set and the world that made 'the mullions and flagged floor', 'the enormous kettles' and the 'burnished brass'; but her moral stamina, her 'composure', that 'sadness without bitterness' with which she endures the death of her husband, comes to her from the past. She is 'ballasted' by love and custom 'against the merely new'—whatever has not stood the test of time—and, in a sense, against time itself, 'the tide / and shift of time'. Planted in tradition, sustained by belief and principle, she is not an isolated unit but part of a whole order which serves as a second and larger self. This is not my metaphor but one that Tomlinson uses in 'A Prelude' (CP p. 59), which is the prelude to this collection and the poem that immediately precedes 'Return to Hinton'. There, however, it is a metaphor not for the individual in time but for the individual's life in space: the poem celebrates, as explicitly or implicitly all Tomlinson's poems do, the 'reign of outwardness', where, he writes, the life of the land is as it were 'a self one might inhabit'. Continuity of idea and value, which holds together and gives form to the life of successive generations, is an application in the dimension of time of the spatial concept of wholeness, the whole being the setting for each object contained within it. Personal reality inhabits the larger human reality, which, if its informing idea holds good, transmits the 'more than bread' of human knowledge and wisdom to its individual members. The widow's 'qualities' are 'inherited', but inheritance is to be understood as not a mere receiving but a taking hold on what tradition teaches. It corresponds to Eliot's idea of the artist's relation to the literary tradition, but it also parallels Tomlinson's account in a later poem, 'Swimming Chenango Lake' (CP p. 155), of how the swimmer makes a place for himself in the sustaining element of water: he at the same time surrenders himself to its 'embrace', 'its coldness / Holding him to itself', and takes possession of 'that space' in water which 'the body is heir to'—'For to swim is also to take hold / On water's meaning'. In 'Return to Hinton' the relation of the farmer's widow to the rural tradition that sustains her—of heir to inheritance—is essentially the same:

> Your qualities
>   are like the land
>   —inherited:
> but you
>   have earned
>   your right to them
> have given
>   grief its due
>   and, on despair,
> have closed your door
>   as the gravestones tell you to.

As the oxen's contentment was a 'consent to submission', so her 'composure', the gift of a disciplined life, given and won, is an assent to the grief as one of the terms of existence, an unavoidable part of the *whole* of life; it is giving 'grief its due' but not letting it take *all*.

The poem pays tribute to this 'second world' of the farmer's widow, glimpsed like a vista into the past through the 'open door', but it is not a world which in its present form the poet could or would want to enter. She is already an anachronism; her son continues to work the farm, but, the poet asks, 'proud of his machine' (a tractor)—a different 'pride'—'will he transmit / that more than bread' that had sustained her to future generations? The poet's sympathetic alliance with her is in honour of the original source of her 'composure' and acknowledgment that in their different ways they are joined still in antagonism to the contemporary world:

>   Narrow
>   your farm-bred certainties
>   I do not hold:
>   I share
>   your certain enemy.

The charge of narrowness is supported by reference to a life lived according to the precepts of a 'chapel gospel', thin gruel with which to maintain the health of a long tradition. She is the widow of that order as much as she is a literal widow. The word of English civilization, which is in her life a prayer text above the piano, lapidary morality and a vigorous if culturally impoverished version of the Christian faith, one form of life among the many, the all, that comprised the original fullness, 'England of the Bible'—this 'word' is for Tomlinson the potential of the English language itself, 'generous / rich and nervous' like the land, continuously reinvigorated by the strenuous labours of the poets.

Sandwiched between poems of rural life there are three poems in *A Peopled Landscape* with industrial settings: 'Canal' (CP p. 64), 'John Maydew, *or* The Allotment' (CP p. 65), and 'Steel' (CP p. 67). It will be ten years before he will again take up this subject-matter and these themes: nature despoiled by an uncreating will, its only monuments 'the pyramids of slag'; a blackened, mechanized world, where an unvaried mathematic of straight lines and 'saw-toothed' (CP p. 64) angularities declares a brutal disregard of the human. In the rural England of the 1950s there were vestiges of an older order for Tomlinson to record, but there were, of course, none in the towns created or transformed by the industrial revolution; for these were the social and physical manifestations of the mass civilization that supplanted it. An uprooted population of agricultural labourers left their fields and villages for the mills and crowded grimy terraces of these manufacturing towns.

This history is implicit in the portrait of John Maydew (under which name Tomlinson commemorates his father); a veteran of the Great War, he has spent 'forty years / of mean amends' in the power of the industrial machine. (Like 'Return to Hinton', this poem is written in the form invented by Williams, a tripartite line that isolates the smaller rhythmical units within the line, pausing momentarily over them but maintaining a fluidity of discourse. Williams's 'new measure', in Tomlinson's practice, is made to submit to additional controls. The divisions break up a verse movement that is surprisingly close to iambic metre; no one unit is rhythmically the same, they are separately expressive, but the metrical thread binds them to the unfolding syntax and sentence structure of the poem. And notice, in the following quotation, how rhyme, half-rhyme and assonances also stitch together the flowing sense.) Emerging each evening from the factory where 'by day, he makes / a burrow of necessity', Maydew seeks expression for essential instincts, left unsatisfied by his daily work, in cultivation of his allotment. On the slopes of the town

>   an acrid drift
>   seeps upwards
> from the valley mills;
>   the spoiled and staled
>   distances invade
> these closer comities
>   of vegetable shade,
>   glass-houses, rows
> and trellises of red-
>   ly flowering beans.

There he and his kind find refreshment for their equally 'spoiled and staled' lives.

>   This
>   is a paradise
>   where you may smell
>   the cinders

of quotidian hell beneath you;
   here grow
      their green reprieves
for those
   who labour, linger in
      their watch-chained waistcoats
rolled-back sleeves—
   the ineradicable
      peasant in the dispossessed
and half-tamed Englishman.

Dispossession has fashioned this 'half-tamed Englishman', a man of famished instincts, stunted humanity. Cut off from the natural springs of life, his tragedy is not to know the fully awakened life of the senses; this is his lost Eden. Here, among growing things, are 'the night's / refreshed recesses', but

Tomorrow
   he must feed its will,
his interrupted pastoral
   take heart into
      those close
and gritty certainties that lie
   a glowing ruse
      all washed in hesitations now.

'Heart' means both feeling and courage—the one deadened, the other broken down, by the daily grind. John Maydew must 'take heart', humanity, into a world that has none; where there are only the 'close' (airless, stifling, confining) and 'gritty certainties' of life reduced to the economic facts of production. These 'certainties' should be set against the living 'farm-bred certainties' of the widow in 'Return to Hinton': 'narrow' they may be, but they are rooted in the realities of a natural and human existence. 'Work is necessary', and knowing this the oxen consent 'to be useful'; but when it requires a daily suspension of living then there can be no voluntary consent to its necessity. Life is both livelihood and living, life used and life for itself, work and freedom; the demands of both must be met. Without the freedom there is no growth and without that there is stagnation.

> A thoughtful yet unthinking man,
>   John Maydew,
>   memory stagnates
> in you and breeds
>   a bitterness; it grew
>   and rooted in your silence.

'Thoughtful yet unthinking', he is full of thoughts that cannot flow, out of the past into the future, out of a remembered past into a future of possibility. In Tomlinson's poems, as we have seen, life presented is habitually arranged for the eye and the mind into foreground and background, the near and the far. In this poem the life of here and now, the 'closer comities' of John Maydew's garden space, has its small compensations, but there is no future, no possibility, only 'the spoiled and staled distances'. The closing down of prospects, in that last phrase, is mirrored later in 'those close and gritty certainties' and the 'burrow of necessity'. As we learn from 'Skullshapes', the mind understands the present in the light of 'that which it remembers' and the other light of what is imaginable, and it is a vision of the latter that guides the artist's hand when he adds to 'lines of containment, lines of extension' and by his 'search beyond the instant discloses a future'. That extension of life depends upon the opportunity for a relation with the other world of nature, where 'space is possibility';[2] it depends upon the possibility of that 'something else' than the man-made for which the 'discriminating / swans', in 'Canal' (CP p. 64), are seeking. The 'spoiled and staled / distances' are at once that natural world plundered and polluted and the closed down prospects of human life generally. John Maydew's 'memory stagnates' because it is rooted in the 'silence' of suppressed, unexpressed life, a poor soil that breeds nothing but 'a bitterness'—a bitterness that answers to, as it is directly connected with, the 'acrid drift' of smoke from 'the valley mills'. It is the reverse side of inertia, the 'stoic lethargy' remembered by the poet a decade later, in 'The Marl Pits' (CP p. 248), as 'the one reply / To horizons and to streets' that shut out 'water, light and air', that 'blocked them back / In a monotone fume, a bloom of grey'. The contrary of John Maydew's silence is the 'silence' of 'The Hand at Callow Hill Farm', which is the essence of the man and signifies an unexpressed sufficiency: 'a reticence / Of the blood, whose calm concealed / The tutelary of that upland field'.

The inner dispossession is the foreground preoccupation of the poem, but in the background is the social history outlined above. John Maydew's unflowing memory is historical as well as personal: the cultural memory, too, stagnates in him. The 'ineradicable' instincts of the peasant in John Maydew lack nourishment because socially he is an uprooted peasant, or the descendant of one, exiled from the 'green' world of growth, not to know what the farmer's widow has known, 'the seasons' sweet succession'. The lines suggest that these peasant instincts lie dormant in all Englishmen; in this instance the name, which has a medieval ring to it, with its associations of spring and morning, carries us even further back (like Genesis in 'Return to Hinton') to immemorial sources, beginnings. John Maydew's peasant nature is cowed and dulled, the peasant has lost his peasantdom, and man has lost his cultural kingdom; he is the daily prisoner, this dispossessed Englishman, of an unnatural world. The image is explicit in 'quotidian hell' and 'green reprieves', and as a latent presence converts 'watch-*chained* waistcoats' of old-fashioned solid worth, ironically, punningly, into emblems of servitude. The image is latent too in the very word, 'allotment', that designates his piece of 'green'. 'The Allotment' is, pointedly, an alternative title for the poem, and as such draws attention away from the thing, described but not named in the poem, to the action in the word, and with the action the general sense of one's lot in life. Carlyle thundered somewhere about 'the stinted allotments of earthly life' and is so quoted in the Oxford English Dictionary; as this strip of land is John Maydew's allotted space, his measure of the 'comities' of life, so these 'forty years' of an unflowing existence are his allotted destiny. A toad, a half-tamed creature 'that takes / into a slack and twitching jaw / the worms he proffers it'—slack, like the 'dispossessed / and half-tamed Englishman', with the inertia of a broken spirit—is an image for that destiny. When it 'looks up at him / through eyes that are / as dimly faithless / as the going years', it wears the 'look' of social betrayal and 'forty years / of mean amends'. The toad 'looks up at him' waiting to be fed; so, as night approaches, 'the valley gazes up / through kindling eyes'; it is 'a glowing ruse' now, but 'tomorrow / he must feed its will'. The toad, 'a seamed and lunar grey' like the landscape, is at once cause, agent and product of John Maydew's destiny, an image for the social cause, industrial agent and human product of dispossession.

* * * * *

From the start the example of American 'free verse' has been a liberating force in Tomlinson's writing. Stevens is a conspicuous presence in *The Necklace* (1955). The short line free-verse poem on the American model appears also, though less frequently, in *Seeing is Believing*, but is more prominent in *A Peopled Landscape* (1963), most of which was written after the poet's first visit to the United States. This collection is notable, in particular, for its successful adaptation to the English voice, as in 'John Maydew', of the three-tier line devised by Williams. The experiment with this verse form made possible a more cursive, discursive but measured utterance. It produces a counterpoint between diversity of pitch and pace in the rhythmical units and some kind of aural equality between them as signalled by the typography. The regularity of the tripartite divisions in effect converts the line into a grid that measures and sets off the irregular contours of voice movement.

In all Tomlinson's collections, early and late, there are poems written to other measures than those of so-called *free* verse. They occasionally obey accentual-syllabic conventions, but more frequently, as we have seen, the movement is that of accentual metre. The proportion of 'free' to 'metrical' verse varies from volume to volume, but it is higher in *American Scenes* (1966), written after a year spent at the University of New Mexico, than in any other collection. American measures for American experiences? Hardly, since the measures have since become part of Tomlinson's poetic repertoire; but nowhere else in his work does his short free-verse line attempt so consistently, and accomplish with such verve, the task that Williams set himself of drawing 'many broken things into a dance': in no collection does he dedicate himself so wholeheartedly to the imaginative transmutation of the minimal, the marginal, the anecdotal and the inconsequential.

American Scenes also announces a new subject matter—the land, chiefly the desert landscapes of the Southwest, the people, behaviour and talk of the United States—but the frame of thought and system of values by means of which he orders his material, albeit adjusted to the new circumstances, remain essentially the same. 'Las Trampas U.S.A.' (CP p. 124) illustrates all this, and is at the same time an attractive example of Tomlinson's English use of the American short free-verse line. It is a beautiful and original poem, an exquisite invention, characteristic in the treatment of its subject—the display of its significance—and in the part played by the lineation in that treatment. In lines of two to six syllables, using a largely monosyllabic vocabulary, it sets out the bare bones of a situation with a lean delicacy of humour. Marianne Moore, in her poem 'The Past is Present', speaks of Hebrew poetry, and by implication her own verse, as 'prose with a heightened consciousness'; her method is frequently, by a dry, spare itemization and analysis of facts, to build up to a point where a poetry of celebration takes over. Similarly, as down its stretched length the slowed-down narrative of Tomlinson's poem spells out in deliberative minuteness its prosaic details, the accumulation and anatomization gradually induce that heightened consciousness and lead to a finale of muted lyricism, which casts back over the whole process the humorous kindness and watchfulness of poetry. The bare bones, one might say, have 'suffered a sea-change into something rich and strange'.

The poet is a visitor seeking entry to the local church; the poem recounts the stages of his protracted negotiations. First he approaches an old Hispanic woman 'for the key / to Las Trampas church'; she refers him to three men working and they send him to a fourth 'hoeing a cornfield / nearby'—the repeated question each time delicately adjusted, in phrasing and in the emphases arranged by lineation, to the stages of the occasion—until finally with a flourish he is admitted. There is the comedy of language. He first makes his request in English but, says the woman in Spanish, she does not speak English, and so the poet repeats the question in careful Spanish. He walks over then to the three men 'preparing to ask / them in Spanish', but 'Hi, they say / in American' and he replies (with British two-syllable expansiveness) 'Hello'. He asks his question in Spanish and they relay it to the previously unmentioned fourth in Spanish. The poet thanks the three men and 'they / reply in American / You're welcome'. The poem has reproduced in careful notation the 'bittiness', the broken quality, of these communications ('many broken things' drawn 'into a dance'); now suddenly the verse begins to flow and rhyme:

> I go
> once more and
> await in shadow
> the key: he
> who brings it is not
> he of the hoe, but
> one of the three
> men working, who
> with a Castilian grace
> ushers me in
> to this place
> of coolness out
> of the August sun.

'Castilian grace' merely names—and suggests a European provenance for—the modest ritual of *civility* which constitutes the whole event. In an address, 'The Poem as Initiation', delivered at Colgate University in 1967 to accompany a reading of 'Swimming Chenango Lake', Tomlinson maintains that there is 'a ceremonial aspect to a poem': the poem is 'a ceremony of initiation' into an imagined experience. 'In the poet's weighing and measuring' (counting syllables and accents, 'calling attention to the intricate meshing of words') 'there is a dwelling on the inner rhythm of events that is as fundamental and primitive, if you like, as ritual. And like ritual, the poem dwells on an event to force us to a consciousness of the meaningfulness of that event'. 'Las Trampas, U.S.A.' *is*, in this sense, a ceremony, the consciousness pausing contemplatively over each stage of the occasion, and is *about* the ceremony which is the visible and audible sign of civility. The 'place of coolness' is a church; it is not there for any part it plays in the life of Christianity, but neither is its presence an accident. The visitor—and the reader with him—undergoes, as it were, a rite of passage, which has earned him entry into not so much a place as a condition: if it is not the *peace* that passes all understanding, it is respite for the body and the spirit from the oppression of a southern summer sun. The conditions are disparate and yet they stand in a comparable relation, it seems, to the 'central calm' (CP p. 36) of objects that rebukes the subjective frenzy of Van Gogh's representations of them, or to 'the equitable core of peace' from which the voice of the flute draws 'reason's song' (CP p. 9). 'This place / of coolness'—the 'key' to which the visiting poet seeks—is where races, languages and manners are differentiated but at the same time related and harmonized by reciprocal courtesies.

Civility, as a mode or code of behaviour, is a learned system of relations, a second nature. All this is on display in 'Las Trampas U.S.A.', and yet it is not only the spare form that distinguishes the treatment of the theme here from its treatment in 'At Delft' or 'On the Hall at Stowey' or 'Return to Hinton'. The evidence of civility, too, must in the nature of the case be sparse; although the courtesy of these Spanish-Americans—holders of the 'key' to the church's 'coolness'—is full of a 'grace', humanity tempered by a social tradition, there is just a hint that it is not home-grown. The poet's praise—for as so often in Tomlinson's work this *is* a poem of praise—is for a civility that has flourished in such unexpected and, as it would appear to the European mind without this disproof, unpromising circumstances. In the poem entitled 'Idyll' (CP p. 149) and located in 'Washington Square, San Francisco', appreciative surprise turns into a question. The poet quotes a text inscribed along the lintel over the door of a church for Italian Catholics; they are the first words of Dante's *Paradiso*: 'La Gloria di Colui che tutto muove PER L'UNIVERSO penetra e risplende'. Noting that the brilliance of a

Californian January sun 'throughout the square / flatters the meanness of its architecture' and that beyond the square the sound of traffic in this American city 'tugs the ear / towards it' and provides 'a constant ground-bass / to these provincialisms of the piazza / tasting still / of Lerici and Genova', he wonders how the coherence of civilization can result from such anomalies. This is not the 'melting pot' of popular conception, the melting down of ethnic differences into a common product, but a miscellany (which Canadians have delicately preferred to call a 'mosaic'); and so the poet is moved to ask:

> How
>   does one spell out this
>   *che penetra e risplende*
> from square
>   into the hill-side alley-ways
>   around it, where
> between tall houses
>   children of the Mediterranean
>   and Chinese element
> mingle
>   their American voices?

The poet sees this mingling nevertheless, without irony, as subject for an idyll:

> the old men sit
>   in a mingled odour
>   of cheroot and garlic
> spitting;
>   they share serenity
>   with the cross-legged
> Chinese adolescent
>   seated between them
>   reading ...

For within the square, if not yet beyond it, there is, in

> this poised quiescence, pause
>   and possibility in which

> the music of the generations
>   binds into its skein
>   the flowing instant.

What Tomlinson finds in these American scenes are the right initial combinations, the seeds, the *possibility* of civilization.

The full title of this collection is *American Scenes and Other Poems*. The first third of the book is given over to English themes and landscapes; the other two thirds are American, nearly half of these scenes located in what Tomlinson has called *America West Southwest*, under which title in 1970, at the invitation of San Marco Press, New Mexico, he brought together the thirteen poems from *American Scenes* (1966), another five from *The Way of a World* (1969), and three previously uncollected pieces which have not been reprinted since. The most interesting of these are the desert and Indian poems, the best of which are from *American Scenes*. They offer a new outlook on the theme of civilization. In his Preface to *America West Southwest* Tomlinson draws attention to Lawrence's exhortation to 'break through the shiny sterilized wrapping' with which 'our trite civilization' protects us from the real Southwest and 'actually *touch* the country'. Tomlinson does not cite *St Mawr*, but it is there, in that story of the struggle to withstand the 'malevolence' of desert and mountain and to wrest a subsistence from, and plant a human meaning in, the 'crude wild nature' of New Mexico—it is in this novel that such pioneering ventures are presented as radical 'enterprises at civilization'; in Lawrence's conception—and this is how it is represented in Tomlinson's desert poems too—civilization is the primal nisus of the human spirit.

The spare, choppy verse of 'Las Trampas U.S.A.', lines that break up the sequence of sense into gobbets of sound, the minimal and for the most part rudimentary diction—these are the linguistic equivalent, I said, for the sparsity of evidence from which we may infer a whole tradition of civility; these broken fragments are, so to speak, the oases in a cultural desert. The literal desert is the instance here of nature—nature at its least hospitable—as the intractable material on which man must none the less make his impressions, the inhuman medium in which the creative spirit must operate.

The desert of the American Southwest in this group of poems is the hostility, the poverty of nature against which humanity sets its will and the devious, patient negotiation with which it pursues its purpose, conformed to the barest necessities, of building the 'city' of man.

> Here, to be,
> is to sound
> patience deviously
> and follow
> like the irregular corn
> the water underground.

The subject, and the title of the poem from which this, the penultimate stanza, is taken, is the 'Arizona Desert', discussed in Chapter 2. As in 'Las Trampas U.S.A.' the humour appreciates at the same time as it acknowledges the exiguity of the civilities celebrated, so 'Arizona Desert' (CP p. 121) places an ironic limitation on, but in no way depreciates, the civilizing enterprise. From the perspective taken in my previous discussion of the poem I may have over-emphasized the role of irony in the last stanza. Hopi villages that revert 'from mud and stone ... to the dust they humanize' 'mean / marriage' not merely in quixotic defiance of the reality, and 'Hopi / means peace', peace now not the memory or prospect of peace. For civilization, in triumph or defeat, retains its meaning: it *is*, in intention and performance, a marriage of man with nature, a peaceful accommodation to the land. Tomlinson underscores this point in his Preface to *America West Southwest*: 'The magnificence was [for the English visitor] a fact, but so was the sense of an attunement between people and place ... If you couldn't overlay all the region's magnificence with the *merely* human, the human had at the same time taken a purchase on the region, had married with it.'

'The Cavern' (CP p. 120) is the first of the series of desert landscapes in *American Scenes*. Introducing the new perspective on the civilizing enterprise, it begins with the recognition that the humanizing of nature cannot take the form of appropriation or conversion but is, rather, 'an attunement between people and place'.

In 'Arizona Desert' the metamorphoses of human perception are ironic victories, illusions of life refuted by the facts: 'the layers / of flaked and broken bone' which 'unclench into petals' flower to the eye only; 'a dead snake / pulsates again' in a mock-resurrection 'as, hidden, the beetles' hunger / mines through the tunnel of its drying skin'—giving, in the way of nature, life not to itself but to the scavengers of the desert. Yet, as 'The Cavern' repeatedly demonstrates, the eye cannot but transform what it sees: in the inhuman shapes of water-worn and encrusted rock, for example, it sees human images:

> Hard to the hand,
> these mosses not of moss,
> but nostrils, pits
> of eyes, faces
> in flight and prints
> of feet where no feet ever were.

The mind tries to think itself into the unthinkable but misses the reality; these images

> elude the mind's
> hollow that would contain
> this canyon within a mountain.

The poem concedes, insists, that this 'boneyard landscape' is resistant to the imagination; nevertheless, while we are enjoined to 'obliterate / mythology', anthropomorphisms, from our minds, nature is not actually depicted as irreclaimably alien; it is approachable, and we are encouraged to explore the possibility of relationship. In verse that has released itself from the controls of accentual metre, in which typography alone cues the reader to reproduce in mental performance emphases and inflections of the voice, we are instructed to penetrate deeper into the interior of the cavern:

> Not far
> enough from the familiar
> press
> in under a deeper dark until

> the curtained sex
> the arch, the streaming buttress
> have become
> the self's unnameable and shaping home.

Having left behind the 'familiar', the human domain, we reach the 'unnameable', that which is not for man's ownership or use, and there a meeting takes place, a meeting, it seems, of equals: man has pressed, and earth has consented to become his 'shaping home'. Earlier, using the metaphors by which language necessarily translates the world, the poet has put this question:

> Pulse of the water-drop,
> veils and scales, fins
> and flakes of the forming
> leprous rock,
> how should these
> inhuman, turn
> human with such chill affinities?

Turning them into reflections of the human is not the way. Earth is *not* man's creature that he can form the things of nature into images of himself; at the same time nature must not, before death, make a thing of man. It is a relationship, where the cave of earth is the frame, the host and the place of generation; for this 'unnameable and shaping home' is nature as female receiving and containing the creative seed of man. It is, again, a marriage, in which the sexual is sacramental: this hollow, not 'the mind's / hollow that would contain' the world, is at once womb and natural cathedral; the same combination of analogies recurs in 'The Shaft' (CP p. 306), in which the poet describes another venture into the earth's interior.

But in some of the poems in this series there is a bias towards another view of the civilizing enterprise. In all these poems death is the canvas on which human endeavour is painted—death as inanimate matter, the lifelessness of what has never lived, at its bleakest in these arid landscapes, and death as the consequence of the desert's inhospitality to life. The '*dry* orange ground' has its accompaniment of 'cowskull' and 'the layers / of flaked and broken bone'; the 'dead snake' lives again only as it feeds the beetles tunnelling through its *drying skin*; the 'mountain-interior' has both its 'limestone stair' and its 'boneyard landscape'. This is not the exterior world of objects viewed neutrally as one half of a relationship—as what is 'bodied over against one' and 'As something one has to do with' (CP p. 11): it is that world as it is presented in 'The Snow Fences' (CP p. 108)—one of the English poems in *American Scenes*—man's adversary, an exterior known to the 'aching skeleton' as a 'levelling zero'. It is a 'nowhere' where 'No flowers / grow' (the opening words of 'News from Nowhere', one of the uncollected pieces in *America West Southwest*); it is what one finds 'On the Mountain' (CP p. 123): 'Nobody there: / no body', where 'nobody sees' and 'nobody climbs', and where

> Somebody
> finding nobody there
> found gold also:
> gold gone, he
> (stark in his own redundancy)
> must needs go too
> and here, sun-warped
> and riddled by moon, decays
> his house which nobody occupies.

With this as the ground bass for all the desert poems—occasion here for sardonic word-play and a verbal spareness that mocks the condition—we are amply prepared for a different attitude to the presence of man in the landscape. We encounter it first in 'A Death in the Desert' (CP p. 122); 'in memory of Homer Vance', this poem speaks of the death of a desert dweller. Homer was the arresting name of the old Hopi doll-maker; Tomlinson met him one summer sitting like an 'Olympian'—another kind of Olympian, Greek god rather than poet—'in his cool room on the rock-roof of the world', and he was dead when the poet returned in the autumn. 'There are no crosses / on the Hopi graves', the poem begins, to signify victory over death; neither religion, Christian or pagan, nor art—the doll-maker's or Homer's or Tomlinson's—could put him, where in his Olympian exaltation he had already seemed to be, 'beyond the snatch / of circumstance'; the circumstances of his particular death, 'beating a burro out of his corn-patch', had indeed been as commonplace and as momentous as any other death. There was no Cross, and no miraculous crossing (as of the Israelites through the Red Sea)—no myth of deliverance from the common fate—and, for the poet, 'the week / that lay / *uncrossably* between us' (the Christian-Mosaic reference is, I think, latent in the word)

> stretched into sand,
> into the spread
> of the endless
> waterless sea-bed beneath
> whose space outpacing sight
> receded as speechless and as wide as death.

This passage, the conclusion to the poem, with its rhymes, echoes and repetitions, its seamless, slow-paced movement miming endlessness, and the gradual lengthening of its lines, expands with the sense outward over the horizons of the imaginable into an infinity of space, which is also the inexpressible and a kind of eternity. The opening lines about the Hopi graves are followed, not by words of limitation, but a description of the desert that salutes its magnitude and its awesome *magnificence* (Tomlinson's word for the region in the Preface to *America West Southwest*):

> The sky
> over the desert
> with its sand-grain stars
> and the immense equality
> between desert and desert sky,
> seem
> a scope and ritual
> enough to stem
> death and to be its equal.

Sky and desert, here, as heaven and earth in another frame of thought, make up a totality; their infinity encompasses and contains the finiteness of a mortal existence. This is not to say that death *is* defeated. If 'to stem / death' meant to check or prevent it, then this seeming, however magnificent, would be an illusion; but it doesn't, although 'seem' invites us to make the mistake before correcting it. For 'the immense equality / between / desert and desert sky' not only to *seem* but to *be* death's 'equal', 'stem' must have the sense of going counter to or resisting (as a ship stems or breasts the current or a bird an opposing wind); in that sense the *idea* of a totality is in the mind equal to the idea of death. That unknowable *totality*, which we have encountered before in Tomlinson's poems, is what is, in the poem's last line, 'as speechless and as wide as death'—not identical but comparable, and equal. The thought of it, like death, is beyond the scope of language; which is why 'scope and ritual' are coupled— ritual rather than words to articulate its scope. Reality is the whole: the particulars of experience are parts of the whole; death is a part and has its place in this totality of desert space. Time is included: it was the interval between seeing the man alive and hearing of his death, a week that seems to be neither life nor death, that 'stretched into' that 'endless' immensity, dissolved into the infinity of space: an endlessness of time and space. 'Uncrossably' acknowledges the mystery of what lies between. I called it a *kind* of eternity because the word also denies the validity of the Christian claims symbolized by the Cross. The vision is, for all that, religious. As in the poems of perception space is primary—space representing the whole of possible sense experience, of which particular sensations, particular objects of perception, are instances—so in this poem his theme is the total landscape, comprehending earth and sky, and the life-and-death of the man (at once commonplace and momentous) is an incident in the full story of that landscape.

Tomlinson has always responded to something other than the human reality. In 'Something: A Direction', the final poem of the sequence 'Antecedents' (*Seeing is Believing*, 1958; CP p. 54) it is simply what is 'not you'; in a language no less definite but which opens the thought to feeling, it is the 'given grace' of objects, the title-phrase of a poem in *American Scenes*. In Tomlinson's poems, as we saw in 'The Cavern', otherness usually presupposes a relationship with it, a subject-object relation: what constitutes the 'given grace' of two plain white cups is that one is both 'challenged and *replenished* by / those empty vessels' (CP p. 155). But the last lines of 'A Death in the Desert', a sort of coda that assimilates and then moves on beyond the conclusion of the man's life, are penetrated, permeated—I have in mind the words from the *Paradiso* quoted in 'Idyll'—by an entranced wonder at their vision of an endless universe, a serene absorption in the thought of that endlessness *without reference to man*. In two other poems of the series, 'Arizona Highway' (CP p. 133) and 'Two Views of Two Ghost Towns' (CP p. 144), we are even reminded to a certain extent of Rupert Birkin's picture, in Lawrence's *Women in Love*, of 'the world destroyed'; he finds it 'a beautiful clean thought, a world empty of people, just uninterrupted grass, and a hare sitting up'. I have previously cited Lawrence's commendation, in *St Mawr*, of the civilizing enterprise; this vision of Birkin's is Lawrence in another mood, but, in appearance contradictory, the two ideas do not in fact exclude each other—nor do they in Tomlinson's work. They are reconciled in Lawrence's conception, expounded in *St Mawr* itself, of creative destruction: 'Creation destroys as it goes, throws down one tree for the rise of another ... Man must destroy as he goes, as trees fall for trees to rise. The accumulation of life and things means rottenness. Life must destroy life, in the unfolding of creation.' If we discount the momentary misanthropy, the exasperation that charges Birkin's exultant version of 'wiping the slate clean', the family resemblance between his visionary picture and Tomlinson's view of a real ghost town, a view more soberly contemplated, is clear enough:

> Why speak of memory and death
> on ghost ground? Absences
> relieve, release. Speak
> of the life that uselessness
> has unconstrained.

The sheer satisfaction in the idea of 'absences' is given more emphatic expression a few lines later, bringing it closer to the mood of Birkin's own emphatic assertion:

> *Keep off*
> the warning says, and all
> the mob of objects, freed
> under the brightly hard
> displacement of the desert light
> repeat it.

Keep off, it says, and objects displaced from their human frame, cleansed of human association, become themselves again in the 'brightly hard / ... desert light':

> clear
> of the weight of human
> meanings, human need,
> gradually
> houses splinter to the ground.

(The notion of displacement recurs a decade later in 'Foxes' Moon' [CP p. 250], where colourless moonlight is the displacing agent.) There is pleasure for Tomlinson—this is in the second of the two views—in a dry desert air that 'tastes of sparseness'; it goes with the absence of decoration on 'the graveyard stones'. Sparseness is what I noted in 'Las Trampas U.S.A.'—a sparseness in the civilities of the occasion which, in view of Tomlinson's own appreciative use of the word here, it would be prudent to regard now, not as a sign of inferiority (by comparison with their Castilian precedent), but as the mark of their authenticity. Absence of the human, sparseness of life elicit a positive imaginative response from the poet that becomes in 'Arizona Highway' an exultation in the self's (temporary) obliteration as he travels 'the telegraphed desert miles':

> To become the face of space,
> snatching a flowing mask
> of emptiness
> from where the parallels meet.
>
> One is no more
> than invaded transparency.

The replenishment, if it can be called that, is of a different order from what is provided, in 'A Given Grace', by 'those empty vessels'—though emptiness is an element in both experiences.

In these desert landscapes, ruled nakedly by death, the poet celebrates—in tones of rapt tranquillity and self-forgetful, wondering admiration—not simply the otherness of nature, but a world without man, a lifeless, life-denying world with which there is no possibility of human relationship. It is presented as a purifying, liberating experience. This vision recurs at intervals throughout Tomlinson's work, but after *American Scenes* never again, perhaps, are the sharp contradictions so starkly displayed. 'The Fox' (CP p. 109), in the same collection, finds a similar paradox in an English snowscape. The poet came upon the fox 'kneeling / in snow'—brought to its knees, rather, for, as it turned out, 'the thing was dead'. But the only difference between its life and its death is 'its stillness'; the snow-drift, 'domed at the summit', had the likeness of a skull, 'as if the whole / fox-infested hill were the skull of a fox', as, conversely, its 'scallops and dips / of pure pile' were a mocking reminder of the animal's fur. 'Clambering between its white temples', the temples of the hill's skull, where 'each / missed step was a plunge' at its invisible centre, he sees the appearance that 'rippled and shone', fears the 'blinding interior', but recognizes that they are surface and core of the same thing: the 'beauty' of snow whose 'stillness'—scalloped, 'rippled', furred—dissembles the movement of life is no more 'pure' than the smooth sculpted lines 'scarped' by the wind 'into a pennine wholly of snow'. There is, no doubt, replenishment in the thought, but it is offered not, this time, for our admiration but as an enigma, and is phrased as a question: 'but what / should I do with such beauty / eyed by that' skull-shaped hill—embrace or renounce it, thrill with delight or, seeing the skull beneath the skin, shudder in horror? Had the fox knelt in reverence or enforced submission, and, as one seemed to penetrate the space between the skull's *temples* (the pun is unavoidable) perilously close to the hill's terrifying 'interior', did 'the crosswind' that 'tore / at one's legs' require from the poet, too, reverence or submission or both? Or does this make a distinction where no distinction exists?

NOTES

1. Alexander Pope, 'Moral Essays: Epistle IV', 23–24.
2. 'Preface', *Collected Poems*, p. vii.

Chapter Four
Manscapes 1969–1978

In this and the previous chapter I am giving equal attention to the changes of direction in Tomlinson's development and to the continuity of thought and outlook. I introduced the sequence of 1950s and 1960s poems with a discussion of 'Oxen: Ploughing at Fiesole', in *Seeing is Believing*, since one can observe there the process by which an ethic of perception is transformed into an ethic of attitude and action. I turned then to poems concerned with civility and civilization in this and the succeeding collection, *A Peopled Landscape*. The preoccupation with this theme persisted in *American Scenes*, but the very different landscapes and cultural circumstances of the New World required a different approach and produced a different emphasis. Finally, in the desert poems and 'The Fox', I noted a transition from a focus on the civilizing enterprise to the theme of being.

The Way of a World (1969), the successor to *American Scenes*, contains by general agreement many of Tomlinson's finest poems. 'Swimming Chenango Lake', a well-known and frequently anthologized poem, is referred to briefly in this chapter; others I have discussed in the first two chapters: 'Eden', 'Adam', 'In the Fullness of Time', 'A Sense of Distance' and 'Skullshapes', which is just one of a remarkable series of prose poems.[1] My list would also include—although they are not treated in this book—'Words for the Madrigalist' (which once, however, had a place in Chapter 1) and 'The Chances of Rhyme'. Two others, 'Assassin' and 'Prometheus', with which a new subject-matter, revolutionary politics, entered Tomlinson's poetry, will be discussed at length.

I begin with 'Descartes and the Stove' (CP p. 196), however, since it shares the theme of being with 'The Fox' and the desert poems in the previous collection and its moral vision with the political poems that are its neighbours in *The Way of a World*. The poet has returned from the relative informality of style and presentation, the jagged edges and the imagistic shorthand, of *American Scenes* to an ampler rhetoric, a more urbane tone and intellectual diction, a no less imagistic but carefully conducted, developed argument. It is not free verse: the lines, as also in 'Prometheus' and 'Assassin', have the approximate regularity of accentual metre—a four-beat line with the occasional addition of a fifth. Nevertheless it is preoccupied with the same antinomies as the free-verse poems of the previous volume: the disparity and the accord of living and dead, the visible and the invisible, the nameable (Adam's privilege) and the unnameable, beauty and terror. The paradox thus repeated and rephrased is condensed into a single formulation in 'Face and Image', a kind of manifesto poem for *American Scenes*, where the poet protests the impossibility of distinguishing between 'the theme [the mind's representation] / and being of all appearances'.

Descartes determined that 'there must be some general science ... a universal mathematics', which 'should contain the primary rudiments of human reason', a science capable of 'eliciting true results in every subject'.[2] Against this vision, which came to the philosopher in his 'snow-bound' room, of a world proved by reason, to the exclusion of all other evidence, Tomlinson opposes the no less incontrovertible facts of the phenomenal world. The poem is, as it were, his answer to the man who said: 'I am convinced that [such a science] is a more powerful instrument of knowledge than any other that has been bequeathed to us by human agency, as being the source of all others.'[3] Starting from the existence of the mind and doubting all that could not pass the test of reason, Descartes proceeded to infer the existence of an external world. Tomlinson is writing poetry not philosophy and his business is not to prove but to persuade; when I say, therefore, that he reverses Descartes' procedure, I am not, of course, suggesting that Tomlinson means to 'prove' the existence of the mind by the existence of the world, or to prove anything. I shall not be misunderstood, then, if I put the opposition between the philosopher and the poet in this way: whereas Descartes worked from the inside out, Tomlinson in this poem works from the outside in. So the poem begins with the stove *thrusting* its belly at the philosopher in brazen sensual invitation and ends with his refusal to recognize in the body's involuntary, unarguable response to the heat's persuasions the undeniable evidence of his senses. Here are the opening lines:

> Thrusting its armoury of hot delight,
>   Its negroid belly at him, how the whole
> Contraption threatened to melt him
>   Into recognition.

And this is the conclusion:

>   The great mind
> Sat with his back to the unreasoning wind
>   And doubted, doubted at his ear
> The patter of ash and, beyond, the snow-bound farms,
>   Flora of flame and iron contingency
> And the moist reciprocation of his palms.

Looking inward, 'the great mind' turns its back on the truth embodied in 'the unreasoning wind'—the rhymes giving ironic accentuation to the antithesis. But there, in the world outside the mind, is where Tomlinson first looks for reality, the (non-human) law of being and finds an image of its necessity in the winter sunset: 'All leaned / Into that frigid burning, *corded tight* / *By* the lightlines as the slow sun drew / Away and down' (my emphasis). From Cartesian doubt follows Cartesian dualism, the division between mind and matter, subject and object. In the language of metaphor the distinction is often ignored, and is so ignored and, characteristically, subverted in Tomlinson's first sentence; for the 'hot delight' of the stove is also the 'hot delight' of the body's response, the objective and the subjective reference being indistinguishable.

Both the primacy of the object and the elimination of the distinction between the objective and the subjective—they become, in a sense (see the passage from 'The Poet as Painter' quoted below), equally objective—are, as I said, familiar positions in Tomlinson's thought. Where 'Descartes and the Stove' resembles 'The Fox', however, is in its representation of being as at once dual and single: the duality of life and death, yet a singleness of being. It is, on the one hand, sensuous, sensual, black, the 'flame' of life, the 'blaze' of the sun; on the other hand, it is the white world of winter death—the imagery and the polarities are remarkably Lawrencian. In the imagery of heat and feeling the outer and the inner realities fuse, the world welcomes its creatures: 'flora of flame', it would *draw* the subject to it, threatening to 'melt' the philosopher's theoretic resistance to its 'hot delight'; as though the stove's heat (likewise the 'blaze of day' and the efflorescence of summer) were trying to encourage in the introspective thinker that 'objectivity' which, in 'The Poet as Painter', Tomlinson finds supremely exemplified in Cézanne: not the 'objectivity of nineteenth century positivistic science ... which supposed a complete division between the observer and the observed' but 'an outward gaze that would *draw* the sensuous world closer to the inner man and that would narrow the gap between abstraction and sensation, intellect and thing'.[4] In the imagery of winter cold is reflected the immutable rule of physical law; it creates a frigid, rigid, stark, 'snow-*bound*' world of 'iron contingency'—that is to say, a government of inflexible indifference. There are, it seems, two realities, an inside and an outside, the one warm, the other cold; the first would softly, meltingly persuade; its contrary, offering no such overtures, binds with cold and tight cords of light and an inexorable 'iron' law. They alternate, as day and night; in the night-time it is the world of 'badger and fox', who 'wind / Through the phosphorescence' of moonlit snow—the 'phosphorescence' acting, for the poet, like the 'hard desert light' to make the familiar strange. They alternate, or simply life hardens into death, as does 'the boughs' *nerve net*' when 'starkened' by snow. But the imagery also demonstrates that they are obverse and reverse of the same reality. Descartes' 'footprint' in the snow 'had turned / To a firm dull gloss', the impression of life rigidified into an image of death, but in what follows—'and the chill / Lined it with a fur of frost'—the image adds a reminder, a 'dull' reminder, of its opposite, and the stiff foot-print with its lining of fur, at once hard and soft, cold and warm, 'dull' and fine, has become now an image of life-and-death. The two realities meet and combine into one when the extremities of cold and heat are identified as 'that frigid burning' of 'the last blaze of day', the sun setting over a snowscape. One word for that single overarching reality is 'anonymity': the evening 'shadow, now, / Defined no longer' but 'dragged everything / Into its own anonymity of blue / Becoming black'. We may be reminded of 'Tramontana at Lerici' (CP p. 27)— 'Dark hardens from blue ... A tangible block ... One is ignored / By so much cold suspended in so much night'—but there is an important difference. Blue hardens into dark and has become 'a tangible block' by which 'one is ignored'—this is a logical sequence, a straightforward statement; but an 'anonymity of blue / Becoming black', dwelling first on 'blue' and then drawing attention to the state of transition, is comparatively a conundrum—what, where is the anonymity? It should, we feel, belong exclusively, as it does in the earlier poem, to the 'black' of night, the shadow that no longer distinguishes surfaces from recesses as it blends into general darkness; but by emphasizing the process of 'becoming' ('blue / Becoming black') it extends its application to include the 'blue' of day. The self-evident anonymity of night—what you can't see you can't name—is, this seems to say, the perfection of an anonymity not patent but already potential in the day. The 'unnameable', all that falls outside human jurisdiction, is—in the words of 'The Cavern'—the ultimate 'shaping home' of man. The other words used by Tomlinson to identify the single reality that embraces contraries is 'unreasoning'. If the wind is distinguished from mind by its indifference to reason, the same is no less true of the fire in the 'belly' of the stove: neither the wind outside—unmindful of, insensible to human desires—nor its contrary, the 'flame' of sensual gratification, is amenable to human reason. 'Anonymity' and 'unreasoning' point in the same direction, to the boundaries that mark the limits of Adam's power. Black is basic for Tomlinson, as he discovered when he made productive use of his obsession with it in the black-and-white graphics of the 1970s reproduced in *Eden* (1985). The painter's obsession has its source, he tells us, in the domination of black in the townscapes of his youth, in the blackened houses, smoky air, sooty allotments, slag-heaps, cinderpaths of the industrial Midlands. The word has none of these associations in the poem, but it is noticeable that the two blacks, the hot ('negroid') black of the stove and the cold black of the winter night, constitute between them the one (unnameable, unreasoning) world of the given and unquestionable.

With 'Assassin' and 'Prometheus', as I have said, a new subject-matter entered Tomlinson's poetry. The theme of revolutionary idealism—the Russian Revolution and its aftermath provide the scene and the characters in these two poems—is treated again a decade later in three poems about the French Revolution. There are no more than a handful of poems concerned with revolutionary politics but they stand out and have attracted a good deal of merited attention. They stand out but are not isolated from their neighbours. The fanaticism of a Mercader, Trotsky's assassin, or a Lenin or for that matter of Trotsky himself, author of *The Defence of Terrorism*, and the apocalyptic idealism of a Scriabin or a Blok are, in Tomlinson's thinking, linked by their imperious single-mindedness to Descartes' subjection of life's multiplicity and variety to the despotic rule of reason. Stripping away the differences of subject-matter in 'Assassin' and 'Descartes and the Stove', we find essentially the same structure of thought, a confrontation of two opposed visions of the world: the poet's and the, in certain respects, similar visions of the two principals, the assassin and the philosopher—on the one hand a reality known 'naturally', the world of phenomena, the truths of time and space apprehended by the senses, and on the other a conceptual diagram of reality.

As I have argued in previous chapters, Tomlinson's peculiar originality is rooted in the interdependence, the interfusion, of moral and sensory experience in his poems. I have been at pains to make clear, therefore, that the distinction between poems of perception and poems on human themes has a limited usefulness. How limited the distinction is and potentially misleading is strikingly demonstrated by a poem like 'Assassin' (CP p. 161). The first thing to notice in this poem, then, is the poet's deployment of a morality of right perception, right relations with phenomena, to judge the mental state of a revolutionary idealist acting according to the logic of his beliefs. His sin is the will to exempt himself from time and place, from sounds and sights, and substitute for a full sensory reality the partial, abstract world of a Marxist future, 'the deed's time, the deed's transfiguration', ruled by a theoretic intelligence: 'The gate of history is straiter than eye's or ear's'. The poem is the self-revelation of Mercader as he mentally re-enacts the murder. In imagination he had anticipated and steeled himself against the visual horror:

> Blood I foresaw. I had put by
> > The distractions of the retina, the eye
> That like a child must be fed and comforted
> > With patterns, recognitions

but he could not dismiss so readily the importunities of the ear, the unnerving rasp of papers or 'the animal cry' of the dying Trotsky. He might urge himself to

> > put down
> This rage of the ear for discrimination, its absurd
> > Dwelling on ripples, liquidities, fact
> Fastening on the nerve gigantic paper burs.

but mere self-exhortation cannot eliminate 'fact', cannot expunge the death-cry of his victim:

> Fleshed in that sound, objects betray me,
> > Objects are my judge: the table and its shadow,
> Desk and chair, the ground a pressure
> > Telling me where it is that I stand.

He tries to disengage himself from the totality of relations that constitutes reality, the *gestalt* of perception, the whole that determines the nature of its component parts. In this attempt he inverts the priorities of the ethic-aesthetic that has governed Tomlinson's practice ever since 'Poem' (CP p. xix), in *Relations and Contraries*, vowed total alertness to the fullness of sense experience. The mental mechanism of *gestalt* is described in 'Skullshapes' (CP p. 191), also from *The Way of a World*: 'The senses, reminded by other seeings, bring to bear on the act of vision their pattern of images; they give point and place to an otherwise naked and homeless impression.' For Trotsky's assassin, however, such 'patterns, recognitions' are nothing but 'distractions' from a purpose which for its accomplishment must reduce the whole phenomenal world to 'one placeless cell' holding only himself and his intended victim. In 'The Farmer's Wife: at Fostons Ash' (*A Peopled Landscape*, 1963; CP p. 70) the poet, viewing the stored 'riches' of home, yard and orchard, assures his hostess that 'fact / has its proper plenitude / that only time and tact / will show, renew'; but for Mercader 'fact / Fastening on the nerve' is simply an irritant, an irrelevance, a mere obstruction to the clean execution of idea—'I wiped / Clean the glance and saw / Only his vulnerableness'. He rejects all that Tomlinson means by place: 'the self's unnameable and shaping home' in 'The Cavern' (CP p. 120) or, as it is in 'A Prelude' (CP p. 59), a larger 'self one might inhabit'. The swimmer in 'Swimming Chenango Lake' (*The Way of a World*, 1969; CP p. 155) 'reaches in-and-through to that space / The body is heir to, making a where / In water'; for him, 'to move in its embrace' is 'to be, between grasp and grasping, free'. But the visible and palpable reality of space and its objects in Trotsky's room, as it were the geography of being— 'Telling me *where* it is that I stand / Before wall and window-light'—is the assassin's enemy and judge. Time, too, for Mercader is an annoying irrelevance: Marxist 'history' would telescope time. Projecting himself upon a future posited by Marxist theory, he in effect denies the reality of the present, the plenitude of fact: 'I am the future and my blow / Will have it now'.

The surprise of the poem is the virtual identity of two worlds, human and perceptual, and of two moral codes, the ethic of perception and an ethic of action. The surprise is doubled in intensity by the device of the dramatic monologue: the poet's judgements are reflected in the reversed mirror-image of the assassin's mind. Properly perceived, the world, for Tomlinson, is objects 'fleshed' in human awareness. Because Mercader had 'put by / The distractions of the retina' and sought to 'put down' the discriminations of the ear, because his 'imagination . . . held all at its proper distance'—'proper' according to this counterview of propriety—those objects now 'betray' him by reasserting their unignorable reality. What is by Tomlinson's standards the restoration of wholeness and proportion is for the Marxist fanatic a 'fall' from the Eden of idea into the world of phenomena:

> But the weight of a world unsteadies my feet
> And I fall into the lime and contaminations
>   Of contingency; into hands, looks, time.

'The Way of a World' (CP p. 165), a close neighbour of 'Assassin' in this collection, pictures 'the seed, the gull' pulled between two forces, 'two / Gravities that root and uproot the trees'; 'the weight of a world' is the gravity that roots trees, that draws all things to the centre.

'Prometheus' (CP p. 156) refers to the tone-poem of Scriabin completed in 1910, inspired by the legend of the Titan's theft of fire from the gods and the liberation of mankind from their oppressive rule; the poem, a note informs us, also refers generally to the composer's 'hope of transforming the world by music and rite'. The utopian dreams of romantic art and of revolutionary ideology are disquietingly close: both aim at the total transformation of human life. Listening to a radio performance of the work, the poet hears in its 'mock last-day of nature and of art' the 'consequence' of such dreams in the real events of the October Revolution—which Scriabin did not live to see—and in the further consequences of those events:

> Trombones for the transformation
> That arrived by train at the Finland Station,
>   To bury its hatchet after thirty years in the brain
> Of Trotsky. Alexander Nikolayevitch, the events
>   Were less merciful than your mob of instruments.

The inordinate aspirations expressed in such music and such poetry —Alexander Blok, symbolist poet turned rhapsodist of the Revolution, is cited—has a direct relation, if not one of simple cause and effect, to the institution of tyranny, which purports to perform the impossible; 'men of extremes' in the world of imagination, like Lenin in the world of action, by their dreams they made themselves unwitting accomplices of systematic terror. 'History' is not as Mercader conceived it. The tone-poem, subtitled 'a poem of fire', is *fin de siècle* poetry ('You dreamed an end / Where the rose of the world would go out like a close in music') but out of Lenin's 'merciless patience grew / The daily prose such poetry prepares for', and that 'daily prose' is the logical conclusion of imaginative excess, at once the accomplishment and the disappointment of such poetry's hopes: 'Chromatic Prometheus, myth of fire, / It is history topples you in the zenith'.

The network of relations plotted by 'Prometheus' is more intricate than that attempted by 'Assassin'. The poet's judgement of revolutionary idealism in the latter is refracted through the medium of the assassin's mind: in the former the judgement is conveyed directly to the reader, but it is based, though less transparently, on the same expanded ethic of perception. This ethic, as it is presented in 'The Poet as Painter', has regard for two principles, objectivity and fullness of perception: a self-forgetful objectivity, a receptivity to the whole field of perception and a consciousness of objects *in* their respective settings. In Tomlinson's words, it is 'an ethic distrustful of the drama of personality of which romantic art had made so much, an ethic where, by trusting to sensation, we enter being, and experience its primal fullness on terms other than those we dictate'.[5] Simply, it rests on the truth of facts. As in 'Descartes and the Stove' the poet sets the truth of sensation against philosophical reason, so in 'Prometheus' he sets the truth of facts against artistic idealism and political ideology. Mercader encounters reality as a fall from the sealed Eden of idea 'into the lime and contaminations / Of contingency; into hands, looks, time'. The atmospheric disturbances and the resulting distortions which accompany the radio reception of this performance of Scriabin's music, described in the opening stanza of 'Prometheus', are an image for 'contingency'—the unpredictable, incalculable variables of event and circumstance—and anticipate the imminent interferences of history:

> Summer thunder darkens, and its climbing
>   Cumulae, disowning our scale in the zenith,
> Electrify this music: the evening is falling apart.
>   Castles-in-air; on earth: green, livid fire.
> The radio simmers with static to the strains
>   Of this mock last-day of nature and of art.

The musical imitation is challenged by the reality: this doomsday, which in the Christian Apocalypse and romantic imagination envisages, after judgement, a re-creation of the world, is confronted by the bleaker Yeatsian vision of the Second Coming, in which 'things' merely 'fall apart', 'castles-in-air' succumbing to the 'green, livid fire' of the storm and the Revolution to come. The reality grows: not only atmospherics, but also 'Too many drowning voices cram this waveband', which, as the nightmare vision intensifies, in turn become 'the babel of continents'. Tomlinson has always distrusted, along with romantic self-regard, the ready recourse of romantic art to myth and symbol. Writing at a time when neo-romantic poetics were still influential, he began a poem of the 1950s, 'The Castle', with the gruff assurance that 'It is a real one—no more symbolic / Than you or I' (CP p. 43). All his references in 'Prometheus' to the tone-poem are founded on the conviction that with the 'myth of fire' Scriabin shields himself from the truths of time and history. His charge against romanticism casts myth and symbol as the culprits. In the passage which confronts the Promethean myth with the facts of the October Revolution, 'symbolled' (if the verb existed) would be the aural twin of the first word:

> Cymballed firesweeps. Prometheus came down
>   In more than orchestral flame and Kérensky fled
> Before it. The babel of continents gnaws now
>   And tears at the silk of those harmonies that seemed
> So dangerous once.

In human affairs the measure of truth must be a cool, moderate, compassionate sense of human possibility and limitation, a human scale of measurement. This is precisely what is lacking in the dreams of Scriabin and the schemes of Lenin. The composer's apocalyptic vision has its counterpart in its historical 'consequence': both are catastrophic; the gathering storm depicted in the first stanza, 'disowning our *scale*', is an image for both. Scriabin and Lenin are guilty of inattention or indifference to the facts, specifically the human facts, that make up the total situation.

> I set Lenin's face by yours—
> Yours, the fanatic ego of eccentricity against
> The systematic son of a schools inspector.

The contraposition assumes a basis of resemblance: a warp or partiality of view. The composer's 'eccentricity' is that his centre is the 'ego' rather than the world of his perception; eccentric because egocentric—the equivalence is mimed in the assonance that joins the initial syllables of the two words. Lenin's centre is his system, the theoretical map of reality that guides his actions. Each ignores the human dimension, the artist perhaps inadvertently, the politician by design: the man of unconstrained imagination forgets or spurns the finite terms that govern any human undertaking; the man of unlimited power uses human life as an instrument of his abstract purpose. Both believe that it is possible to wipe the slate clean and start afresh, though they have different conceptions of that pristine state. According to Scriabin's aesthetic programme,

> Each sense was to have been reborn
> Out of a storm of perfumes and light
> To a white world, an in-the-beginning—

a white world in which are fused and dissolved all the colours of history. But the unvisionary truth is that 'In the beginning, the strong man reigns'; a reminder to Trotsky, who should have known, but a lesson Lenin had no need to learn. 'In the beginning', properly, is part of the vocabulary of religious imagination; it goes behind history. Tomlinson, who has his own interest in pristineness, in 'primal being', remembers this usage when in his next collection, *Written on Water* (1972), he insists that 'The light of the mind is poorer / than beginning light' and that beginning light 'dispenses / imperial equality to everything / it touches, so that purple / becomes common wear' (CP p. 216). The phrase resonates with implications of a divine or quasi-divine power. The substitution of a human agency, vowed to perform the impossible, is necessarily the substitution of baffled violence for creation.

Both Scriabin and Lenin were inspired by the dream of an egalitarian Utopia; the 'transformation' by music and rite postulated by the composer, transposed into the key of politics, 'arrived' with prosaic punctuality at the Finland Station when Lenin returned from exile. The illusions of utopian thought are exposed in the poem by an appeal to the facts of history and the juxtaposition of idea and 'consequence'. One consequence was the policy of terror in post-revolutionary Russia, and this is part of what Tomlinson means by 'the daily prose'—produced, as it was, by 'a merciless patience'—of Lenin's dictatorship. But it is not the whole meaning. Ultimately, it is not idealism but density of numbers that brings about a sort of equality: 'Population drags the partitions down / And we are a single town of warring suburbs'. It proves to be sameness rather than equality, a oneness without distinction or distinctions; the other consequence, then, of Scriabin's and Blok's 'poetry', a large part of what comprises 'the daily prose' of Lenin's creation, was the featureless anonymity of life in a collectivist state. This is not the coherence of a civilization, which recognizes and fosters difference; not the city of man but an uncentred conglomerate, 'a single town of warring suburbs'. The two consequences, terror and homogenization, are given equal weight in the poem.

Notwithstanding the gulf between revolutionary and gradualist politics, there are parallels, which as the poem proceeds move into the foreground. England has been spared the terror, but collectivism is almost universal and the counterpart in post-war England of Lenin's clean slate is a uniform dreariness and cultural amnesia. The poet's reflections have all been prompted by the performance of the tone-poem *Prometheus*. When the music comes to an end, in the penultimate stanza, he addresses Scriabin and Blok: 'History treads out the music of your dreams / Through blood, and cannot close like this / In the perfection of anabasis. It stops'. The pronoun and the tense of the verb in that last sentence are elusive; and after cessation what follows, if not a world renewed? The music stops; history, this particular episode, must reach its conclusion; revolution, the translation of dreams into history, habitually runs and will run its course, but 'cannot close like this': the process of (musical and political) transformation will have a different outcome. The climax will be an anti-climax: 'The trees / Continue raining though the rain has ceased / In a cooled world of incessant codas'. The conflagration of revolution and the fiery poetry of utopianism are followed, in this 'cooled world', by the drab prose of uninflammable fact:

> Hard edges of the houses press
>   On the after-music senses, and refuse to burn,
> Where an ice-cream van circulates the estate
>   Playing Greensleeves, and at the city's
> Stale new frontier even ugliness
>   Rules with the cruel mercy of solidities.

That terror should be a logical consequence of idealism without 'gravity'—idealism in flight from, rather than grounded in, reality—indeed demonstrates the dangerous irresponsibility of such dreaming. It is not immediately so obvious that the numb life of a council estate, whose 'ugliness / Rules with the cruel mercy of solidities', offers the same kind of refutation. Hard-edged, solid, this is, after all, reality of a sort, if only the reality of a failed egalitarian ideal: it has its compensations, and is surely preferable to a world built, with 'a merciless patience', on the Leninist model. This, at any rate, is for Donald Davie the significance of the final stanza. From an investigation of the poem's 'political implications', in *Thomas Hardy and British Poetry* he draws a provocative conclusion: 'Tomlinson, when he thinks politically, lowers his sights and settles for second-best just as Hardy and Larkin do—but more impressively than either because so much more aware of, and pained by, the cost' (p. 79). His account of the poem is interesting and suggestive but his conclusion, I am convinced, misreads Tomlinson's intentions and misjudges the overall effect of the poem. Granted that it ends with the description of a 'second-best' reality, and let us also concede that there is no other image in the poem to represent a possible alternative to the murderous idealism of a Lenin: yet showing us the 'second-best' is not the same as settling for it. A 'cruel mercy' may be easier to bear than a 'merciless patience'—preferable on that score—but are we being asked to choose between them? The oxymorons, surely, make the phrases equal—the second merely a reversal of the first. The picture we are left with in the last stanza is of a dead or dying world; it has 'ceased', except for the 'incessant codas'. Codas are addenda to the natural end; the aftermath is a kind of posthumous life, no more desirable than the 'daily prose' of the new dispensation in Soviet Russia.

In 'Canal' (CP p. 64), the sinuous grace of swans 'unsteadying' the water is a living repudiation of the rigid verticals and horizontals of street and chimney on either bank: 'the discriminating / swans that seek / for something else' are an image for unrealized possibilities of life denied by the setting. Such an image, it is true, is missing from 'Prometheus'; but it would seem facile in a political poem. Nevertheless, if we read the tone properly, we feel the absence of that image as a potential presence. That the unlovely houses 'refuse to burn' is as much a reproach as evidence of suburban imperviousness to incendiary fanaticism. 'Refuse' is a gesture of surly stubbornness, disclosing a kind of grim complacency; it is the response of a dampened, unignitable imagination in a world cooled, as it were, by the banality of ice-cream and canned nostalgia. The 'hard edges' are resistant not only to the fires of revolutionary poetry but to poetry *per se*: unfired, unlit and, to invoke another favourite image, unawakened. We are reminded that Tomlinson has a positive use for images of heat and light—the examples are everywhere; he has a preoccupation, too, with thoughts of 'a white world, an in-the-beginning'. In 'Prometheus' the 'cooled world' contradicts the 'myth of fire': it is the disillusion that succeeds illusion, the death after fever. One need only recall the *complementarity* of 'coolness' and 'burning' in his praise of the two white cups reflected in the polished mahogany of the table-top in 'A Given Grace' (CP p. 115) to recognize—undeclared, but latent in the negatives of this passage—the passions and convictions, the possibilities, that stir Tomlinson's imagination:

> Though common ware,
> these rare reflections,
> coolness of brown
> so strengthens and refines
> the burning of their white,
> you would not wish
> them other than they are.

The 'given grace' of the cups includes the passionate, incandescent quality of the subject's response to the sight of them. It is a 'burning' that is enhanced and improved by its containment within the medium of cool, discriminating thought (a metaphorical addition contributed by the pun on 'reflections').

Scriabin's 'orchestral flame' and the apathy of 'a cooled world' are, we might say, the parodic analogues of passionate imaginative response and cool reflection in 'A Given Grace'. We are meant to notice the difference between Tomlinson's and the composer's aesthetic. The second stanza of 'Prometheus' begins: 'We have lived through apocalypse too long: / Scriabin's dinosaurs!' This is not only a statement about political idealisms and their consequences but also a poetic manifesto. (It is a minor association, but not irrelevant, that twenty years before this poem was written, a group of poets calling themselves the New Apocalypse issued *their* revolutionary manifesto.) Tomlinson is 'against extremity' (the title of a poem in the same collection as 'Prometheus'), against eccentric-egocentric politics and poetics of the clean slate. He has no sympathy for the poetry of apocalypse, but neither does he respond with a Larkinesque poetry of disappointed romanticism, a poetry of resigned ('second-best') realism. In the lines that set out Scriabin's aesthetic programme, quoted earlier, we glimpse—unstated but operative—the intermediary position of the poet. They give a grandiose, mythical rendering of Tomlinson's own Edenic vision. They gain in piquancy of interest when set alongside such poems in *The Way of a World* as 'Eden' and 'Adam'. The difference is that his artistic fiction is 'for the improvement of truth' (CP p. 33)—for reformation rather than transformation of sense experience. In Scriabin's transcendental dream, 'Each sense was to have been reborn'. Tomlinson's vision remains earthbound; 'reborn' would not be his word, but 'born' —quickened, awakened, brought to its sharpest natural alertness. His objective is to experience the world as it reveals itself to be to a trained keenness of perception—that is his Eden. Refusing to burn, suburban mentality denies itself the possibility of such an experience.

The political theme reappeared nine years and three collections later, in *The Shaft* (1978). Two poems in a section entitled 'Histories' are portraits, at dramatic moments of their lives, of Charlotte Corday, assassin of Marat, and Danton, characters who played decisive parts in the French Revolution. Studies of revolutionary idealism and ambition, they are of the same kind as 'Assassin' and 'Prometheus', bringing to bear upon the choices and actions of their protagonists the ethic of perception fashioned into an instrument of political judgement by the earlier poems; it is therefore appropriate to break the chronological sequence and consider the two groups of poems together.

While the characterization of Marat's assassin, in 'Charlotte Corday' (CP p. 275), is distinctly more sympathetic than that of Trotsky's, Mercader and the French girl are recognizably of the same type. An enemy of tyranny, the selfless heroine who gave her life for others, delivered a 'faultless blow', and at her trial and execution exhibited a 'composure none could fault', Charlotte Corday had, and is represented as having, 'impressive strength', yet in terms of the poem's (Yeatsian and Lawrencian) morality, her faults ran deep: she had made a voluntary contraction of her full humanity and subjected it to an idea. When she came to murder 'her tyrant' she saw not the man, who had 'a mildness in him, even', but a Julius Caesar: she was 'A girl whose reading made a heroine—/ Her book was Plutarch, her republic Rome'. Not only had she lopped her feelings to fit her 'whole / Intent' (a maimed wholeness) but, in her blinkered single-mindedness, she had no clear whole view of the political situation the outcome of which she had wished to determine—'How should she know / The Terror still to come?' Tomlinson points to the conflict in her between idealism (possession, in her case, by idea *and* ideal) and a full human responsiveness and awareness by means of one telling detail that recalls 'Assassin'. Unlike Mercader, she is that paradox, 'a daggered Virtue', 'innocence' directing a murderous 'intent', one who also ' "believed her death would *raise up* France" ' (my emphasis) but, as Mercader's prepared impassivity was not proof against the sound of Trotsky's rustling papers and his animal death-cry, so the poet conjectures that her 'composure' was almost breached by an unforeseen human incidental, the cry with which Catherine Marat at the trial 'broke off her testimony'.

'For Danton' (CP p. 278) passes the same judgement upon its protagonist. Danton has invested the whole of himself in the partial satisfaction of enjoying 'perfect power'—partial in that in the pursuit of political power he has forfeited the 'contrary perfection', the power of 'seeings, savourings'. Not only has he exchanged a general for a specialized humanity but, now that he realizes his mistake, he seeks the missed satisfaction of the senses with an equally unbalanced intensity:

> He fronts the parapet
> Drinking the present with unguarded sense:
>
> The stream comes on. Its music deafens him
> To other sounds, to past and future wrong.

The diagnosis of his moral sickness is inherent in the figure-ground composition of the picture: his egoism—he 'thinks that he and not the river advances'—is set against the background of moral 'consequence' acted out, metaphorically, in the inexorable progress of the river, an image for time and fate; the snatched pleasure of the river's 'music', as he listens from the bridge's parapet, is set against 'other sounds' of 'past and future wrong'.

The implied standard in 'For Danton' is that of a rounded life. A rounded life—one that has given equal expression to diverse inclinations, each subordinated to a sense of the whole of which it is part—is also a full life, which needs for the realization of its possibilities a certain length of years. Early in his life, before leaving for the metropolis, Danton had made a choice between powers and is pictured at the end of his career paying a last visit to his birthplace. He had 'Returned to this: to river, town and plain, / Walked in the fields and knew what power he'd lost', seeking, too late, to reverse that choice and give to his unnurtured senses now 'a life he has *no time* / To live' (my emphasis). Like Charlotte Corday he has sacrificed fullness of humanity to the partiality of a conceived ambition; his will to power requiring the death of a king, and her idealism the assassination of Marat, their motives lie closer together than from their respective histories and personalities we should suspect. In both, the sacrifice of fullness entails the cutting short of their lives, voluntary on her part, involuntary on his. Of Corday, as she approaches the scaffold, the poet asks: 'What unlived life would struggle up against / Death died in the possession of such strength?' 'Unlived life', in its double sense, is Danton's tragedy too: on the one hand, tracts of personality uncultivated, experience unexplored, on the other, the lost years needed for such cultivation and exploration. For the rounding of life, we infer, time is important; life needs to be lived out: without quantity, a certain number of years, a certain quality of life is hardly to be achieved; 'ripeness is all'.

Though thematically and morally the poems about revolution, Russian or French, are closely connected, in poetic mode—in the poet's relation to his subject-matter and the manner of conveying his judgements—the two sets are quite distinct. In the earlier poems the voice is combative, the verse vigorous, the language strong. They are direct indictments, attacking the premises of revolutionary thought and action—in 'Prometheus' by open confrontation, in 'Assassin' by the self-condemnation of dramatic monologue, where the tight-lipped ferocity of Mercader's own words, enacted in gripped, muscular rhythms, rebounds upon the speaker. In the later poems it is a voice of dispassionate contemplation, mingling judgement with empathy, that questions the thoughts of Danton and Corday. The attitude is ironic rather than antagonistic. The disparity between the foreground of the characters' partial, subjective readings of reality and the impersonal background of time's 'links of consequence', of history, which is the poet's knowledge of the whole story, is the gap which in these poems admits not accusation but irony; the gap, for instance, between Corday's intention, which was 'to have brought peace', by her 'faultless blow', and 'the Terror still to come', the future she could not foresee. The irony is at once cool and sympathetic. The guillotine,

> the blade
> Inherited the future now and she
> Entered a darkness where no irony
> Seeps through to move the pity of her shade:

this side of death irony and pity are companions, and what she can no longer feel (for Marat's widow) the poem, contemplating the words and actions of Charlotte Corday, provides.

* * * * *

Tomlinson's is a poetry of negotiations; it is full of metaphors that imply a negotiated association or partnership—pacts, truces, treaties, leases—a vocabulary which, used equally for historical and perceptual phenomena, implies the whole civilizing enterprise of man. Nature as 'the weight of a world', the force of facts, and history as consequence and contingency were of no interest to the revolutionaries; they thought and acted as if there were no world of objects independent of man or events outside his control. It was there to be appropriated, mastered and turned to human use. But the world must be acknowledged. Man must act in it and towards it as the swimmer in 'Swimming Chenango Lake' (CP p. 155) does, who, having studied the 'geometry of water', tells himself that 'he has looked long enough, and now / Body must recall the eye to its *dependence*' (my emphasis). Swimming is an act of negotiation: it is 'making a where / In water', but also it is 'a possession to be relinquished / Willingly at each stroke'; 'Human, he fronts it and, human, he draws back / From the interior cold'. Water—'the ungovernable wave' (CP p. 9)—is Tomlinson's recurrent image for what is 'beyond the clasp of words' (CP p. 311), cannot be fixed, possessed or contained, for what is out there to be negotiated with. In 'The Poet as Painter', recalling his childhood in the Potteries, a 'region of smoke and blackened houses, of slag-heaps, cindery ashes, pitheads, steelworks', he writes: 'The element that touched most persistently on the imagination there of the child as growing artist, was water', the water of the canals and the water that filled the marl pits. Water—sea, lake, river, pond—fascinates both the painter and the poet; for 'he who looks into water, and into the changing world of perception which water represents, looks into the heart of time'. It is at once 'the baptismal element', the promise of refreshment, and, 'full of metamorphoses', the instability of life. [6]

I left the chronological sequence in order to bring together and compare the treatments of revolutionary politics in *The Way of a World* (1969) and *The Shaft* (1978). But, returning to it, we come to *Written on Water* (1972). Although the title refers specifically to the subject-matter of no more than a handful of its poems, it has a general significance applicable to the whole collection—and much of Tomlinson's work. The title-poem—it is the last poem in a sequence of six 'Movements'—is a meditation on the meaning of water:

> 'Written on water', one might say
> Of each day's flux and lapse,
>   But to speak of water is to entertain the image
> Of its seamless momentum once again.

There is a mystery here: 'a music of constancy' murmurs under 'its liquid friction / Of small sounds'. It is 'hard to read / The life lines of erratic water', but the 'multiplicity' of sounds even in a 'still pool' is 'a speech behind speech'; we return to it 'as though to clarify ourselves / Against its depth, its silence'. Tomlinson has perhaps an additional reason for choosing this title for the whole collection: it describes the paradox of art, which endeavours to give a kind of permanence to the impermanent.

I have selected four poems from *Written on Water* to illustrate the part played by negotiations in Tomlinson's thinking. The first two, 'Rower' and 'Mackinnon's Boat', are seascapes; 'The Compact: at Volterra' and 'Machiavelli in Exile' take the theme into other scenes and times.

'Rower' (CP p. 203) begins with a languid scene—a sheltered bay at a time of slack tide, only stirred into life by the sudden appearance of the rower.

> A plotless tale: the passing hours
>   Bring in a day that's nebulous. Glazes of moist pearl
> Mute back the full blaze of a sea,
>   Drifting continually where a slack tide
> Has released the waters.

A scene without focus—until the rower breaks into the frame:

> Already his world
> Is sliding by him. Backwards
> He enters it, eyes searching the past
> Before them: that shape that crowns the cliff,
> A sole, white plane, draws tight his gaze—
> A house, bereft so it seems of time
> By its place of vantage, high
> Over cleft and crack.

Plotting (in one sense) the space between shore, cliff and boat, and (in another sense) the otherwise eventless stretch of time, he introduces clarity of purpose and direction into an aimless, 'nebulous' day, turns 'a plotless tale' into geometry and narrative. The rower's imposition of a plot, a human sense of purpose, upon 'that want of purpose / In sky and water', corresponds to the poet's endeavour in this and all his poems, as he describes it in 'The Poet as Painter', to catch the 'fleeting freshness' of sense experience 'and unite it to a stable form'.[7] Man as artist, creator of meanings, does not simply suffer 'the passing hours', but makes time pass: like the rower he plots life's day, taking his bearings on the past and aiming for the future, cutting a track between memory and possibility. If the rower's exertions are directed to a 'consummation of the will', then human will and effort stand here in bold contrast to the random motions of the released waters.

It appears that nature and man represent the contrary poles of aimless inactivity and active purpose. Negotiation, however, is a two-way process. In reality the rower's exertions establish a relation-in-tension with the element in which they are applied, in opposition to and collaboration with the resistant non-human world. The rower 'cuts athwart' the 'ripple' out in the bay, but at the same time his oars make a 'liquid counterpulse' to 'the pull and beat' of the sea. The aim is to complete the half-circle of the bay with the reverse half-circle of the boat's track, giving the natural world its human complement. Moreover, nature's motions are not all random:

> It seems nothing will occur here until
> The tide returns, ferrying to the shore its freshness,

> Beating and breaking only to remake itself
> The instant the advancing line goes under.

Conversely, in the life of man rest is the natural end (and rebeginning) of work: 'satisfaction gathers to surfeit, strain / To ease'. The rower's alternation of activity and suspended activity reproduces the natural rhythm of tide and slack tide.

The poem salutes human will but indicates its subordination to the larger pattern of nature: man and nature pursue different if complementary purposes, but when, 'pleased by his exertions', the rower 'abandons them / Riding against rested oars', he is '*subdued* / For the moment to that want of purpose' (my emphasis) in the natural scene. The appearance of a privileged timelessness presented by that landmark of the past, by which the rower plots his course, is shown for the illusion it is when confronted with the reality of tide (and time) mirrored in the closing lines:

> Out of the coherent chaos of a morning that refuses
> To declare itself, it comes plunging in
> Expunging the track of his geometries.

The man, facing expectantly in 'the direction the tide will take', is prospectively content to be 'subdued'; the poet, by his appreciative participation in the tide's virtual self-declaration, enacts his own 'consent to time'.[8] Nature has pattern and even purpose (since 'want of purpose' distinguishes the inactivity specifically of a *slack* tide), though it obliterates human patterns and is oblivious to human purpose. It has no plot, no line of narrative with beginning, middle and end: its pattern is cyclic, a perpetual making, unmaking and remaking, its purpose is renewal, refreshment. Only to the eye of man is this 'forenoon all melting *redundancies*'; it seems to him aimless and meaningless only because nature on this 'nebulous', 'drifting' morning, the nature of light and movement, 'refuses to declare itself'. At a time when to the human observer it is no more than 'a plotless tale', the 'full blaze' of light is muted, the tidal rhythm is unapparent. A seeming 'chaos', in fact nature, as it were reading an invisible score, is a 'coherent' whole. The concealed fullness at the beginning of the poem is answered by the revealed wholeness in its conclusion.

If we were to compare Tomlinson with Wordsworth, we should have to say that Tomlinson's is a poetry of will and purpose rather than of 'wise passiveness'. If we compare Tomlinson with himself, however, then there are distinctions to be made—between, for instance, the earlier and the later poems. *American Scenes* (1966) was in this respect a turning-point in his career. The poem that opens the collection, 'Face and Image' (CP p. 107), sounded one new note, which has since become a keynote, in Tomlinson's poetry. There is in the nature of things, the poem argues, a disparity between what is perceived and the perception of it, between face and image; but, he concludes,

> To love
> is to see,
> to *let be*
> this disparateness
> and to live within
> the unrestricted boundary between. (my emphasis)

Since that poem, in his various treatments of man in the world the compulsion to master experience has notably diminished. In the relation of human will to what it cannot govern, the mood is never possessive and is frequently one of *letting be* what must be. The intention is neither protest nor elegy but, as in that stanza from 'Face and Image', an affirmative realism; the mood is relaxed but not lax.

'Mackinnon's Boat' (CP p. 199) details the activities of a fisherman's day. There are two fishermen, Mackinnon and Macaskill, and, stretched in the prow, a dog. The polarities of the human and the non-human are more strongly marked and demonstrated more thoroughly than in 'Rower'. The theme of negotiation is treated with a corresponding directness. The two environments, land and sea-world, are mutually repellent: the 'flailing / Seashapes pincered to the baits' die in the air, 'their breath all at once grown rare / In an atmosphere they had not known existed'; the dog, a solipsistic landlubber, 'stays / Curled round on himself: his world / Ignores this waste of the in-between, / Air and rock'. By their work, however, the fishermen are made experts of 'the in-between', as it were professional intermediaries between human and non-human realities. The poem highlights on the one hand the encounter, the transaction, and on the other the absolute discreteness of the two realities and in particular the impenetrable otherness, inconceivable to the human mind, of the sea-world. This sea gives back not even a ragged, twisted *image* of the boat: 'Black, today / The waters will have nothing to do with the shaping / Or unshaping of human things ... The visible sea / Remains a sullen frontier to / Its *unimaginable* fathoms' (my emphasis). The general theme is familiar but the poem has taken on new subject-matter. Describing not only the sea and the light but also the journey out to the nets, the hauling in of the catch, the ruthless disentangling of unwanted 'Crabs, urchins, dogfish, and star', and the rhythms of each task, the poem is about 'the dealings' of man with this 'underworld' and the meaning of physical labour. The conception of not-self is extended to include, along with the otherness of water and its creatures, the impersonal self that engages physically with its environment and makes its livelihood by its efforts. In their work the fishermen are anonymous, their anonymity corresponding to, and joining while it lasts, a reality that bears no human imprint. 'Making a time / Where no day has a name, the smells / Of diesel, salt, and tobacco mingle': human purpose and pleasure, we might say, mingle, in a temporary, evanescent blend of smells, with the salt that tastes of the non-human element and of oblivion, that 'at last must outsavour name and time / In the alternation of the forgetful waters'. Serving a purpose beyond themselves, they are—like the separate stages in their rapid undoing, retying and new-baiting of the traps (and like a Tomlinson poem)—'The disparate links of [a] concerted action'. The self-annulment of physical labour is also a release from self into a common human world. When 'Their anonymity, for a spell, / Is at an end', each one is 'Free to be himself once more / Sharing the rest that comes of labour', their cooperation in the impersonal task both reinvigorating their individual freedoms and renewing the human bond. The *wholeness* of this human-inhuman world is presented as an interdependence of independent realities. The *wholesomeness* of living 'within / the unrestricted boundary between' (to revert to the wording of 'Face and Image' [CP p. 107]) consists in the 'alternation', reproducing the ebb and flow of 'the forgetful waters', of action and inaction, of journeying out from self, the human domain, and returning, refreshed, renewed, to one's selfhood, one's humanity.

The motif of negotiation—the endless process of adjustments and adaptations that constitutes man's relation, his secular, unfinalized covenant, with the world of space and time—finds expression in several other poems collected in 'Written on Water'. In 'The Compact: at Volterra' (CP p. 206) and 'Machiavelli in Exile' (CP p. 214) the imagery is exemplary rather than figurative; historical instances take over from the metaphor of water.

Volterra is built on a small plateau, the steep sides of which are subject to landslips. 'There is a compact / to undo the spot'—and undermine literally the enterprise of civilization—

>   between the unhurried sun
> Edging beyond this scene, and the moon,
>   Risen already, that has stained
> Through with its pallor the remaining light.

Sun and moon divide time between them, but in the period of transition when they are both visible they can be seen, as they are pictured here, to join in the 'compact' of mortality. At the turn of the day sunlight surrenders the world to moonlight, 'the night's derisions' succeed 'the day's delights':

> Unreal, that clarity of lips and wrinkles
> Where shadow investigates each fold,
>   Scaling the cliff to the silhouetted stronghold.

Daily existence is a matter of negotiation (though the word is not used) between the sovereign natural powers of day and night and man, impelled by his 'unreasoned care' for the earth that sustains him and for the work of his hands to till the land and plant vines and 'repair' the daily damage. There is 'this tale of unshorable earth' and there is the story of human endeavour and endurance; the slow dying of the soil contested by man's immemorial cultivation of it: 'Refusing to give ground before they must, / They pit their patience against the dust's vacuity'.

'The Compact: at Volterra' and 'Machiavelli in Exile' are, I indicated, historical instances of what Tomlinson means by negotiation. It would give a more accurate impression of 'The Compact', however, if I said that the perspective *includes* the known history of the place but stretches back through an unrecorded human past into the pre-human phase of our geological era, the 'cenozoic skeleton' of which has been exposed at Volterra by ages of erosion. This length of perspective is essential to its theme:

> The crack in the stone, the black filament
> > Reaching into the rockface unmasks
> More history than Etruria or Rome
> > Bequeathed this place.

Each geological flaw and fault 'unmasks' the full scope and reality of time—'unmasks', therefore, the historical illusion of human dominion. For the ancient 'ramparted town' of Volterra, this cliff-top 'stronghold' perched on the edge of an 'abyss', pays its 'daily / Tribute' of parched soil, 'powdering away', 'trickling down', not to the successive imperial powers, but to the 'vacuity' waiting 'at the town brink' to receive its final 'downfall'. The burden of the first four stanzas is the infirmity of its foundations and the uselessness against the forces of nature of its fortifications. Life in time is as shifting and unstable as water.

No poem of Tomlinson's ends here, however: we must meet time's gifts and risks—as 'In the Fullness of Time' (CP p. 163) insists, we greet the future with 'our consent to time', and the last two stanzas of 'The Compact' exemplify and analyse, in the farmers' specific settlement with circumstance, the spirit of such a consent. Despite incessant 'rumours of downfall', 'the cicadas / Chafe on', displaying the same heedless persistence as the human inhabitants when they 'Till up to the drop that which they stand to lose'; and the grapevine that 'entwines the pergola / Gripping beyond itself' is an image of the vinegrower's own helpless dependence on forces outside his control but necessary trust in a nature that may yet betray him. There is an element of blind faith in this 'consent to time', but that is not to say recklessness. It is represented as a dogged 'patience' ('They pit their patience against the dust's vacuity'), infused with a kind of love; there are sexual overtones in the picture of 'Their terraces, fondling the soil together' but the final word for it is 'care'. 'Care' is care felt and care taken; the word combines the ideas of love and patience:

> as if
> Unreasoned care were its own and our
> Sufficient reason, to repair the night's derisions,
>   Repay the day's delight, here where the pebbles
> Of half-ripe grapes abide their season,
>   Their fostering leaves outlined by unminding sky.

'Unreasoned care'—care that precedes reasoning and is motivated by a deeper 'reason'—is an imperative more unquestionable than the obligation to weigh the odds and count the cost. It gives rise to opposite but complementary responses to the terms of existence: resistance with practical measures, and something like piety, the repayment of a debt of gratitude for what life has bountifully provided. 'Consent to time', we might say, combines the notions of assent and dissent; it leaves room, precisely, for negotiation. When, in summary, Tomlinson writes, 'all live / At a truce, refuted, terracing', the agreed or accepted truce between man and nature is a relation-in-tension rather than a compromise: human purpose 'refuted' by 'the incursion of the slow abyss', yet continuing in its cultivation, human 'terracing', of the hillside, to assert itself against the 'unminding' (unthinking, unfeeling, *un*fostering) sky.

In 'Machiavelli in Exile', the former defence secretary and plenipotentiary for the Florentine republic—dismissed from office, imprisoned and tortured when the Medicis returned—is portrayed in his final years of banishment to his country estate at San Casciano, where, debarred from active politics, he wrote his chief works of political theory, notably *The Prince*. This, his best-known work, in which the 'ideal' ruler depicted is seemingly modelled on Cesare Borgia, is the only one referred to directly in the poem. Like the rural portraits in *A Peopled Landscape*, this poem is a eulogy; unlike them, however, and like 'Assassin', it is a political portrait. Whereas those are embedded in English cultural history and the unnamed characters, the childless 'Farmer's Wife: at Fostons Ash' (CP p. 70) and the widow addressed in 'Return to Hinton' (CP p. 59), are, as embodiments of a traditional rural civilization in decline, submerged in their representative functions, Mercader and Machiavelli are actors on the public stage. What is dramatized in their stories is the individual's relation not so much to his historical setting as to his political ideology: their convictions, hopes, choices and actions have a significance not tied to a particular time and place.

'Machiavelli in Exile' offers another historical instance of man negotiating a place for himself in the world of space and time and securing some room for manoeuvre among its determining forces. There is the same balance here as in 'The Compact: at Volterra' between human assertion and unprotesting submission to the terms of existence, but the conditioning forces are different. In my account of 'The Compact' I referred to the farmers' settlement with circumstance, the chances of geography and geology that governed the lives of the town's inhabitants: Machiavelli's fate is the result of what both 'chance and character have brought him to'. Chance, moreover, is not in this case represented by the accident of locality but by the actions of others that have placed him there, while character is a factor that plays no part in 'The Compact'; 'character' refers to the former statesman's preferences and choices and their consequences. He was betrayed by his enemies but he is equally 'self-betrayed': the two causes are intricately interwoven and in combination have determined his present condition.

The poem contains a dialectic of freedom and necessity.

> A man is watching down the sun. All day,
> Exploring the stone sinew of the hills,
> For his every predilection it has asked
> A Roman reason of him. And he has tried
> To give one, tied to a dwindling patrimony
> And the pain of exile.

'Watching down' figures more than detached observation: it is as if the man is willing the sun to do what the sun in any case will and must do;

it describes an act of participation, even identification. It is the sun that explores, but on first reading that line we take it to be the man, and in the next line 'his' delays a little longer our discovery of the true subject in 'it'; the effect of making us wait for the main clause is a temporary uncertainty that invites us to identify exploring sun with watching man. Later, in the fourth stanza, the poem speaks in overt metaphor of 'the sun that lit his mind'. The eye, following the sun's path, moving with the same searching motion as the sun's, sees what it sees, knows what it knows; man and sun are, as it were, of the same mind. What the light reveals and the mind learns is 'the stone sinew', the hard binding substance, of life. Every mere partiality, subjective predisposition to favour certain attitudes and courses, must be brought to the test of present fact. The sun of strict truth has also demanded (this asking is imperative) that 'every predilection' justify itself by reference to the public interest, especially the need of strong, decisive government. Machiavelli, who is represented as one who has met this demand for 'a Roman reason', is later enrolled among 'that courtly ancient company / Of men whose reasons may be asked'. In 'watching down the sun', an act signifying vigilance rather than resignation, and in his readiness to give reason and take responsibility for his choices, the man is at the same time identifying himself with the dictates of necessity and exercising his freedom. 'Tied' necessity rhymes with and complements its opposite, 'tried', the exercise of free will.

The two parts of Machiavelli's life, as they are presented in the poem, were of a piece. As a public servant of the republic, we know by inference from the style and content of the exile's thoughts, he lived by certain convictions; banished for acting upon them, discredited, without political influence, in circumstances of limited external freedom, yet he remains true to those convictions. His practice was consistent with his theory: giving priority to reasons of state, his policies and actions were in accordance with that belief; he was never passive in the midst of events. Excluded from the political arena, he is still not passive: his acquiescence in his fate is depicted, paradoxically, as an expression of will. The word used to describe the way he takes his fate is 'choose': if it is to spend his remaining days in the society of 'Such men as endure history and not those / Who make it', then he chooses—the verb is active—because, of necessity, he 'must choose' such men, his provincial neighbours, for 'his day's companions'. The politician made decisions and instigated actions; no longer free to act directly, the writer, declaring and exercising an internal freedom, acts with words, indirectly, to influence the future.

> The sun that lit his mind now lights the page
> At which he reads and words, hard-won, assuage
> What chance and character have brought him to.

Those three syllables—'words, hard-won'—effortful in sound as in sense, enact the continuity between present words and past deeds, the writing and the life: 'hard-won' testifies at once to literary labour and moral stamina; in effect they are a single identity, for, it says, such words have been lived, are the reward and expression of a life-time's single-minded tenacity of will. The politician and the writer are the same man. Though Machiavelli is powerless himself, 'Borgia shall be praised' by him for using power (for he 'moved and, moving, saved by sudden action'), and the Florentines, who 'despite their words' put factional interests before the interests of state, must be condemned for obstructing action. 'Despite their words': this is a key phrase. Borgia moved swiftly and thus *saved* by action: the Florentines were indecisive and, failing to act in unity against their foreign enemies, endangered the republic; they failed to act and, furthermore, their deeds were at variance with their words. Not only, we are to assume, did Machiavelli, when he held public office, practise what he preached, but the writer's words, in the aftermath of his political career, are the direct outcome and true reflection of the convictions that informed his policies.

'What chance and character have brought him to' has not been enough to silence him. In the 'book' of his last years there is 'defeat' and there is 'victory'.

> Adversity puts his iron pen in hand,
> First torture, then neglect bringing to bear
> The style and vigilance which may perfect
> A prince...

Adversity and neglect having completed his own education, the resulting 'style and vigilance' (a phrase which, like 'hard-won', does not distinguish between the life and the work) may do the same for Machiavelli's ideal ruler. Adversity and neglect are the cards that life has dealt him; he must make do with what he has. This is not fatalism or even stoicism but the willingness to employ his freedom as his conditions permit. The 'given' is always the body of acted intention; exile and political impotence are from one point of view privations, but they are also none the less the concrete form of Machiavelli's freedom. This distinction rests on the broad base of other distinctions common in Tomlinson, between the actual and the possible, memory and imagination, what is and what might be. Outwardly a prisoner of circumstance but inwardly free, 'Released from tedium, poverty, and threat', the exile's freedom is 'tempered by / The memory of its opposite'. This is the memory of particular events, but the statement also implies a general truth. The hopes that are generated by this knowledge of inner freedom must be accompanied by a recognition of constraints upon that freedom, 'else too soon / Hopes are a mob that wrangle for the moon' (like those of the revolutionary idealists, in 'Prometheus' [CP p. 156], whose hopes were given musical expression by Scriabin's 'mob of instruments'). Machiavelli is admired in this poem for living this recognition without abandoning his own ideals. His acquiescence in his fate carries a note of challenge, an 'amen' mixed, so to speak, with a 'nevertheless'; he makes his indictment of the Florentines, accepts and defies his punishment, all in the same breath:

> The work of France and Spain others begin—
> Let him who says so exercise his powers
> With dice and backgammon at a country inn.

The limits on action are acknowledged, but this is none the less to live, as his 'day's companions' do not live, 'in the light of possibility'. They 'quarrel at [and with] their cards' but do not act: he accepts the hand that fate has dealt him without complaint and acts. 'Their fate is bound by their own sleeping wills'; whereas they 'endure history', he is resolved to maintain his position among 'those / Who make it'.

'The light of possibility', Tomlinson's characteristic phrase, is associated by him with Petrarch's *grazie divine*; the words occur in a line of verse misquoted by Machiavelli in a letter and copied from that source by Tomlinson—*Tarde non furon mai grazie divine* (Divine graces were never late). His companions are 'gods who do not know they're gods'; allowing their wills to become inactive and to atrophy, they have forfeited that part of divinity in them: he, on the other hand, tells his correspondent that he puts his trust in *grazie divine*. How literal, or orthodox, was Machiavelli's understanding of the words we do not know, and Tomlinson is not inviting us to speculate. All we do know is that 'the light of possibility' is 'the sun that lit his mind' (which is also the sun of necessity in the poem's first line), and that this is an image for the divinity in man, but that it is as much a matter of human will as of openness to the operations of grace. Paganism, humanist pride and at least the terms of Christian doctrine blend in the poem's creation of its concept of freedom within necessity, victory in defeat.

* * * * *

The Way In and Other Poems (1974) will provide the concluding instances for this survey of Tomlinson's manscapes. 'Manscapes', as I explained in the opening paragraph of Chapter 3, is a term adapted from Tomlinson and used by me as a convenient label for all those poems which are direct treatments of human experience. Tomlinson himself, however, restricted its application to a group of poems about the urban universe, published in *The Way In and Other Poems* (1974), their setting—with a few exceptions—his home town Stoke and generally the industrialized region of the West Midlands. In a sense, then, my survey of Tomlinson's 'human' poems ends where it began. For in this collection a missing factor, the poet's early environment, is supplied; the result, for the reader as for the poet, is a refocusing of his poetic material. As an introduction to the industrialized 'manscapes' of *The Way In*, it will be necessary, therefore, to review the major themes of these two chapters.

Civilization, in Tomlinson's conception, sampled in the previous chapter, lacks health if it is not nature-centred; it presumes a negotiated alliance between the human and the non-human. He finds evidence of what he calls 'civility' among the aboriginal peoples of the American Southwest, in the two faces of the English rural tradition, that of the landowning class at Stowey and of the yeoman class at Hinton, and in Vermeer's images of bourgeois Delft—where we are 'the guests of objects' and *'as in a landscape*, / All that is human here stands clarified / By all that accompanies and bounds' (CP p. 32; my emphasis). Negotiation, I have suggested in the present chapter, is invariably, for him, a manifestation of that civility, the civilizing spirit—exemplified as much in the daily work of the fishermen, those intermediaries between man-world and sea-world, and the Volterran compact with geology, as in Machiavelli's accommodation with political circumstance in the human world. Human nature is fully human only when it is rooted in physical nature. The modern city that banishes the natural world by the same act depletes the humanity of its citizens: it is at once a denaturing of the outer and the inner life. Those who, like John Maydew, give their evenings to the cultivation of their allotments disclose the lingering traces of 'the ineradicable peasant in the dispossessed / and half-tamed Englishman' (CP p. 66). This city is our common condition; its streets are 'the meagre / Streets of our dispossession' (CP p. 159), our exile not from a mythical Garden but from a real nature, a possible Eden. The revolutionary idealists are enemies not merely of an established order but of civilization *per se* when they seek, as Mercader sought, to reduce the whole phenomenal world—the eye's 'recognitions', the ear's 'discrimination'—to 'one placeless cell' (CP pp. 161–62). For place is 'the self's *unnameable* and shaping home' (CP p. 121), and Trotsky's assassin whose mind is sealed in an Eden of idea, pledged to perform the impossible, who acts in the *name* of 'history', is judged by the geography of being: 'the ground a pressure / Telling me *where* it is I stand' (CP p. 162). The human world, like the natural world, is a 'fortuitous / Full variety'. Civilization, the city of man as a human centre, takes into account, and fosters, difference: but, as the mind-set of Mercader is 'one placeless cell', so 'the daily prose' of Lenin's utopianism, which is also the world we live in, is 'a single town of warring suburbs' (CP pp. 156–57)—an uncentred, fractured, frictional sameness.

In 'John Maydew' Tomlinson portrayed his father and the industrial machine that had made him an embittered prisoner of an unnatural world. Twenty years later, in 'Poem for My Father' (CP p. 367), he associates himself with his father's 'sense of an exile'. In his father's life he identifies, and reads as a warning, the forces that shaped his own early life—and, ultimately, the lives of all of us. And yet the *poet* was fortunate to have lived his formative years close to the generative source, to have breathed its 'familiar, sedimented air' (CP p. 248), felt the intimate warmth of the factory wall as a 'black, pulsating ... comforting brick beast', the mines underneath threatening to undermine the houses of 'Gladstone Street'. Without the pressure of this lived history he would not have needed to imagine its contrary, his natural Edens, with such exactness and intensity. This is the recognition that accompanies his poetic re-immersion in the 'manscapes' of his youth. Tomlinson's artistic roots are in the world of natural phenomena, but his personal roots were in the 'ravaged counties' (CP p. 247) of the West Midlands: this is what we learn, for the first time, from the poems of *The Way In*. The late return to the scenes of his youth recorded here is a return, so to speak, from the natural landscapes he has chosen for his adult life, and the created habitat of his poetry, to the violated landscapes of his personal beginnings. Past memories and present impressions speak to him 'of all that seasoned and imprisoned' (CP p. 248) the person and the artist in this environment; it is evident from the resulting poems, exploring as they do the connection between the exterior-interior world of the child and schoolboy and the mental terrain of the subsequent poetry, that this encounter of past and present has generated a different understanding of the poet he has become.

Nature is confronted with its man-made substitute in these poems, but the relation discovered in the imagery is not merely one of opposition: these 'manscapes' appear as grotesque, parodic reflections of the natural world. The 'heights and distances' (CP p. 257) mentioned elsewhere in this collection, prospects and perspectives that are a recurrent feature and preoccupation of Tomlinson's poetry, are absent from these scenes; the distances and colours of 'light and air' have vanished behind 'a monotone fume, a bloom of grey': yet hills and valleys have their ghastly counterparts in the pits and slag-heaps of this 'landscape of disembowellings, underworlds / Unearthed among the clay' (CP p. 248), and equally in the inhuman 'towers' of the new structures, the 'mannerless high-risers' (CP p. 241) of the modern city. In two of the poems the natural world makes a brief, dispirited appearance to adumbrate a comparison. 'By ash-tips ... the hills / Swell up and free of it to where ... / The cows stand steaming in an acrid wind': this is 'At Stoke' (CP p. 243) and these are the constituents of the 'single landscape' in which he lived as a boy and which has lived ever since in the imagination of the man. The comparison is most poignant in 'The Tree' (CP p. 247), in the picture of a child, under 'a colourless damp sky', shovelling away snow from a city pavement, who

> knows nothing of the pattern
> his bent back lifts
> above his own reflection:
> it climbs the street-lamp's stem
> and cross-bar, branching
> to take in all the lines
> from gutter, gable, slates
> and chimney-crowns to the high
> pillar of a mill chimney.

For the 'pattern' ascending, branching upwards, grows out of him like a tree:

> there in the topmost air
> and eyrie rears that tree
> his bending sends up
> from a treeless street.

In this 'grey-black' (CP p. 243) landscape and 'sedimented air' (CP p. 248) hills are begrudged their cramped liberty; skies are 'a colourless damp' or else 'the milky sky of a dragging afternoon' (CP p. 243) that seems more like the absence of sky; horizons 'block ...

back' that other world of 'water, light and air' (CP p. 248). Hill, sky, horizon, and the tree that soars only in the visionary eye of the observer are images of possibility against which the failures of vision revealed equally in man's destructions and his creations are measured.

In these poems Tomlinson reflects upon the relation between the Edens of his nature poems and the 'manscapes' of his origins. I have already quoted phrases from 'Hokusai on the Trent' (CP p. 243). In the opening lines the poet considers—only, later, to reject—the notion that 'This milky sky of a dragging afternoon' over the River Trent is 'a painter's sky', conveying a painter's 'vision of a lack, / A thwarted possibility that broods / On the meanness and exclusion'. It is a relation of opposition: what belongs to the elemental world is excluded by these scenes. Not merely a thwarting but a mockery of possibility, opposition is expressed, I have suggested, in what seems a style of cynical parody. The poem quickly abandons the fancy of 'a painter's sky' for the taste of reality, and asks: 'what painting could taste of such dragging afternoons / Whose tints are tainted, whose Fujiyamas slag?'

The meaning of this sky is the meaning of the 'single landscape', 'a land / Too handled to be primary', described in 'At Stoke' (CP p. 243), a landscape both actual and mental—one that formed the horizon of his early life and one that has been retained by memory to become the setting for, and a foil to, his experience of all subsequent (exterior-interior) landscapes: 'Every tone / And turn [picture and poem—the 'turn' of verse] have had for their ground / These beginnings in grey-black'. He has discovered that the 'vision of a lack', the meaning of that 'single landscape', is the 'ground'—because 'the first in feeling'— of his total mental gestalt; not 'primary' in the sense of pristine but, since 'first in feeling' for the man, the 'foundation' in personal history of the artist's outlook. Its importance is not simply historical, however, not simply that it has made an indelible impression on the poet's imagination: 'This place, the first to seize on my heart and eye, / Has been their *hornbook* and their history' (my emphasis). 'The years return' the poet (in 'The Marl Pits'; CP p. 248) 'To tell of all that seasoned and imprisoned', the surprising word being 'seasoned': for, though indeed the place starved the senses of their proper food, the word tells us that it also fortified the growing artist's will and ripened something in him; as 'hornbook', therefore, it taught him the rudiments of what 'heart and eye' were missing and fostered in him the desire to know and possess this contrary, this refutation, of his daily experience, an elsewhere of the imagination.

The 'patched battlefield' of Stoke where nature is but an irruption of 'discouraged greennesses' among ash-tips and cinders, though the poet 'thought it once / Too desolate, diminished and too tame / To be the foundation for anything', was nevertheless 'the first to seize on [his] heart and eye' (CP p. 243); the poet's 'vision of a lack, / A thwarted possibility' in the 'milky sky of a dragging afternoon' (CP p. 243) over the Trent is a vision of something that not merely the eye but the whole being needs and is denied. The disfigurement of the landscape, in 'At Stoke', and the lethargy of 'dragging afternoons', in 'Hokusai on the Trent', are at the same time an oppression of the spirit and an offence to the eye; they do violence both to outer and inner nature, the physical world and the psyche. What is implied in these two poems is a stated theme in 'The Marl Pits' (CP p. 248). The close streets and smoke-hazed sky of Stoke 'blocked ... back' the very 'water, light and air' that were to become recurrent presences and indispensable components of his poetic world; diminishing space, the exterior image of possibility, and narrowing the natural horizons of vision and feeling, they accordingly occluded too the interior prospect of human satisfactions in all their possible fullness of realization. These 'manscapes' substituted for the 'water, light and air' of nature 'marl pits', a 'bloom of grey', a 'sedimented air'; correspondingly, free enjoyment of the elemental—water, light, air—gave way to a 'stoic lethargy' that 'seemed the one reply / To horizons and to streets that blocked them back'—a human 'air', an attitude, clogged with inertia. The violence we do to the world about us is at the same time a violence done to ourselves, they are one and the same thing: the need *for* the natural is the need *of* the natural, for a cleansed vision, wider horizons, a fuller humanity.

The awareness of this contrary possibility is related specifically, in 'The Marl Pits', to the origin and direction of Tomlinson's poetic impulse. Prisoner of an almost natureless world, whose citizens responded and could only respond to their privation with the 'stoic lethargy' of a deadened sense and unawakened feeling, he recalls: 'It was a *language* of water, light and air / I sought—to speak myself free' (my emphasis) of such an existence. The water that seeped up from underground to fill the pits 'In slow reclaimings, shimmers, balancings' was, like his poetry, 'a second nature' (the natural world returning from exile and, as it were, Adam of the fallen city given a second chance), affording glimpses of, and the incentive to restore, a primal perfection: 'As if kindling Eden rescinded its own loss / And words and water came of the same source'. In seeking a way out of 'the horizons and streets' of Stoke and a way into the full reality of space, his quest was for a language of both outer and inner freedom: poetry, for him, was to be a welling-up of suppressed nature to fill the hollows left by man's gougings of the earth, a nature that the 'eye' sees and the 'heart' feels.

The major poem in this group is the title-poem of the collection. The poems are set principally in the industrial Midlands but the townscape in 'The Way In' (CP p. 241) is not the Stoke of his youth: it is Bristol, viewed from the car in which he is making his 'way in' to the University from his home in the Gloucestershire countryside. The poet's 'vision of a lack' is imaged here entirely in human terms: the poem describes the reconstruction of the city undertaken in the 1960s and 1970s but presents it as the destruction of 'civility', the social form of Eden. As elsewhere in post-war Britain, the demolition of old working-class neighbourhoods and their replacement with highrise buildings changed the 'face' of Bristol at a bewildering speed and with brutal thoroughness.

> I thought I knew this place, this face
>   A little worn, a little homely.
> But the look that shadows softened
>   And the light could grace, keeps flowing away from me
> In daily change; its features, rendered down,
>   Collapse expressionless, and the entire town
>
> Sways in the fume of the pyre. Even the new
>   And mannerless high risers tilt and wobble

> Behind the deformations of acrid heat—
> A century's lath and rafters.

Tomlinson does not pretend that the doomed streets of mid-Victorian houses have retained, a century later, anything but the dimmest, stalest memories of civility; but the 'place' has a 'face' still and that 'face' is not 'expressionless', and the expression it wears has acquired with time and daily familiarity all the associations of home, the home that is a retiring, modest presence, at once hidden and visible, in its 'homely' features. The signs of civility are, however faded, recognizable, whereas the 'mannerless high risers', lacking a manifested human identity, have not yet joined the human world; Tomlinson can only wonder with a mild scepticism, therefore, whether the occupants of 'the new blocks'—'those who have climbed into their towers'—'will find that civility I can only miss'. The suggestion of privileged aloofness and insulation in the word 'towers' would seem to rule out that possibility even as the thought is tentatively entertained.

The erasure of the old—the mushrooming of the new—has created a population of virtual refugees, 'A race in transit, a nomad hierarchy', a condition of rootlessness. Tomlinson notes a couple gleaning the ruins, as if it were 'Their punishment to number every hair / Of what remains'. The woman, 'a sexagenarian Eve', survivor of a lost hope, a lost paradise, is an image of what even exceeds loss, the total amnesia of lack. The tone is unsentimental but not—a possible misreading—contemptuous of the couple: they have a representative role as sufferers of a general condition. 'The place had failed them anyhow'; the pair are attached to what has gone but cannot recall why, nor can they find what they have forgotten in 'the new blocks', which were in any case 'not built for them'; their fate is to remember and not to remember and she is, rather than the fallen Eve, a 'mindless Mnemosyne':

> She is our lady of the nameless metals, of things
> No hand has made, and no machine
> Has cut to a nicety that takes the mark
> Of clean intention—

things drained of all their human virtue—

> at best, the guardian
> Of all that our daily contact stales and fades,
> Rusty cages and lampless lampshades.

She inherits merely the '*dismantlings*' of a neighbourhood; 'guardian' of the 'nameless', of things that bear no human imprint and, 'lampless', are no longer lit with the light of human possibility. The poem's vocabulary rings with the sound of loss—'expressionless', 'nameless', 'mindless', 'nameless', 'lampless'—and where the word of loss is missing the notion is not: placeless is 'this time / And dusky space we occupy together', not a neighbourhood but a limbo, where 'together' signifies proximity not relationship.

In this poem, more than the other 'manscapes', the poet appears as a sufferer-participant in the condition he deplores; it is the 'dusky space we occupy *together*'. The poem begins with 'The needle-point's swaying reminder' to the commuting motorist not to exceed the speed limit; and other checks and appeals—'Kerb-side signs / For demolitions and new detours, / A propped pub, a corner lopped'—commanding his attention, eliciting carefully judged responses, 'all / Bridle the pressures that guide the needle'. The final stanza returns us to the poet-driver negotiating the morning traffic and the first line is repeated. Behind the literal 'pressures' applied by 'the flexed foot' to the accelerator, guiding, controlling the vehicle's progress, as the driver manoeuvres his 'way in' and through the barely familiar scenes of the rapidly changing modern city, are interior pressures suffered and received—oppressions, impressions—and pressures of inwardly bridled feeling in response to sights seen and insights into their meaning; they compel the poet in his journey through this literal, unmythic *waste land*, the ruins of a lost civility, towards a final question: 'Is it patience or anger most renders the will keen?' for 'This is a daily discontent. This is the way in'.

'The vision of a lack, / A thwarted possibility' in 'Hokusai on the Trent' (CP p. 243) implies, I said, an interior to match the exterior condition. The complement of the ruined city of man, in 'The Way In', is a crushed spirit, of a lost civility a loss of heart; the disappearance of the very idea of civility demonstrated by the *'mannerless* high risers' is reflected in the blank amnesia of the 'mindless Mnemosyne'. Likewise, the contrary sense of what is lacking is there not only in the physical evidence of loss imaged in the poem but also in the poet's 'flexed', flexible tone of finely controlled involvement. In Chapter 2 I drew attention to a connection between this poem and 'Eden' (CP p. 159) in *The Way of a World* (1969), specifically in that instance to the references in the second stanza to the opening lines of the earlier poem; my purpose was to illustrate the adaptation of the Edenic motif to the social world. 'The Way In' does more than extend the theme, however; in one respect at least it shows a change of mind. 'Is it patience or anger most renders the will keen?' directly questions a statement in 'Eden', the assertion that, if we are to seek repossession of what is lost, 'there is no / Bridge but the thread of patience, no way / But the will to wish back Eden'. It would seem, since 'the way in' is 'a daily discontent', that the question answers itself; certainly there is more of anger than resolute patience in the voice that speaks these stanzas. Anger that sharpens the will to resist and to speak for the contrary hope provides the counter-movement in the poetic voice to the triumph of the inhuman and the defeat of the spirit witnessed in the hopelessness and passivity of the working-class couple. Anger was Tomlinson's response in *Seeing is Believing* to the 'suburban' disfigurement and neglect of the Hall at Stowey, and for similar reasons; but a comparison reveals, what might be missed in a reading of the earlier poem by itself, a simpler counterpoint of praise and blame, where anger stops short at indictment and we hear in the poet's voice more of repugnance and indignation, motions of personal recoil, than of the accompanying 'sadness' he also claims to feel. In 'The Way In' anger is, rather, the expression of the creative will; something we can feel throughout the poem, but which is also the implication of a contrast arranged by a piece of word-play: the demolition of the city, whose 'features, *rendered* down, / Collapse expressionless', is answered by an 'anger' that—surely more than 'patience'—*'renders* the will keen'. What is missing from the new city, which the poet's voice supplies, is the *manner* that the high risers notably lack; the point is developed further when the poet insists: 'It will need more than talk and trees / To coax a *style* from these disparities'. The *poem's* 'style' is not a single thing, but in all its variation of tone it speaks with the voice of impassioned will, of (precisely) 'bridled' passion, the voice of will provoked by 'a daily discontent' and focused by anger; it speaks 'the resolved soul', we might say, if Marvell's phrase can be separated from some of its specifically Christian meanings.[9] It is a style that stands for undiscouraged, unremitting but also undeluded resistance to the inhuman.

The way of 'daily discontent' is the poet's 'way in' to the modern city, the 'way in' to our daily condition. Tomlinson's daily journey takes him from a natural Eden, a stone house beside a stream in a Gloucestershire valley, into the heart of an inferno, where an 'entire town / Sways in the fume of the pyre'. In the journey of his life, as we have seen, it was the other way round. Set this with its companion poems, the 'manscapes' of an industrialized land, and give this group of poems their place in Tomlinson's work as a whole, and we may understand the title-phrase differently. His return to the 'ravaged counties' of the Midlands and the redirection of his attention from landscapes to the dehumanized townscapes of modern Britain have brought him this recognition: the 'way in' to his preferred subject-matter, the goad to his Edenic theme, is now, as it was initially, a 'daily discontent' with its contrary—the condition he identifies, in 'The Poet as Painter', as 'the tragic fall from plenitude in our own urban universe'.[10]

NOTES

1. See Donald Wesling, 'Process and Closure in Tomlinson's Prose Poems' in *Charles Tomlinson: Man and Artist* (1988).
2. Haldane and Ross (eds), *Philosophical Works*, p. 13
3. *Ibid.*, p. 11.
4. *Eden*, p. 14.
5. *Ibid.*
6. *Ibid.*, pp. 10–11.

7. *Ibid.*, p.13.
8. CP p. 164.
9. Andrew Marvell, 'A Dialogue of the Resolved Soul and Created Pleasure', in *The Poems of Andrew Marvell* (London: Routledge and Kegan Paul, 1952; ed. Hugh Macdonald), p. 3.
10. *Eden*, p. 15.

Chapter Five
A Saving Grace

A saving grace in so much certainty of stone.
'The Gap'

The preceding chapters offer a series of partial perspectives, in a sequence contrived to allow Tomlinson's poetry to unfold its 'logic', the principle of its coherence. The purpose of those chapters was expository; its pursuit would have been incompatible with a consistently historical treatment of this poet's work. The distinction between nature poem and human poem, having served its purpose, can now be dropped. Since this study has been, intentionally, sparing in its references to the later work, this chapter will explore ways of viewing the poetry of the 1970s and 1980s as an entity.

It goes without saying that the poems of the 1970s and 1980s built on foundations laid in the 1950s and 1960s. There are no clear historical divisions in Tomlinson's work. In the evolution of his poetry the later simply modifies and extends the earlier. As he said in an interview with Michael Schmidt in 1977, 'the underlying continuity is the important thing'.[1] Nevertheless, to characterize the later work, we need to take note of what differences do exist between that and the earlier; talk of modifications and extensions implies a particular conception of what has been modified and extended. A description of the second twenty years therefore requires, for comparison, a characterization of the first twenty—not, I should add, as a fixed thing but as a process of development. In this brief overview of the earlier work I shall be recalling qualities and aspects of the poetry discussed in the previous pages, but not hitherto related to period and viewed in a historical perspective.

Not counting *Relations and Contraries* (1951), which Tomlinson regards as prentice work, he published two collections in the 1950s, *The Necklace* in 1955 and *Seeing is Believing* in 1958 (reissued with additions in 1960). Early influences in the formation of his personal style were the clean line and phrasing of the American modernists, Pound, Stevens and Marianne Moore (William Carlos Williams made his mark later) and the reasoned structures, civilities and conceptual diction of the eighteenth-century English poets. Linguistic control, the ordering of confusion, and the tempering of expectations to realities, submission of the eye to the objective world and of the mind to a consciousness of limits—a literary regimen of chastening, corrective severity—were largely what these poems recommended and vigorously practised. The stance was firmly and sometimes truculently anti-romantic. Such convictions and strategies produced verse notable for its crisp sensuousness, energy and incisive intelligence. These were the qualities of his poetry that struck one most forcibly in the 1950s—by virtue of their intrinsic appeal but also because they stood out in sharp contrast from the neo-romanticism of the 1940s. Most contemporary reviewers failed to notice, however, the already plentiful evidence in *Seeing is Believing* of the will and ability to pursue a larger ambition.

The contrast offered by Tomlinson's poetry in the 1950s to that of a miscellaneous group of poets writing at the same time and known for a while as the Movement should have been sufficient indication of the size and direction of that ambition. These poets were also trying out alternatives to the various romanticisms that prevailed in the poetry magazines of the period. But Tomlinson's poetic programme had as little in common with the drily reasonable or matter-of-fact realism of the Movement as with the vatic grandiosities of Dylan Thomas and his imitators. Some of the group—notably Thom Gunn and Donald Davie—developed and moved on; only Philip Larkin remained a Movement poet. At his best he was, of course, considerably more than its outstanding talent but for that very reason, because of the individuality as well as the representativeness of his achievement, it is useful to consider the differences between Larkin's and Tomlinson's work. 'The Less Deceived' (1955) introduced into contemporary British poetry a distinctive voice and outlook, a manner that blended a 'faithful and disappointing' photographic realism with its complement, a disappointed romanticism.[2] Although Tomlinson acknowledges a debt to the nineteenth-century tradition of *perceptual realism*, beginning with the early Romantics, Wordsworth and Coleridge, he is, as we have seen, unsympathetic to the subjectivist strain in romanticism and his early poetry was in reaction against the romantic revival of the mid-1930s and 1940s. He rejected the current forms of romanticism, but he also spoke out against the Larkinian school of realism. Indeed, his polemic against neo-romanticism, it is clear now, is less significant for an understanding of his poetry than his opposition to the literary ethos associated with Larkin's name. If, in the 1950s, to be 'less deceived' was, for Larkin, the grey limit of realistic expectation, Tomlinson's 'seeing is believing' spoke for disciplined hope, announcing the conditions for and proclaiming the possibility of fulfilment; the titles of the two collections epitomize the contrariety of their contents. Larkin's theme was the disparity between reality and desire: Tomlinson's was neither the self and its emotions—which is not to say they are absent from his verse—nor a fixed, adversarial reality, but the larger reality that exceeds and includes man, the reality of nature and—more extensively in the 1960s—of history, and the story of man's accommodations with the world of space and time. It might be said that he chose to measure the scope of being rather than trace, like Larkin, 'the graph of pain'—poetry, he was to declare in the 1970s, is precisely 'the will to exchange the graph of pain / Acknowledged, charted and repeated, for the range / Of an unpredicted terrain' (CP p. 270). The choice signalled his conscious repudiation of the literary milieu for which Larkin became the unofficial laureate.

Reviewing *Seeing is Believing*, in 1955, Donald Davie pointed out that Tomlinson's 'exquisitely accurate register of sense-impressions' was 'never for its own sake', but was a means of 'discipline and control', and that it controlled 'an exceptionally passionate and wholehearted response to the world, a world that bore in, not just on the five senses, but also on a man's sentiments, a man's convictions'.[3] For this reason, I would add, his voice carried what was in the 1950s an unfamiliar note of authority. It was a poetry grounded in objectivism, but an objectivism that 'speaks / To celebrate' the given world (CP p. 235). The *passionate* response to, and absorbed interest in, the life of the senses and the intention of celebration revealed an early affinity with Hopkins—significantly, like Tomlinson (and Marianne Moore), an admirer of Ruskin. Neither romantic nor simply in retreat from romanticism, Tomlinson brought to sense experience, moreover, an Augustan vigour of mind. The 'accurate register of sense-impressions' is the foundation of his poetry but on this foundation, as Davie maintained, he has built a human world. Accuracy of eye and ear, which lies in the proper relation of foreground to background, part to whole, usually implies also in these poems the tempering of emotion to its object and the clarity and impartiality of the judicious mind. It is, in a word, normative poetry: it seeks to define norms—where it is possible, and where it is not, acknowledging the fact; norms of sensory perception, of feeling and thinking, ultimately of human being.

If my description of Tomlinson's early anti-romanticism has suggested that in the 1950s he barricaded himself behind the ramparts of a defensive neo-classicism, the poems themselves, of course, leave no such impression. Indeed they suggest the contrary: the tone in 'Through Binoculars' (*The Necklace*) or 'Tramontana at Lerici' (*Seeing is Believing*) is assertive, even combative, rather than defensive. 'The tempering of expectations to realities', in my formulation of his literary agenda, is not meant to suggest an unduly self-limiting exercise in asceticism but to identify Tomlinson's determination to castigate in others and eschew for himself mere subjectivity—the unreal and the impossible. It would perhaps clarify matters if the poetic principle in question were defined alternatively as the measuring of expectations by the yardstick not of a reduced but an expanded reality, the yardstick of both the actual and the potential. In saying, further, that he chose to measure (what in fact cannot be measured) the scope of being, my intention was to indicate both the scope and the paradox of Tomlinson's ambition. In the alternative definition and by this paradox I am proposing that 'measure' is practised in the interests of liberation not constraint. The measuring eye in 'Ponte Veneziano' (CP p. 19), 'Stripping the vista to its depth', is also the perceiving intelligence that 'broods on the further light' and, having stripped the vista to its depth, tunnels into unmeasured and immeasurable prospects beyond. In different versions, this image of the penetrant mind that uses keenness of sensory perception as a tool of the prospecting imagination recurs in poems of the 1960s and 1970s. The note of praise and celebration, when it is sounded, is clearer and more confident in the last gathering of the 1960s, *The Way of a World* (1969); this, too, continues to be heard in the 1970s.

The objectivist component in Tomlinson's ethic of perception was most prominent in the poetry he published in the 1950s. 'Observation of Facts' (CP p. 11), in *The Necklace*, one of several objectivist manifestos to be found in the early collections, bases its argument on a baldly asserted, absolute distinction between objective and subjective seeing:

> Style speaks what was seen,
> Or it conceals the observation
> Behind the observer: a voice
> Wearing a ruff.

Poems should present, as this poem seeks to present, 'fact stripped of imagination'—imagination here conceived solely as the expression of the self-conscious observer. A tree, a house, a room has 'facets of copiousness'; only by an act of disinterested attention can the artist, so to speak, enable reality to present itself: 'Those facets of copiousness which I proposed / Exist, do so when we have silenced ourselves'. The objectivist premise has remained an integral part of Tomlinson's thought, but it is no longer a matter for polemical enforcement. The challenging insistence by several poems in *The Necklace* and *Seeing is Believing* on the *irreducible* otherness of objects, the *stubborn* separateness of facts, was a tactical insistence in response to the provocation of the neo-romantic subjectivist poetic of Dylan Thomas and others in the 1940s and 1950s. Objectivism, moreover, was never the whole story; the poems of the 1950s had also other things to say. In all but a few of even the earliest poems the emphasis was not so much on otherness as on the relationship, the interaction, between self and not-self, subject and object. This is invariably so in the collections of the 1960s. In essentials Tomlinson's poetic world remained the same during the next two decades. The reader's impression that, nevertheless, something has changed can be attributed, I think, to a shift in mood that began in the late 1960s and established itself in the 1970s; there is a difference of temper in the later poems. They show, I believe, an acute sense that the double—at once objective and subjective—awareness constitutes a paradox; the awareness creates an exhilarating tension between two ways of seeing the world—as at the same time having an independent existence and depending for its meaning upon the observer. 'At the Edge' (*The Flood*, 1981; CP p. 324) speaks of the secrecy of nature, the interest for the questing eye of distances and recesses, 'The offscape, the in-folds, secreted / Water-holes in the boles of trees', an interest partly supplied by the opportunity for conjecture.

> Edges are centres: once you have found
>   Their lines of force, the least of gossamers
> Leads and frees you, nets you a universe
>   Whose iridescent weave shines true
> Because you see it, but whose centre is not you.

The contraries of self and not-self entail others: what is apparent to the observer and what is hidden from him, the perceived part and the divined whole; contraries that are in fact complementarities in that they are mutually exclusive viewpoints which are yet both true. Each polarity expresses the same paradox, that the world has its centre simultaneously inside and outside the subject; edges are centres for the viewer but do not cease to be edges too, and the world's centre is 'not you': the netted universe is private and common, particular and general. The heightened sense of tension between equally valid but discrepant viewpoints is not the only difference between the earlier and the later poetry disclosed by this poem. If we compare two statements, one from 'At the Edge'—'whose centre is not you'—and the other from 'Something: A Direction' (CP p. 54), the last poem of the sequence 'Antecedents' in *Seeing is Believing*, we find that, though their meanings are essentially the same, the intentions of the statements are in some respects contradictory. Both poems are about relationship, the proper relationship, between self and the world. The earlier poem insists on the distinction between subject and object as a warning against the solipsism of a Symbolist poetic ('the shut cell of that solitude'): 'Sun is, *because it is not* you; you are / Since you are self, and self delimited / Regarding sun' (CP p. 54; my emphasis); having made this 'acknowledgement' of boundaries and limits, 'released . . . from prison / To powers, you are new-found / Neighboured, having earned relation / With all that is other'. 'Acknowledgement' of the distinction is as fundamental in 'At the Edge' as it is in 'Antecedents', but the later poem celebrates 'release' not from the 'prison' of solipsism into a world of relationship, but from the constraints imposed by objectivism upon the divinations of the (subjective) imagination: self refuses to be 'delimited' and the lines ring with the excitement of trespass.

The double focus in Tomlinson's poetry upon the thing itself and the whole of which it is a part or sign is reflected in the 'sensuous abstraction' of his diction—a potential of the French language which, he told Michael Schmidt,[4] he envies. More to the point, when we remember his early interest in eighteenth-century verse, an interest he shared with his friend and mentor Donald Davie, is the fact that 'sensuous abstraction' names a generally recognized quality of Augustan poetry. 'Foxes' Moon' (*The Way In*, 1974; CP p. 252), which studies the transformation by moonlight of an English landscape and assimilates the disparity between the two Englands to the incongruity of the foxes' night world with the adjacent human world ('These are the fox hours cleansed / Of all the meanings we can use'), exemplifies this quality in Tomlinson's verse:

> The shapes of dusk
> Take on an edge, refined
> By a drying wind and foxes bring
> Flint hearts and sharpened senses to
> This desolation of grisaille in which the dew
> Grows clearer, colder.

The imagery, factual and figurative, is precisely, incisively sensuous, but even in the thought-connections that link 'edge', 'refined', 'drying', 'flint', and 'clearer, colder' the control of the abstracting mind is noticeable; in 'this desolation of grisaille' it is overt and elegantly definitive. The confrontation of the fact and its interpretation is yet more striking a few lines later:

> They nose
> The garbage of the yards, move through
> The *white displacement* of a daily view
> Uninterrupted. (my emphasis)

Representing the poetic search, in 'Movement II' (*Written on Water*, 1972; CP p. 234), as a 'Grasping for more than the bare facts warranted', Tomlinson could easily be naming the motivating principle in a language of 'sensuous abstraction'. We might recognize this principle at work also in another image in 'At the Edge'. Watching the movements of a wren darting in and out of its hole, 'It made me', the poet remarks of its visible energy, 'measure all the force unspied / That stirred inside the bank'. The extension of the concrete into the abstract is a similar leap of imagination, spurred by the (paradoxical) need and will to measure the invisible and immeasurable.

Tomlinson has always worked to incorporate in one vision the near and the far, the data of sense experience and the 'something else' (CP p. 65) of imagination; repeatedly his poems explore outward from the known to the edges of the known and just beyond. 'At the Edge' gives us that movement in the rapid transition from 'the wheel of a web' to a netted 'universe'. But the delight in the 'unspied', the attraction of hiddenness as such, is, I think, a new mood. The unspied is the realm of more-than-fact, closed to the eyes, open to the mind; what is beyond or within, 'secreted', is an irresistible invitation to the activated imagination. The delight felt is a delight in pure possibility, in the speculative power and play of imagination that knows its hyperboles for what they are. The truth of poetry's 'web' is a play of 'iridescent' light, the 'universe' it nets a universe of gossamer tenuity; it is a mirror world created by the poet's breath:

> this floor of water
> On the wood's floor (knock with the breath
> And enter a world reverted, a catacomb
> Of branching ways where the roots splay).

The poem celebrates moments of liberation from the bounds of the known world ('The least of gossamers / Leads and frees you') and the intuition—but not the lasting knowledge—of another world.

I have been assembling evidence of a shift in mood in Tomlinson's later work, a refocusing of an existing poetic world. The mystery of hiddenness now holds the poet's attention more than the prospect of replacing mystery with knowledge. Imagination has been given greater licence to spin its tenuous webs of momentary coherence—and to live contentedly in this poetic dwelling. It appears that an attitude of agnosticism, in its general sense, has become more prominent. Those words of reservation and circumspection characteristic of Tomlinson's approach to metaphor, 'as if' and 'it seems', are, I believe, a little more insistent, as though to highlight the aspect of illusion in the workings of imagination. In 'At the Edge' I noted the delight shown in what cannot be *known* directly or with certainty. I would add that this corresponds to the poet's growing preoccupation with what cannot be *said* singly, firmly, unambiguously—and with how to say it. It is the theme of 'Nature Poem' (*The Shaft*, 1978; CP p. 295). The creative confusion of perception, 'this sound / Of water that is sound of leaves', nature's 'stirrings and comminglings . . . recall / The way a poem flows':

> No single reading renders up complete
> Their shifting text—a poem, too, in this,
> They bring the mind half way to its defeat,
> Eluding and exceeding the place it guesses,
> Among these overlappings, half-lights, depths,
> The currents of this air, these hiddenesses.

The poems in *Seeing is Believing* have the same manner of terse authority as their title: the tone is positive, the disciplined eye and mind take command; they are distinguished by their sensory and mental clarity, strictness of moral discrimination and generally by the strenuous clearing of a ground of certainty in a world of lax behaviour, disordered emotion and confused understanding. A good deal of this remains in his later work but it has been modified to make a place for uncertainties and confusions. In the 'Arden' of in-between in which we live—the seasons of time and nature housing memories or hopes of a timeless Eden—'the contraries / Of this place are contrarily unclear: / A haze beats back the summer sheen / Into a chiaroscuro of the heat'. For Arden is where the real and the possible interpenetrate and distinctions blur; 'the depths of Arden's springs', supplied by underground streams from their source in Eden, 'convey echoic waters—voices / Of the place that rises through this place'. 'In Arden' (*The Shaft*, 1978; CP p. 305) finds in this rich confusion of what is there with what is not there, the real with the imagined, a reason for celebration. 'A Self-Portrait: David' (*The Shaft*, CP p. 278), concerned to express the same sense of double reality (in a formula that recalls 'the place that rises through this place'), is on the other hand cautionary: 'This is the face behind my face', expressing a truth that 'puts by / The mind's imperious geometry';

> distrust
> Whatever I may do unless it show
> A startled truth as in these eyes' misgivings,
> These lips that, closed, confess 'I do not know'.

Celebratory or cautionary, the deepest place in these poems is where there is not finality but an open question. 'In the Balance' (*The Shaft*; CP p. 289), for example, sets the finality of a winter landscape after a snowfall—its photographic immobility and clarity of definition—against the questions it raises and the doubts it leaves in the observer's mind: 'Will it thicken or thaw, this rawness menacing? / The sky stirs: the sky refuses to say'. The sky is poised between fixity and change:

> Brought to a sway, the whole day hesitates
> Through the sky of afternoon, and you beneath,
> As if questions of weather were of life and death.

'The *whole* day hesitates': since nature is, as we have seen, 'a shifting text', the wholeness of nature is composed of shifting parts. If wholeness is always unpredictably rearranging itself or induces that expectation, then 'you beneath', the reflective mind, must copy that hesitancy in sensitive attunement to the nature of things; and this holds true, too, for 'questions . . . of life and death'. Nature—likewise a nature poem—is a 'shifting text'; its shades and secrets 'bring the mind half way to its defeat, / Eluding and exceeding the place it guesses'; and if the 'stirrings and comminglings' of a summer day 'ask to be / Written into a permanence', the permanence of a poem is not stasis—'a poem flows', life in its verbal translation is 'not stilled / But given pulse and voice' (CP p. 295). A poem, in this view, has the changing permanence of life renewed with each new reading. The aim, then, is 'not to seize the point of things'—an earlier statement of his position (CP p. 76)—but to catch the fugitive hint of Eden from the stream of time. Tomlinson uses this image, without making it as overtly metaphorical as I have made it, in 'Departure' (*The Shaft*; CP p. 289) when he reminds his recent guests of the 'stream / Which bestows a flowing benediction and a name / On our house of stone' and adds:

> it is here
> That I like best, where the waters disappear
> Under the bridge-arch, shelving through coolness,
> Thought, halted at an image of perfection
> Between gloom and gold, in momentary
> Stay, place of perpetual threshold,
> Before all flashes out again and on
> Tasseling and torn, reflecting nothing but sun.

As it is a 'place of perpetual threshold' for the stream, so for the contemplating mind it is a threshold between the known and the imagined.

The mind must practise a delicate hovering of attention to catch its images, but it is only a 'momentary stay against confusion' (to complete the quotation from Frost)[5] and the image is willingly relinquished, allowed to dissolve in the rush of waters. The poet balances appreciation of the mind's reflection, the stilled image, and enjoyment of the stream's flash of movement—'reflecting nothing but sun'. The stream bestows upon the house two things, as separate and as inseparable as a baptism and a christening: 'a *flowing* benediction' and an *unchanging* 'name', as fixed and permanent as the stone of which the house is built. The certainty of stone receives its benediction from the *living* flow of water. The clumsily sensitive movement of the stream is in immediate contrast with that of the jet which carries his guests to their destination, the trail of which 'is scoring the zenith / Somewhere': the language of water, 'pushing / Over a fall, to sidle a rock or two / Before it was through the confine', feeling its way pliantly over and round obstacles towards its freedom, is more exemplary for the mind and will than the imperious rhetoric of the jet-plane's insensibility to its surroundings. 'Certainty of stone' is a phrase I have borrowed from another poem in *The Shaft*, 'The Gap' (CP p. 308). What, asks the poet, is the meaning of your delight in noticing, casually as you are driving by, a gap in the stone wall 'Where you'd expect to see / A field-gate', through which

> All you see is space—that, and the wall
>   That climbs up to the spot two ways
> To embrace absence, frame skies:
>   Why does one welcome the gateless gap?
> As an image to be filled with the meaning
>   It doesn't yet have? As a confine gone?
> A saving grace in so much certainty of stone?

The answers are inherent in the question: the wall thus lets in the whole expanse of space, releases imagination to its task of filling absences, opening vistas of possibility. To frame is not to contain skies—they are uncontainable; the gap creates a view the value of which is that it gives the eye freedom. It takes you beyond certainty, whether of stone or the oblivious certainty of a jet's flight, and leaves you in one of two conditions: either it is the agnostic's confession, 'I do not know', or it sets you 'at the edge' or on the threshold of 'a saving grace', your redemption from the merely known. For Tomlinson, however, they are not distinct conditions but alternative names for the invitation to the imagination potential in any encounter of the familiar with the unexpected. Living at the frontier of the known and the unknown is its own justification: 'The Gap' emphasizes not the 'after-knowledge and its map' generated by the encounter but 'the moment itself, abrupt / With the pure surprise of seeing'. The sudden invasion of the mind by the awareness of what is beyond its grasp is in itself a liberation and an enlargement.

    Tomlinson's poems are a dialogue between order and disorder, clarity and confusion; these are alternative expressions of essentially the same antithesis, the wording of which declares a preference for the first term over the second. This is how the antithesis worked in the earlier collections, but the later poetry permits a reformulation which removes the evaluative bias: the distinction now is between the mental translation and the immediate experience, which is to say, between the abstract and the concrete. The concrete and immediate, or the unclear and fortuitous experiences, are the (literally) inconceivable and unnameable at the edges of the known and named. 'In both graphic and poetic art'—this is Tomlinson in 1979—'I like something lucid surrounded by something mysterious'; and again, in the same essay, 'The Poet as Painter', he writes: 'A human measure, surrounded by surprises, impenetrables and unknowables, but always reasserting itself, this could be a salutary aim' for the artist.[6] The centrality for Tomlinson of the human measure does not in consequence banish what is not measurable to the peripheries of the poems; in the poems of the 1970s and 1980s, moreover, the surrounding mystery has become increasingly important. The glimpsed 'image of perfection' caught momentarily from the flowing stream, in 'Departure', is immediately lost again in the tangle of the waters, 'Tasseling and torn, reflecting nothing but sun'. 'The Gap' celebrates the abrupt surprise, divested of explanation, that admits the limitless world. The unending flow and change of time and the infinity of space represent what exceeds the compass of the framing eye or the naming tongue.

The objective 'mystery' is for the subject 'uncertainty'. Tomlinson's agnosticism is like Keats's negative capability, a capacity for 'being in uncertainties, mysteries, doubts, without an irritable reaching after fact and reason'. When Keats judges Coleridge to be 'incapable of remaining content with half-knowledge' and confidently supposes that philosophical scruple would prevent him from using 'a fine isolated verisimilitude caught from the penetralium of mystery',[7] we are reminded, without forgetting the differences, of Tomlinson's fascination with 'impenetrables and unknowables' and, in 'At the Edge', the special interest expressed in the penetralia of nature. In 'The Miracle of the Bottle and the Fishes' (*The Return*, 1987, p. 18) Tomlinson discerns in cubist painting a precedent for his own 'agnostic' receptiveness to the influx of sense experience. His subject is a still life by Georges Braque, in which the painter has contrived that the composition (or decomposition) should bring about a disorientation in the viewer corresponding to what, in 'The Gap', Tomlinson called 'the pure surprise of seeing':

> We do not know
> with precision or at a glance
> which is space and which is substance,
> nor should we yet.

'We do not know', in this instance, welcomes a gift to the imagination: we are looking at a 'piled-up tabletop'—a bald, matter-of-fact description of the basic ingredients of this pictorial concoction—but the eye is at the same time reminded of grander appearances:

> One might even take it for
> a cliff-side, sky-high
> accumulation opening door on door
>
> of space.

This confusion of the eye is liberating for two reasons. First, the disordering of a mental set is potentially a re-ordering, initiated not by the mind but the world itself; the mind, released from its presumptions, is at once 'delighted and disordered'—the verbs imply not only simultaneity but identity—delighted and disordered 'by the freshness of the world's own weather'. And this is to affirm, against the presumption of man's homelessness in an alien universe, a conception of human dwelling, one that depends for its realization not on the 'taken measure' of the appraising mind but on tentative conjecture and exploratory diffidence.

The second reason why visual ambiguity in a painting might have on the viewer a liberating effect is that it encourages the active cooperation of the eye in the creation of the pictured world, teaching it not merely to look *at* (objects on a table) but to see *into* (the relation between them or the relation between their 'substance' and the surrounding 'space'), teaching the spectator to become a participant in the world of his experience. *Not knowing* 'which is space and which is substance', 'the eye must stitch / each half-seen, separate / identity together'. The painter's compositional surprises are devices for unsettling and unstaling visual expectation and then, the poem implies, instruments of initiation: we learn from Braque what it feels like to become (in Wordsworth's phrase) 'inmates of this active universe'.[8] To remove boundaries and open doors of perception is 'To enter space anew'; to re-experience is, furthermore, as if to re-create:

> To enter space anew:
> to enter a new space
> inch by inch and not
> the perspective avenue
> cutting a swathe through mastered distance
> from a viewpoint that is single.

Poems, like paintings, are acts of attention; the art of attending, in both senses of the word—paying attention and being in attendance, observation and presence—is the theme of the first part of the poem. The painting's lesson in the art of seeing is at the same time the poem's lesson in the art of dwelling, of being at home in the natural world.

The stitching together of unclear and obscurely related identities, by which we come to know them both separately and as parts of a whole, is to enter into the 'shifting text', which is none the less a readable text, of the natural world. It is a complete world but it cannot be comprehended from a single viewpoint; to forfeit the clear simplicity of 'the perspective avenue' is to lose mastery of a two-dimensional illusion and to 'stumble' into the palpable reality of a three-dimensional world. The 'new space' entered is a space perceived from every possible viewpoint, but it is also a space that you discover not with the eye only but—through the eye—with the whole body, kinaesthetically. As Tomlinson explains in 'The Poet as Painter': 'Painting wakes up the hand, draws-in your sense of muscular co-ordination, your sense of the body'; poetry likewise 'brings the whole man into play and his bodily sense of himself'.[9] Braque is represented in the poem, therefore, as aiming, not at a 'mastered distance', but at closeness and immediacy of experience:

> Touch must supply
> space with its substance and become
> a material of the exploration
> as palpable as paint,
> in a reciprocation where
> things no longer stand
> bounded by emptiness.

The eye learns from the sense of touch—the eye through the brush manipulating paint on canvas—to feel its way, near-sightedly, 'inch by inch' into the dimensions of space, to feel the reality of space. The world then ceases to be 'things . . . bounded by emptiness', as it was in the disposition of a single perspective, and becomes substance: the 'substance' of space and the substance of 'things' exist 'in a reciprocation'—the indefinite article hinting also at a reciprocal relation between the 'I' exploring and the world of his or her sense experience. Touch closes the distance between eye and world, it brings direct knowledge; lacking the distanced perspective of single vision, however, it cannot *command* experience. Sureness of touch has nothing in common with mental facility or certainty—the facility, for example, of 'a mind / in collusion with its spectres' or the certainty of a mind supplied with ready-made ideas and judgements: 'refusing to travel straitened / by either mood or taken measure', the eye at close quarters with reality

> must stumble, it must touch
> to guess how much of space
> for all its wilderness
> is both honeycomb and home.

Vision that accepts the tutelage of tactile knowledge comes by trial and error to a more intimate awareness of the world as man's natural home. Only by this stumbling-exploratory, never fixed or final reading of the world's book—a blind awareness among mysteries, uncertainties—may we hope to recognize in this natural 'wilderness' what signs there are that 'space [is] possibility', sweet sustenance of human enterprise, 'the self's unnameable and shaping home', the promised land of man's 'own inheritance'.[10]

'Coombe', also from *The Return* (p. 44), is about landscape not painting, but it teaches essentially the same lesson in the art of dwelling. The poem starts with 'the secrecy of this coombe', as 'At the Edge' starts with 'secreted / Water holes in the boles of trees'; but the attraction of the hidden is, in 'Coombe', the attraction of life known at close quarters. There is the same contrast here as in 'The Miracle of the Bottle and the Fishes' between spectatorial and participatory vision. The contrast is preceded in part I of 'The Miracle . . .' by an investigation of the grace of not knowing, displayed as a favouring precondition for the preferred mode of being discussed in parts II and III of the poem—the direct knowledge of participatory vision. This is a premise rather than a theme of 'Coombe'. The coombe is a secret presence within the larger wilderness of Dartmoor; conversely, the larger whole is invisible from the interior of the coombe. Only from the 'crest' of the hill or in the high perspective commanded by the 'buzzard's eye' might one take spectatorial possession of the terrain. But 'Climb / To the crest and the river has lost itself / Down in the leafed-round dip', and if 'In a buzzard's eye / It might all lie one map', a map abstracts and flattens-out the landscape, losing, like the hill view, the dense particularity of the scene. The poem opposes to the map of reality the reality itself, substituting for instant, finished knowledge the intimate, experimental process of getting-to-know. The landscape is not there but here: it is '*this* coombe' and '*our* territory', and 'we' do not master it, like the buzzard', from a distance:

> we
> Take in our territory by inches then by bursts,
>   More like the heron who stands, advances, stands
> Firm in the sliding Torridge that divides
>   The sheer of the woodslope from the packed cornland.

Braque enters the 'new space' opened up by the process of painting 'inch by inch', and the key verbs to describe the mode of entry are 'stumble', 'touch' and 'guess'. 'We' also explore 'our territory by inches', *'take in* our territory'—take it in to ourselves—as it were with the whole body; the process is slow but sure like the heron's fishing technique, the slow sureness—difficult labour followed by intuitive, seemingly effortless 'bursts' ('miracles' of chance or 'guess' or inspiration)—with which a poet discovers his text, a 'shifting text' like the water-world of 'the sliding Torridge' patiently fished by the heron. In the recesses of the coombe one does not see the full expanse of Dartmoor but one feels, kinaesthetically, as weight and pressure its inner forces:

> The secrecy of this coombe is weighted through
>   With the pressures of the land that does not show
> Over its ridge—the massing of the moors,
>   The withstanding of the cliff and the inland sweep
> And drop whose encompassing granite hand
>   Extends us the deep lines of its palm
> Through softer soils that a river
>   Silvers and darkens between.

It is as if the secrecy of the coombe guards by condensing into itself the undisclosed identity of moor, cliff, granite, soil, river, the whole varied region spread around it. With the same 'silences / It kept from the Romans with' it protects itself from the comparably imperialist incursions and predatory designs of the spectatorial view; it gives up its deeper reality, extending graciously and generously an open 'palm', revealing its *'deep* lines', only to 'us' who make it 'our territory', our home, by closing the gap between eye and thing and ceasing to be strangers in the land.

Perceptual, or epistemological, agnosticism—the basic uncertainty hailed as 'a saving grace' that liberates the imagination—includes a specifically religious agnosticism, one that underlies all his poetry but is overt only in his later work. Yet here, too, agnosticism rings with the tones not of doubt but of affirmation. Sacramental language has long been a feature of Tomlinson's verse; what is new is that the Christian associations of certain keywords in his poetic vocabulary, discreetly used, are now firmly separated from their supernatural significance. 'To See the Heron' (*The Shaft*, 1978; CP

p. 296) catches a moment of visual perfection in language that, as the poem proceeds, gradually increases its religious charge—'To see the heron *rise*: . . . this / *raised* torch . . . this leisurely sideways / wandering *ascension*', for which the autumn trees are waiting 'to unite / their various brightnesses'—but no sooner has the heron's resurrection been accomplished than it is immediately restored to its natural body and its natural purposes: it is 'risen' but, stripped of poetry, this means only that it's in flight and, unsurprisingly, in quest of food and, as its eye travels the stream, 'wondering where / to stoop, to alight and strike'. This is not cynicism but the unfolding of a paradox: the bird is both its natural self and, for the human viewer, a vehicle of revelation. The disparity is a fact, and an occasion for thanksgiving for both its 'realities' rather than for distinguishing preferentially between them. The heron's blue 'is darkening now / against the sullen sky blue'—that is, a sky resistant to both miracles and poetry—and, as it goes and the moment of perfection fades, the poet, not expecting to resolve the paradox of appearances, bestows a blessing on it, an acquiescent valediction, 'so let it go'.

> To see the heron rise
> detaching blue from the blue
> that, smoking, lies along
> field-hollows, shadowings
> of humidity,

and its 'raised torch' of blue 'set off'—intensify by contrast and thus kindle—'that blaze . . . of autumn trees' is to see its rising 'unite'— while retaining its difference communicate its glory to—'their various brightnesses'. Not only are the words I have italicized, 'rise', 'raised', 'ascension', terms of Christian doctrine, but the imagery of fire—'smoking', 'torch', 'blaze'—is traditional metaphor in both the Jewish and the Christian Scriptures for the 'glory', the perfection, of God. And yet, as we have seen, in the poem the revelation of perfection is transitory; the heron's risenness is figurative not transfigurative, poetry not doctrine. The paradox has the same elements as that represented by the gulls in 'The Faring' (*The Shaft*; CP p. 291), which were, in the poet's recollection of an extraordinary day, at the same time birds in a storm 'above seasonable fields', 'intent / On nothing more than the ploughland's nourishment', and seeming messengers from an 'unending sea' of space, whose presence for the participant observer 'rhymed here with elsewhere'.

The religious question is treated more directly in the 1980s. In several poems of *The Flood* (1981), for example, poetry is being offered, plainly, as a sufficient 'recompense' for the failed promise of revealed truths. In the poem actually entitled 'The Recompense' (CP p. 319) the poet records how he and his companion 'climbed the darkness' to view the comet predicted for that night; they 'waited' but 'no comet came, and no flame thawed / The freezing reaches of [their] glance'. 'Unwillingly' then they took themselves and their disappointment back down again, but, facing in the opposite direction, found in the 'climbing brightness' of the 'risen moon' 'recompense for a comet lost': forfeiting the hoped-for prodigy, they turned instead to the opportunity of self-transcendence afforded by the mere 'rarenesses' of sense experience: for we

> Could read ourselves into those lines
>   Pulsating on the eye and to the veins,
> Thrust and countercharge to our own racing down,
>   Lunar flights of the rooted horizon.

In his fine elegiac sequence 'For Miriam' (CP p. 317), in the same collection, he recalls how he played the advocate for traditional Christianity against the heresies of an eccentric woman preacher, not as a believer but as a 'pagan' pleading for 'poetry forgone'. In the light of his own sacramental imagery, it is interesting that he should muster all his 'rhetoric' to defend specifically the doctrine of the Incarnation.

'To See the Heron', 'The Faring', 'The Recompense' and 'For Miriam', if they are not products of religious belief, are none the less, in one sense of the word, religious poems. The religious affirmation in them is merely—and quite literally—relocated. There are other poems, however, that proclaim their 'paganism' not by appropriating and revaluing the language and images of Christianity but by pitting 'beauty of the earth' against a discredited faith, substituting (to continue the quotation from Stevens's 'Sunday Morning') '*things* to be cherished' for 'the *thought* of heaven' (my emphases).[11] 'Under the Moon's Reign' (CP p. 251), which gives its title to a group of poems in *The Way In* (1974), is the first of Tomlinson's poems to do this:

> Twilight was the going of the gods: the air
>   Hung weightlessly now—its own
> Inviolable sign. From habit we
>   Were looking still for what we could not see—
> The inside of the outside, for some spirit flung
>   From the burning of that Götterdämmerung
> And suffused in the obscurity.

If, like the pharisees, 'we would see a sign', the obscurity of that Götterdämmerung had thrown us into such confusion that we were looking in the wrong place: the air now, unsymbolic, mythless, godless, was its 'own ... sign'. The miracle we can expect to follow such a twilight, and which is about to take place, is the transformation of earth and sky wrought by a risen moon. 'Under the moon's reign' all is drawn 'into more than daylight height' and the 'heavens'—the real heavens, not 'the thought of heaven'—are 'transfigured'; but the moon's transfiguration of the scene is effected by 'no more miracle than the place / It occupied and the eye that saw it': 'more than daylight height' indicates, in a favourite construction (cf. 'more than earth', 'more than bread', 'more than the bare facts warranted'[12]), that the seeming miracle of its 'steady lightning' is not other than, but an extension of—in this case a literal heightening of—the world of sense perception.

'Under the Moon's Reign' alludes to the gods of Scandinavian mythology; 'Teotihuacán' (*Notes from New York*, 1984; CP p. 385) is *about* the rival gods in the polytheistic religion of the Toltecs, a Mexican people whose chief city, named in the title, was abandoned in the eleventh or twelfth century. These are the divinities of *vanished* religions but the subject in both poems is one Tomlinson shares with Stevens—and, before him, Nietzsche: religion itself, its death and its aftermath. 'Now the gods are dead' and the priests who served them, a thousand years later on the slopes up to the pyramid we meet their successors, 'a priesthood of vendors', and with their *idolitos*, all equally 'genuine' (a commercial echo parodying the original rivalry?), 'It is the gods they are selling'. But at least the air is again itself, unburdened by divinity, as after the destruction of the Northern gods:

> Now the gods are dead
> their houses greet a sky
> freed of their weight.

Under a godless sky a thus enlightened vision will notice the remarkable resemblance between the 'flat-topped pyramids', monuments to exploded beliefs, and the flat-topped cones of the extinct volcanoes that crowd the horizons of 'this high terrain', which therefore 'opens its fastnesses to a mythless sun'; 'mythless' for obvious reasons, but also because this chief pyramid of Teotihuacán is named the Pyramid of the Sun.

'In San Clemente' (*The Return*, 1987; p. 4) returns us to Europe, a church in Rome; but the poem works with the same antithesis, elaborated so that we have more than the simple contrast between an other-worldly religion and the naturalistic pieties Tomlinson calls pagan. There are layers of reality; the foundations of the church constitute but the latest stage of a stratified history. Beneath the Christian site is the older shrine of Mithras, and below that, below everything,

> the roar
> Of subterranean waters pouring by
> All of the centuries it takes to climb
> From Mithras to the myth-resisting play
> Of one clear jet chiming against the bowl
> In the fountained courtyard and the open day.

The reality of water is flux; the 'subterranean waters' are primal, formless reality and *all* the centuries of time. Above that, far above—we imagine the passing of eras—are the ages in which the gods were formed, represented here by Mithras—as much for the identification by pun of myth and religion as because Mithraism was Christianity's major competitor in the Roman Empire. But at the top of this ascent, and not merely as the last stage in an evolutionary process but as a truth waiting at every stage to be recognized, is 'the myth-resisting play' of the fountain. The centuries—and we—'climb' out of the primal flux into history, but the reality of water moves with us and in us and we are not to be separated from it—for 'he who looks into water, and the changing world of perception which water represents, looks into the heart of time.'[13] 'The humid cave / Of Mithras' bull and shrine' reveals the proximity of these 'subterranean waters', but the 'roar' of the waters finds an echo in the roar of the Mithraic bull, bringing it perhaps closer than Christianity to that source. Above ground, in the light of day, the fountain, a spring straight from the source, plays *outside* the church. The clear, 'chiming' music of the single 'jet' of water in the courtyard and the 'open day' oppose in each corresponding detail the vague, booming resonance and confinement of 'the sonorous dark beneath'. By a building-up of facts a metaphor of the free, spontaneous imagination gradually emerges, unarticulated, as it were forming itself. 'In San Clemente' takes us from the waters under the earth 'pouring' uncontrollably by, upward through the cave of Mithras and through the foundations of the church, until they burst out with the force of a single, concentrated 'jet' into the civilized enclosure of a Roman courtyard, free-flowing yet making music by the repeated 'chiming' of its falling waters against the sides of the containing 'bowl': the procession of images brings us, once again, to the threshold of metaphor. The poem that precedes this one in *The Return* compares art to a fountain, 'a Roman fountain'; this is explicit confirmation of what we begin to feel as we plot the 'intricate meshings of words'[14] and add up the images of 'In San Clemente' and calculate the metaphoric sum. Other memories enter into our sense of the poem. Art is play, the 'daylong play' of light—resisting, let us say, the darkness of myth—and it is openness, like the space of possibility revealed by 'a field gate . . . flung wide' (CP p. 308) open in a length of stone wall. But, as always for Tomlinson, art is channelled force, clarity of thought and sensation, and a 'myth-resisting' spontaneity and free 'play' that yet accepts the resistance of solid stone for the making of its civilized harmony of precisions.

In several poems the confrontation between naturalist and supernaturalist views turns to satire. The satirical note is not absent from 'Under the Moon's Reign' but it is heard more frequently and is more pronounced in the poems of the 1980s. A satirical intention gradually insinuates itself, for example, into the offhand anecdotal narrative of 'San Fruttuoso' (*The Flood*, 1981; CP p. 334). The poet takes the ferry in rough seas; divers don their rubber suits and slip underwater: the two actions alternate. The poet's is a world of sun, bodies, 'an ill-lit sky' and violent motion: the divers 'assume / alternative bodies', pursuing purposes—'whatever it is draws them downwards'—that Tomlinson treats throughout with an affectation of polite puzzlement and incredulity. His incredulity fastens on the image of the sunken statue of Christ somewhere in the water under him, around which he imagines the divers circling. That the word 'alternative'—the 'alternative bodies' assumed by the divers—is a coldly disdainful substitute for 'resurrected' becomes apparent in the poet's fantasy of the divers, 'buoyed up by adoration', performing 'slow-motion pirouettes / forgetful of body, of gravity'—and we may be sure that *gravity* also means 'proper seriousness': 'all weight gone', they

> levitate now
> around the statue,
> their corps de ballet
> like Correggio's sky-
> swimming angels, a swarm
> of batrachian legs.

The poem begins with salt—'Seasalt has rusted the ironwork trellis'—and towards the end, thankfully after the uncertainties of his passage, the poet reaches the quay 'with salted lips': the salt of corrosive time, then, the acrid taste of unignorable reality, in the presence of which the charming antics of the levitating divers seem, appropriately, the merest *levity*. It is in keeping that, in an implied comparison with the 'baroque ecstatic devotion' of the circling divers in the postcard of *Cristo del Mare*, Tomlinson should show a humorous preference for the mother who 'has the placid / and faintly bovine look / of a Northern madonna'.

Tomlinson's satirical treatment of Christian iconography in his play on the words 'levitate' and 'gravity'—the *levity* of angels and divers released from *gravity*, the levity of human behaviour and emotion generally when they are, so to speak, out of their element—and his quasi-physical ascription of the divers' angelic buoyancy, absurdly, to an ecstasy of adoration: these manoeuvres are characteristic of his dealings with Christian art in the poetry of the last decade. In the chronological reading of any major poet, and especially of a body of work like Tomlinson's notable for its intellectual coherence, one finds that one is listening to a tacit conversation between the later and the earlier poems; it is not possible to read the poems in isolation from each other. 'In the Gesù' (*The Return*, p. 5), for example, a short, trenchant poem published six years after 'San Fruttuoso', gains from its kinship with the thought of that poem and poems like it, satirical or not, and from earlier poems with no direct bearing on the religious theme, an added depth and weight, an increase in poetic authority. 'Adoration' in the first line links back to the 'ecstatic devotion' of the balletic divers.

> All frescoed paradise in adoration,
> Saints choir the unanimity each atom feels,
> And hearts that cannot rise to the occasion
> Are spurned to earth beneath angelic heels.

We are helped to calculate the precise force of 'unanimity', too, by our recollection of its contrary in 'To See the Heron', the momentary harmony among the '*various* brightnesses' of an autumn scene effected by the heron's addition of its touch of blue, the visual unity that is not sameness. As unanimity among the saints is made to betray fanaticism, and as 'the church triumphant' depicted here is equated with the despotism to which fanaticism leads, albeit 'the despotism of the dove', so the ironic voice of continence, the voice 'against extremity',[15] that, speaking for 'hearts that cannot rise to the occasion', invokes the norm of strictly human possibility, reduces transcendence to an 'occasion' and diagnoses an unfitness for angelic heights as an insusceptibility to spurious emotion. There are other connections between this and earlier poems. The naturalized 'rise' recalls the 'risen' heron; the 'resistless certainty' of the church triumphant brings to bear upon the question of religious belief the poet's counter-belief in the 'saving grace' (CP p. 308) of a wondering, questioning, receptive uncertainty. The poem's final judgement, in its eighth and final line, on this painted image of absolute faith, certainty as a power-wielding force, is that it shows 'The empire of love without love's comity'. 'Comity', a word that appears early in Tomlinson's poetry and recurs at intervals in a variety of contexts, and always as a touchstone of sanity, applies to religious bigotry and coercion the same standards of civilized thinking, the necessary sensitivities and reciprocities of social intercourse, that he has applied consistently throughout his work to the whole field of human conduct.

We know with our senses; we cannot make images of a life we do not know, an after-life or alternative life, except with materials from the world of sense experience. This basic dilemma—the unbridgeable gap between the life of the senses and the life we imagine and, in any comparison between them, the trite theatricality of the latter—provides the major satiric opportunity in Tomlinson's recent satires on religious otherworldliness. In 'San Fruttuoso' the 'solid' reality of 'deck' and 'dock', of 'sea-roll and sea-chop' and 'the buck of the boat', of flesh, 'bone and blood' converts into dreamlike silent comedy the weightlessness and 'staggeringly / slow-motion pirouettes' of the underwater rubber-suited swimmers; 'In the Gesù' lets us feel the overheated excitement—'all frescoed paradise'—of the Christian artist's imaginings and the simple melodrama in the scornful flick of the angelic heels. This gesture of arrogant dismissal links this poem to another in *The Return*, 'Catacomb' (p. 15), where, a small but significant connecting detail, it is reproduced, or paralleled, by the capuchin who 'stands guard' at the entrance 'gate and stairhead' to this underground city of 'eight thousand' embalmed dead as the poet and his companion are leaving it: never taking his eyes from his book, contemptuous, it seems, of the unconverted and the merely curious, 'His disregard / Abolishes us as we pass beyond the door'. The imputed contempt of the capuchin for the uninitiated is a more reticent but unmistakable implication in the earlier description of his predecessor at the gate, who, unprovided with reading matter, 'withdraws to contemplation' in a supercilious unwitting parody of the Lady in Eliot's *Ash Wednesday*. The verbs—'withdraws', in its created context, as much as 'abolishes'—give to the hackneyed antithesis of worldly and unworldly a satirical twist. In their unworldiness the capuchins have lost not 'the world' but reality; the taciturnity of the contemplative friar betrays kinship not with a life beyond this life but with 'The silence throughout this city of the dead'. The life 'beyond the door' to which the poet returns is life out under the sun—which, on the coast of Sicily, 'Comes burning off the bay / Vibrant with Africa'—not, as in the pious cliché, the putative life of the immortal soul. These details that characterize the friars refer us to the larger theme of the poem: the rival attractions of this world and an imaginary world of the spirit. A sly verbal repetition, echoing across forty lines, contrasts the minimal, as it were entombed, life of the first capuchin, whose 'eye / Glides with a marvellous economy sideways / Towards the stair, in silent intimation / *You may now descend*', with 'the world's great wonders':

>   if once a year
> The house of the dead stood open
>   And these, dwelling beneath its roof,
> Were shown the world's great wonders,
>   They would *marvel* beyond every other thing
> At the sun.   (my emphasis)

The sun is the true mystery; in comparison, the sideways glide of the friar's eye is a conjuring trick. The larger theme is present as an implied question, posed wittily by the embalmer's art: are these bodies, variously clothed in

> Mob-cap, cape, lace, stole and cowl,
>   Frocked children still at play
> In the Elysian fields of yesterday—

are these lifelike dead 'costumed for resurrection' or does embalmment, so to speak, embody nostalgia for the life they are leaving? Either explanation would be plausible, but the poet's description of them leaves no doubt in the reader's mind that their strongest motive was the desire to perpetuate the Elysium of life as they had known it: 'caught / Forever in their parting pose', 'Dressed for the promenade they did not take'. It is, presumably, because the 'solidity the embalmer would counterfeit' would indeed be a counterfeit if an image of the resurrected body were intended that the second capuchin's mind is 'Averted from this populace whose conversion / Was nominal after all': for 'conversion' applies simultaneously to a turning of the spirit and to the transmutation of the physical body.

I have said that in Tomlinson's later poetry religious agnosticism rings with tones not of doubt but of affirmation. The gap opened by a gate 'flung wide' in a stretch of stone wall is, to the eye that sees it, an image of freedom: an irruption of space as if it were an access of possibility, release from the confinement of the known, from foreknowledge of the expected and, after the moment of perception 'abrupt / With the pure surprise of seeing', from the finality of 'afterknowledge and its map' (CP p. 308). Uncertainty becomes a positive: a newness and immediacy of experience that transcends the closure of certainty. The developments that have taken place in Tomlinson's work since the 1960s, aside from the accretions that come with new experiences in the work of any poet who remains poetically active, comprise, I have suggested, refocusings, reslantings of existing interests and attitudes. It is clear that the mood of his poetry shifted somewhat in the late 1960s and early 1970s, but if we take the 'terse authority' (my earlier characterization) of *Seeing is Believing* as representative of his early manner, then words like 'tentativeness' and 'hesitancy', 'uncertainty' and 'confusion' in a description of his later work, though applicable, would by themselves seriously misrepresent the nature of the difference between the two periods. If one were to attempt a single definition of the difference between early and late Tomlinson, it would not take the form of a distinction between early confidence and late loss of confidence: the distinction would be, rather, between different kinds of positiveness. I will not, however, even attempt such a definition. There will be less risk of simplifying generalization if I juxtapose a poem of the 1980s, 'Thunder in

Tuscany' (*The Flood*, 1981; CP p. 339) with a comparable poem of the fifties, 'Ponte Veneziano' (*Seeing is Believing*, 1958; CP p. 19), and let the comparison stand as a concrete exemplification of the shift in mood, which it would be just as accurate to call a change of viewpoint. Both poems depict figures in postures that express and affirm exemplary attitudes. In 'Ponte Veneziano', the fixed gaze of the two human figures, 'tight-socketed in space . . . / Stripping the vista to its depth', projects strength of mind and will: undistractable concentration, unrelaxing singleness and tenacity of purpose, strictness of judgement, a disciplined commitment to what is necessary and, as 'It broods on the further light', to the utmost of what is possible. Staring into the circle formed by a bridge-vault and its reflection,

> They do not exclaim,
> But, bound to that distance,
> Transmit without gesture
> Their stillness into its ringed centre.

In contrast with the steady light and stillness of 'Ponte Veneziano', the scene of 'Thunder in Tuscany' is cinematically dramatic and the stone figures, far from being 'without gesture', are almost flamboyantly expressive: lightning illuminates a facade of 'statues listening', giving fragmentary glimpses of features 'Taut with the intent a body shapes through them / Standing on sheerness outlistening the storm'. The 'stillness' of the Venetian figures epitomizes the peculiar quality of their attention, a stoicism. If there is an element of stoicism in the attitude of the Tuscan statues, their 'taut' posture reveals more than endurance or resilience: it also projects tension and challenge. The illusion of an abyss conveyed by 'sheerness' may justify the suggestion that the attitude in which these figures are caught 'outlistening', looking to survive with knowledge of something beyond, the storm is an image of post-Christian daring.

NOTES

1. *PN Review*, 5:1 (1977), p. 35.
2. See 'Lines on a Young Lady's Photograph Album' and my comments in 'Philip Larkin and Charles Tomlinson: Realism and Art' (*The New Pelican Guide to English Literature*, 8: *The Present*, ed. Boris Ford).
3. Donald Davie, *The Poet in the Imaginary Museum* (Manchester: Carcanet New Press, 1977; ed. Barry Alport), p. 66.
4. *PN Review*, 5:1 (1977), p. 35.
5. Robert Frost, 'The Figure a Poem Makes', in *Collected Poems, Prose and Plays* (New York: The Library of America, 1994), p. 777.
6. *Eden*, p. 20.
7. John Keats, in a letter written in December 1817.
8. *The Prelude* (1850), Book II, 254.
9. *Eden*, p. 18.
10. *The Prelude* (1850), Book XI, 145–48.
11. Wallace Stevens, *The Collected Poems of Wallace Stevens* (New York: Knopf, 1974), p. 67.
12. The phrases are from 'At Holwell Farm' (CP p. 39), 'Return to Hinton' (CP p. 59), 'Movements II' (CP p. 234).
13. *Eden*, p. 13.
14. *The Poem as Initiation*.
15. The title of a poem in *The Way of a World* (CP p. 163).

Chapter Six
Art and Mortality

It was in the 1980s that Tomlinson revisited the region of Northern Italy in which he had written his first characteristic poems, those published in *The Necklace* in 1955. A poem written a few years after his first visit, 'Up at La Serra' (*A Peopled Landscape*, 1963; CP p. 78), recalls the landscape and the people of the place; its principal character is the young poet Paolo Bertolani. In the poem sequence 'The Return' (*The Return*, 1987; p. 7) describing his return visit, Tomlinson speaks more directly of their friendship:

> Two things we had in common, you and I
> Besides our bitterness at want of use,
> And these were poetry and poverty.

In 'Up at La Serra', with its refrain of *Soldi soldi*, we hear of Bertolani's 'deprivations' but not of Tomlinson's; accustomed to the personal reticence of his poems, we are startled by these confessions of a 'bitterness at want of use', a 'youthful sickness' of perhaps self-pitying resentment, 'cure' of which 'came in part', he says, from what 'I grew to know' living in that place: after the storms that greeted his arrival, 'a time of storms' to match the mood of that time of life, he writes, 'I felt the sunlight prise me from myself'. Returning to Serra thirty years after his first visit, Tomlinson discovered that Bertolani had never left. The second poem of the sequence records a walk with him from Serra to Rocchetta. Taking in the scene once more, confronting the remembered image with 'all that meets the eye and all that does not', with what has persisted and what has not, he reflects on their common reverence for 'those lesser deities / We still believe in', to whom both poets have dedicated their poetry—'For place is always an embodiment / And incarnation beyond argument'. The poets had shared 'poetry and poverty': now, 'returning' brings general recognition of riches and abidingness but also of losses and impoverishment. Man is poisoning the earth. The fireflies were in danger of extinction, though 'Under the vines the fireflies are returning': but some things are beyond return. Where they pause in their climb to La Rocchetta, their 'lookout lies above a poisoned sea': the poets are united not only in their belief in the gods of earth but also in their belief that 'We have lived into a time we shall not cure'. The sequence, in part, celebrates the renewal of a friendship, but that return signifies both a sharing of hopes and fealties and a shared sense that the times and time are adverse. Turning to the personal life, the second poem of the sequence balances its ending between gain and loss; coupling praise of the dedication and achievement of poetry, Paolo's, with the communication of a death:

> But climbing to La Rocchetta, let there be
> One sole regret to cross our path today,
> That she, who tempered your beginning pen
> Will never take that road with us again
> Or hear, now, the full gamut of your mastery.

The poem sequence itself 'climbs' to a finale of affirmation; it does not, however, ignore the several, including contrary, meanings of 'return'. We have the return of the past to the present, but we are forewarned also of 'the last submission and return' to earth. 'The soundless revolution of the stars / Brings back the fireflies and each constellation', but 'We wait now on the absence of our dead': wonder and acquiescence weave a counterpoint in this last poem of the sequence. And the whole sequence is filled with such counter-pointings: contraction to self and expansion by sunlight into the wide, open day ('sickness' and 'cure'); poetic 'mastery' and the final 'submission'; creation and destruction, time's regenerations and what time cannot cure.

'The Return' is a major poem of summation; it is not my purpose to give a full account of it. I have focused on one aspect of the poem simply to introduce and epitomize the antitheses of Tomlinson's poetry written in the 1980s. They are reflected in the titles of the two parts of this chapter: 'The Affirmations of Art', which discusses poems about the imagination in general and poetry in particular, and

'Against the Autumn', which notes an increased preoccupation with last things.

The Affirmations of Art

Tomlinson's poetic thinking has always included thinking *about* poetry, *about* art. He has found it necessary repeatedly to ask himself: 'What is it for / this form of saying?' (CP p. 221). As the poet's relation to his experience has over the years gradually changed, so has the question been asked and answered in different ways. The positive agnosticism of the later poetry—an unknowing which, acknowledged, is a gift of the imagination, a synonym for self-forgetful attention and enlargement of view—has had a bearing, therefore, on the way the question has been asked and answered in the 1970s and 1980s. During these years he wrote several poems about 'this form of saying', and about the imagination in general, which comprise, it seems to me, his most comprehensive treatment of the subject.

The place to start, however, is with *The Poem as Initiation*, a prose piece written two decades earlier. Its theme is ceremony, which Tomlinson maintains is an aspect of 'what the poem is and what the poem does', as ritual is an aspect of religion. Setting aside the distinction between the reading of a poem and the poem itself, we can say that the performance of a poem, or the performance that a poem is, is a ceremonial act in that it is a form of words corresponding to—in some sense, reproducing—the reality it celebrates. With the word 'ceremony' Tomlinson poses the question of the relation between 'the intricate meshings of words', which is the 'life' of a poem, and life itself, beyond the reach of words. The poem is specifically 'a ceremony of initiation'. 'It leads us into and through and out on the other side of an imagined experience'; but the imaginary parallels the real—'is pointed outwards ... towards life at large, towards the possible meaningfulness of life at large'. Living and making or reading poems are different things, but Tomlinson defends ceremony as the enactment of 'the inner rhythm of events': pointing outwards not only and not simply to life, but to the meaningfulness of life supplied by the mind, and not simply to its meaningfulness—as if meaning is inherent in the fact—but to all the possibilities of meaning that present themselves to speculative thought. But because it *is* a matter of forms and formalities ceremony also has its limit. Tomlinson cites an instance from the initiation rite of the Hopi Indians. Masked figures impersonate the tribal spirits, and are believed to be what they seem by the Hopi children, but at the culmination of the rite 'the spirits remove their masks and the child sees that those he had taken for gods are only metaphors for gods: they are his uncles and kinsmen ... The Hopi removal of masks confesses the limit of ceremony.' In dramatizing its own fictiveness, 'the ceremonial act is always indicating something greater than itself, something of the indivisible and thick texture of reality, something undefinable, yet out there around us ... We can never *know* all that reality, but the rite of the poem has, so one hopes, brought us into closer relation with it.'

What relation the 'life' of a poem has to that reality is one of the questions Tomlinson has addressed in his poetry. In *The Poem as Initiation*, delivered as a Convocation address at Colgate University in 1967, though he does not minimize the disparity between 'an imagined experience' and 'life at large', or ignore the limits of art, Tomlinson's message to his audience, phrased moderately as a working hypothesis, is that the 'ceremony' of a poem points towards 'the possible meaningfulness' of life outside the poem. The poems themselves, however, are not general statements but concrete occasions; they are not always concerned, or not directly, with the question of meaningfulness. They are more particular but also, frequently, immoderate and teasingly equivocal in their celebrations of imagination and poetry. 'A Rose for Janet' (*The Return*, p. 39), for example, is a playful poem about the serious *play* of poetry; it sets out verbally and in typographical mime the paradox of the poetic act. A poem moves as if alive, and the poet shows it moving in the expansions and contractions of his lines:

>   I know
>   this rose is only
>   an ink-and-paper rose

> but see how it grows and goes
> on growing
> beneath your eyes.

The life of this mimic rose, no less than that of 'a rose in flower', is 'perennial', except that its revival occurs whenever the reader chooses to 'resurrect it':

> whenever you repeat
> this ceremony of the eye
> from the beginning
> and thus
> learn how
> to resurrect a rose...

The 'ceremony of the eye' rehearses the ceremony of the poem itself. Repeating the 'ceremony of the eye / *from the beginning*'—the phrase has a whiff of wizardry about it, suggesting that instructions must be followed to the letter if the magic of poetry is to work—repeating the ceremony, the reader learns how to conjure up at will the rose of a poem, a mimic reality with its problematic relation to the world 'on the other side of [the] imagined experience'. Tomlinson claims that 'in the poet's weighing and measuring' of an occasion 'there is a dwelling on the inner rhythm of events'—that is, on the inner dynamic of the occasion, its deeper reality: yet he also says that poetry is a masquerade, its realities 'only metaphors'. I have brought Tomlinson's consideration of the function of ceremony in poetry into a discussion of this poem not because I mean to ignore its playful wit and light urbanity, but precisely to illuminate these qualities of the poem. In 'A Rose for Janet', as in the prose meditation on ceremony, Tomlinson hovers between bold claim—though not 'a rose in flower', the poem's 'rose of spaces and typography' blooms with a comparable life: it 'grows', and to read is to 'resurrect' it, to bring it back, as it were, to bodily life—between this claim to reality and the candid confession that it is an ersatz rose. The poet at once deprecates the inferior 'life' of the poem ('it is *only* / an ink-and-paper rose') and boasts of its superior reality ('but see how it grows...'); or rather, he pretends to deprecate and pretends to boast: the urbanity, the poise, of the poem is this blending of undervaluation and overvaluation, which dramatizes the paradox of poetry and the impossibility of measuring how much, or in what sense, it is truth or illusion.

Poems of the 1970s and 1980s not only draw attention to the element of illusion in the truth of poetry but express relish of the disparities between fact and appearance exploited by poems; as, for instance, between bales of hay and the 'scattered megaliths' they resemble ('Hay', *The Flood*, 1981; CP p. 323). On the sky-line at nightfall they seem to be—and this is what so delights the imagination—

> A henge of hay-bales to confuse the track
> Of time, and out of which the smoking dews
> Draw odours solid as the huge deception.

The metaphor, in confusing the two things, thereby wins a victory over time: the megalithic appearance in evening light is as 'solid' as the thing itself and at the same time a 'huge deception', a deception which is appreciatively embodied in the 'lavish' sensuousness of the whole poem—'The air at evening thickens with a scent / That walls exude and dreams turn lavish on'. Imagination, says 'Hawks' (*Written on Water*, 1972; CP p. 215), enables us to do the impossible: namely, to share, though we cannot understand, the ecstasy of birds, which 'after their kind are lovers', and, in defiance of our earth-bound limits, 'ride where we cannot climb the steep / And altering air, breathing the sweetness / Of our own excess'. The poet is doing what many poets have done with their skylarks and nightingales, eagles and wind-hovers, but never with quite this contented poise between doing it and knowing it can't be done. Specifically, the sense of immoderateness, of overstepping limits, in 'excess' is qualified by the etymological sense, appropriate here, of simply 'going beyond' (of 'exceeding the place it guesses' in 'Nature Poem' [CP p. 295]); going beyond ourselves, 'we are kinned / By space we never thought to enter': that kinship and that entry are at once real and illusory, the claim to them is at once sober truth, carefully measured in the language, and intemperateness. The poem is both a confession and a celebration of the imagination's inordinacy.

'In New Mexico' (*Annunciations*, 1989, p. 5) is also about inordinacy, though not explicitly, a disorder relished. The eye looking at clouds above a sandy beach, as when it watched the hawks, feels empathetically, or creates, a kinship with the upper space of light and air. The clouds appeared suddenly, as if from nowhere:

> Where had the clouds come from? A half-hour since
>   There was none, then one, the size
> Of a man's hand that unclenched, spread, grew
>   In no time into an archipelago on blue.
>
> They grew out of each other and multiplied.
>
>   The inter-breedings,
>   The feathery proliferations of cloud-boats
> Careless of anchorage, set out in flotilla
>   Over this dry sea-bed they pied with their shadows
> Until they covered the entire sea above.

The behaviour of clouds—self-generating, shape-changing, proliferating—is nothing so obvious and clumsy as an allegory of the imagination: the clouds are clouds, seen in New Mexico, and yet the cumulative effect of twenty-seven lines of description, recording their appearances and actions in images that convey at once the findings of an attentive eye and the delighted involvement of the whole man in what he sees, is the gradual adumbration of a parallel. To the human eye the metamorphoses are metaphors, and seem to say that by grace of wind and light-and-shadow the world has become no less imaginary than real: as imaginary as 'cloud-boats' or 'an archipelago' of cloud-islands, as real as the 'rocks' on the beach and the 'eagle' that held solitary sway before the invasion of the clouds. Summarizing its several impressions of this insubstantial world of air and cloud, light and shadow, the poem discloses, with an urbane wit, its connivance in these inversions of reality: 'Throughout the vagrant disorder of the sky / Excess was to be the order of the day'. 'Disorder', 'excess' and 'vagrant', words that *should* appeal, censoriously, to norms of order, restraint, steadiness, are here without their underpinning of righteousness: disorder is indistinguishable from delight, as it is in 'The Miracle of the Bottle and the Fishes'—discussed in the previous chapter (p. 225)—and, as in 'Hawks', excess is sweet; vagrancy, for the wandering of the clouds, has in consequence a sort of gipsy licence. The world of space, in its largesse, gives itself to the unrestrained imagination. Freedom is the keynote of the poem: the 'cloud-boats' are *'careless* of anchorage', 'archipelago' invokes a geography of roving and discovery. Space 'offered its unfilled miles' to the proliferating clouds, as, in 'The Gap', the 'gateless gap' in a stone wall is a 'space' waiting 'to be filled with the meaning / It doesn't yet have' (CP p. 308). Clouds turn the already insubstantial air into a counter-world of fantasy: on the ground, cloud-shadows seemingly dematerialize even the substance of rocks—'The ground was no more than a screen / Onto which the heavens could project themselves / And alter it all at will'. No longer literal air and sky, they are now 'the heavens' of the gods with the power to make the earth a 'screen' for their shadow-thoughts, their imaginings: triumphant imagination has supplanted the solid world. 'True', the poet concedes, 'You could pick up a stone and feel / That was a tight world still'—perhaps as the young Wordsworth 'grasped at a wall or a tree' to be assured of its material existence and save himself from the 'abyss of idealism'[1]—but nothing else in the scene has offered that assurance. The world belongs now to the wind. The poem confronts the certainty of stone, finally and conclusively, with an image of the world cast loose and in tatters: 'the white / Seed of the cottonwood', shaken from its tree-anchorage by the same wind that has been shaping and re-shaping the clouds, 'Was drifting across the sand like shreds of sky'. Twenty years earlier, in 'The Way of a World' (CP p. 165), Tomlinson was in no doubt that the 'weightless anarchy of air' swept by an autumn gust needed the 'counterpoise' of a firmly rooted and resistant tree. As a matter of fact the possibility of a similar judgement is latent in the images of the 'drifting' cottonwood seed and a sky 'in shreds', and must occur to the reader, momentarily, as he reads those last lines of the poem; a possibility that justifies the glancing reference to Wordsworth's defence against 'idealism'. And yet the balance of sympathies has changed since 'The Way of a World'. In the 1970s, 'the gateless gap' that liberates the eye and opens space is, as we saw, 'A saving grace in so much certainty of stone'. Stone might signify, even in the 1980s, 'a tight world'—sealed and secure, if precariously—but 'tight' also recalls its contrary at the beginning of the poem, the '*un*clenched' hand pouring out, filling the sky with, cloud-shapes; the contrast with that open-handed, lavish prodigality discovers in the hard, compact shapes of stone, rather than a reassuringly firm, steady reality, a sense of confinement and narrow (tight-fisted) meanness.

The metamorphic imagination finds its justification in the ways of the world, of the natural world itself—in the ways of wind, for example, or the ways of light-and-shadow. Wind has been in the past—'In New Mexico' makes an exception—an instrument of chaos to be resisted; light, however, always speaks for the imagination. Everywhere in Tomlinson's art—in his graphics and his poetry, and no less conspicuously in his earliest poems than in his recent work— light, changing appearance, transfiguring fact, points to other possibilities than those realized, to other extensions of the real. The word for its activity, its mission in the world, is play—but, as in art (as in 'A Rose for Janet'), it is serious play:

> The light, in its daylong play, refuses
>   The mountains' certainty that they
> Will never change . . .

This is 'Above the Rio Grande' (*Annunciations*, 1989; p. 6), a kind of sequel, but also a counterweight, to 'In New Mexico'. By its illusions and transformations the light lightly brings into question the mountains' delusion of permanence. The play of light parallels the wizardry of art, the *mind* at play. Light

>   shifts and shows
> Even the cloudshadows how to transform
>   The very stones by opening over them
> Dark wings that cradle and crease their solidity—
>   As if to say: I gather up the rocks
> Out of their world of things that are merely things,

>   I call dark wings to be bearers of light
>   As they sail off the shapes they pall.

On the other hand, although light seems to dissolve matter, and its emissary shadows to change its substance, the stones and rocks nevertheless remain. The contraries of light and matter are matched by a duality in the mind: it responds to the light, but another part of the mind responds with equal conviction to this assertion of material reality. 'The rocks remain to tell what [light] is',

>   and only so
>   Can they both flow and stay, and the mind
>   That floating thing, steady to know itself
>   In all the exceedings of its certainty.

The serious play of art, which finds in the world's own weather the sanction for its excess, exemplifies the will to live beyond the mere fact of existence. It is a form of poetry's 'Grasping for more than the bare facts warranted / By giving tongue to them' (CP p. 234); it finds its unlikely match in the composure of the farmer's widow at Hinton, who is sustained by the 'more than bread' of inherited tradition (CP p. 60). 'Possibility' is Tomlinson's deliberately moderate, persuasively reasonable word for what is affirmed so diversely in his celebrations of metamorphic imagination. If, as he writes in the Preface to *Collected Poems*, in his poetry 'space represent[s] possibility', then perhaps the space in which light and wind-spread clouds work their transformations represents a further range of possibilities.

In some reflections on the Borghese Gardens in Rome Tomlinson turns from the transgressions of metamorphic imagination to the power of redress and renewal intrinsic to the products of imagination; reflections which reveal the deep affinity between play and grandeur of imaginative ambition. Cardinal Borghese's seventeenth-century estate—villa and gardens housing his collection of antique statues—is now a park surrounded and intersected by the modern city. 'In the Borghese Gardens' (*The Return*, 1987; p. 1) refers to 'the cardinal's great dream'; whatever that was literally, the poem intimates by its images that the cardinal aspired, with his sculptured gods and goddesses in a pastoral setting, to marry the worlds of nature and myth, time and eternity. It was a great dream and, surely, one that was inordinately so. Time brings its changes—the original 'parterres redesigned, gardens half-gone'—

> Yet Pluto's grasp still bruises Proserpine,
> Apollo still hunts Daphne's flesh in stone,
> Where the Borghese statuary and trees command
> The ever-renewing city from their parkland.

This is Tomlinson's revised version of Rome as the Eternal City. These are time's renewals: it gives and it takes away. 'Rome is still Rome', and that is a city of gains and losses: 'Spray-haloed traffic taints your laurel leaves / City of restitutions, city of thieves'. Yet the embodiment of the cardinal's dream commands the city, apart but potent. Essentially his dream is the artist's vision of Eden, a temporal and natural Eden. The human lovers described in the first stanza, unlike their divine counterparts, lie under the temporary protection of the Borghese pines, which merely blinds them to—does not exempt them from—the gathering 'storm that must drench them soon': yet, the storm having broken and spent itself, the poet feels he has reason to celebrate the 'healing artifice' of the cardinal's creation; with which phrase, moreover, he names the office of art:

> Lovers, this giant hand, half-seen, sustains
> By lifting up into its palm and plane
> Our littleness: the shining causeway leads
> Through arches, bridges, avenues and lanes
> Of stone, that brought us first to this green place—
> Expelled, we are the heirs of healing artifice.

The stonemason's art has made the 'arches, bridges, avenues and lanes / ... that brought us first to this green place': art, paving the way, has opened to us Eden and, lifting us to its height, has granted us its protection. The rain that, as we learn in the final stanza, has 'quenched' the ardour of the young lovers has, on the other hand, made the causeway shine: contraries of rain and sun, inescapable fact ('the storm that *must* drench them soon') and imagination, complement each other; it is the rain that intensifies the scent of Eden, which fills the parkland and spills over and out into the city beyond its borders:

> here the parkland ways
> Reach out into the density of dusk,
> Between an Eden lost and promised paradise,
> That overbrimming scent, rain-sharpened, fills,
> Girdled within a rivercourse and seven hills.

We live between loss and promise, and art is the intermittent reminder or harbinger, extending its influence—which is its gift of saturated, heightened perception—into the 'density of dusk' between one day and another, one visit and the next. It is patently impossible to 'translate' into fixed quantities—as this commentary presumes to do—the elusive suggestiveness of these last two stanzas as they shift back and forth between planes of meaning. The 'dusk' is literally the day's end, figuratively our banishment from the Garden of Eden, our unawakened senses, and the city outside the gardens of art. The 'green place' hovers between Eden and 'Eden' (Tomlinson's Eden of time and place), art and parkland; we were 'expelled' from the first only, but the promised land we inherit is at once Canaan, the natural world, the creations of myth and art, and the cardinal's bequest to the human city.

The Gardens' ambiguous presence within the city poses once again, for Tomlinson, the question of relation, between art and life, between the Eden of art and the city of man. The association of art with civility, civilization, is frequent in Tomlinson's poetry. It is a lightly suggested, elusive theme, for example, in 'The House in the Quarry' (*Annunciations*, 1989; p. 29). The unaccountable presence of a solitary house in this working quarry, a house still lived in and cared for, with tended vines and melons growing and a table set out 'As though, come evening, you might even sit at it / Drinking wine'— the incongruity of such a presence amidst the waste created by, and the daily activity of, a marble quarry is the subject of the poem. 'What is it doing there, this house in the quarry?'—the first of a series of questions put by the poem. The answer is that 'it stands its ground'; an unlikely, bizarre manifestation of human creativity—man the settler and cultivator of the land—it 'stands' *against* the devastations both of man and of time: though 'the dust lies heavy along its sills'— the dust of the quarry, the dust of time—yet a 'dusty pergola keeps back the blaze / From a square of garden'. (It should be said that to convert, as I do here, the faint murmur of other meaning stirred by the repetitions of 'dust' and 'dusty' into an overt metaphor of mortality, though unavoidable, is to sacrifice the poem's teasing lightness of touch to the convenience of commentary.) The fantasy, suggested by these signs of civility, that, 'come evening', the house expects to 'repossess / Its stolen site' lies in apposition, and implicit comparison, to 'the unshaped marble' waiting 'to be quarried here': a comparison between a civility restored and a poem composed.

'The House in the Quarry' also reworks the dialectic of fiction and reality pondered in *The Poem as Initiation*. If art is an extension of the real into the possible, then the reality of *this* waste land would seem to be infirm ground on which to set the ladder of imagination—the light of possibility being, rather, the light of impossibility, Wordsworth's 'light that never was on sea or land'. By analogy with the insouciant bravura displayed in the gestures of home-making and house-keeping in the midst of ruin, the poem must be an act of quixotry; a quixotry related, however, to the 'unreasoned care' of the farmers in 'The Compact: at Volterra' (CP p. 206)—'Refusing to give ground before they must, / They pit their patience against the dust's vacuity'—and to the resoluteness of those, in 'Snow Fences' (CP p. 108), who, encountering 'the snow-shrouds of a waste season' and evidence of time's effacement in 'the nameless stones' of a Saxon burial ground, 'are fencing / the upland against those years, those clouds'. Clearly we are meant to take heart from this latest exemplar of the shaping spirit: 'All things / Seem possible in this unreal light'— the reclamation of this 'stolen site' (an Eden of civility not so much lost as confiscated) no less than the shaping of a poem from these stolen materials. The pursuit (there is point, as we shall see, in asking whether it is indeed the pursuit of a lost Eden or, rather, a future paradise) is an enterprise to be wondered at, incredulous of—this is the tone of the poem's questions—but the poetry invites us at the same time to succumb to the enticements of its affirmative unrealism.

And this is because time contributes not a little to the constructions of the human mind. 'And will they taste then', this improbable crop of grapes,

> Of the lime-dust of this towering waste,
> Or have transmuted it to some sweetness unforeseen
> That original cleanliness could never reach
> Rounding to insipidity?

Either seems possible, but, retained or 'transmuted', the taste of mortality is also the taste of human aspiration. The second question returns us to the Borghese Gardens, the alternative of Eden or paradise, and implies a preference. It asks whether time itself is not the agent that transforms the eventual 'insipidity' of prelapsarian Eden, the unsullied grape, into the 'sweetness unforeseen' resulting from a blend of grape and added dust which is the fermented paradise promised at the end of time.

The Poem as Initiation offers two descriptions of art: art as 'only metaphor', a masquerade, and, where Tomlinson's principal emphasis falls, art as pointing to the possible meaningfulness of life at large, as indeed a ceremony of initiation. My discussion of his treatment of this theme in the poetry started with poems of exuberant imagination, flaunting the free play of poetry, in which the relation to life is, at most, implicit in the tone—the extravagance on the threshold of undoing itself—or briefly explicit as an appendage. 'In the Borghese Gardens' has not lost its awareness that a belief in art's value for life is vulnerable when it speaks of its ministry of 'healing artifice'; the awareness merely complicates what is notwithstanding a celebration of its restorative potential for the human city. 'The House in the Quarry' is more playful but, while humorously noting the inequality between the forces of art and civilization and the destructive power of its opponent (Samson and the Philistines?), its questions point firmly towards the parity and identical worth of civility and poem.

The same conjunction holds in 'Revolution' (*The Return*, 1987; p. 7), where it is used to stage a confrontation between two sets of values, one inherent in the political meaning of the title-word, the other brought to bear by an appeal to the etymological sense. By their opposition the poem gives to the poet's artistic ethic, identified with the second meaning, a polemical edge and, in spare verse and small compass, a surprising range and depth of life-significance. The scene is the Spanish Steps in Rome's Piazza di Spagna. The 'double stair' supplies an image for the movement and motivation that differentiate the poet's values from those of revolutionary doctrine: for it is possible to make a circuit (a revolution) of the Steps, 'down, up and back', and *return* to your starting-point.

In the title-poem of the collection, which commemorates Tomlinson's 'return' to the place of his poetic self-discovery, the word refers, as we have already seen, to more than a journey—more than the literal journey back to Serra or memory's retrospect. It is not only a return *to* the past but, in the renewal of his friendship with the poet Paolo Bertolani, to whom the poem is addressed, a return *of* the past. The poem repeatedly flows out from and back to the word, in all its senses, and to the idea of return in a wide range of applications. The road travelled after thirty years, for example: 'I could not draw a map of it', he writes,

> And yet I know
> Each bend and vista and could not mistake
> The recognitions and recurrences
> As they occur, nor where. So my forgetting
> Brings back the track of what was always there
> As new as a discovery.

The returns of memory are rediscoveries of what was only temporarily lost, renewals of a faded freshness. The experience of return, in this poem, is one thing and many—many returns, not all happy but ministering, in a complex balancing, to an overall acceptance of the ways of time, a comprehensive re-pledging of the poet's covenant with time and place, a hallowing of rootedness.

The full significance and importance of this return, the bringing back of 'what was always there', becomes clearer if we link this theme to Tomlinson's claim for Cézanne's ethic of perception, the artistic ethic he adopted as a basis of his poetry: 'It seemed to me a sort of religion, a bringing of things to stand in the light of origin.'[2] The shape of the 'double stair', returning you to where you started from, in 'Revolution', is an ironic-playful image of art's 'bringing of things to stand in the light of *origin*'. Political revolution is the opposite process: a disavowal of the past, a disruption of connectedness. The poem opens with this contrast.

> REVOLUTION it says
> painted in purple along
> the baluster of the Spanish
> Steps and yes
> you can return
> by the other side
> of this double stair...

The painted slogan is a gesture of brutal impatience, a call to an instant Eden. Sidestepping the challenge of the word, in the guise of courteous concession ('and yes') to an unintended meaning ('you can return') the poet coolly sets aside its peremptory vehemence, the verse exemplifying, in its uninterrupted, unruffled pace and its matching urbanity of tone, the patience, the civility, necessary to restore or rediscover Eden. The Eden one rediscovers or restores is not the Eden of the 'sun-browned / drop-outs'—the only revolutionaries in sight—'who litter the ascent' as if they had tried and failed. Even this modest instance of a return to Eden—involving, as we shall see, 'recognitions' and 'recurrences' like those described in the title-poem, a restoration of the memory and a renewal of the experiences of 'what was always there'—even this is a labour leaving you as you climb 'a little breathless', which, working in and with time, assents to its conditions. The difference between their Eden and the poet's is the distance between two senses of 'flights': solipsists, 'their flights are inward / unlike these', the flights of stairs,

> unfolding by degrees
> what was once a hill,
> each step a lip
> of stone and what they say
> to the sauntering eye

> as clear as the day
> they were made
> to measure out and treasure
> each rising inch
> that nature had mislaid.

Art, the mason's or the poet's, declares here its allegiance to outwardness, the plenitude of the given and primary, and through nature to the Eden that is, equally, a given.

The drop-outs are in flight *from* the external world: the flights of stairs are a formal expression of art's attachment *to* it. The revolutionary flight is precipitate: art's movement is, in all senses, measured, measured by the divisions of the stairs and of the verse, an even-stepped and -staged, regulated progress of slowed-down contemplation. For, the poem continues, 'only art / can return us to' the real Eden. This was not, the lines announce with a teasing authority, a paradise lost but one that, carelessly, 'nature had mislaid'—and a careful art therefore has the power to restore. It is only temporarily or circumstantially lost, 'mislaid'—either hidden from us by nature (hence Tomlinson's fascination with the hidden in such poems as 'At the Edge' [CP p. 324]) or an Eden we have lost sight of. Art seeks the Eden in nature; art therefore follows—follows rather than copies—nature, as the Spanish Steps literally, step by step, follow but do not reproduce the shape of 'what was once a hill'. The flights 'were made', and poems are made, not simply to imitate and ornament the natural fact but 'to measure out and treasure'—to enable the mind to pause and deliberate over, to prize and store up in memory—'each rising inch' of the fact. As the stone mason measures out the gradient by converting it to geometry, so the poet brings to the rhythms of speech and thought the measure of verse, a measuring that, as the poem demonstrates, is no less a measuring *out*. For 'to measure out' is to add up, inch by inch, part by part, the sum of something, to take its measure, to mark it out, furthermore, with a suggestion of laying it out for appropriation—which is also a connotation of 'treasure'.

The transposition by art of content into form, the replaying of nature in a different key, is, in Tomlinson's representation, a process of lingering, savouring attention by which the given of nature becomes the possession of the mind, and what the mind receives is what 'nature had mislaid', its true, its Edenic self. One must use words like 'appropriation' and 'possession' with reservation, however; Eden is not there for the taking, it is there only for 'the sauntering eye' commended by Thoreau:[3] not the intent, narrowly focused gaze in pursuit of the visible but a relaxed attentiveness, open and receptive, one that does not anticipate the things it will see but waits for the world to present itself. Art's recovery of what had been lost through inattention is not so much a taking possession as an entry *into* possession accomplished by a process of self-submission, as the act of swimming in 'Swimming Chenango Lake' is at once 'to take hold / On water's meaning' and 'to move in its embrace' (CP p. 155). To 'the sauntering eye' 'each step' is a 'lip / of stone': the script is not man's but nature's, and nature utters (outers) its Edenic self only to the eye-and-mind that waits for it to make itself known; the appropriate manner of attention, this waiting for, is therefore an attendance upon, a waiting upon, the word of nature.

What has been 'mislaid'—whether by nature or man—is re-experienced, its existence reconfirmed, in the translation of art:

> for only art
> can return us to an Eden where
> each plane and part
> is bonded, fluid, fitting, and
> fits like this stair.

Nature mislaid its Edenic self in perhaps another sense—laid it wrongly, presented an imperfect picture of itself in a number of discrete, partial, momentary impressions. Art's peculiar task and privilege is, in that case, to make the thing itself and the image of it match. This poses a problem. We remember, from 'The Poet as Painter', that in 'painting where the presence of the external world is strongly felt', such as Cézanne's, the problem for the artist is 'how to reconcile sensation and form without bullying your picture into a wilful unity', for sensation is momentary and form is not; and, we are told, the problem is the same for the poet, or for the sort of poet who, like Tomlinson, tries to catch 'the fleeting moments of sensation' and unite 'this fleeting freshness to a stable form'.[4] These observations, based on the assumption that the artist's objective is to make the mutable immutable, the transient permanent, tell us much but not enough; the motive cited—to create 'a stable form where others may share' the experience of 'this fleeting freshness', to make the momentary truth permanently available to a succession of readers— is, as it were, a social motive and not one that resolves the enigma of the relation between the stability of the form and the instability of the content. The poem implies another explanation. The difference between nature as we know it and the Eden in nature is the difference between the 'fleeting moments of visual sensation' and the reality of nature-in-itself. Cézanne is reported by his friend Joachim Gasquet as saying—and Tomlinson quotes him—that 'Nature is always the same, but nothing remains of it, nothing of what comes to our sight'; Cézanne insisted that 'our art ought to give ... the appearance of all its changes' but 'ought to make us taste it eternally'.[5] Cézanne means more by 'eternally' than Tomlinson means by 'stable form': his aspirations for art are less modest than those expressed by Tomlinson in his essay. Yet in 'Revolution', surely, the poet wants to claim more for artistic form than that it makes the fleeting experience indefinitely repeatable. 'Nature is the same', wrote Cézanne, even though its appearances are constantly changing; we encounter the same thought in the form of a paradox in Tomlinson's poems: 'the shapes of change' in 'The Way of a World' (CP p. 165), 'a geometry of water' in 'Swimming Chenango Lake' (CP p. 155). Tomlinson seems to believe as firmly as Cézanne, then, that the stability of artistic form discovers in the fleeting an eternity of change. Tomlinson's name for that eternity is Eden. The mis-laid Eden postulated in 'Revolution' needs art to re-lay it—converting nature into a fluid geometry. The natural Eden imaged ('restored') by art is, therefore, at once nature and human artefact. 'Bonded'—the bonding of stones—is the poem's instance of man's cooperation with nature, a mastery gained by a deft dependence; 'fitting' similarly blends the suggestion, created by its apposition with 'fluid', of a natural coming together of interlocking shapes with a hint of human agency and more than a hint of human-aesthetic approval. 'Only art / can return us to' this particular Eden because only art can assume the fluidity of nature and at the same time, in its stable form, compose an analogue of nature's sameness, its eternity.

In 'The Poet as Painter' Tomlinson describes 'Cézanne at Aix' as 'a kind of manifesto poem'. 'Fountain' (*The Return*, p. 3) stands in a similar relation to his later work as 'Cézanne at Aix' stands to the poems of *Seeing is Believing* and *The Necklace*. In the thirty years that separate the two poems Tomlinson's art has indeed developed, and the view of art to which in the 1980s he would win his reader's assent is more complex, has wider implications than that for which he campaigned in the 1950s; correspondingly, the later poem is a tighter and more intricate web of thought.

> Art grows from hurt, you say. And I must own
> Adam in Eden would have need of none.
> Yet why should it not flow as a Roman fountain,
> A fortunate fall between the sun and stone?
> All a fountain can simulate and spread—
> Scattering a music of public places
> Through murmurs, mirrors, secrecy and shade—
> Makes reparation for what hurt gave rise
> To a wish to speak beyond the wound's one mouth,
> And draw to singleness the several voices
> That double a strength, diversify a truth,
> Letting a shawl of water drape, escape
> The basin's brim reshaping itself to fill
> A whole clear cistern with its circling calm,
> And the intricacies of moss and marble
> With echoes of distance, aqueduct and hill.

Tomlinson would have us consider not the personal origin but the 'flow' of art. If it begins in 'hurt', this is simply because all things begin there. Not all the consequences of Eden's loss are ruinous, however. The Christian believes that the original sin and exile from divine grace set in motion the action of redemption and restoration. For Tomlinson, too—making his own use of the concept of 'a fortunate fall'—the luck outweighs the lack. Since art is in time, it flows as a fountain and as time flows; but the compensation is that it resembles specifically a *Roman* fountain: civilization and the 'healing artifice' of art are, both, fruits of the Fall—'Adam in Eden would have need of none', neither art nor civilization. As in 'The House in the Quarry', time is represented as an enabling agent. The poem grants that there is a causal relation between 'art' and its half-rhyme 'hurt' but not that 'Art *grows* from hurt'. Substituting the notion of contingency—that some precondition, some 'hurt gave rise / To' the artistic impulse—for the metaphor of growth, Tomlinson hints a distinction, that art is initiated by hurt but is not organically determined by it. There is no necessary connection between the prompting hurt and what the poem says: art does not *grow* out of but—the rhyme points a contrast—*flows* away from, spreads beyond, hurt. Art speech is, precisely, the 'wish to speak *beyond* the wound's one mouth', and everything it is and does, 'between the sun and stone', transcends its personal origin.

The central theme of the poem is the 'public' existence of art and its relation to the natural and human worlds. The relation is paradoxical. A poem is at once a fiction and a 'truth'. The fountain flows *like* time, *like* life: a likeness, a pretence, a simulation of reality; a 'music' of 'mirrors' and 'echoes'. Another paradox is that it makes its 'music of public places' out of undertones, latencies, hiddennesses; an interior life not of the poet but of language. We, the poet and his readers, meet publicly in the privacies of words. Art's healing power lies in its ability to 'speak beyond' the personal history and in doing so to create a common world exterior to the self out of the interiority of words. It makes 'reparation'—for a particular felt lack, for imperfection generally—by the *all* it can 'simulate and spread': an act of inclusion by metamorphosis (translation of the world into word) but also an act of extension. 'All' collects the plurals—'murmurs', 'mirrors', 'echoes', 'the several voices'—into a 'singleness', a single 'music' of several 'places', a single 'shawl of water', 'a strength', 'a truth'; and this oneness confronts 'the wound's one mouth' with its contrary. Whatever the voices of a poem are—mingling as they do interior and exterior, voices of the medium and voices of 'public places', of 'distance, aqueduct and hill'—the united strength and diversified truth of their single utterance is art's reply to the separated, estranged self, proudly nursing its pain, excluding the world.

What 'Fountain' claims poetry should be—repairing the poverty of self, supplying a lack—this poem consummately is. Tomlinson's impersonality is a creed not an evasive manoeuvre; the whole of his personality enters into his poetic embodiment of it. The 'flow' of the verse in 'Fountain' exhibits the poise of an alert, proportionate intelligence in alliance with an unself-conscious intensity of feeling—a self-forgetfulness which is a total self-engagement with what is 'beyond' self. Although it begins in easy, open urbanity, it builds up into the intricately plotted, richly orchestrated celebration of a mystery. The style of the first four lines is one of courteous debate in which weighty matters—Eden and the Fall—are handled with a light dexterity and equability. With a mock-concession ('And I must own . . .')—conceding the undeniable with an amused civility that murmurs 'but of course'—the poet disarms his disputant by granting him his point and changing the grounds of dispute; from a position of vantage, he can now make his counter-claim with a negative question ('why should I not. . .?') that presents his opponent with the dilemma of having to agree or, perversely, to contest a manifestly reasonable alternative. The alternative view of art becomes, half-way through the third sentence, an alternative view of life, where lower-case 'a fortunate fall'—its field of operation the space 'between the sun and stone'—naturalizes the supernatural; at the same time the conversational-persuasive manner moderates into a tone of reflective soliloquy. The fourth line replaces the Christian content of the paradox but borrows its authority, preparing it to be a serious image for a different affirmation. Without severing its connection with the reasoning and reasonable manner of the first two sentences—indeed, building upon it—having asked its question, the poem proceeds, through the winding, elusive syntax of its final sentence, to 'darken' meaning and deepen the tone. That last long sentence *flows*, generously and with incremental power, but it flows 'through . . . secrecy and shade': it is light not sluggish—has buoyancy and momentum—and at the same time it is charged with piled-up meaning; the words have clarity but, I would suggest, a clarity that leaves dark spaces for the mind to puzzle over.

The poem begins discursively: the first word names its subject, the first sentence is a statement and the second is a counter-statement, framed as a question, which introduces the fountain as a similitude for the named subject, art. Yet the poem is not a proposition and the relation of image to meaning is not equational. The analogy is continuously surprising and at times elusive. The reality of the fountain comes before any meaning it may acquire in the unfolding of its attributes; the mystery celebrated is in the first place the mystery of 'a Roman fountain'. The image is not *applied* to the subject: the facts of the image *discover* the poet's thought for him, resisting conversion into the algebra of idea; it is a living process of thinking, which can therefore be endlessly relived by the reader. The evasive intention of the poem—evasive of neat correspondences—is evident in the teasing circularity of its pivotal statement: what art does 'Makes reparation for what hurt gave rise / To a wish to speak beyond' hurt. This is not the simple antithesis between art and hurt that 'reparation' might suggest, since the personal hurt was not only what needs mending but also the prompting impulse for art's pursuit of impersonality; the 'reparation' performed by art is potential in the hurt because it is inherent in the wish to 'speak beyond' generated by the hurt.

I have said that the poem becomes the celebration of a mystery, and that meaning is not so much elucidated as darkened. The keyword is 'simulate'. Does the artist make a simulacrum or a counterfeit? The word refuses to choose between the two possibilities, two judgements of the act of making likenesses: that art reflects, or that it creates a substitute for, reality. The intention, it would seem, is to display the paradox of art. The poetic *counterfeit* is the *truth* of translation (of world into word). Art simulates 'a truth': that is, it *persuades* a 'public' that this is a truth in which its members can come together. The dissimulation is in the means of persuasion: it is an art of suggestion and illusion ('Murmurs, mirrors, secrecy and shade'). Art has an objective life, indubitably, but the relationship between word and world, art and reality, is problematic. 'Simulate' is the keyword but 'spread'—'All a fountain can simulate and spread'—carrying the image of flowing water, is equally important; reinforced by 'scattering' and 'public places', it would seem to imply a public existence, a daylight reality, for art. It is an impression the poem means to create, and yet it does so by sleight of hand, for 'spread' *refers*, surely, not to the public diffusion of art but to its 'shifting text' ('the ways a poem flows', compared in 'Nature Poem' [CP p. 295] to the 'shifting text' of an August landscape): the 'several voices', metamorphoses, 'intricacies' and ramifications of art, verse's *diversification* of 'a truth'.

All analogy—figurative imagery or the correspondence of sound to meaning—is in this sense dissimulation: the correspondences *pretend* to demonstrate the truth of what the poetry 'says'. Tomlinson means to expose the pretence but without discrediting the result. The long, trailing last sentence, copying the 'flow' of temporal and logical consequences, imitates poetry's diversification of meaning. We read the sentence with the expectation that at each stage of the process image and meaning (fountain and art) will match exactly and thereby seem to *explain* the 'healing artifice' of art. But the correspondences are partial; they leave spaces for questions. How can art belong to the public realm ('of'—not in—'public places') and be at the same time secret and private? We know the stages of the spring's passage by way of the fountain to the surrounding cistern, but how does poetry make its parallel journey from 'hurt' to 'calm'? This is to ask what constitutes the 'calm' created by art and how art can be a 'reparation' for pain and loss—is it simply the act of utterance (outering)? These questions are not unanswerable, but they are not answered: the poem, instead, presses the reader to enquire among the word-relations for possible explanations, promising no certain solution.

Even as in the last sentence image and meaning stand slightly apart from each other, so the sound of the words tends to convey something other, something more than their referential content, augmenting the sense. Finding in art 'a wish to speak beyond the wound's one mouth / And draw to singleness the several voices', the *words speak soberly* of manyness and singleness, a language of logical relations, while, beginning with that second line, the *music sings* of facility and fusion. The sound of the next line, with its balance and burliness—'That double a strength, diversify a truth'—again keeps close to the sense; but, in describing the movement of water from basin to cistern and the absorption of the distant landscape into its 'circling calm', the assonance and the rhymes in the next two lines and the sibilants of the concluding lines, together, serenade the perfection of smooth-flowing, concerted power, release and serenity. The music traces for the ear, beneath the meanings of the words, a progression from difficult birth to a fullness and freedom overflowing into a clarity and calm that extends beyond itself, includes within itself the outside world; a progression that translates the 'meaning' of the fountain's flow and hints a collateral application to art. But the words that give us that other meaning plainly—'hurt', 'speak', 'mouth', 'voices', 'truth'—are at the beginning of the sentence; from there on the analogy retires into the shadows, a putative presence of uncertain significance. The music would convince us that the analogy of spring water rising through a man-made fountain in a Roman square and falling in a single, powerful jet of many sounds, filling a basin and spilling over the rim in one smooth, gliding motion to fill again the waiting cistern, a flood becoming calm clear water, a medley of sounds becoming silence and echoes—that this analogy of 'a Roman fountain' demonstrates in every detail the action of art: but the music 'proves' more than the words will confirm.

    This is, I think, deliberate. We are reminded of a statement in 'The Poet as Painter': 'In both graphic and poetic art, I like something lucid surrounded by something mysterious.'[6] The mystery of art is the elusiveness of its 'truth'. 'Fountain' is a poem about art, which uses its own art to draw attention to the elusiveness of the reality it endeavours to catch in words. What it reveals is the impossibility and yet the necessity of translating world into word (or paint or musical sound). Since the subject of the poem is poetry itself, the poem grows into a celebration of the mystery of its own form, which is the mystery of its relation to reality. The poem makes the reader aware of the mystery by creating a sentence the syntax of which deliberately obscures, and obstructs the reader's attempt to apprehend, its structure. The length, complication and catenary organization of this sentence, offering no foreseeable, easily identifiable grammatical structure, keeps us in suspended, baffled anticipation of its completion. In effect the sentence is a succession of shifting subjects, under continuous reorganization as it moves from one to the next; this syntactical flux is calculated to 'bring the mind *half-way* to its defeat' (CP p. 295). By adding to the difficulty *we* have in translating the flow and sounds of water into the diversity and eloquence of art, the elusive syntax would seem to demonstrate the difficulty intrinsic to *any* act of linguistic translation. The process of mystification here resists but does not nullify the mind's efforts to solve the problem of the sentence. The intention is to create, in counterpoint to the triumphal progress of the poem's music, an energizing state of strenuous uncertainty.

The value of a poem is in the process of thinking which in submitting ourselves to the reading of it we are made to undergo. This poem refuses to gratify the mind's craving for abstract patterns, for a neat ordering and containment of experience. We are sent out, uncertain of our destination, on a trailing sentence of connections, moving us further and further away from the initiating 'hurt', and when we arrive—with a feeling of having arrived—at the clarity and 'calm' of the water in the outer cistern, we discover not an end but 'echoes of distance', and the continuing trail disappears with its questions—specific questions about the relation of the fountain to the aqueduct and of the 'echoes' to the 'voices' and a general question about the relation of art to nature—into the landscape beyond the formal conclusion of the poem. The poem's 'logic' does not close down meaning: gaps and enigmas open the poem to the reader and give him or her a participatory, speculative presence in it.

'Against the Autumn'

The reason why Tomlinson at the time when he was writing the poems of *Seeing is Believing* wanted his poetry 'to take its ethic of perception from Cézanne' was, he explains in his essay 'The Poet as Painter', that it is 'an ethic distrustful of the drama of personality of which Romantic art had made so much, an ethic where, by trusting to sensation, we enter being, and experience its primal fulness on terms other than those we dictate ... It seemed to me a sort of religion, a bringing of things to stand in the light of origin, a way, even, of measuring the tragic fall from plenitude in our own urban universe.'[7] I have cited this essay a number of times and have quoted these statements more than once. The essay, prefixed to *Eden* in the mid-1980s, was based on a lecture given in 1979; the poems of the following decade suggest reasons for looking at these sentences once again. Tomlinson's poetry has always borne the strong imprint of a particular sensibility—a cast of mind and modes of feeling, a general outlook, specific views and beliefs, impressions and responses that are peculiarly his; in this sense of the word his poems have always been markedly personal. This is not to say, however, that they act out 'a drama of personality'. His more recent poetry is no more self-conscious than it ever was but is perhaps less sparing of personal reference than before, and in some remarkable poems personal history and the personal life are central. Above all, the thought of time running out and the final victory of death, recurrent in these collections, is an added note which, in his reviewing of themes, cumulatively makes a difference. The theme of 'being' is focused now more on the idea of conclusion than the idea of origin.

Once our ears are attuned, we hear this note of mortality, howbeit quietly sounded, everywhere in these poems. I have taken the title-phrase of this section, with its implications of beleaguerment and resolute resistance, from 'Poem for my Father' (*Notes from New York*, 1984; CP p. 367), though this personal motif is far from conspicuous in that poem. It begins with an 'I' and recalls feelings about 'countryside' shared with his father, but the poem, as usual, faces outward, its subject industry's destruction of our natural world, which is linked here to the devastation and disruption of the Great War; the idea of time running out *for the poet*—that is, in its personal application—is only a secret presence waiting to be noticed. Once it is recognized, however, it adds a note of personal urgency to the poem.

Comparison of Tomlinson's poems about the scarred landscape, the 'patched battlefield' (CP p. 243), of the industrial Midlands in which he spent his youth with the earlier portrait of the man he calls 'John Maydew' (CP p. 65), to be later identified as the poet's father, a countryman dispossessed and condemned to live out his life bound to this circle of *unnatural* sights and smells, reveals the biographical sources of his major theme: in his father's sense of exile from the Eden of nature he discovered a mirror of his own. It is clear, too, that the father's 'bitterness' over what is felt to be history's betrayal and a stolen birthright has been passed on to the son and—though the note of personal bitterness itself is rare in Tomlinson's poetry—fuels both the occasional anger of his earlier poems and throughout his work the compulsive intensity of his Eden quest. The young man's 'bitterness at want of use', as remembered in 'The Return', looks back to and chimes with the father's bitter consciousness of powers unused, thoughts and feelings unexpressed. The diagnostic portrait of John Maydew implies a passionate indictment of our time but the poem's feeling-content is not referred to the circumstances of the poet's life. In 'Poem for my Father' Tomlinson exchanges impersonal analysis for first-person statement about their shared sense of exile and their common turning to an unspoiled nature for its temporary reversal. The personal mode adopted is one of unhistrionic, matter-of-fact, direct report, but in adopting it the poet is licensing a greater measure of 'subjectivity' in the linking of fact and feeling:

> I bring to countryside my father's sense
> Of an exile ended when he fished his way
> Along the stained canal and out between
> The first farms, the uninterrupted green,
> To find once more the Suffolk he had known
> Before the Somme.

Already in this first sentence—'Eden' is mentioned later—'exile' carries insinuations of the biblical Fall. Such imagery is, of course, not unusual in Tomlinson's poetry. The Christian tropes of Eden and Fall, imprisonment and liberation were at work, for example, in his description of the water-filled 'marl pits' of the Potteries as 'a second nature', an Eden restored, and of how the young artist sought to 'speak' his imprisoned spirit and senses 'free' of a denatured world with 'a language of water, light and air' (CP p. 248); similarly, John Maydew's evening 'pastoral' out on the allotment was pictured as a 'paradise' above the 'quotidian hell' of the valley mills that owned his days (CP p. 65). But these were avowed metaphors; 'Poem for my Father' is nearer to myth than metaphor. The opening statement loses as it advances, line by line, its initial character of objective report. The Staffordshire 'countryside', on the one hand, and the post-war 'urban universe', on the other, are in process of being converted into the mythic polarity of old order and new age, the battle of the Somme being the abyss that separates the two worlds. For most of the poem the boundary between myth and history is blurred:

> For everything we see
> Teaches the time that we are living in,
> Whose piecemeal speech the vocables of Eden
> Pace in reminder of the full perfection,
> As oaks above these waters keep their gold
> Against the autumn long past other trees
> Poised between paradise and history.

Though the poem identifies the 'aftermath' of the Somme as 'the time that we are living in', what has been lost is measured against the imagined 'full perfection' of an Eden, whose 'vocables' and measure are those of poetry, not against the facts of a pre-1916 Suffolk or a pre-war England. The oaks, like the poem, are also 'Poised between paradise and history', and in the simile 'their gold' is a 'reminder' of more than a summer gone. At this point the suspended distinction between history and myth is restored and the historical and mythic viewpoints are presented in opposition to each other. The 'gold' is at once a natural autumn sight and an unseasonable colour, timeless witness (gold remembered or envisioned) of a 'full perfection' that the oaks 'keep . . . / *Against* the autumn'—in spite of, as if hoping to hold back, the movement of time. The preposition 'against' brings a new emotion into the poem; with the strong suggestion of holding out against something, against the coming winter, at this point—as I began the discussion of this poem by saying—it brings the poet into the poem. One half of its visible theme could be translated fairly accurately as 'the tragic fall from plenitude in our own urban universe'; the private wish and fear secreted in that one phrase, 'against the autumn', give a personal point and intensity to the contrary vision, complementing the sense of loss, of an unfallen, accessible Eden. The chief pleasure offered by this poem, for me, is the grace with which it balances its equivocations and mingles its currents of meaning—personal, historical and mythic—in one *fluency*. It is the pleasure, as in 'Fountain', of a created mystery.

Tomlinson's poetic shaping of his material in the 1980s can always be profitably compared with earlier shapings of the same material. For his resumption of familiar themes is invariably a re-examination, and to each new viewing he brings the clarity and confidence learned from previous encounters. A style that can, as in 'Poem for my Father', compass with apparent ease the different registers of strong, plain directness, stately grandeur and mythic resonance is achieved, presumably, not without effort and practice. The effect of subtle simplicity that such a poem has on a reader who knows the whole work is partly due to his sense that the earlier explorations of that material are, so to speak, included or, even, consummated in the later treatment of it. 'At Huexotla' (*The Return*, 1987; CP p. 31), for example, recalling a visit to 'the poorest / church in Mexico', reminds us of other poems that confront religion with the challenge of Tomlinson's naturalism. The poet and his companion are drawn to this church by 'the sound of the place'; not the sound of bells, though it seems to come from the bell-towers, but the flute-notes of 'caged birds hung' on either side of the altar. The obvious comparison, in this instance, is with the poet's visit over twenty years before to the church of 'Las Trampas U.S.A.' (CP p. 124), where, too, the building is a focus not of a Christian sanctity but of what Tomlinson presents as its natural and human counterpart. Instead of the 'peace' that is 'not of this world', it offers 'coolness'—coolness to temper the savage heat of a southern 'August sun', and coolness as a symbol of the temperate comities of a tiny social ritual, as it were a rite of initiation preceding and culminating in the poet's admission to—its only title—'this place of coolness'. In 'Las Trampas U.S.A.' a natural and human good replaces a transcendent good. There is more in the anecdote of the caged birds, however, than a substitution of rapturous birdsong for (say) the oblation of praise and thanksgiving: the poem links, and plots the relationship between, the two kinds, the two sources of joy. Despite its poverty—and this is presumably the reason for mentioning it— even this church must have its portion of gold, gold for the glorification of God: it was not gold, however, that set the birds singing but 'sun on gold', 'the alchemy of light transmuting', unlike the old alchemy, 'gold to song'. Light is not, here, the symbol but the rival of God. It is as though gold of divinity is only a reflective medium of the light, and worship of a Supreme Being a deflection of praise from the true mystery of being, manifested in and by the light:

> for it was the light's
> reflection had set
> those cages in loud accord
> and only night would staunch it.

The choir of caged birds sings the poet's own hymn to the real light of the universe and, like the poet, will continue to sing until night stops them. There may be a memory of Edward Thomas's thrushes, in 'March', who filled the last hour of the day with 'their unwilling hoard of song' to 'keep off silence / and night'; like Thomas, at any rate, Tomlinson here, as before in 'Poem for my Father', gives to his images an undertone of personal feeling and lets his poem end with the anticipation of the end of poems and the conclusion of life. 'Staunch' is in some ways a surprising word. Its root meaning is 'stop the flow of' but in current English, the application confined usually to the flow of blood, it always carries the suggestion of relief. For this poet, surely, the ending of the flow of poetry is not to be thought of as a relief from pain. Yet we cannot mistake the metaphor: the flow of song is at the same time a flowing away of the singer's life-blood. From what point of view consistent with his general outlook, then, could Tomlinson conceive poetry to be an *open wound* for death to close? Art, he insisted in 'Melody' (CP p. 269), is not complaint, not the voice that cries 'I am dying, I am denying, I, I...', but the reply to it: 'It is the will to exchange the graph of pain / Acknowledged, charted and repeated, for the range / Of an unpredicted terrain'. Nor is life the incurable suppurating wound for which the mastery of one's art is the only compensation. Yet in its affirmations his poetry has never flinched from the thought of extinction: the 'unpredicted terrain' includes, in the sequel to these lines of 'Melody', 'the dark immensity' and 'unfathomable silence' of the final sea. The poet of the 1980s would not repudiate an earlier statement, that man as artist, 'tutelary spirit / Of his own inheritance, speaks / To celebrate' (CP p. 235); the birds respond to the reflected light with the 'loud accord' of wholehearted celebration. But they are *caged* birds who sing as though they are free, who celebrate what will not last as though it will; that sense of fatality, a poignancy, has become part of the music of celebration. Since there is no God to staunch the wound of time—time running out—night invests itself in robes of divinity and performs that office. Night, in 'At Huexotla', is the partner of light; they are the two halves of a single mystery, the one completing the other.

Night is at once the complement and the contrary of light; the 'gold' of autumn oak leaves is related in one aspect to the meaning of autumn, but of the autumn we hold out 'against' it is the antithesis. In 'At Huexotla', as in 'Poem for my Father', the contrary—night or winter—does not simply, or entirely, contradict the affirmation of life: it brings to an end, and instinctively we resist it, but, as I have tried to show, it also contributes something to the 'theology' of naturalism. The theme of mortality is in each instance a brief tail-note; it arrives without fanfare, more as a supplement to than an expected culmination of its plot. 'At Huexotla', for example, begins with the church's poverty and a hint of something else, both in the first line:

> Tall on its mound, el Paupérimo—
> the poorest
> church in Mexico
> and the smallest.

Raised up, this tiny church—it has, we learn, 'a minute interior'— aims to impose. The poet and his companion are drawn not by an appearance but by the mysterious 'sound of the place'. The next five stanzas 'quicken' with the visitors' eagerness to reach the place in a crescendo of mounting expectation of learning the alternative to this poverty, a solution to the mystery of this music. The expectation is fulfilled in the penultimate stanza, where alternative and solution prove to be one and the same: the glory of sunlight on the gold ornament, and 'the alchemy of light transmuting / gold to song'. This is the climax of the poem, the celebration of light as lord of the universe and generator of praise in his grateful subjects, and it continues from this stanza into the first three lines of the next and final stanza. Only in the last line of the poem does 'light' meet its adversary 'night'; the contrary arrives almost, it seems, as an afterthought. But it is not that: it is a new factor to be reckoned with and included. One line fills in, quickly, as it were casually, the whole background to art's celebration of life.

In the same collection, *The Return*, 'The Night Farm' (p. 47) follows a similar plot line: a scene is encountered, the life in it celebrated, with images of light and fire, the last line adding the contrary image of the dark. The farm, with its 'flaring panes', seemed like 'the first house' of 'a city hidden in the hill',

> A forge, it might be, from which the fire pulsed out
> Above the steep descent of streets whose veins
> Of light wound down into the hill heart.

The fantasy is an occasion for honouring 'the ardent geometry of dwelling'. The oxymoron, characteristically, joins inner fire to outer form, life to art. It is an old and recurrent theme: the passion man brings to making a home for himself in nature. Not new but new in the degree of emphasis is the picture of life as the hidden elemental force, revealed, from which the city of man receives its creative vitality; at once the internal life of the body (pulse and veins) and the subterranean life of the physical universe, where the metaphorical 'veins' are also water channels and geological deposits of earth's previous upheavals. The 'flaring panes' of the farmhouse windows had suggested an outpost of a hidden city; they 'were also telling / Of the ardent geometry of dwelling / And'—the last line follows—'the purity of the dark from which they shone'. This names for the first time the *ground* of darkness against which the *figure* of light stands out.

The imagery of life makes its statement only in relation to the framing, containing whole, and yet, once again, the thought expressed, and so serenely, is unexpected and disquieting. The 'purity' of night equals and answers the pure fire of human ardour and the clean forms of human geometry; this post-climactic ending contrives a not unforeseeable but none the less unforeseen completion, effects a sudden lengthening, deepening of perspective.

In *Notes from New York* (1984), the smaller part of the collection that contains his observations of the city, Tomlinson casts a sometimes quizzical or sardonic eye over the streets and vistas of Manhattan, adjusting lifelong preoccupations and a formed outlook to a new subject matter in poems of poised humour and surprising perspectives. All show the alertness and zest characteristic of his poetic record of sense experience. In two of them, 'The Landing' (CP p. 355) and 'On Madison' (CP p. 357), the poet's keen appreciation of life keeps company with an awareness of an end to it. In 'The Landing' it is one detail among several but the image for it, sunset over Manhattan viewed from the arriving plane, is the focal point of the poem; familiar motifs, as in 'The Night Farm', congregate around that central fact. The poet still 'speaks / To celebrate' (CP p. 235), and the life celebrated is that which human beings and animals have in common; the poem begins and ends with it: 'Banking to land, as readily as birds / We tilt down in', and the tall buildings are 'eyries of the town'. But the high view that enables the poet, as so often before, 'to see / The total and spreading scope' of the landscape below, as it were life itself, and the light 'That catches on spire and pinnacle and then / Shafts out the island entire' is one that shows 'The Passaic flowing with fire towards the sun'—the source of life—'Just when one thinks the sundown over and done'. The echoes that mingle the contrasts of 'sun' and 'sundown', of 'sun' and 'done' express a relish of life sharpened by a simultaneous apprehension of its impermanence. Manhattan 'is holding on to the rays / Of a tawny strip of sun of late afternoon', and the poet, too, is 'holding on' with all the tenacity, the unwillingness to let go, that the phrase suggests.

In 'The Landing', time is running out; the poem 'is holding on to' a brief moment between day and night, a *now* in danger of slipping into *then*. Walking north 'On Madison', it is again, for the poet and his wife, 'the end / Of a winter afternoon'; but the poem is concerned less with time running out than its correlative, space closing in, an effect produced by the mist rolling in over the island. A *here* of immediate human experience matters more at this moment than the mystery of an inhuman *there*. With greater urgency than before, in these two poems Tomlinson takes hold on the reality of here-and-now. This is a winter scene and by faint implication, I am suggesting, also a winter life. We are divided by the invasion of mist from the further 'reaches' of space—from the island's 'surrounding' water and from all that lies above and 'beyond the mist-lopped towers'. As the vista of vision closes down, so the rivers, rendered alien as they disappear from sight, seem more insistently to 'Assert their right to the island they enclose'. 'The unseen'—what is concealed from us by, and as if embodied in, mist—'Presses upon us at this hour' as an unseen menace. Horizons shrink to an island within an island. The ethic of perception outlined in Tomlinson's 'Preface' to his *Collected Poems*—'where space represented possibility and where self would have to embrace that possibility somewhat self-forgetfully'—is still in effect, but we have here an added truth, that space in winter cannot so easily represent possibility. Civilized man may 'savour the wine of the solitude of spaces', but the metaphor implies that it is a comparatively rarified pleasure. The plural 'spaces' is there to remind us perhaps of *Le silence éternel de ces espaces infinis m'effraie* (an echo of Pascal—if that is what it is—sufficiently muted to secure the allusion against portentousness): they are wine to the imagination but their primary significance is that they are unpeopled, they are the feared 'homelessness beyond the mist-lopped towers'. Even as the imagination pays homage to that 'solitude', 'in the same instant' our bodies

>   choose the street
>   That seems like a home returned to, grown
>   Suddenly festive as we enter it
>   With the odour of chestnuts on the corner braziers.

There have been other adjustments to Tomlinson's habits of thought. Once 'a bringing of things to stand in the light of origin'—

beginnings, the creative mystery—was 'a way of measuring' humanity's 'fall from plenitude'.[8] Now the measure is more likely to be the *full* circle that assimilates first to last things, creation to destruction. 'Near Ceibwr' (*Notes from New York*; CP p. 376) muses over the disappearance of the local castle. Its stones have 'gone into the cliff'; to the 'rocks that recall the origins of earth' the ephemeral existence of the castle and its makers is unmemorable. The permanence of matter is the impermanence of sensate life. The now 'unguarded threshold stones'—which were, in any case, no defence against time—lie near 'the roots / Of the bracken', part of the earth again. Rooted in earth and its natural cycle, no more than the primordial rocks can the plants feel the mortality that afflicts its rootless creatures: they

> Are deaf to the searching whisper of the sea
> That startles our ears with the very tone
> That flowed up to the sentry looking down.

The 'tone' of life that flows from human past to human present is a continuous awareness of death.

Height and range are prized by Tomlinson; the metaphors express the poetry's compelling aspiration to wholeness of vision. It is characteristic that, with 'The Landing', the series of New York poems should open on an aerial vision of Manhattan, the aeroplane passengers 'the only ones to see / The total and spreading scope' of the sun's last rays. These are the high, ranging views, commanding breadths and depths of time or space, taken by many of Tomlinson's poems. Their ambition is large but not inordinate: the vistas of possibility represented by this imagery of space are not endless, and the poems have given equal, often simultaneous attention to the natural boundaries of expansion. Therefore, in qualifying its celebration of the view from Carrara's 'marble mountain' down into its quarries—'so much of space and depth gathered at one glance'—'Carrara Revisited' (*Annunciations*, 1989; p. 28) is doing nothing new; its disquieting reminders, warnings against hubris, differ from the reservations expressed in earlier poems only in the downright statement of them. But this is enough to mark a change of position: the balance of confidence and misgiving has tipped, in this poem, decidedly towards the latter. High above the marble quarries, our echoing steps

> Make us seem gods whom that activity
> Teems to placate. But not for long. The hawk
> Stretched on the air is more a god than we,
> And sees us from above as our eyes see
> The minute and marble-heavy trucks that sway
> Slowly across the sheernesses beneath us, bend on bend,
> Specks on an endlessly descending causeway.

We recognize in the last image a metaphor for the descent towards death, over which the watching hawk presides. The switch of perspectives—whereby 'we' on our Olympian height surveying our domain become in turn minute specks under the surveying eye of the hawk—is paralleled by a similar reversal earlier in the poem: the eye sees 'space and depth' but the ear hears something less gratifying—

> the unbroken separation
> Of fragile sounds from solid soundlessness—
> The chime of metal against distant stone,
> The crumple and the crumble of devastation
> Those quarries filter up at us.

The solidity of stone is transferred to the 'solid soundlessness' on which the sounds of metal against stone impinge. Reality is the silence underlying all this human activity. This sort of reversal has been from the beginning a key strategy in Tomlinson's verse.

> From the palace flanking the waterfront
> She is about to embark, but pauses.
> Her dress is a veil of sound
> Extended upon silence—

this is one of several images in 'Venice' (CP p. 3) that subordinate the *figure* to its *ground*. But in these instances the figure-ground denotation of sense experience is for exploring its texture and shape, exhibiting its full possibilities and conveying the poet's delighted and total assent to the 'reality' thus displayed. The sharpening of perception and enlargement of consciousness are an unqualified good. In 'Carrara Revisited' the 'separation' of the parts from, and their subordination to, a whole that is more than the sum of its parts has more ominous implications than in those earlier poems. The deeper 'silence' that sets off and gives distinctiveness and elegance to the sound of the woman's dress and the moment of pause, in 'Venice', is a benign mystery, related to the quiet of the evening landscape, in 'Farewell to Van Gogh' (CP p. 36), deepening into the 'central calm' of night. The 'sounds' of the quarry, on the other hand, are 'fragile' and partake of the general fragility of human life, and the solidity of this 'soundlessness' is that of infrangible rock and represents an eternity that means danger and ultimately death.

There are poems now that *toy*, at once playfully and fearfully, with images of disaster. 'The Way Through' (*The Return*, p. 49) is explicitly about images as distinct from realities: the 'reflection' in a rock pool at the mouth of the cave, and what that reflection resembles and the consequent fear it awakens. For it 'Reads like a gap in the floor of the rock / That you could fall through', an image 'that speaks of falling day by day by day / Through a space which does not yet exist', that leads to a vision of a final *Dies Irae*. Again solidity is in question: 'The image refuses to believe / You are more solid than this downward way'. Even as the image is being accused of practising illusion, the illusion grows in reality until, as endless falling and the last day, it becomes the only reality—like the 'solid soundlessness' of 'Carrara Revisited'. 'What Next?' (*The Return*, p. 46) recalls a real event, a flood of rain that caused a landslip near the poet's home, but the emotion of the poem is attached less to the immediate experience than to the possibility raised by the question repeated in the title, 'what next. . .?'. The poem makes a sustained comparison between the successive phases of the landslip—the first jerky motions of the hill slope breaking away, the steady pouring of rain and mud, the final 'tidal wave of clay'—and the movement of a film: at first

> like the several
> frames of an unsteady
> film that then

> came right
> unexpectedly, to go on
> pouring forth its smooth
> successive images
> of rain, mud, rain
> until the film again
> (a montage unintended)
> cut and the whole
> slope was coming away . . .

The language of 'frames' and 'images' removes the actuality to a safe distance, to be viewed with a mixture of ironic incredulity (can this *really* be happening?) and voyeuristic satisfaction ('that then / came right / unexpectedly'). Not until we reach the title-question in the final line, however, do we grasp the full significance of the assimilation of a happening in process to a film of it. The images are at once literal and figurative, indeed prefigurative; from behind the description of things seen, a potential danger that left the poet and his wife, nevertheless, 'high and dry' in their as yet unthreatened 'hill-top house', emerges a metaphor foreboding the unthinkable, hidden in the final question and ellipsis. Film is a shared dream, and the narrative sequence is dream-like in its alternation of the gratifyingly predictable and the alarmingly unpredictable. The dreamer plays with his fears, masked in symbols; by translating the stages of the event into moving pictures the poet has done the same. We are shown an art that tames reality knowing that it is doing so, that seeks security in taut, nervous rhythms: an art that 'plays with' the disparity between the reality and its conversion into word and image. The disparity between the 'picturesque' view of the flood and what it is ominous of, thus brought to our attention, marks the boundary line between human power and impotence.

The play in 'The Way Through' and 'What Next?' is a way of registering the distance between the mirrors and metaphors of art and the immediacy of life—'play' meaning pretence, without implications of game or humour. It just touches on comedy, however, in the second of these poems; where the last lines express an amused appreciation of the human plight dramatized in the 'perplexed nervous domesticity' of these safe but anxious householders; 'perplexed' waits to link up three lines later with the defensive bewilderment of its lightly mocking rhyme 'what next ... ?' The anecdote of 'The Tax Inspector' (*The Return*, p. 30) is entirely in the mode of comedy. As frequently in this and other recent collections, the poem engages in implicit dialogue with earlier work; defining its comedic view of life and death partly by comparison with the view of this world and the next imaged in the baroque iconography of a wooden frieze of martyrs described in 'Weeper in Jalisco' (*American Scenes*, 1966; CP p. 148). For the poet has returned, he says, to 'the chapel / Of hacked saints' first visited in the 1960s. The Christian view embodied in this carving is reduced, in the earlier poem, to a diagram of simple faith: 'They / are in paradise now / and we are not'. The world is a prison from which martyrdom has won them a

>   blood-
> bought, early resurrection
> leaving us this
> tableau of wounds, the crack
> in the universe sealed
> behind their flying backs.

The description bears the irony of the poet's disbelief in the diagram, but the weeping woman referred to in the title is none the less the voice of the suffering world,

>   the voice
> those wounds cry through
> unappeasably bleeding where
> her prone back shoulders
> the price and weight
> of forfeited paradise.

Tragedy is exchanged for a genial humour in 'The Tax Inspector', which facilitates the invited comparison to 'Weeper in Jalisco' by using the same verse form: a short line of two accents—and any number of unstressed syllables—that can swell to three or four accents or cut back to one; the later poem, allowing itself more freedom of expansion and retraction, has a greater range of tone and feeling.

> I had been here before.
> I came back
> to see the chapel
> of hacked saints.
> It was shut.
> A funeral filled
> the body of the church:
> small women with vast lilies
> heard out the mass: the priest
> completing communion
> wiped wine
> from his lips and from
> the gold chalice
> which having dried
> he disposed of: the event
> was closed.

The chapel of martyrs is temporarily 'shut'; but it always spoke of a closed world, and its statement is curtly set aside. In its place we have the funeral and a different attitude to life and death. Death requires ceremony, and the performance is dutiful, but matter-of-fact: something that must be done—and finished with. The verbs articulate a chain of neat conclusions: the mass 'heard *out*', communion completed, the wine and chalice 'disposed of', an event 'closed'. Typography, separating rhythmical units, activates tensions within the sentence; thus the spondaic 'came back', expressing deliberated purpose, crosses over a bridge of pedestrian iambics ('to see the chapel') to an abrupt encounter with its rhyme and spondaic match, the intractable assertion of 'hacked saints'. Assonances and internal rhymes—'priest completing', 'wiped wine', 'disposed ... closed'—confirm finalities. Juxtapositions—of sounds, of rhythms—do the work of metaphor; as when the soft-breathing 'f's and rippling middle syllables of 'funeral filled' supply the life missing from the bleak 'It was shut'. The stirrings of analogical meaning awaken a dormant opposition between the mutilated bodies of the martyred saints and the 'body of the church', architectural space translated into living beings. The life growing—typographically and semantically—in lines six to nine, and held in suspension until the priest has finished his business, bursts out in the following sentence: the rite concluded, the organ suddenly 'broke into a waltz' and the dead man's work-mates (*compañeros de trabajo*) 'shouldered the coffin forth / to daylight'. The rhythm and diction have fitting weight and solemnity, but 'daylight', like the unsolemn music, heralds a return to everyday life. Death is given its due but life takes over, with undiminished enjoyment:

> The waltz
> seemed right as did
> the deathmarch, the woe
> of the inconsolable brass . . .

The light gaiety of the waltz and the heavy pomp of sorrow divide the occasion between them, but not, as pretended, equally. The doleful 'o's of inconsolable woe blown by the brass exaggerate grief; in the poet's vowels we hear the 'overblown' note of comedy. Consider the parallel and contrast between the *inconsolable* music of the deathmarch and the *unappeasable* anguish of the weeping woman in Jalisco. The wounds that cry through the woman's voice are 'unappeasably bleeding' because the mythic diagram is implacable, the gap between imperfection and perfection infinite; notwithstanding the poet's dissent from the creed assumed in the polarity of suffering world and 'forfeited paradise', there is no irony, let alone comedy, because, given her belief, there is no self-indulgence, in the woman's unappeasable sorrow. Comedy in 'The Tax Inspector' discloses a view that eschews such extremes; it does not dismiss the thought of death but accommodates it, as part of the life that goes on. It is comedy that has the 'small women' dwarfed by their 'vast lilies', devout expression of grandiose intent, and patiently waiting to resume their ordinary selves; comedy, too, that appreciates the celebrant's deft dispatch of his duties. The ordinary world takes charge. Led by the band, the mourners proceed to the *campo santo*, the sweating *compañeros* 'under the bier, / swaying it like a boat'—an image that adds a touch of homely paganism to the scene.

> And this was the way—
> a banner declaring
> what work he and his *compañeros*
> had once shared—
> the tax inspector,
> ferried across on human flesh,
> was borne to burial.

Again comparison with 'Weeper in Jalisco' makes the point for us. The weeper carried 'the price and weight' of the Fall on her shoulders: the tax inspector's colleagues shoulder the weight of one dead man. Reality is simply the sharing of life and the sharing of death, without myth; a burden borne by all—'ferried across on human flesh'.

The thought of death insinuates itself quietly but firmly into these poems; only in retrospective reflection, looking back over the poem, listening to its echoes, do we begin to recognize it—briefly or obliquely acknowledged—as a large pervading presence. While the poem is, apparently, speaking of something else, suddenly, in a hint or an image, the thought intrudes or is dangled as an ostensible afterthought. There are other poems in these collections, however, in which death is the undisguised single theme, focused in images of the inhuman world, of the vertigo of space, of winter and snow, of danger and destruction. 'The Peak' (*The Return*, p. 22), 'Night Fishers' and 'The Glacier' (*Notes from New York*; CP pp. 374, 373) record very similar memories. In 'The Peak' the poet and his companion, making their descent, are 'faced' at each turn of 'the snail-shell road-bend' with the same vision of 'the mountain-head':

>   Ice
> Had scooped and scraped the rock
> That climbed up to it, rivered
> By waters no foot had walked beside.

'Night Fishers' recalls a precipitous climb to a place where they could 'fish the bay': 'the grasp at slipping rock unnerved / All thought'. In

'The Glacier', 'The glacier's edge, eating at the track' is a constant reminder of danger. In these memories the poet is brought to the 'frontier' of human existence—is 'fronted' by a lifeless world and experiences with shocking intimacy the terrors of the inhuman, the precariousness of life, the frailty of flesh. The vision of the mountain-head repeated at every turn of the road assumes for the poet now the quality of 'a dream or a damnation'; the terrors were not so *personally* close in the poetry of the preceding decades. Each poem ends in safety—'night-bound we fished on unharmed'—and in 'The Peak' and 'The Glacier' that safety is their return to the generative earth, 'the soil which fructifies / In the plains a wide and level shore'. But a summary statement of their common plot—a journey to the furthest edge of the human followed by a grateful re-entry into the living world—mislays the mood of these poems: the menace of impending disaster is the keynote—like the glacier, 'overshadowing our minds' even after the return. And, although 'the lowlands opened to receive us, / Brought us the first sun free of mountain shadow', 'The Peak' concludes:

> From above the snow-line, and above the snow,
> Something was tracking us, measuring our return
> Past the stone certitude of barn on barn.

These poems re-explore familiar themes in order to register a change. As we have seen, encounters with the inhuman world are not, here, invitations to a negotiable relationship, as they were, in the form of accommodation or resistance, even in the desert poems of *American Scenes* (1966). In the earlier poetry eye and ear, taking hold on the natural world, were frequently represented as taking the measure of sense experience—as they still do in the 1980s, in such poems as 'Revolution' (*The Return*, p. 2) where the Spanish Steps 'measure out and treasure / each rising inch' of the gradient to please the eye of the mason. In 'The Peak' the roles are reversed, power changes hands, and death is the measure of our meanings, questioning the 'certitude' of our creations and the stored harvests of our cultivated soil.

Death is yet closer in 'Night Fishers'. That night, space and time withdrew their consolations: space was simply a fathomless drop between 'clefts we over-leapt', and the perilous, unnerving climb 'thrust out of time / And into now the sharp original fear / That mastered me then'. The feared total loss 'then' obliterates 'now' all memory of gains: 'The catch / I scarcely recollect'; he remembers only the crisscrossing of torch beams,

> so the mind
> Recalling them, still seems to move
> Inside a hollow diamond that the dark
> As shadows shift, threatens to unfacet:
> It was no jewel, it was the flesh would shatter.

'And yet it did not'; they arrived and fished in safety. 'The night... lay round / Thick with silence':

> And unalarmed, I could forget
> As night-bound we fished on unharmed,
> The terrors of the way we'd come, put by
> The terrors of return past fault and fall,
> Watching this calm firmament of the sea.

The last half of the poem—eighteen lines ending with those just quoted—describes an insulated world, a scene of soothing illusion. The words that would claim immunity from the dangers of the ascent and the return in effect insist, as it were inadvertently, upon their presence. 'Thick with silence' and 'night-bound' are phrases that raise the very spectre of menace they purport to exorcise. 'Calm' is not the finality its placing would have us believe. The core of reality that was once, in *Seeing is Believing*, the 'central calm' belied by the 'violence' of Van Gogh's art (CP p. 36) has become, in 'Night Fishers', a brief interlude between 'terrors'.

Danger is a subsidiary theme of 'The Glacier'. The poem's subject is the barrenness of the terrain, its focus the lifeless world itself.

> We climbed that day
> Up into a region where the mist
> Stagnated over beds of slate—a waste
> Of mountain ground we had approached
> Through grass and moss, themselves as grey

> As the accumulating dust (for it was summer)
> That soiled the trickling glacier where it lay.

Their attention was divided between the waste ground, the crumbling 'blades' of slate beneath their feet, and, above, 'the source that fed a slow / Continuous water out of ice and snow / Into this carious mass', the 'source' that 'Coiled along the ledges with a hold / Slackened by thaw, then frozen firm by cold': 'We trusted that faint line / To take us back and down'. *This* waste land is one half of nature, one meaning of mortality: decay, attrition ('The glacier's edge, eating at the track'), a monotone of grey, stagnation, death. The other half, the other meaning, is generation, 'the soil which fructifies', the trickle of water from 'the source' of life—and what this region cannot show, the variety and distinctions of life, signified in 'The Peak' by 'the *demarcation* of ploughland, vineyard, meadow' (my emphasis).

'Waste'—of life, of possibilities—has been a constant preoccupation in Tomlinson's work. His poetry resists and redresses 'waste' and affirms its opposite, in the natural and human worlds. To define these contraries we need a variety of pairings: fecundity and aridity, abundance and lack, completeness and void, plenitude and poverty, *fulfil*ment and un*fulfil*ment, use and disuse (we recall the young poet's 'bitterness at want of use'), life and (Lawrence's term) anti-life. In 'The Snow Fences' (*American Scenes*, 1966; CP p. 108), the nameless 'they' are erecting fences against 'the snow-shrouds / Of a waste season'—the 'levelling zero', the 'anonymity' of death. Nature regularly wastes life, but men waste their lives, wilfully or haplessly, in obedience to no law; 'Last Days of the Miser' (*The Way of a World*, 1969; CP p. 179) portrays a man afflicted with 'the taste of time / wasted'. The same word is used for the natural process and human failure; men wasting time and their lives are thereby allying themselves with the natural forces of destruction. 'On the Hall at Stowey' (*Seeing is Believing*, 1958; CP p. 40) is explicit. The poet has discovered that the derelict sixteenth-century house had been refashioned recently to suit 'a suburban whim'; 'What we had not / Made ugly', he comments, 'we had laid waste', by our abandonment of the house and with it five centuries of continuous civilization—'Left (I should say) the office to nature, / Whose blind battery', outdoing human blindness, 'completes by persistence/ All that our negligence fails in'.

Human activity affirms, by imitating, the creativity of nature (the other meaning of mortality); a poem sets itself against the inevitable depletion of life. There are limits to what art, what the civilizing enterprise can accomplish. The only poem written before the 1980s to give prominence to the inevitability of failure *and* to let recognition of the fact reflect a personal discontent is (I think) 'After a Death' (*The Way In*, 1974; CP p. 253), a meditation on the recent death of the poet's mother. Death has left 'A little ash, a painted rose, a name'—and a 'husk of moon' in the 'winter blue' of a January sky, that 'hangs / Fragile at the edge of visibility'. The eye, drawn to this 'sudden frontier' between the visible and the invisible, 'Asks for a sense to read the whole / Reverted side of things'. But 'Verse / Fronting' the 'blaze' of a 'blinding sky', retracing 'the path of its dissatisfactions', is 'only certain that / Whatever can make bearable or bridge / The waste of air, a poem cannot'. Verse by its very nature and name cannot comprehend (in both senses) the '*reverted* side of things'; by the same token life cannot comprehend death. Confronted with its impotence, Tomlinson's poetry leaves traces of its discomfiture in 'The Glacier', as in other poems of the 1980s. 'Waste' is never a simply descriptive word, as 'desert' might be. It names an absolute condition, and in Tomlinson's usage it does more than name the condition; it conveys, with variations of application and emphasis, the horror of what it is: an absolute negation, a void, absence of life, of meaning and purpose. The discomfiture noticeable in recent collections shows in 'The Glacier' where the horror *of* waste becomes an expressly personal horror *at* waste. 'This *carious* mass', keeping a fastidious distance from what it describes, 'the blackened razors of the slate / Crumbling as they cut' the slithering feet of the climbers, contains its disgust in Latinate technicality. (The manner is Eliot's, and 'carious' perhaps remembers Eliot's representation of another rocky desert region, 'Dead mountain mouth of carious teeth that cannot spit'.) The veiled revulsion is then nakedly revealed in the poem's last vision of the glacier, as 'a *sordid* glistening' that 'outwaited our descent'. 'Sordid' is more an emotive than a descriptive word; it recoils from waste as from an obscenity; it would reject the scene as if to say, this is a non-world, which unaccountably and inadmissably exists.

'The Glacier' illustrates a central paradox of Tomlinson's poetry. It is at once a poetry of minute particulars and of large general meanings. Tomlinson's first allegiance is to the literal, the actual. The world has 'facets of copiousness'—a memorable phrase from an early poem, 'Observation of Facts' (CP p. 11)—and the task of art is to reveal them, or, rather, to make them reveal themselves. 'Style speaks what was seen', without the intrusive 'I'; for 'Those facets of copiousness . . . / Exist . . . when we have silenced ourselves'. He notes in the painting of Constable 'the labour of observation' and 'the unmannered / Exactness of art' (CP p. 33). Remembering the excesses of the neo-romantics, he has eschewed facile recourse to myth and symbol. In 'The Castle' (CP p. 43), he brusquely dissociates his castle from Kafka's—'It is a real one—no more symbolic / Than you or I'—and, in 'Frondes Agrestes' (CP p. 35), Ruskin's rose—'Gathered up into its own translucence / Where there is no shade save colour, the un-symbolic rose'—from 'the symbolic rose' of Yeats's art.[9] Tomlinson has found means, nevertheless, through rather than despite scrupulous attention to the fact, of intimating something more than the fact. Recognizing and deploring, in the meagre utility of 'the iron sheds' that mar his approach to the derelict Hall at Stowey, the meanness of our times, and faced with 'its opposite', the pride and durable stonework of house and barns, he begins to speak of them, in loose anger, as 'unwarrantable / Symbols of. . .', but interrupts his incipient vehemence with 'no; let me define, rather/ The thing they were not, all that we cannot be, / By the description, simply of that which merits it: / Stone' (CP p. 40). A descriptive poet? Yes. When he asks the question of Constable, however, his answer includes an important qualification: 'A descriptive painter? If delight describes . . .'. The painter wanted his art to be considered a branch of science, which 'should be pursued as an inquiry into the laws of nature'. But Tomlinson's poem discovers in Constable a fruitful ambivalence: on the one hand, admiring facts because 'governed by laws', on the other, 'Representing them (since the illusion was not his end) / As governed by feeling'. Not description for its own sake, then: for the poet, as for the painter, representation is an embodiment of 'the total and accurate knowledge / *In a calligraphy of present pleasure*' (my emphasis), 'the illusion persuading us / That it exists as a human image' (CP p. 30).

Displeasure is the predominant feeling in 'The Glacier'. But it is the same paradox. We are conscious, as always, of the poet's determination to make a full and faithful rendering of the concrete reality, to give us first the truth of fact and let the truth of feeling compose itself out of the noted and scrutinized minute particulars of time, place and circumstance. The mountain 'region' of mist, slate and a dust-soiled 'trickling glacier' and the approach to it, described in the opening lines, is, like Tomlinson's castle, or a region of Dante's *Inferno*, 'a real one'. The phenomena of desolation are particularized, the lay-out of the ground and the sequence of the event are plotted; the connecting threads of sense and imagery are strengthened by the interlace of outer rhymes ('day', 'grey', 'lay') and inner half-rhymes ('mist', 'waste', 'dust'). Words in the passage that have stirrings of figurative meaning— 'region', 'stagnated', 'waste', 'grey'—refer, nevertheless, primarily to the physical conditions; the 'human image' shadowed forth, the human significance, needs no further accentuation because the scene is so exactly and completely there that its symbolic life seems to be a natural outgrowth, feeding on the substantiality of the literal images. Three of the keywords depend on close proximity and consequent interaction for their symbolic potential: 'a *region* where the mist / *Stagnated* over beds of slate—a *waste*. . .'. 'Region' has an indeterminate expansiveness, hospitable to mythic suggestion. 'Stagnated' can apply to human as well as physical inertia. 'Waste' needs for the moment no further comment. 'Grey' is first, here, a dominant shade of the terrain, and three kinds are listed and distinguished: the grey of mist, behaving, furthermore, in a specific way, the grey of vegetation, also specified, and the grey of 'the accumulating dust'; the presence of the last must be, and is, explained ('for it was summer') and what it does must be, and is, circumstantiated—it 'soiled the trickling glacier'. The truth of fact has to be demonstrated before the symbolism of grey—a property of death and dying—can be brought to bear, its meaning reinforced by the repetition of its echoing rhymes. The word 'source', used later in the poem, has an evident symbolizing intention: the contrary of aridity and stagnation, the source of water is the fountain of flowing life, in this barren landscape reduced to a slow trickle. But it is characteristic of Tomlinson's method and indicative of his priorities that the reason given for keeping an eye on 'that source' is the literal one, to guide them 'back and down' the mountain, and not what is implied by his phrasing, 'searching the source', to discover in order to take his bearings from the springs of life. With the reality solidly established, symbolism can, so to speak, take place and the poem can even take on without strain allusions to the waste lands of other poets. 'Carious', as we have noted, links Tomlinson's 'waste / Of mountain ground' to the desert scene in 'What the Thunder Said'. Perhaps, too, this 'region' of 'mist' and of 'ice and snow' derives some of its mythic resonance from Coleridge's Antarctica, a 'land of ice' in the prose synopsis of 'The Ancient Mariner', of 'mist and snow' in the poem.

* * * * *

The poems we have been examining, under the heading 'Against the Autumn', view life from its end or in anticipation of the end; the mood is apprehensive. It is not, however, the only mood in these late collections, even in poems written from the same perspective. Death is the plain subject of 'The Beech' (*Notes from New York*, 1984; CP p. 370), for example, but not, ultimately, its theme: it uses the end-view, not to project a sense of imminent disaster, but to re-affirm the defeated human purpose and at the same time awaken the imagination to what lies beyond, encompasses, and nourishes the human world. It begins on an obituary note with news of the beech tree's destruction by winter storms, but before the sentence has finished memory has made it the occasion for celebration:

> Blizzards have brought down the beech tree
> > That, through twenty years, had served
> As landmark and as limit to our walk.

To the eye accustomed to the tree's presence in the landscape, an eye at home in its perceptual world, the beech was not only an assertion of natural life, finally 'brought down', but seemed especially to measure the extent of the human domain and to make the landscape legible to the human eye. The metaphors that describe the living tree elaborate its human meaning. In spring its buds were 'A galaxy of black against a sky that soon / Leaf-layers would shut back': that is, the buds were a part of and apart from space, a galaxy by definition *in* the sky but seen as standing out *against* the background of sky; and in full leaf of summer the tree would not merely confront but insulate itself against a limitless expanse of sky. Even in winter, perhaps especially in winter, the tree figures a humanly centred world:

> The naked tree
> Commanded, manned the space before
> And beyond, dark lightnings of its branches
> Played above the winter desolation.

The homophonic relationship of 'commanded' and 'manned' would persuade us that, in these circumstances, to command is at once to occupy and to humanize space. When mastery becomes, despite the season, play it demonstrates the power of human freedom. The tree felled, 'the place' is left 'uncitadelled / A wrecked town centred by no spire'.

> At night
> As the wind comes feeling for those boughs
>   There is nothing now in the dark of an answering strength,
> No form to confront and to attest
>   The amplitude of dawning spaces as when
> The tower rebuilt itself out of the mist each morning.

Death is, in this last sentence as in the first, the poem's subject; yet, though it begins with 'nothing', it concludes with the memory of the tree's daily re-creation of the human world. The keyword is 'answering'. The tower rebuilding itself each morning and the 'dawning spaces' are equal and complementary. This landmark, this image of human presence, no longer stands; the fact remains, nevertheless, that the universe exists in, receives its meaning from, the human eye and mind: it needs the human witness as much as humanity needs to be filled with its 'amplitude'.

The awareness of mortality, prominent in 'The Beech', is there too in 'After the Storm' (its successor in *Notes from New York*; CP p. 371) but lightly signified, late in the poem, in the image of the sun appearing for a brief hour before 'going under' the covering of cloud. The reference is subordinated, and assimilated, to a picture of the valley as a theatre in which primal forces, light and water, meet to play their cosmic parts. 'Waters come welling into the valley / From a hundred sources . . . rustle and rush / In their teeming gulley after the storm'; but

> Where the sun
> Is going under it seems to impose
> That silence against which the streams keep telling
> Over and over in the ebbing light
> In their voices of liquid suasion, of travelling thunder
> From what depths they have drunk and from what heights.

A single silence is what lies 'under' the multiple 'voices' of the streams. The *under*silence is linked directly to 'the *ebbing* light', but also to the 'sources' of the living water—preceding the suasive 'rustle and rush' of streams and the noise of thunder. The silence of the end joins the 'depths' and 'heights' of the beginning. Death does not lose any of its finality by this assimilation but is incorporated into a total vision of elemental processes.

The first six lines of the poem speak generally of the water-sources of this valley. The middle section, detailing the history of one hour of sun, is characteristic of Tomlinson's method in the way its metaphorical meanings are founded on a scrupulously accurate charting and substantiation of the facts:

> Today—just once—the sun looks forth
>   To catch the misty emanations of our north
>   Rising in spirals underneath the hill:
>   Here, like a steaming beast, a house
>   Emerges into its beams, the mist
>   Smoking along them into a vapour veil
>   That trails up into soaked branches
>   Sending down shower on shower.

The facts of the scene compose an elemental order of interdependent energies. The day is polarized between 'heights' and 'depths' on upward and downward lines of motion: straight falling lines of light and rising spirals of mist; the moist spirit of the north trailing *up* into the 'soaked branches' sending showers of raindrops *down*. Stirrings of myth animate the naturalism. Sun from the south and northern mist, contraries, mingle forces and 'a house / Emerges', like some 'steaming' primeval creature born of fire and water.

These are not the only poems in which the end-view, marking the limit of human being and human possession, is absorbed into a larger vision. It expresses—as Michael Edwards has said, in a perceptive review of *Annunciations* (1989)—a 'religious' sense of life. 'His poetry', he writes, 'looks to this world to provide the "religious" sense of life which Christianity for him can no longer sustain ... The "annunciation" of a larger-than-life presence in the world, of a reality which has preceded us and will outlast us, of a mystery ceaselessly entering local chance and circumstance, comes not from beyond but from within the world, often in the form of light from the sun and moon.' *Annunciations*, he proposes, 'is the book in which Charles Tomlinson makes explicit what has always been the case', the naturalistic focus of his 'religious' sense of life.[10] It is surely not, however, the first book in which Tomlinson has been *explicit* about this. I could have taken my own examples from any of the collections published in the 1980s, and, as it happens, I have found them principally in *Notes from New York* (1984). Let me add to 'the amplitude of dawning spaces', to the 'depths' and 'heights' and the underlying 'silence' another example from that volume of Tomlinson's peculiar 'religious' tone and vision, the closing lines of 'In December' (CP p. 372). After a day of fog filling up space, dissolving 'all distinctions', all differences into one 'grey lava' of 'gliding apocalypse', the world is restored to itself and 'by midnight the sky is clear'. What is restored—and this is the concluding vision—is the proper relation of the human and the suprahuman, a horizon that holds things apart, maintains distinctions, clearing and defining a human place, at the same time as it surrounds earth with the expanding mystery and order of the cosmos:

The horizon is keeping its distance and its nearness
Between the glittering of earth and galaxies,
Worlds within worlds encircling our walls
From the recesses and recessions of winter skies.

The 'mystery' of life is life itself. The paradox of this 'religious' vision is that it finds life to be a 'larger-than-life' matter. 'Confluence' (CP p. 371), belonging to the group of poems in *Notes from New York* which also includes 'The Beech', 'After the Storm' and 'In December', is perhaps the most impressive embodiment of that vision. The poem follows the stream of life from its beginnings as an 'emerging spring' to within 'calling' distance of the end, the final sea; following its progression, 'the mind' contemplates more than a life—'Creation overleaping its seven days', the mystery of the original deed made continuous and incessant. The changing state of the stream, which is also of the participant mind, as it passes from hill to valley, by 'sandstone, moorslope, shales and scarp', towards the estuary, charts a 'moral landscape'[11] established in the earliest collections. The 'hillside stream unearths itself', declaring freedom from its matrix, taking possession of the intangible upper world of sound and thought, 'its urgent voice / Laying claim to the air and bearing down / On all that lies below'. It voices, in other words, 'the more possessive and violent claims of personality' that Tomlinson's poetry has expressly renounced.[12] Filling 'the air' with its urgency, claiming 'all', the voice of 'the emerging spring' loses *all* in unfocused, unchannelled 'querulousness'. Freedom is conditional: it is learning what is possible and choosing a direction from among the possibilities offered and following it. To become a stream the spring must find 'a bed to flow into'; finding it is 'submitting / To go the way a valley goes'. There is no way but submission; choosing among ways of submitting is freedom. As the yoked animals, in 'Oxen: Ploughing at Fiesole' (CP p. 19), 'consent to submission' without feeling compelled, so 'the mind', studying the ways of water', goes *with* the water feeling free, / Yields itself to the sea's gravity'. With the word 'gravity' the poem moves from a moral to a 'religious' perspective. For the mind surrenders not simply to necessity—the pull of gravity—but to what is of fundamental and ultimate seriousness, which includes but is not confined to the fact of death (the grave). Death is in the poet's mind not as the close of an individual life: the end-view is absorbed into a total view of life-and-death. Water rises out of the earth and empties into the sea; life and death are joined by the image, which is in the first place an image of plenitude:

> New the sound that *fills* the mind's ear now,
>   Each vein and voice of the watershed
> Calling to the estuary as they near...
>   a singleness
> Out of all the confluences pours on
>   To a music of what shapes, what stays and passes
> Between this island and its seas. (my emphasis)

'Now' is the changed time—a 'now' made 'new'—after 'The querulousness of the emerging spring' and specifically the now of late middle age from which the poet is viewing this flow of life. 'New', supported by the line's weight of solemn welcome, echoes a Christian motif—a new earth if not a new heaven. The present flows 'downhill' but with a new music, the music of creation, in its ears; a single music harmonizing many notes; life in its natural fullness pouring into the surrounding seas, 'calling' to its natural end, its match and mate. The verse itself is a calling and answering of sounds, a music of confluence that gathers and converges and opens out into a finale of virtual praise and thanksgiving for an unconfined, continuous act of creation. And 'creation'—'Creation overleaping its seven days'—is the word: invoking even as it omits a Creator.

* * * * *

This chapter began by noting a certain relaxation of personal reticence in Tomlinson's later poetry. My first illustration was drawn from the poem sequence 'The Return', the title-poem of its collection. 'Winter Journey', another four-part sequence from the same volume (*The Return*, p. 33), provides my last example—and the conclusion to this book. It is written as a sort of letter-journal to his wife, Brenda, during her brief absence from home; the 'winter journey' is literally hers. The poet imagines her passage through cold and dark across a snow-covered landscape; the images compose the familiar *lifescape* of his recent work. 'The Return', addressed to a fellow-poet, is a poem of friendship. 'Winter Journey' is in effect, though not formally, a love poem. Each poem of the sequence has a circular plot: the poet turns to his wife in the first line and returns to her in the close, each closing reference an anticipation of *her* return to him, the last a ceremony of welcome. The lines between share with her what he has seen and heard, felt and thought while 'alone in the house': a fearful then comforting dream about her journey, his memory of 'our flood' (a forewarning of life's ultimate defeat), the wonders nevertheless of the night-sky that she is not there to see, lastly the descent from sunlight to twilight to firelight and his domestic preparations for her arrival; experiences of his solitude, but all speaking to him of their shared life at the same time as they tell over the elements of his poetic universe.

The sequence is a love poem and something more than a love poem. It does not need, conventionally, to praise Brenda or name feelings, since all is referred to her and included in his love of her. (Most of Tomlinson's books are dedicated to his wife and all, as he says in the Preface to *Collected Poems*, were written for her in the first place.) 'Winter Journey' makes no proclamations but lets us see that the whole enterprise of his poetry is founded on this shared life, its moral being centred in the reality of this love. The poet's sense of what life is is their joint sense of what life is together. 'Alone in the house', therefore, Tomlinson's thought, in the second poem of the sequence, is of mortality. He recalls 'our flood', when the house received its counter-baptism of 'muddy flux', and, listening to the stream now, he hears again the reality of water 'beneath all these appearances':

> That night
> The wave rose, broke, reminded us
>   We cannot choose the shape of things
>   And must, at the last, lose in this play
>   Of passing lights, of fear and trust.

Brenda's absence explains the bias of memory towards loss and 'last' things, but, in its response to what is symbolized by water, the poem is balanced equally between 'fear and trust', fear of the end but a continuing trust, nevertheless, in 'this play / Of passing lights', in the chances and changes of life. As the flood, notwithstanding its suggestion of general disaster, is *'our* flood', so, in the first poem, the poet's fear, revealed in an anxiety dream, is fear specifically for his wife's safety; the recovered trust in life is the reassurance of reading news of her arrival in the letter she was writing even as his fear was forming into dream-images of snow and mist endangering her 'moorland drive'. His dream and her letter coinciding, the dream seemed eventually to feel the benign influence of her 'midnight pen', 'Turning the threats from near and far / To images of beauty' and the terrors of a winter night to 'propitious dark': what makes the sinister 'propitious' is, plainly, the survival and efficacy of their love. Tomlinson's is an outward-looking art that has consistently resisted 'the more possessive and violent claims of personality' and embraces the 'possibility' of self-extension represented by space 'somewhat self-forgetfully'. This statement[13] recommends, however, not the repudiation but the discipline of self. The poetry's energy and 'passionate' response to the given world reveal the strong, tacit presence of a *personal* sureness and steadiness. It is clear in 'Winter Journey', moreover, that the personal strength of his work is sustained and fortified by—is the product of—this relationship of mutual dependence. Art is possibility—an equation made and defined in the prose poem 'Skullshapes' (CP p. 191); underlying Tomlinson's poetic art is the created possibility of the shared life. In the lifescape of 'Winter Journey' life is the gift of love, at risk.

The *now* of this poem sequence, as of other poems examined in this chapter, is winter; night, adding to the symbolism, has fallen or is imminent. But the poem's imaginal life is, as always, situated between contraries, defining the poles of existence: winter and summer (the unpredictable dangers of a snow-covered landscape measured against 'the calculable expectations summer in such a place / Might breed in one'), dark and light, threat and beauty, harm and safety; fear and trust are the antithetical attitudes that correspond to these conditions.

'Between' is where Tomlinson's poems take place, between the feared end and the savoured present. Having reminded Brenda of 'our flood', he describes the stream 'lapping past its stone flank now', 'close to the source and gathering speed' but safe—and gracious, catching the world for him, 'Netting the air in notes, letting space show through / As sound-motes cluster and then clear'. They speak to him, nevertheless, not only of possibility but of necessity, and he attends to what they also 'have to say / Of consequence and distance'. In the conclusion of this second poem the poet turns to his wife again: 'Waiting, as I wait now, I wish you could hear / The truce that distils note-perfect out of dusk'. The perfection of the moment is sufficient reason for celebration but 'truce'—a truce between contending eventualities—recognizes and defines precisely the limits of perfection. 'Waiting' is another poised word. It is at once an activity and a condition: he is waiting *for* Brenda's return and he is just waiting, as one *must* wait for whatever should befall—in the dark of winter and the 'dusk' of a day's end perfection must be counted a grace and not one of the 'calculable expectations summer... / Might breed in one'. The posture of waiting joins up with a previous image of suspended action, a component of the ominous dreamscape of the first poem:

> My eye took in
> Close-to, among the vastnesses you passed unharmed,
> The shapes the frozen haze hung on the furze
> Like scattered necklaces the frost had caught
> Half-unthreaded in their fall.

This is an instance of 'threats' turned to 'images of beauty' by the intervention, as it were, of Brenda's written words; the motion is, however, caught in mid-fall and is waiting its completion. It is caught between, and it is a truce between, creation and destruction. The waiting, in the second poem, is divided between, or combines perhaps, the dispositions of trust and fear. Throughout the sequence, 'between' is a situation that favours combination rather than division: the imagery works to persuade us that suspension between alternatives can be a relation of complementarity. When the poet tells his wife that he could not close

>   his dreaming eye
> To the thought of further snow
>   Widening the landscape as it sought
> The planes and ledges of your moorland drive,

does 'widening' *dis*close fear or trust? Does not the word greet a 'widening' of perception as much as it sounds a note of warning? The responses are not mutually exclusive. The simultaneity of answer and recognition, glad answer to the invitations of the world tempered by recognition of its prohibitions and determinations, is the distinguishing mark of Tomlinson's 'consent to time'. The third poem of the sequence is an announcement of vocation, at the heart of which is the poet's declared belief in the mutuality of dark and light, uncertainty and faith.

> Though bidden by darkness to the feast of light,
>   I came as one prepared, and what I could not name
> Opening out the immensity flame by flame
>   Found me a celebrant in the mass of night,
> Where all that one could know or signify
>   Seemed poor beside the reaches of those fires,
> The moon's high altar glittering up from earth,
>   Burning and burgeoning against your return.

Like all paradoxes, the equation of 'the mass of night' with 'the feast of light' is only seemingly self-contradictory. The night displays 'in clarity' of moonshine and starlight 'the lesson of the sky'; conversely, starlight opens out the dark 'immensity' of night. It is the darkness of 'one's ignorance' that makes one a worshipper of the light, the reverence of the unknowing responding to the mystery of the unknown. '*Bidden* by darkness'—it is his calling—the poet is a priestly 'celebrant *in* the mass of night' but a 'celebrant' *of* 'the feast of light'. This is the 'little certainty and much surmise' of a religious agnosticism.

Finally, in imagery of fire and winter cold, the sequence is an affirmation of life in the midst of death. The night before Brenda's expected return Tomlinson begins the third poem: 'I must tell you of the moon tonight / How sharp it shone'. The moonlight is 'sharp', and the sky is a crisply clear 'revelation' of starlit space, because '*cold burnt* back the mist'. Uniting opposite intensities of sensation, this metaphor makes us feel as paradox what the full scene conveys as picture: at the core of cold and darkness, a universe of death, are the stellar 'fires', unquenchable life, 'Opening out the immensity flame by flame'. In preparation for his wife's arrival, the poet tells her in the fourth and last poem,

> I pile the hearth
> With the green quick-burning wood that feeds
>   Our winter fires, and kindle it
> To quicken your return.

Fire is, as it were, the quick of winter—*their* winter fuelled by 'the quick-burning wood' of their lives. 'Quick' combines the ideas of transitoriness and, reinforced by 'green', of vitality; the burning is at once the burning up of life and the burning that is life itself. By kindling the fire, therefore, the poet means not only to hasten Brenda's return but by bringing her home to make the fire of life burn the more intensely.

Setting out the 'relations and contraries' of a whole view has been Tomlinson's purpose since this title identified the contents of his first pamphlet of verse. Contraries are prominent in 'Winter Journey'; in the examples I have discussed they are a means of presenting a balanced awareness or a state of complementarity. The concluding poem of the sequence, which I quote in full, takes us beyond oppositeness, transcending or dissolving antinomies—and, possibly, the images of fire and cold, in the third poem as well as the last, are not what I have made them seem, complementary opposites, but are made to dissolve or transcend the distinction.

> I lay the table where, tonight, we eat.
>   The sun as it comes indoors out of space
> Has left a rainbow irising each glass—
>   A refraction, caught then multiplied
> From the crystal within our window,

> Threaded up to transmit the play
> And variety day deals us. By night
> The facets take our flames into their jewel
> That, constant in itself, burns fuelled by change
> And now that twilight has begun
> Lets through one slivered shaft of reddening sun.
> I uncork the wine. I pile the hearth
> With the green quick-burning wood that feeds
> Our winter fires, and kindle it
> To quicken your return when dwindling day
> Must yield to the lights that beam you in
> And the circle hurry to complete itself where you began,
> The smell of the distance entering with the air,
> Your cold cheek warming to the firelight here.

It is a 'dwindling day' but its completion is a return, and the human 'lights' herald a new life not an ending, an enhanced life to light the dark and warm the winter cold. As twilight merges day into night, so art, imaged as the hanging crystal, gathers promises of the day into its celebration of the candlelit, firelit night to come. Distance enters the house; space leaves its sunprint. The crystal brings indoors the gifts of chance, the outer life of the day, and, 'fuelled by change', burns with the inner life of the house: the 'vastnesses' of space and the privacies of the hearth are conformed to the same life. Like a (Tomlinson) poem, the crystal multiplies light's variety, plays with the flame-life of the human presence, yet, 'constant in itself', combines and concentrates their separate powers. The change of light and life, entering, reflected in, transmitted by the faceted but unchanging form of art, becomes thereby the substance of permanence, yielding this conundrum: change constitutes constancy.

The most important thing to say about 'Winter Journey' is that, as I began by saying, it is a love poem; a love poem, however, that assimilates the personal subject of love poetry to the general themes of Tomlinson's work. The exploration of possibility which art is is intimately related, in the emphases, balances and affirmations of this poem and—I am suggesting—of his other poems, to the sense of possibility *created* by a life sustained and fortified by love. In my previous discussion of the poem I have intimated that the part played by Brenda, her presence in the poem, is also more specific and more special. I interpreted 'truce', in the second poem, as a truce between creation and destruction. He is addressing Brenda in those closing lines, and the word also conveys, I believe, a personal message. He first summarizes the lesson of 'our flood':

> We cannot choose the shape of things
> And must, at the last, lose in this play
> Of passing lights, of fear and trust;

and then turns to his wife:

> Waiting, as I wait now, I wish you could hear
> The truce that distils note-perfect out of dusk.

'Truce', here, seems more than temporary; beyond its strict sense, it gives an impression of firmness and lastingness, and that is not only because it is 'note-perfect': it is a consequence, I think, of the virtual slant rhyme that joins it to 'trust' two lines before. That the words rhyme in sense as well as sound is confirmed by their etymologies, in which they are also cognates of 'truth', 'troth', and the archaic 'trow': all derive from an Old English root meaning belief, faith, pledge. 'Truce', for Tomlinson, signifies more than a suspension of hostilities. Alone and waiting for his wife's return, he wants *her* to hear the 'note-perfect' music of 'truce' because it sounds the note—is a pledge—of their common faith, their life together. If 'faith' suggests something more than personal fidelity—and that is my intention—the word gives an accurate impression, I believe, of what this poem is about: it is a general declaration and a particular act of faith, which consigns his poetic universe to his wife's safekeeping. An act of faith concludes the first poem as it does the second. His dream fears were dispelled by the 'firm prints' of her writing hand inscribing its message on his dreaming consciousness and, by her *saving* intervention, now, he tells her,

Flowed to the guiding motion of your hand
As though through the silence of propitious dark
It had reached out to touch us across sleeping England.

He has entrusted to her the direction of their life's dream, which moves now under the power of her conjuring hand. Her 'touch' cancels distance, conquers separation, and night loses its terrors. Her firmness affirms the reality of life and steadies him against fears of death. In the third poem faith looks at 'darkness' and finds 'light'. Tomlinson begins the poem by telling Brenda of the moon that night, 'how sharp it shone', adding: 'You have been gone three days', a period of time which in myth prepares for some extraordinary culmination. 'Though bidden by darkness to the feast of light', nevertheless, like the wise virgins in the parable, he writes, 'I came as one prepared', and the mass he celebrates has a carefully unfocused but evidently preparatory relation to the 'return' of his wife: 'The moon's high altar glittering up from earth, / Burning and burgeoning against your return'. The parable alluded to is one of a group whose common theme is the advent of the heavenly kingdom. One hesitates to say bluntly that the woman addressed has been given a role that combines the bridegroom Christ of the parable with the returning Christ of Revelation, though the hieratic language and the rhythms of high ritual are strong inducements. The veiled analogy, the glimpsed possibility, must be noted but must not be given sharper definition or more emphasis than the poet himself has given it. The last poem of the sequence leaves no doubt, however, that Brenda is the culmination, the awaited advent. She shares with the crystal of art the power to dissolve antinomies: she joins the end to the beginning and the far to the near. But imagery and rhetoric teasingly hint at a mythic role for her. Like the 'rainbow irising each glass', left by the sun, she is a gift from the distance, a promise brought home. Her lights—'the lights that beam [her] in'—take over, triumphantly, from the light of 'dwindling day'. The poem's conclusion gives to her alone victory against the day's ending, against the autumn: her entrance, her return, mimes the defeat of death.

NOTES

1. Prefatory note to 'Ode: Intimations of Immortality'.
2. *Eden*, p. 14.
3. Thoreau, *The Journal*, 13 September 1852.
4. *Eden*, p. 13.
5. *Ibid.*, p. 14.
6. *Ibid.*, p. 20.
7. *Ibid.*, pp. 14–15.
8. *Ibid.*, p. 15.
9. W. B. Yeats, 'Meditations in Time of Civil War: II The House'.
10. *The Times Literary Supplement*, 22–28 December 1989.
11. Tomlinson's phrase, in a commentary on *The Necklace* in *Poems in Folio*, quoted on the dustcover of *Seeing is Believing*.
12. 'Preface', *Collected Poems*, p. vii.
13. *Ibid.*

Bibliography

WORKS BY CHARLES TOMLINSON

Poetry

Relations and Contraries. Poems in Pamphlet 9. Aldington, Kent: Hand and Flower Press, 1951.
The Necklace. Oxford: Fantasy Press, 1955. Reprint. London and New York: Oxford University Press, 1966.
'Solo for Harmonica'. Poems in Folio 7. San Francisco: Westerham, 1957.
Seeing is Believing. New York: Mcdowell, Obolensky, 1958. Reprint (with one poem excluded and fourteen poems added). London: Oxford University Press, 1960.
Versions from Fyodor Tyutchev, 1803–1873 (with Henry Gifford). London and New York: Oxford University Press, 1960.
A Peopled Landscape: Poems. London and New York: Oxford University Press, 1963.
Castilian Ilexes: Versions from Antonio Machado, 1875–1939 (with Henry Gifford). London, New York and Toronto: Oxford University Press, 1963. Reprint. Harmondsworth: Penguin, 1974.
Poems: A Selection by Charles Tomlinson. With Austin Clarke and Tony Connor. London and New York: Oxford University Press, 1964.
American Scenes and Other Poems. London and New York: Oxford University Press, 1966.
The Matachines. San Marcos, Texas: San Marcos Press, 1968.
To Be Engraved on the Skull of a Cormorant. London: The Unaccompanied Serpent, 1968.
Penguin Poets 14. Alan Brownjohn, Michael Hamburger, Charles Tomlinson. Harmondsworth and Baltimore: Penguin Books, 1969.
The Way of a World. London, New York and Toronto: Oxford University Press, 1969.
America West Southwest. San Marcos, Texas: San Marcos Press, 1970.
Ten Versions from 'Trilce' by César Vallejo (with Henry Gifford). Cerrillos, New Mexico: San Marco Press, 1970.

Renga: A Chain of Poems. Co-author with Octavio Paz, Jacques Roubauld and Eduardo Sanguineti. Paris: Editions Gallimards, 1971; Mexico: Joaquin Mortiz, 1972; New York: George Braziller, 1972; Harmondsworth: Penguin, 1979.

Written on Water. London: Oxford University Press, 1972.

The Way In and Other Poems. London, New York and Toronto: Oxford University Press, 1974.

The Shaft. Oxford, London and New York: Oxford University Press, 1978.

Selected Poems 1951–1974. Oxford, London and New York: Oxford University Press, 1978.

Airborn/Hijos del Aire. Co-author with Octavio Paz. Mexico: Martin Pescador, 1979; London: Anvil Press Poetry, 1981.

The Flood. Oxford, New York, Toronto and Melbourne: Oxford University Press, 1981.

Translations. Oxford and New York: Oxford University Press, 1983.

Notes from New York and Other Poems. Oxford and New York: Oxford University Press, 1984.

Collected Poems. Oxford and New York: Oxford University Press, 1985. Except 'Poem' from *Relations and Contraries* this edition begins with *The Necklace* and ends with *The Flood.* The 2nd edition, 1987, adds *Notes from New York.*

The Return. Oxford and New York: Oxford University Press, 1987.

Annunciations. Oxford and New York: Oxford University Press, 1989.

The Door in the Wall. Oxford and New York: Oxford University Press, 1992.

Attilio Bertolucci: Selected Poems, translated by Charles Tomlinson (bilingual edition). Newcastle upon Tyne: Bloodaxe Books, 1993.

Jubilation. Oxford and New York: Oxford University Press, 1995.

Selected Poems. Oxford: Oxford University Press, 1997; New York: New Directions, 1997.

Translations of Tomlinson's Poetry

Poemas, [65 pages] selecção e tradução de Gualter Cunha. Lisbon: Cotovia, 1992. Bilingual edition.

Sette Poesia di Charles Tomlinson, [21 pages] translated by Ariodante Marianni. Cittadelli, Italy: Biblioteca Cominiana, 1992.

La huella del ciervo [*The Track of the Deer*], [28 pages] translated by Juan Malpartida. La Laguna, Tenerife: El Castillo, 1994. Bilingual edition.

Charles Tomlinson: Gedichte, [329 pages] translated by Joachim Utz. Heidelberg: Mattes Verlag, 1994. Bilingual edition.

En La Plenitud de Tiempo, [14 pages] translated by Jordi Doce. Gijon, Normadas: Orviedo, 1994.

La insistencia de las cosas: Antologia, [224 pages]. Madrid: Visor, 1994. Bilingual edition.

Charles Tomlinson in Italia, [282 pages]. Milan: Garzanti, 1995. Bilingual edition.

Poemas Portuguesas / Portuguese Pieces by Charles Tomlinson, [44 pages] translated by Gualter Cunha, with a preface by Charles Tomlinson. Lisbon: Relogia D'Agua Editores, 1996. Bilingual edition.

The Fox Gallery / La Galeria del zorro. Mexico City: Ediciones el Tucan de Virginia and Vuelta, 1996.

Parole e Acqua, translated by Franca Morandi. Lugo: Edizione di Bradipo, 1997. Bilingual edition.

Graphics

Words and Images. London: Covent Garden Press, 1972.
In Black and White: The Graphics of Charles Tomlinson. Cheadle, Cheshire: Carcanet Press, 1976.
Eden: Graphics and Poetry. Bristol: Redcliffe Press, 1985.

Anthologies Edited

Marianne Moore: A Collection of Critical Essays. Englewood Cliffs, New Jersey, and London: Prentice-Hall, 1960.
William Carlos Williams: A Critical Anthology. Harmondsworth: Penguin, 1972.
William Carlos Williams: Selected Poems. Harmondsworth: Penguin, 1976; reprinted 1983.
Octavio Paz: Selected Poems. Harmondsworth: Penguin, 1979.
The Oxford Book of Verse in English Translation. Oxford and New York: Oxford University Press, 1980.
Poems of George Oppen. Newcastle upon Tyne: Cloud, 1990.

Eros English'd: Classical Erotic Poetry in Translation from Golding to Hardy.
Bristol: Bristol Classical Press, 1992.

Interviews

Interview with Peter Orr, 1961. In *The Poet Speaks*, edited by Peter Orr. London: Routledge and Kegan Paul, 1964.
'Robert Creeley in conversation with Charles Tomlinson'. *The Review*, 10 (January 1964), pp. 24–35.
Interview with Ian Hamilton in the series 'Four Conversations'. *London Magazine*, 4:6 (November 1964), pp. 82–85.
'An Interview with Charles Tomlinson', by Jed Rasula and Mike Erwin. *Contemporary Literature*, 16:5 (Autumn 1975), pp. 405–16.
'Charles Tomlinson in Conversation' with Michael Schmidt. *PN Review*, 5:1 (October 1977), pp. 35–40.
'Words and Water: Charles Tomlinson and His Poetry'. Interview with Alan Ross. *London Magazine*, 20:10 (January 1981), pp. 22–39. Reprinted in *Charles Tomlinson: Man and Artist*, edited by Kathleen O'Gorman. Columbia: University of Missouri Press, 1988.
'Charles Tomlinson at Sixty: In conversation with Richard Swigg'. *PN Review*, 14:3 (November 1987), pp. 58–61. Reprinted in *Charles Tomlinson: Man and Artist*, edited by Kathleen O'Gorman. Columbia: University of Missouri Press, 1988.
'A Human Balance: An Interview with Charles Tomlinson', by Bruce Meyer. *The Hudson Review*, 43:3 (Autumn 1990), pp. 437–48.
'The Poet of the Eye'. Interview with Jordi Doce. *Agenda*, 33:2 (Summer 1995), pp. 22–30.

Notes on his Own Poetry

[*A Peopled Landscape*]. The Poetry Book Society Bulletin (Summer 1963).
[*American Scenes*]. The Poetry Book Society Bulletin (April 1966).
[*Written on Water*]. The Poetry Book Society Bulletin (Christmas 1972).
Introductory Note on 'Swimming Chenango Lake' and 'Assassin'. In *Let the People Choose*. Edited by James Gibson. London: Harrap, 1973.
[*The Way In and Other Poems*]. The Poetry Book Society Bulletin (Autumn 1974).
[*Selected Poems*]. The Poetry Book Society Bulletin (Summer 1978).

[*The Shaft*]. The Poetry Book Society Bulletin (Spring 1978).
[*The Return*]. The Poetry Book Society Bulletin (Winter 1987).

Cassettes

Keele Recordings. Department of English, University of Keele, Keele, Staffs. ST5 5BG.
Charles Tomlinson: The Complete Poems 1955–1989 [*The Necklace* to *Annunciations*]. Tomlinson's readings of his poems, 1989. (Individual collections and a selection of his poetry are available separately.)
The Modern Age: Hugh Kenner and Charles Tomlinson in Conversation. 1988.
Octavio Paz Talks to Charles Tomlinson. 1989.
Charles Tomlinson Reads 'The Waste Land' by T. S. Eliot. 1989. Recorded together with two talks by Tomlinson, 'Eliot, Pound and *The Waste Land*: The Narrative of a Relationship' and 'Reading *The Waste Land*'.

Memoir and Letters

Some Americans: A Personal Record. Berkeley and London: University of California Press, 1981.
'Selections from the Correspondence of William Carlos Williams and Charles Tomlinson, 1957–63'. Introduction by Hugh Kenner and Charles Tomlinson. *The American Poetry Review*, 21 (November/December 1992), pp. 27–30.
The Letters of William Carlos Williams and Charles Tomlinson, edited by David Magid and Hugh Witemeyer; introduction by Hugh Kenner. New York: Dim Gray Bar Press, 1992.

Published Lectures, Articles and Reviews

'Mr. Pound on Literature'. Review of *Literary Essays of Ezra Pound*, edited by T. S. Eliot. *Spectator*, 192 (19 February 1954), p. 212.
'Coleridge: "Christabel" '. In *Interpretations: Essays on Twelve English Poems*, edited by John Wain. London and Boston: Routledge and Kegan Paul, 1955.
'Pages from an Italian Journal'. *Poetry*, 89 (1956), pp. 183–87.
'Abundance, Not Too Much: The Poetry of Marianne Moore'. *Sewanee Review*, 65 (1957), pp. 677–87.

'The Case of L. H. Myers'. A Review of *L. H. Myers: A Critical Study*, by G. H. Bantock. *Sewanee Review*, 65 (1957), pp. 136–40.

'The Middlebrow Muse'. Review of *New Lines*, edited by Robert Conquest. *Essays in Criticism*, 7 (1957), pp. 208–17.

'The Poetry of Christina Rossetti'. *Poetry*, 89 (1957), pp. 385–90.

'Rock Bottom'. Review of *Poets of the 1950's: An Anthology of New English Verse*, edited by D. J. Enright. *Poetry*, 89 (1957), pp. 260–64.

'Poet without an Audience'. Review of *The Letters of William Blake*, edited by Geoffrey Keynes; *William Blake's 'Vala'*, edited by H. M. Margouliouth; *William Blake: The Finger on the Furnace*, by Laura DeWitt James. *Poetry*, 90:5 (August 1957), pp. 321–25.

'Street Ballads'. Review of *The Common Muse: An Anthology of Popular British Poetry XVth–XXth Century*. *Poetry*, 91 (1958), pp. 400–02.

'Now, God Help Thee, Poor Monkey'. Review of *Poor Monkey: The Child in Literature*, by Peter Coveney. *Sewanee Review*, 66 (1958), pp. 490–94.

'Edward Thomas'. Review of *The Last Four Years*, by Eleanor Farjeon, and *As It Was and World Without End*, by Helen Thomas. *Poetry*, 95:1 (October 1959), pp. 52–54.

'Studies in Chinese Literature'. *Yuan Mei*, by Arthur Waley; *The Nine Songs: A Study of Shamanism in Ancient China*, by Arthur Waley; *The Way and its Power, A Study of the Tao Tê Ching and its Place in Chinese Thought*, by Arthur Waley. *Poetry*, 93:6 (March 1959), pp. 408–12.

'Rimbaud Today'. Review of Rimbaud, by C. A. Hackett. *Essays in Criticism*, 9:1 (January 1959), pp. 93–102.

'Poetry and Silence'. Review of *The Poetry of Boris Pasternak*, edited and translated by George Reavey; *Poems by Boris Pasternak*, translated by Eugene M. Kayden. *Poetry*, 96:2 (May 1960), pp. 108–11.

'America: Imagination and the Spirit of Place'. *National Review*, 11:6 (1961), pp. 86–87.

'And the Eyelids are a Little Weary'. Review of *Collected Poems*, by Lawrence Durrell. *Poetry*, 98:1 (April 1961), pp. 53–55.

'Last of Lands'. *New Statesman*, 61 (28 April 1961), p. 674.

'Poetry Today'. In *The Pelican Guide to English Literature: The Modern Age*, edited by Boris Ford. Harmondsworth: Penguin, 1961.

'Pull Down Thy Vanity'. Review of *Essays and Introductions* by W. B. Yeats. *Poetry*, 98 (1961), pp. 263–66.

Introduction to *The Collected Poems of Ronald Bottrall*. London: Sidgwick & Jackson, 1961.

'Poets and Mushrooms: A Retrospect of British Poetry in 1961'. *Poetry*, 100 (1962), pp. 104–21.

'Magisterial Eye'. Review of *The Darkening Glass: A Portrait of Ruskin's Genius*, by John D. Rosenberg; *The Lamp of Beauty: Writings on Art by John Ruskin*, by Joan Evans. *Sewanee Review*, 70 (1962), pp. 220–28.

'Black Mountain as Focus'. *The Review*, 10:10 (1964), pp. 4–5.

'Pictures from Brueghel'. *Times Literary Supplement*, 21 May 1964, p. 435.

Guest editor. 'Robert Creeley in Conversation with Charles Tomlinson'. *The Review: Black Mountain Issue*. 10 (Jan 1964).

Guest editor. *Agenda*: special Louis Zukofsky issue. 3 (December 1964).

'Wilfred Owen'. *Poetry*, 106 (1964), pp. 41–43.

Review of *Imitations*, by Robert Lowell; *Three Hundred Poems: 1902–1953*, by Juan Ramon Jimenez, translated by Eloise Roach; *Twenty Poems of César Vallejo*, translated by John Koepfle, James Wright, Robert Bly; *Sun Stone*, by Octavio Paz, translated by Muriel Rukeyser; *Ballad of the Buried Life*, by Rudolf Hagelstange, translated by Herman Salinger; *Sonnets to Orpheus*, by Rainer Maria Rilke, translated by M. D. Herter Horton. *New Mexico Quarterly*, 33 (Winter 1964), pp. 457–60.

'The Tone of Pound's Critics'. Review of *Poet in Exile*, by Noel Stock; *Ezra Pound and Sextus Propertius*, by J. P. Sullivan; *The Confucian Odes of Ezra Pound*, by L. S. Dembo; *The Poet as Sculptor*, by Donald Davie. *Agenda*, 4:2 (October–November 1965), pp. 46–49.

'Yeats and the Practising Poet'. In *An Honoured Guest: New Essays on W. B. Yeats*, edited by Denis Donoghue and J. R. Mulryne. London: Edward Arnold, 1965.

'Elizabeth's New Book'. Review of *Questions of Travel*, by Elizabeth Bishop. *Shenandoah*, 17 (Winter 1966), pp. 88–91.

'Experience into Music: The Poetry of Basil Bunting'. Review of *Loquitur*, *The Spoils* and *Briggflatts*, by Basil Bunting. *Agenda*, 4:56 (1966), pp. 11–17.

Review of *The Poetry of Robert Frost*, by Reuben Brower, and *The Comic Spirit of Wallace Stevens*, by Daniel Fuchs. *Critical Quarterly*, 8:i (1966), pp. 92–93.

'Dr. Williams' Practice'. Review of *The W. C. Williams Reader*, edited by M. L. Rosenthal; *Penguin Modern Poets*, 9: Denise Levertov, Kenneth Rexroth, William Carlos Williams; *William Carlos Williams: A Collection of Critical Essays*, edited by J. Hillis Miller. *Encounter*, 29 (November 1967), pp. 66–70.

Review of *The Old Glory*, by Robert Lowell. *Critical Quarterly*, 9 (Spring 1967), pp. 90–91.

The Poem as Initiation: An Address Delivered at Phi Beta Kappa Convocation,

Colgate University. Hamilton, New York: Colgate University Press, 1968.
'Marianne Moore and her Critics'. Review of *The Complete Poems of Marianne Moore*. *Agenda*, 6:34 (1968), pp. 137–42.
'After Mistah Kurtz'. Review of *Poets of Reality*, by J. Hillis Miller. *Encounter*, May 1968, pp. 85–87.
'Wilfred Owen as Correspondent'. *Agenda*, 6:2 (1968), pp. 66–70.
Review of *Letters of Wallace Stevens*, edited by Holly Stevens, and *Stevens: Poetry of Thought*, by Frank Doggett. *Critical Quarterly*, XI:i (1969), pp. 94–96.
'Of Native Things'. Review of *The Autobiography of William Carlos Williams*. *The Listener*, 81 (20 February 1969), p. 242.
'A Rich Sitter: The Poetry of Lorine Niedecker'. Review of *North Central*, by Lorine Niedecker. *Agenda*, 7:2 (1969), pp. 65–67.
'Poetry and Possibility: The Work of Robert Duncan'. Review of *The First Decade*, *Derivations*, *The Opening of the Field*, *Roots and Branches*, by Robert Duncan. *Agenda*, 8:34 (1970), pp. 159–70.
'The State of Poetry—Symposium'. *The Review*, 29–30 (1972), pp. 48–51.
'Europe from America'. Review of *William Carlos Williams: The American Background*, by Mike Weaver. *London Magazine*, 11:6 (February/March 1972), pp. 166–68.
'Not in Sequence of a Metronome'. Answer to a Questionnaire on Rhythm. *Agenda*, 10:4 (1972–73), pp. 53–54.
'An Introductory Note on the Poetry of George Oppen'. *Grosseteste Review*, 6:14 (1973), pp. 233–39.
'Fate and the Image of Music: An Examination of Rosenberg's Plays'. *Poetry Nation*, 3 (1974), pp. 57–69.
'The Poet as Painter'. An Address to the Royal Society of Literature, 16 October 1975; published in *Essays by Divers Hands: Innovation in Contemporary Literature*, n.s. 9, edited by Vincent Cronin. Woodbridge, Suffolk: Boydell Press, 1979. Reprinted in *Eden* (1985) and in *Charles Tomlinson: Man and Artist*, edited by Kathleen O'Gorman (1988).
'Poet as Painter' [an extract from 'The Poet as Painter', 1975]. *Eden*. Cheadle, Cheshire: Carcanet Press, 1976.
'To Begin: notes on Graphics'. *Eden*. Cheadle, Cheshire: Carcanet Press, 1976.
'Image and Chance: from a Notebook'. *Eden*. Cheadle, Cheshire: Carcanet Press, 1976.
'The Poet as Translator'. Review of *The Violet in the Crucible: Shelley and

Translation, by Timothy Webb. *Times Literary Supplement*, 22 April 1977, pp. 474–75.

'Europeans in English'. Review of *Rites of Passage*, by Edwin Morgan. *Times Literary Supplement*, 18 March 1977.

'From Amateur to Impresario'. Review of *Muthologos: The Collected Lectures and Interviews*, by Charles Olson; *A Guide to the Maximus Poems of Charles Olson*, by George F. Butterick; *Charles Olson*, by Paul Christensen; *Olson's Push*, by Paul Sherman; *Charles Olson*, by Robert Von Hallenberg. *Times Literary Supplement*, 14 December 1979, p. 135.

'Dove sta memoria: in Italy'. *Hudson Review*, 33 (1980), pp. 13–34.

'The Poet as Translator'. *Times Literary Supplement*, 26 September 1980, pp. 1067–68. This is the same as the introduction to *The Oxford Book of Verse in Translation*.

'Isaac Rosenberg of Bristol'. *Local History Pamphlets*, 53. Bristol: Bristol Branch of the Historical Association, 1982.

'Looking Out for Wholeness'. Review of *The Complete Poems 1927–1979*, by Elizabeth Bishop. *Times Literary Supplement*, 3 June 1983, p. 575.

'Overdoing the Generosity'. *Times Literary Supplement*, 25 March 1983, p. 286.

'Some Aspects of Poetry Since the War'. In *The New Pelican Guide to English Literature: The Present*, 8, edited by Boris Ford. Harmondsworth: Penguin, 1983. Revised and updated in the revised edition of that volume, retitled *From Orwell to Naipaul*, 1995.

Poetry and Metamorphosis (the Clark Lectures, delivered at Cambridge University). Cambridge, London and New York: Cambridge University Press, 1983.

'The Sense of the Past: Three Twentieth-Century Poets'. [David Jones, Basil Bunting, Geoffrey Hill]. The Kenneth Allott Lectures 3. Liverpool: Liverpool University Press, 1983.

'Of Charles Reznikoff'. In *Charles Reznikoff: Man and Poet*, by Milton Hindus. Orono, Maine: National Poetry Foundation, 1984.

'Out of Liguria'. *London Magazine*, n.s. 23 (February 1984), pp. 73–76.

'Ivor Gurney's Best Poems'. *Times Literary Supplement*. 3 January 1986, p. 12.

'Aerial Vision in the Valley of Vision'. Review of *The Parting Light: Selected Writing of Samuel Palmer*, edited by Mark Abley. *PN Review*, 13:2 (1987), pp. 52–53.

'Wallace Stevens and the Poetry of Scepticism'. In *The New Pelican Guide to*

English Literature: American Literature, 9, edited by Boris Ford. Harmondsworth: Penguin, 1988.

'Some Presences on the Scene: A Vista of Post-War Poetry'. In *On Modern Poetry: Essays Presented to Donald Davie*, edited by Vereen Bell and Laurence Lerner. Vanderbilt: Vanderbilt University Press, 1988.

'The Claims of Lyric'. Review of *The Music of What Happens*, by Helen Vendler. *Times Literary Supplement*, 8–14 July , 1988, p. 757.

'Discovering Cézanne'. Review of *Cézanne by Himself*, edited by Richard Kendall. *Modern Painters*, 2:1 (Spring 1989), pp. 109–13.

'Lives and Works'. Review of *A Serious Character: The Life of Ezra Pound*, by Humphrey Carpenter. *Hudson Review*, 42 (Summer 1989), pp. 191–200.

'Poetry and Friendship'. Review of *Becoming a Poet: Elizabeth Bishop with Marianne Moore and Robert Lowell*, by David Kalstone. *Parnassus*, 16:2 (1991), pp. 102–07.

An Address in Honor of William Carlos Williams's Induction Into Poet's Corner of the Cathedral Church of St. John the Divine, 25th October, 1992. New York: Dim Gray Bar Press, 1992.

WORKS ABOUT CHARLES TOMLINSON

Books

John, Brian. *The World as Event: The Poetry of Charles Tomlinson*. Montreal and Kingston, London, Buffalo: McGill-Queen's University Press, 1989.

O'Gorman, Kathleen (ed). *Charles Tomlinson: Man and Artist*. Columbia: University of Missouri Press, 1988.

Swigg, Richard. *Charles Tomlinson and the Objective Tradition*. Lewisburg: Bucknell University Press; London and Toronto: Associated University Presses, 1994.

Criticism in Books, Articles and Reviews

Auberlen, Eckhard. 'Does He Care for More than Beauty? Beauty and Cultural Criticism in the Poetry of Charles Tomlinson'. *REAL: The Yearbook of Research in English and American Literature*, 7 (1990), pp. 245–64.

―――. 'The Theme of Death in the Poetry of Philip Larkin and Charles Tomlinson'. *Arbeiten aus Anglistik und Amerikanistik*, 16, 2 (1991), pp. 175–203.

Bachem, Walter. 'Self and Other in Charles Tomlinson's Poetry'. *Yearbook of English Studies* (Greece), 1 (1989), pp. 255–73.

Barker, Jonathan. 'An Awareness of Delight'. *Times Literary Supplement*, 17 July 1981, p. 816.

Beaver, Harold. 'Crossing Rebel Lines'. *Parnassus*, 10 (Spring–Summer 1982), pp. 117–24.

Bedient, Calvin. Review of *Written on Water*, by Charles Tomlinson. *New York Times Book Review*, 29 April 1973, p. 7.

—————. *Eight Contemporary Poets*. London, New York and Toronto: Oxford University Press, 1974.

—————. 'Poetry Comfortable and Uncomfortable'. Review of *The Shaft*, by Charles Tomlinson. *Sewanee Review*, 87 (1979), pp. 296–304.

Berger, John. In Schmidt (ed.), 'Charles Tomlinson at Fifty: A Celebration', 1977.

Bergonzi, Bernard. Review of *Poetry and Metamorphosis*, by Charles Tomlinson. *Encounter*, 61 (July–August 1983), pp. 79–81.

Bewley, Marius. 'Poetry Chronicle'. *Hudson Review*, 17 (1966), pp. 479–93.

Bolt, Sydney. 'Not the Full Face'. *Delta*, 40 (1967), pp. 4–9.

Brown, Merle. 'Intuition and Perception in the Poetry of Charles Tomlinson'. *Journal of Aesthetics and Art Criticism*, 37 (1979), pp. 277–93.

—————. *Double Lyric: Divisiveness and Communal Creativity in Recent English Poetry*. New York: Columbia University Press, 1980.

Brownjohn, Alan. Review of *The Way of the World*, by Charles Tomlinson. *New Statesman*, 78 (5 December 1969), p. 830.

Carruth, Hayden. 'Abstruse Considerations'. *Poetry*, 106 (1964), pp. 243–44.

Chamberlin, J. E. 'Poetry Chronicle'. *Hudson Review*, 26 (1973), pp. 395–96.

—————. 'Poetry and Confidence'. Review of *The Way In*, by Charles Tomlinson. *Hudson Review*, 28 (1975), pp. 119–35.

—————. 'Unclenching the Mind'. In O'Gorman (ed.), *Charles Tomlinson: Man and Artist*, 1988.

Ciardi, John. Review of *American Scenes*, by Charles Tomlinson. *Saturday Review*, 41 (27 September 1958), p. 32.

Clayre, Alasdair. 'The Poetry of Charles Tomlinson'. *London Magazine*, n.s. 3 (May 1963), pp. 47–57.

—————. In Schmidt (ed.), 'Charles Tomlinson at Fifty: A Celebration', 1977.

Cluysenaar, Anne. Review of *Written on Water*, by Charles Tomlinson. *Stand*, 14:3 (1973), pp. 70–73.

Cookson, William. 'Charles Tomlinson and Robert Creeley'. Review of

American Scenes and *The Necklace*, by Charles Tomlinson. *Agenda*, 4:56 (1966), pp. 64–66.

Corn, Alfred. 'Fishing by Obstinate Isles: Five Poets'. Review of *Selected Poems 1951–1974*, by Charles Tomlinson. *Yale Review*, 68 (1979), pp. 400–10.

Cox, C. B. Review of *American Scenes*, by Charles Tomlinson. *Spectator*, 216 (20 May 1966), pp. 638–39.

Cunningham, Valentine. Review of *Selected Poems 1951–1974* and *The Shaft*, by Charles Tomlinson. *English*, 28:130 (Spring 1979), pp. 88–95.

Davie, Donald. Introduction to *The Necklace*, by Charles Tomlinson, 1955. Reprint. London: Oxford University Press, 1966.

———. 'See and Believe'. Review of *Seeing is Believing*, by Charles Tomlinson. *Essays in Criticism*, 9 (1959), pp. 188–95; reprinted in *The Poet in the Imaginary Museum*, by Donald Davie, 1977.

———. *Thomas Hardy and British Poetry*. New York: Oxford University Press, 1972.

———. Review of *Notes from New York*, by Charles Tomlinson. *London Review of Books*, 20 September–3 October, 1984.

———. Foreword to *Charles Tomlinson: Man and Artist*, edited by Kathleen O'Gorman. Columbia: University of Missouri Press, 1988.

Deane, Patrick. 'Eden in America and Elsewhere'. Review of *Notes from New York and Other Poems*, by Charles Tomlinson. *Brick*, 22 (Fall 1984), pp. 30–32.

Dibb, Michael. 'Filming "Words and Images" '. In Schmidt (ed.), 'Charles Tomlinson at Fifty: A Celebration', 1977.

Donoghue, Denis. 'In the Scene of Being'. *Hudson Review*, 14 (1961), 233–46.

———. 'The Proper Plenitude of Fact'. In *The Ordinary Universe: Soundings in Modern Literature*, by Denis Donoghue. London: Faber and Faber; New York: Macmillan, 1968.

Duncan, Robert. 'A Critical Difference of View'. *Stony Brook*, 3/4 (1969), pp. 360–63.

Dunn, Douglas. Review of *The Way In*, by Charles Tomlinson. *Encounter*, 44 (March 1975), pp. 85–89.

Eagleton, Terry. 'Structures and Connections: New Poetry'. Review of *The Way In*, by Charles Tomlinson. *Stand*, 16:3 (1975), pp. 73–78.

Edwards, Michael. Review of *The Way of a World*, by Charles Tomlinson. *Adam: International Review*, 340–42 (1970), pp. 52–57.

———. 'The Poetry of Charles Tomlinson'. *Agenda*, 9:23 (1971), pp. 126–41; reprinted in O'Gorman (ed.), *Charles Tomlinson: Man and Artist*, 1988.

———. 'Charles Tomlinson: Notes on Tradition and Impersonality'. *Critical Quarterly*, 15 (Summer 1973), pp. 133–44.

———. 'Renga: Un nuevo género literario?' *Plural*, 23 (1973), pp. 36–37.

———. 'Charles Tomlinson'. *Donald Davie, Charles Tomlinson, Geoffrey Hill*. Milton Keynes: Open University Press, 1976.

———. ' "Renga", Translation and Eliot's Ghost'. *PN Review*, 7:2 (1980), pp. 24–28; reprinted in a revised form, 'Collaborations', in O'Gorman (ed.), *Charles Tomlinson: Man and Artist*, 1988.

———. Review of *Collected Poems* and *Eden*, by Charles Tomlinson. *Times Literary Supplement*, 21 March 1986, p. 308.

———. 'Charles Tomlinson's Seeing and Believing'. In *Poetry and Possibility*, by Michael Edwards. Basingstoke and New York: Macmillan, 1987.

———. 'Providence and the Abyss'. Review of *Annunciations*. *Times Literary Supplement*, 22–28 December 1989, p. 1417.

———. 'Tomlinson'. In *Of Making Many Books*, by Michael Edwards. Basingstoke and New York: Macmillan, 1990.

Elliot, Alistair. Review of *Poetry and Metamorphosis*, by Charles Tomlinson. *Times Literary Supplement*, 14 October 1983, p. 1120.

Enslin, Theodore. 'A Precision of Two Languages'. Review of *American Scenes*, by Charles Tomlinson. *Poetry*, 109 (1966), pp. 112–14.

Erzgraber, Willi. 'Bild und Reflexion in Charles Tomlinsons Gedichtfolge "Under the Moon's Reign" '. In *Tradition und Innovation in der Englischen und Amerikanischen Lyrik des 20. Jahrhunderts*, edited by Karl Josef Holtgen, Lothar Honnighausen, Eberhard Kreutzer and Gotz Schmitz. Tubingen: Niemeyer, 1986.

Falck, Colin. 'Dreams and Responsibilities'. *the Review*, 2 (1962), pp. 3–18.

———. Review of *The Way In*, by Charles Tomlinson. *The New Review*, 1:9 (Dec. 1974): 67–68.

Fenton, James. Review of *The Way In*, by Charles Tomlinson. *New Statesman*, 88 (6 December 1974), pp. 832–34.

Fraser, G. S. Review of *A Peopled Landscape*, by Charles Tomlinson. *New York Review of Books*, 20 February 1964, p. 12.

Furbank, P. N. Review of *A Peopled Landscape*, by Charles Tomlinson. *Listener*, 70 (25 July 1963), p. 141.

Galassi, Jonathan. Review of *Written on Water*, by Charles Tomlinson. *Poetry*, 123 (1973), p. 113.

Garfitt. Review of *The Way In*, by Charles Tomlinson. *London Magazine*, 14:5 (December 1974–January 1978), pp. 100–06.

Getz, T. H. 'Charles Tomlinson's Landscapes'. *Modern Poetry Studies*, 11 (1983), pp. 209–18.

Gibbons, Reginald. 'With So Exact a Care'. Review of *The Shaft*, by Charles Tomlinson. *Agenda*, 16:2 (1978), pp. 52–58.

Gioia, Dana. Review of *Airborn* and *The Flood*, by Charles Tomlinson. *Hudson Review*, 34 (1981–82), pp. 579–94.

Gitzen, Julian. 'Charles Tomlinson and the Plenitude of Fact'. *Critical Quarterly*, 13 (Winter 1971), pp. 355–62.

──────. 'British Nature Poetry Now'. *Midwest Quarterly*, 15 (1974), pp. 323–37.

Gould, Alan. 'Control and Parsimony'. *Poetry Australia*, 72 (October 1979), pp. 54–59.

Grogan, Ruth. 'Tomlinson Material in the Lockwood Library, Buffalo'. In Schmidt (ed.), 'Charles Tomlinson at Fifty: A Celebration', 1977.

──────. 'Charles Tomlinson: Poet and Painter'. *Critical Quarterly*, 19 (1977), pp. 71–77; reprinted as 'Language and Graphics' in O'Gorman (ed.), *Charles Tomlinson: Man and Artist*, 1988.

──────. 'Charles Tomlinson: The Way of his World'. *Contemporary Literature*, 19 (1978), pp. 472–96.

──────. 'Tomlinson, Ruskin and Moore: Facts and Fir Trees'. *Twentieth Century Literature*, 35:2 (Summer 1989), pp. 183–94.

──────. 'Tomlinson, Ruskin and Language Scepticism'. *Essays in Literature*, 17:1 (Spring 1990), pp. 30–41.

──────. 'The Fall into History: Charles Tomlinson and Octavio Paz'. *Comparative Literature*, 44:2 (Spring 1992), pp. 144–60.

Grubb, Frederick. *A Vision of Reality*. London: Chatto and Windus, 1965.

Gunn, Thom. 'Seeing and Thinking'. Review of *Seeing is Believing*, by Charles Tomlinson. *American Scholar*, 28 (1959), pp. 390–96.

Halfmann, Ulrich. ' "Negotiations": Zur Subjekt/Objekt-Beziehung in der Lyrik Charles Tomlinsons'. *Anglia*, 98 (1980), pp. 68–84.

Hall, Donald. Review of *Seeing is Believing*, by Charles Tomlinson. *New Statesman*, 60 (2 July 1960), pp. 27–28.

──────. Review of *Some Americans: A Personal Record*, by Charles Tomlinson. *New York Times Book Review*, 1 March 1981, p. 12.

Hamburger, Michael. *The Truth of Poetry: Tensions in Modern Poetry from Baudelaire to the 1960s*. London: Weidenfeld & Nicolson, 1969.
Hardie, J. Keith. 'Charles Tomlinson and the Language of Silence'. *Boundary 2*, XV:12 (Fall 1986/Winter 1987), pp. 211–35.
Harsent, David. Review of *Written on Water*, by Charles Tomlinson. *Spectator*, 229 (9 December 1972), pp. 926–27.
Harvey, Arthur. ' "Naked Nature" and "Negotiations" '. *New Poetry*, 19 (April 1979), pp. 3–8.
Hayman, Ronald. 'Observation Plus'. *Encounter*, 35 (December 1970), pp. 72–73.
———. In Schmidt (ed.), 'Charles Tomlinson at Fifty: A Celebration', 1977.
Hennessy, Michael. 'Perception and Self in Charles Tomlinson's Early Poetry'. *Rocky Mountain Review of Language and Literature*, 36 (1982), pp. 95–102.
———. 'Charles Tomlinson'. In *Critical Survey of Poetry*, edited by Frank N. McGill. Englewood Cliffs, N.J.: Salem Press, 1983.
Hirsch, Edward. 'The Meditative Eye of Charles Tomlinson'. *The Hollins Critic*, 15:2 (1978), pp. 1–12.
———. ' "Out There is the World": The Visual Imperative in the Poetry of George Oppen and Charles Tomlinson'. In *George Oppen: Man and Poet*, edited by Burton Hatlen. Orono, Maine: National Poetry Foundation, 1981.
Homberger, Eric. *The Art of the Real: Poetry in England and America since 1939*. London: J. M. Dent & Sons, Ltd., 1977.
———. 'The Objectivists'. *Akros*, 17 (April 1982), pp. 42–51.
Howard, Ben. Review of *Collected Poems*, by Charles Tomlinson. *Prairie Schooner*, 63 (Summer 1989), pp. 119–27.
Hughes J. W. Review of *The Way of a World*, by Charles Tomlinson. *Saturday Review*, 53 (8 August 1970), p. 33.
Jennings, Elizabeth. Review of *Seeing is Believing*, by Charles Tomlinson. *London Magazine*, 7:10 (October 1960), pp. 75–79.
John, Brian. 'The Poetry of Charles Tomlinson'. *Far Point* (University of Manitoba), 3 (Fall–Winter 1969), pp. 50–61.
Kenner, Hugh. 'A Creator of Spaces'. Review of *The Necklace*, by Charles Tomlinson. *Poetry*, 88 (1956), pp. 324–28.
———. 'Next Year's Words'. Review of *Seeing is Believing*, by Charles Tomlinson. *Poetry*, 93 (1959), pp. 335–40.

———. Review of *Selected Poems of William Carlos Williams*, edited by Charles Tomlinson. *Times Literary Supplement*, 27 April 1984, pp. 451–52.

———. 'Charles Tomlinson'. In *The Dictionary of Literary Biography* vol. 20: *Poets of Great Britain and Ireland since 1960*, edited by Vincent Sherry Jr. Detroit: Gale Research Co., 1985.

King P. R. *Nine Contemporary Poets*. London and New York: Methuen, 1969.

Kinsella, Thomas. Review of *A Peopled Landscape*, by Charles Tomlinson. *New York Times Book Review*, 24 November 1963, p. 46.

Kirkham, Michael. 'Negotiations'. Review of *American Scenes*, by Charles Tomlinson. *Essays in Criticism*, 17 (1967), pp. 367–74.

———. 'A Civil Country'. In Schmidt (ed.), 'Charles Tomlinson at Fifty: A Celebration', 1977.

———. Review of *Selected Poems 1951–1974*. *Queen's Quarterly*, 86:2 (Summer 1979), pp. 345–46.

———. 'Charles Tomlinson'. In *British Poetry since 1970: A Critical Survey*, edited by Peter Jones and Michael Schmidt. Manchester: Carcanet Press, 1980.

———. 'Philip Larkin and Charles Tomlinson: Art and Realism'. In *The New Pelican Guide to English Literature: The Present 8*, edited by Boris Ford. Harmondsworth: Penguin, 1983. Revised in the revised edition of that volume, retitled *From Orwell to Naipaul*, 1995.

———. 'An Agnostic's Grace'. In O'Gorman (ed.), *Charles Tomlinson: Man and Artist*, 1988.

Koehler, Stanley. 'The Art of Poetry VI'. *Paris Review*, 8 (Summer–Fall 1964), pp. 111–51.

Lattimore, Richard. Review of *The Oxford Book of Verse in English Translation*, by Charles Tomlinson. *Hudson Review*, 35 (1982), pp. 154–58.

Law, Pam. 'Notions of Excellence'. *Poetry Australia*, 47 (1973), pp. 75–80.

Lea, Sydney. 'To Use and Transform: Recent Poetry of Charles Tomlinson' [*The Return, Annunciations, The Door in the Wall*]. *Hudson Review*, 46 (Winter 1994), pp. 731–40.

Lee, L. L. 'Charles Tomlinson as American un-American'. *Contemporary Poetry: A Journal of Criticism*, 2:2 (1977), pp. 11–15.

Lengeler, Rainer. 'Charles Tomlinsons Phanomenonologische Naturdichtung'. In *Englische und Amerikanische Naturdichtung im 20 Jahrhundert*, edited by Gunter and Hans Ulrich Seeber. Tubingen: Narr, 1985.

Levertov, Denise. 'An English Event'. *Kulchur*, 2:6 (1962), pp. 3–9.

Levi, Peter. In Schmidt (ed.), 'Charles Tomlinson at Fifty: A Celebration', 1977.

Lobb, Edward. Review of *Collected Poems*, by Charles Tomlinson. *Cambridge Quarterly*, 16:2 (1987), pp. 162–68.

Longley, Edna. Review of *Poetry and Metamorphosis*, by Charles Tomlinson. *Notes and Queries*, n.s. 32 (1985), pp. 413–15.

Lucas, J. Review of *Notes from New York*, by Charles Tomlinson. *New Statesman*, 107 (22 June 1984), pp. 23–24.

MacCaig, Norman. Review of *Seeing is Believing*, by Charles Tomlinson. *Spectator*, 205 (5 August 1960), p. 223.

——————. Review of *A Peopled Landscape*, by Charles Tomlinson. *New Statesman*, 66 (5 July 1963), pp. 23–24.

Mariani, Paul. 'Tomlinson's Use of the Williams Triad'. *Contemporary Literature*, 18 (1977), pp. 405–15; reprinted in O'Gorman (ed.), *Charles Tomlinson: Man and Artist*, 1988.

——————. 'Charles Tomlinson'. In *A Usable Past: Essays on Modern and Contemporary Poetry*, by Paul Mariani. Amherst: University of Massachusetts Press, 1984.

Marsack, Robyn. 'Elegy and Celebration'. *PN Review*, 8:5 (1981), p. 57.

Marten, Harry. 'Tomlinson's American Relations'. Review of *Selected Poems 1951–1974*, by Charles Tomlinson. *Prairie Schooner*, 53 (1979), pp. 280–82.

Martin, Graham. Review of *American Scenes*, by Charles Tomlinson. *Listener*, 75 (26 May 1966).

Martz, Louis L. Review of *American Scenes*, by Charles Tomlinson. *Yale Review*, 56 (December 1966), p. 496.

Molesworth, Charles. 'British Poetry: Crossing the Borders'. Review of *Written on Water*, by Charles Tomlinson. *The Nation*, 16 (1974), pp. 346–48.

Mott, Michael. 'Recent Developments in British Poetry'. Review of *The Way of a World*, by Charles Tomlinson. *Poetry*, 118 (1971), pp. 102–14.

Murphy, Rosalie (ed.). *Contemporary Poets of the English Language*. London and Chicago: St James, 1970.

O'Driscoll, Dennis. Review of *The Flood*, by Charles Tomlinson. *Agenda*, 19:23 (1981), pp. 79–81.

O'Gorman, Kathleen. 'Space, Time and Ritual in Tomlinson's Poetry'. *Sagetrieb*, 2 (Summer–Fall 1983), pp. 85–98; reprinted in O'Gorman (ed.), *Charles Tomlinson: Man and Artist*, 1988.

Palmer, Penelope. Review of *The Way In*, by Charles Tomlinson. *Agenda*, 13:2 (1975), pp. 66–67.

Pardee, Hearne. 'A Distant Vision: Charles Tomlinson and American Art'. *Partisan Review*, 58 (Summer 1991), pp. 554–62.

Pawling, Geoffrey. 'A Way into England'. *Delta*, 54 (1975), pp. 10–16.

Paz, Octavio. 'The Graphics of Charles Tomlinson'. *Poetry Nation*, 5 (1975); reprinted in *On Poets and Poetry*, by Octavio Paz (1986), in *In Black and White*, by Charles Tomlinson, and in O'Gorman (ed.), *Charles Tomlinson: Man and Artist*, 1988.

Perloff, Marjorie. 'The Duality of the Visible'. In Schmidt (ed.), 'Charles Tomlinson at Fifty: A Celebration', 1977.

Picot, Edward. *Outcasts from Eden: Ideas of Landscape in British Poetry since 1945*. Liverpool: Liverpool University Press, 1997.

Pinsky, Robert. *The Situation of Poetry: Contemporary Poetry and its Traditions*. Princeton: Princeton University Press, 1976.

Ponsford, Michael. 'Charles Tomlinson's Motorway Poems'. *Notes on Contemporary Literature*, 17:4 (1987), pp. 4–5.

──────. ' "To Wish Back Eden": The Community Theme in Charles Tomlinson's Verse'. *The Midwest Quarterly*, 30 (Spring 1989), pp. 346–60.

Press, John. *Rule and Energy: Trends in British Poetry since the Second World War*. London, New York and Toronto: Oxford University Press, 1963.

──────. In Schmidt (ed.), 'Charles Tomlinson at Fifty: A Celebration', 1977.

Pritchard, Willam H. 'In the British Looking-Glass'. Review of *The Way In*, by Charles Tomlinson. *Parnassus*, 4 (Spring–Summer 1976), pp. 225–34.

──────. 'Aboard the Poetry Omnibus'. Review of *Notes from New York*, by Charles Tomlinson. *Hudson Review*, 37 (1984), pp. 327–42.

Rae, Simon. Review of *The Flood*, by Charles Tomlinson. *New Statesman*, 102 (4 September 1981), p. 19.

Raine, Craig. Review of *Selected Poems 1951–1974* and *The Shaft*, by Charles Tomlinson. *New Statesman*, 96 (4 August 1978), p. 154.

Robinson, Peter. Review of *Collected Poems*, by Charles Tomlinson. *London Review of Books*, 20 February 1986

Rosenthal, M. L. *The Modern Poets: A Critical Introduction*. London, Oxford and New York: Oxford University Press, 1960.

──────. 'The American Influence on the Coots of Hampstead Heath'. *Antioch Review*, 22 (1962), pp. 189–201.

──────. 'Contemporary British Poetry: Charles Tomlinson'. In *The New Poets: American and British Poets since World War II*, by M. L. Rosenthal. London, Oxford and New York: Oxford University Press, 1967.

Ruddick, Bill. Review of *The Way In*, by Charles Tomlinson. *Critical Quarterly*, 17 (Summer 1975), pp. 181–85.

Ruthven, Greystiel. 'Charles Tomlinson: An Introduction'. *Gemini/Dialogue*, 3 (January 1960), pp. 30–33.

Saunders, Judith P. 'Charles Tomlinson and the Art of Sustained Allusion'. *The Arkansas Quarterly*, 2:1 (Winter 1993), pp. 30–41.

Saunders, William S. '*A Peopled Landscape*: Discrepancies between Poetics and Poem'. *Delta*, 56 (1977), pp. 10–15.

——————. 'Artifice and Ideas'. *Delta*, 59 (1979), pp. 35–40.

Schlessinger, Sheila. ' "Hawk, Thrush and Crow": The Bird Poems of Tomlinson and Hughes'. *Theoria*, 59 (October 1982), pp. 51–61.

Schmidt, Michael (ed.). 'Charles Tomlinson at Fifty: A Celebration'. *PN Review*, 5:1 (1977), pp. 33–50.

——————. 'In the Eden of Civility'. Review of *Selected Poems 1951–1974* and *The Shaft*, by Charles Tomlinson. *Times Literary Supplement*, 1 December 1978, p. 1406.

——————. *An Introduction to Fifty Modern British Poets*. Pan Literature Guides. London: Pan, 1979.

——————. 'On Charles Tomlinson'. *PN Review*, 13:2 (1986), pp. 70–72.

Sereni, Vittorio. In Schmidt (ed.), 'Charles Tomlinson at Fifty: A Celebration', 1977.

Shapiro, Harvey. Review of *Seeing is Believing*, by Charles Tomlinson. *New York Times Book Review*, 22 June 1958, p. 4.

Shivpuri, Jagdish. 'Charles Tomlinson: Earlier Poetry'. *Siddha* (Siddharth College, India), 12 (1978), pp. 7–22.

Sisson, C. H. Review of *The Oxford Book of Verse in English Translation*, edited by Charles Tomlinson. *Times Literary Supplement*, 3 October 1980, pp. 1093–94.

Skelton, Robin. 'Brittania's Muse Awakening'. Review of *American Scenes*, by Charles Tomlinson. *Massachusetts Review*, 8 (1967), pp. 352–66.

——————. 'Brittania's Muse Revisited'. *Massachusetts Review*, 6 (1965), pp. 829–39.

Smith, William J. Review of *American Scenes*, by Charles Tomlinson. *Harper's* (August 1966), pp. 89–92.

Spears, Monroe K. 'Shapes and Surfaces: David Jones, With a Glance at Charles Tomlinson'. *Contemporary Literature*, 12 (1971), pp. 402–19.

Spiegelmann, Willard. 'The Rituals of Perception'. Review of *Selected Poems 1951–1974* and *The Shaft*, by Charles Tomlinson. *Parnassus*, 7 (Spring–Summer 1979), pp. 151–65.

Srawley, Stephen. 'A Note on Musical and Poetic Rhythm'. *Agenda*, 1011:4 and 1 (1972), pp. 114–22.

Stanton, Richard J. 'Charles Tomlinson and the Process of Defining Relationships'. *North Dakota Quarterly*, 45:3 (1977), pp. 47–60.

Stevenson, Anne. 'Night-time Tongue'. Review of *The Shaft*, by Charles Tomlinson. *The Listener*, 100 (13 July 1978), pp. 62–63.

Swann, Brian. 'English Opposites: Charles Tomlinson and Christopher Middleton'. *Modern Poetry Studies*, 5 (1974), pp. 222–36.

Swigg, Richard. 'Reading the World'. Review of *The Flood*, by Charles Tomlinson. *PN Review*, 6:7 (1982), pp. 63–64.

—————. Review of *Notes from New York* and *Translations*, by Charles Tomlinson. *Times Literary Supplement*, 27 April 1984, p. 452.

—————. Review of *Collected Poems* and *Eden: Graphics and Poems*, by Charles Tomlinson. *Prospice*, 18 (Summer 1986), pp. 130–37.

Thwaite, Anthony. *Poetry Today: 1960–1973*. Edinburgh: R. & R. Clark, Ltd., 1973.

Vendler, Helen. Review of *The Way In*, by Charles Tomlinson. *New York Times Book Review*, 6 April 1975, pp. 45, 29–38.

Watkins, Evan. 'Charles Tomlinson: The Poetry of Experience'. In *The Critical Act: Criticism and Community*, by Evan Watkins. New Haven: Yale University Press, 1978.

Weatherhead, Andrew Kingsley. 'Charles Tomlinson: With Respect to Flux'. *Iowa Review*, 7 (Fall 1976), pp. 120–34.

—————. 'Charles Tomlinson'. In *The British Dissonance: Essays on Ten Contemporary Poets*, by A. K. Weatherhead. Columbia: University of Missouri Press, 1983.

Weber, Horst. *Wahrnehmung und Realisation: Untersuchung zu Gedichten von Charles Tomlinson*. Heidelberg: Carl Winter, 1983.

Weisman, Karen A. 'Tomlinson's "A Rose for Janet"'. *The Explicator*, 50 (Winter 1992), pp. 122–24.

Wesling, Donald. 'The Inevitable Ear: Freedom and Necessity in Lyric Form, Wordsworth and After'. *ELH*, 36 (1969), pp. 544–61.

—————. 'An Avant-Garde Careful and Bold'. In Schmidt (ed.), 'Charles Tomlinson at Fifty: A Celebration', 1977.

—————. 'Process and Closure in Tomlinson's Prose Poems'. In O'Gorman (ed.), *Charles Tomlinson: Man and Artist*, 1988.

White, R. S. Review of *Poetry and Metamorphosis*, by Charles Tomlinson. *Review of English Studies*, n.s. 36 (1985), pp. 601–03.

Wilcox, Joel F. 'Tomlinson and the British Tradition'. In O'Gorman (ed.), *Charles Tomlinson: Man and Artist*, 1988.

Wilkinson, David. 'Charles Tomlinson and the Narrative Voice'. *Dutch Quarterly Review of Anglo-American Letters*, 14:2 (1984), pp. 110–24.

Williams, William Carlos. 'Seeing Is Believing'. Review of *Seeing is Believing*, by Charles Tomlinson. *Spectrum*, 2 (Fall 1958), p. 189.

Wilmer, Clive. Review of *Some Americans: A Personal Record*, by Charles Tomlinson. *Times Literary Supplement*, 5 February 1982, p. 141.

Wilson, Robert Jr. 'Not Awfully Plain'. Review of *American Scenes*, by Charles Tomlinson. *Carleton Miscellany*, 8 (Winter 1967), pp. 103–07.

Wood, Clifford. Review of *American Scenes*, by Charles Tomlinson. *New Mexico Quarterly*, 36:3 (Autumn 1966), pp. 293–294.

Wood, Michael. 'We All Hate Home: English Poetry since World War II'. *Contemporary Literature*, 18 (1977), pp. 305–18.

Young, Alan. 'Rooted Horizon: Charles Tomlinson and American Modernism'. *Critical Quarterly*, 24 (Winter 1982), pp. 67–73.

Young, V. Review of *Selected Poems 1958–1974* and *The Shaft*, by Charles Tomlinson. *Hudson Review*, 31 (1978–1979), pp. 677–92.

Index of Proper Names and Works

'Above the Rio Grande' 251–52
'Adam' 120–21, 169
'Aesthetic' 43, 45, 46, 48, 57, 77
'After a Death' 289
'After the Storm' 294–95, 296
Airborn/Hijos del Aire 2
America West Southwest 158, 159, Preface to 163
American Scenes 18, 40, 153–54, 158, 286
Amis, Kingsley 10
Annunciations 295
'Antecedents' sequence 13, 128, 164, 219
'Appearance' 34, 39, 40, 83
'Arden' 221–22
Aristotle 9, 27
'Arizona Desert' 86, 87–89, 90, 159, 160
'Arizona Highway' 166
Arnold, Matthew 16
'Assassin' 169, 174–77, 178, 185, 187, 196
'At Delft' 77, 128, 132–38, 140, 142, 156
'At Holwell Farm' 109, 110, 117, 121, 128, 134, 138
'At Huexotla' 272–75
'Atlantic, The' 73–76, 77, 113
'At Stoke' 204, 205–06
'At the Edge' 218–19, 220, 221, 225, 259
Augustan poetry 17, 44, 214, 216, 219

Barzun, Jacques 17
Bedient, Calvin 20, 21
'Beech, The' 292–93, 296
'Before the Dance' 108, 110, 113
Berger, John 55, 57

Bertolani, Paolo 243–44, 257
Bertolucci, Attilio 2
Bevin, Ernest 19
Blake, William 53
Blok, Alexander 174, 177, 181
Borgia, Cesare 196
Braque, Georges 226, 227–28

'Canal' 105, 148, 151, 183
'Carrara Revisited' 278–79, 280
'Castle, The' 128, 179, 290
'Catacomb' 238–41
'Cavern, The' 33, 159–61, 164, 173, 176
'Cézanne at Aix' 39, 40, 261, 262
Cézanne, Paul 3, 33, 36, 38, 39, 40, 55, 56, 57, 257, 260, 261, 268
'Chances of Rhyme, The' 169
'Charlotte Corday' 185, 186, 187–88
Christianity 230, 231, 232, 234–35, 237, 238, 264, 270, 282, 295
Clark Lectures, Cambridge 2
Coleridge, Samuel Taylor 7, 17, 53, 215, 225, 292, 'Frost at Midnight' 7
Collected Poems, Preface to 2, 142, 252, 277, 298
'Compact: at Volterra, The' 189, 194–96, 197, 255
'Confluence' 296–97
Constable, John 26, 27, 32, 44, 290 *see also* 'Meditation on John Constable, A'
'Coombe' 229–30
Corday, Charlotte *see* 'Charlotte Corday'
'Crane, The' 128
'Crow' 62–63

329

Dante Alighieri *Inferno* 291, *Paradiso* 18, 156, 165
Danton, Georges Jacques 20, 21, 185, 186, 187
Davie, Donald 1, 5, 16, 17, 182, 214, 215, 216, 219
'Death in the Desert, A' 162–64, 165
Denham, Sir John 129
'Departure' 113, 114–15, 116, 223–24, 225
'Descartes and the Stove' 169–74, 178
Descartes, René 170, 171, 172, 174

Eden 2, 173, 269
'Eden' 51–53, 109, 118, 119, 120, 121, 210, 254
Edwards, Michael 5, 295
Eliot, T. S. 18, 147, 289, *Ash Wednesday* 239, 'Perfect Critic, The' 27, quoted 21, 25, 27, 34, 36–37, *Waste Land, The* 292
'Encounter' 78
Eros English'd: Classical Poetry in Translation 2

'Face and Image' 170, 192
'Farewell to Van Gogh' 57, 58, 59, 60, 61, 107, 108, 130, 280
'Faring, The' 231–32
'Farmer's Wife: at Fostons Ash, The' 176, 197
Flood, The 53, 232
'Flute Music' 58, 83–84, 85, 107, 108
'Focus' 49, 50, 51, 53
'For Danton' 20–21, 186
'For Miriam' sequence 232
'Fountain' 262–68, 272
'Four Kantian Lyrics' 91, 92–93, 106
'Fox, The' 167, 171
'Foxes' Moon' 166, 219–20
French Revolution 174, 185
'Frondes Agrestes' 290
Frost, Robert 223

'Gap, The' 224, 225, 226, 240, 250
Gasquet, Joachim 261
Gestalt psychology 77
Gifford, Henry 10, 11
'Given Grace, A' 40–42, 48, 50, 167, 183–84
'Glacier, The' 285, 286, 287–88, 289–90, 291–92
'Glass Grain' 39, 108, 116–17
'Greeting, The' 78, 113
Gunn, Thom 214

Hamilton, Ian 13, 15
Hand and Flower Press, The 43
'Hand at Callow Hill Farm, The' 132
'Hawks' 248, 250
'Hay' 248
Hegel, Georg Friedrich 27
'Hill Walk' 104, 121, 123–25
'Hokusai on the Trent' 205, 206, 209
Hopkins, Gerard Manley 18, 108, 216, inscape 109, sprung rhythm 53
'House in the Quarry, The' 254–55, 256, 263
'How it Happened' 65, 95, 98, 102
'How Still the Hawk' 63, 66–67

'Icos' 63–64, 65, 66, 91
'Idyll' 18, 156–58, 165
'Images of Perfection' 115–16
'In Arden' 103, 104, 105
In Black and White 2
'In December' 295–96
'In Defence of Metaphysics' 70
'In New Mexico' 249–51
'In San Clemente' 234–35
'Insistence of Things, The' 35–36
'Insufficiency of Earth, An' 106
'In the Balance' 222–23
'In the Borghese Gardens' 252–54, 256
'In the Fullness of Time' 58, 121, 122–23, 124, 195

Index of Proper Names and Works 331

'In the Gesù' 237–38
'In Winter Woods' 50, 56, 111–13
Jaccottet, Jacques 9, 19
Jewish Scriptures 231
'John Maydew' 132, 148–53, 202, 203, 270, 271
Johnson, Dr Samuel *Lives of the Poets* 129
Jonson, Ben 138, 139
Joyce, James 18, 19
József, Attila 19

Kafka, Franz 290
Keats, John 225
Kenner, Hugh 2

Laforgue, Jules 14
'Landing, The' 276, 278
Larkin, Philip 10, 214, 'Less Deceived, The' 214–15
'Last Days of the Miser' 288
'Las Trampas U.S.A.' 103, 154–56, 158, 166, 272–73
Lawrence, D. H. 12, 13, 158, 288, *St Mawr* 165, *Women in Love* 165
Leavis, F. R. 45
Lenin, Vladimir Ilyich Ulyanov 101, 174, 177, 179, 180–81

Machado, Antonio 2, 11
'Machiavelli in Exile' 189, 195, 196–201, 202
'Mackinnon's Boat' 189, 192–94
Mallarmé, Stéphane 14
Marat, Catherine 185, 188
Marat, Jean Paul 185, 186
'Marl Pits, The' 9, 26, 70, 151, 205, 206–07
Marvell, Andrew 21
'Meditation on John Constable, A' 26–27, 32, 53, 102, 142, 290
'Meeting, The' 78
'Melody' 91, 273–74

Mercader, Ramón 174, 176, 177, 185, 187, 197, 202
Merleau-Ponty, Maurice 40
Miller, J. Hillis 12
'Miracle of the Bottle and the Fishes, The' 225–29, 250
Mithraism 234
Moore, Marianne 2, 43, 214, 216, 'The Past is Present' 154
'Movement II' 220
Movement poets 16, 214
'Movements' 92

'Nature Poem' 221, 248, 266
'Near Ceibwr' 278
Necklace, The 1, 25, 44, 45, 83, 107, 153, 213, 217, 243
'Necklace, The' 17
'News from Nowhere' 162
Nietzsche, Friedrich 233
'Night Farm, The' 275–76
'Night Fishers' 285, 286–87
'Nocturnal' 56
'Northern Spring' 141–42
Notes from New York 276, 295

'Observation of Facts' 217, 290
'On a Landscape by Li Ch'eng' 83, 84–85, 89
'One World' 78–79
'On Madison' 276–77
'On the Hall at Stowey' 128, 138–41, 142, 156, 210, 288–89, 290
'On the Mountain' 162
'Oppositions' 78
'Over Elizabeth Bridge' 6, 10, 19, 20
'Oxen: Ploughing at Fiesole' 128–32, 133, 134, 169, 296
Oxford Book of Verse in English Translation 2

Paz, Octavio 2, 58, 122, collaboration with Tomlinson 11, quoted 57, 59, 62, 78

'Peak, The' 285, 286
Peopled Landscape, A 40, 44, 127–28, 132, 143
'Poem' 43, 44–45, 46, 48, 49, 53, 74, 75, 76, 77, 175
Poem as Initiation, The 245–47, 255, 256
'Poem for My Father' 203, 269, 270–72, 273, 274
'Poet as Painter, The' 3, 36, 37–38, 39, 40, 61, 171, 172, 178, 188, 190, 225, 227, 262, 267, 268–69
Poetry Book Society Bulletin 14
'Ponte Veneziano' 64–66, 77, 93–95, 131, 132, 216, 241
Pope, Alexander 138
Pound, Ezra 18, 34, 214, 'E.P. Ode Pour L'Election de Son Sepulchre' 43, *Hugh Selwyn Mauberley* 43
'Prelude, A' 146, 176
'Prometheus' 57–58, 100, 104, 169, 174, 177–84, 187, 200

'Recompense, The' 232
Relations and Contraries 1, 43, 78, 213
Return, The 14
'Return, The' sequence 243, 244, 257, 270, 297, 298
'Return to Hinton' 132, 143–48, 149, 152, 156, 197
'Revolution' 256–57, 258–62, 286
Rilke, Rainer Maria 39, 91
'Rose for Janet, A' 246, 247–48, 251
Rosenberg, Isaac 19, *Trench Poems* 19
Ross, Alan 10, 11
Roubaud, Jacques 2
'Rower' 189–92
'Ruin, The' 128
Ruskin, John 18, 216, 290

'San Fruttuoso' 236, 237, 238
Sanguineti, Edoardo 2
San Marco Press 158

Scandinavian mythology 233
Schmidt, Michael 13, 213, 219
Scriabin, Alexander 100–01, 104, 174, 177, 179, 180–81, 184, 200
Seeing is Believing 1, 25, 31, 40, 44, 45, 107, 127, 128, 132, 213, 214, 215, 217, 218, 221–22, 268
Selected Poems (1978) 2
Selected Poems (1997) 5
'Self-Portrait: David, A' 222
'Sense of Distance, A' 91–92, 110, 113, 169
'Shaft, The' 95, 97–98, 99–100, 101–02, 103, 104–05, 161
Shaft, The 107, 113, 184
Shakespeare, William *King Lear* 68
Sidney, Sir Philip 139
'Skullshapes' 25, 29–32, 33–34, 41, 54, 57, 60, 61, 151, 175, 299
'Snow Fences, The' 86, 162, 255, 288
'Snow Sequence' 111, 113, 115
'Snow Signs' 15, 49, 53, 55
Some Americans 2
'Some Presences on the Scene: A Vista of Postwar Poetry' 16
'Something: A Direction' 164, 218–19
'Steel' 148
Stevens, Wallace 29, 43, 153, 214, 233, 'Sunday Morning' 233
Stoke 7, 9
Swigg, Richard 5
'Swimming Chenango Lake' 15–16, 109, 147, 155, 169, 176, 188, 260, 261

'Tax Inspector, The' 282–85
'Teotihuacán' 233–34
Thomas, Dylan 12, 16, 214, romanticism 43, 217
Thomas, Edward 38, 273
Thoreau, Henry 260
'Through Binoculars' 216
'Thunder in Tuscany' 240–41

Index of Proper Names and Works

Toltecs 233
Tomlinson, Brenda 298, 299, 300, 301, 304–05
Tomlinson, Charles, biography 1–2, 7, critics' underestimate of 2–3, 5–6, 14–15, honours 2, painting 2, 3, publications 1–2, translation 2, 10–11, *see also under names of individual poems and collections*
'To See the Heron' 230–31, 232, 237
'Tramontana at Lerici' 142, 173, 216
'Translating the Birds' 63, 69–70
'Tree, The' 15, 204–05
Trotsky, Leo 174, 175, 180, 202
'Two Views of Two Ghost Towns' 165
Tyutchev, Fyodor 2, 10, 11

'Under the Moon's Reign' 233, 236
'Up at La Serra' 243–44

Vallejo, César 2, 11
Van Gogh, Vincent 156, 287 *see also* 'Farewell to Van Gogh'
'Venice' 43, 46–48, 74, 75, 76, 77, 94, 95, 131, 132, 133, 134, 279, 280
Vermeer, Jan 77, 132–33, 136, 202
Versions from Fyodor Tyutchev 10

Way In, The 127, 201, 203
'Way In, The' 119, 120, 121, 207–11

'Way of a World, The' 59, 60, 61, 79–80, 81, 82, 90–91, 109, 177, 250, 261
Way of a World, The 4, 5, 30, 79, 169, 189, 210, 217
'Way Through, The' 280, 281
'Weathercocks, The' 49, 53, 105
Weatherhead, A. Kingsley 15
'Weeper in Jalisco' 282, 285
'Well, The' 95–98, 102, 103, 104, 105
'What Next?' 280–82
Williams, William Carlos 11, 44, 143, 153
'Wind' 90
'Winter Encounters' 80–83, 92, 93, 107, 108, 110
'Winter Journey' sequence 297–305
'Winter-Piece' 63, 67–69, 86, 124
Winters, Yvor 16
Words and Images 2
'Words for the Madrigalist' 169
Wordsworth, William 15, 17, 38, 40, 92, 105, 192, 215, 'Elegiac Stanzas' 105, *Excursion, The* 89, quoted 53, 227, 255
'Written on Water' 14–15, 189
Written on Water 189

Yeats, William Butler 19–20, 290, 'Prayer for My Daughter, A' 67, 'Second Coming, The' 179